SCATTERED ROUND STONES

Scattered

A UNIVERSITY OF ARIZONA SOUTHWEST CENTER BOOK

JOSEPH C. WILDER, SERIES EDITOR

David Yetman

Round Stones

A MAYO VILLAGE IN SONORA, MEXICO

Published in cooperation with the University of Arizona Southwest Center

UNIVERSITY OF NEW MEXICO PRESS
ALBUQUERQUE

© 1998 by the University of New Mexico Press
All rights reserved.
First edition

Library of Congress
Cataloging-in-Publication Data
Yetman, David, 1941–
Scattered round stones : a Mayo village
in Sonora, Mexico / David Yetman.
p.   cm.
Includes bibliographical references and index.
ISBN 0-8263-1955-6 (cloth) — ISBN 0-8263-1956-4 (pbk)
1. Mayo Indians—Social life and customs.
2. Mayo Indians—Ethnobotany.
3. Mayo Indians—Politics and government.
4. Ethnobotany—Mexico—Teachive.
5. Human ecology—Mexico—Teachive.
6. Teachive (Mexico)—Social conditions.
7. Teachive (Mexico)—Economic conditions.
8. Teachive (Mexico)—Politics and government.
I. Title.
F1221.M3Y47   1998
972'.17—dc21   98-24411
CIP
Designed by Sue Niewiarowski

To Lynn

Teachive

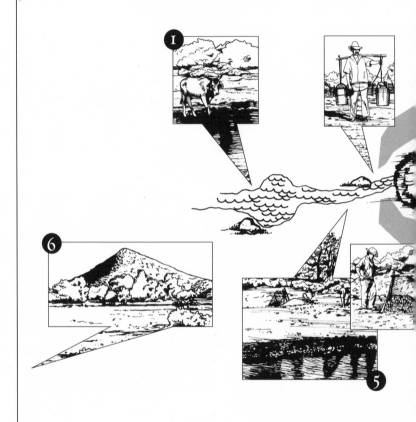

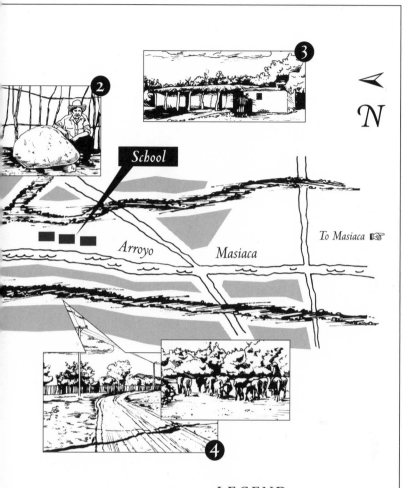

School

To Masiaca ☞

Arroyo   Masiaca

LEGEND

1. *El Aguaje*
2. *La Piedra Santa Cruz*
3. *A typical Teachive house*
4. *The road through town (Teachive Road)*
5. *Gravel diggers*

residential area

Contents

Acknowledgments

This book could not have been written without generous financial support from the Native & Nature company and from Agnese Nelms Haury. Joe Wilder, director of the Southwest Center of the University of Arizona also supported the project financially and provided unflagging encouragement. Tomás Valdés and Rosendo Benegas Reyes of Alamos, Sonora, provided helpful historical information. Manuel Robles of Hermosillo and the personnel of the Archives of the State of Sonora assisted me in locating historic documents about the Masiaca community. Donald Bahr and Nancy Cole made important suggestions for the manuscript. Mary O'Connor provided anthropological information I could not have obtained elsewhere. Thomas Van Devender spent many hours in the field with me and identified many of the plants listed in Appendix B. Vicente Tajia Yocupicio and María Teresa Moroyoqui Zazueta, along with Elvira Tajia Moroyoqui, their daughter, as well as Olivia Blanca, Fausto, Sandra, Francisco, Lupita, and Lulu, their grandchildren, made me feel at home in Teachive.

Scattered Round Stones

The peasantry, which had formed the majority of the human race throughout recorded history, had been made redundant by agricultural revolutions, but the millions no longer needed on the land had in the past been readily absorbed by labor-hungry occupations elsewhere, which required only a willingness to work, the adaptation of country skills, like digging and building walls, or the capacity to learn on the job. What would happen to the workers in those occupations when they in turn became unnecessary? Even if some could be re-trained for the high-grade jobs of the information age which continued to expand (most of which increasingly demanded a higher education), there were not enough of these to compensate. What, for that matter, would happen to the peasants of the Third World who still flooded out of their villages?

ERIC HOBSBAWM, THE AGE OF EXTREMES

I follow don Vicente through a maze of pathways winding among tangled groves of spiny thornscrub and cactus not far from the village of Teachive.[1] *The forest growth is not tall, but it is still more than twice a man's height and of a thickness that hides the horizon in all directions. In the narrow openings the ground is bare and dusty, trampled by a thousand hooves. The shrubs and trees intertwine in an unending thicket, leafless and nearly colorless in the pounding heat of June. Vicente wears* huaraches de tres puntas, *skimpy sandals that leave his feet and ankles perilously exposed to the myriad spines at ground level. I wear thick boots. Vicente's pants are tattered victims of the thornscrub, his shirt a series of patches. His hair is only slightly graying in spite of his more than sixty years. Every few moments he swings his machete.* Thwink, *it goes, and a protruding thorny branch falls to the ground. With the tip of the machete Vicente flips the branch off the path, making the passage easier for me. We turn left, then right, then left again, another right. Paths cross, crisscross, separate, then meet again. Vicente stops and points to a shrub. "Ba'aco," he says. I write it down. "Jícamuchi," he says, indicating another. He points his machete at yet another. "Watch out for this one, David. It is* sa'apo *and it will stain your shirt."* Thwink, *another branch falls to the machete's slash. He stops beside a small tree. "David, this one is called* ono jújuga. *That means* 'huele a sal' [smells of salt]. *It's not good for much, just firewood."*

After a kilometer the dense scrub opens into a clearing. In the center grows an enor-   1 mous palo jito tree, an ancient sentinel a good ten meters tall whose symmetrical shape casts a dark shade. Its crown is round and spreading, its dense leaves freshly turned green, its thick, gray bark rugged and gnarled. The bole, nearly a meter in diameter, rises straight. I am nearly six feet tall. The bottom branches clear my head by a foot. The dense foliage forms a flat ceiling in places, making the tree resemble a huge brown and green mushroom. In the parched landscape of late June it is the only tree that remains green.

Don Vicente and I sit sweating on the trampled, leaf-strewn earth beneath the great jito. He tells me of times long past, of the ancient Mayos, of his grandparents, his parents. "This jito, David, was already a giant when I was a little boy, oh, almost sixty years ago. Everybody called it 'El Jitón,' the giant jito, in those days. All my life and long before I was born the people from around here stopped along the trail—it goes for many kilometers through this monte that has no end[2]—to rest here and take refuge from the heat. Look how fine is its shade!" Vicente smiles when he tells me that Mayos say the shade cast by El Jitón induces a slumber so profound that one who dozes off in its shade may never awaken. I am tempted to lie on the ground and close my eyes.[3]

As is usual, El Jitón bears many small orange fruits. Vicente says they are quite edible. "You cannot eat them raw, David, because they are very bitter. The fruits must be boiled in water to make them palatable." He goes into detail: "When the water begins to bubble, a yellow foam collects on the surface. It must be skimmed off, for this is the bitter element. When no more of the yellow froth develops, the fruits are ready to eat. Add a little sugar. Everyone loves them." El Jitón's fruits are especially tasty. It has been that way for as long as he can recall, and he is a grandfather many times over.

Jito trees grow to be thousands of years old, Vicente tells me. He traces his fingers over the healed scars of ancient attacks by youths and insects. El Jitón's trunk bears witness to generations of mischief, whether idle whittlings by impetuous youths biding their time through the heavy noonday heat, or attacks by wood borers and woodpeckers. Now, Vicente points out, youngsters have carved initials in the tree and attacked it, albeit mildly, with a machete. They lack the respect that children showed in bygone days, he laments. In addition to the danger from vandalism, El Jitón's leaves are stunted from the persistent, withering drought that has lasted nearly a decade. Last year, las aguas (the summer rains) produced only a few sporadic thunderstorms. Las equipatas (the winter rains) produced not a drop. Six months of unvarying drought.

We climb a nearby hill. I look out over the vast coastal plain. Jitos, many as large as El Jitón, form black spots on the gray-brown landscape.[4] None of them are young. "No young jitos are growing to replace the ancient giants," Vicente remarks ruefully. Seedlings are trampled before they reach the age of resiliency. Perhaps with the end of the millennium, the beginning of the end of El Jitón has arrived.

Or perhaps it will outlive Teachive.

I want to know just how old the venerable giant is. There is no easy method to count its years. I thought of the dendrochronologist's core borer, considered extracting a long, thin rod of a sample for a tree-ring laboratory. Dedrochronologists examine such samples and count growth rings to determine the age of a particular tree. I gave up that idea when I recalled that tropical trees such as the *jito* aren't good subjects for tree-ring studies. Their growing season is year-round, so they do not leave countable rings. Maybe it's best that I don't know, anyway. I think that El Jitón was a tree when the land knew no Spanish, only the Mayo tongue.

From the very first, Teachive captivated me. As I walked its dusty streets, hammered by the relentless sun, and then stood in the blessed shade in the ramadas of Teachive's rustic, ancient houses seeing women kneeled before their looms and men passing by driving a solitary cow or burro, I knew I should return. Teachive fulfilled my childhood pictures of Mexico, from its dark-skinned, Indian-featured people, to the plastered, dirt-roofed adobe houses and the cactus-studded surroundings. The rough hills in the background, covered by low forest, provided an air of isolation and timelessness. When I left that day in early May (for I was wandering about the byways of rural Sonora), a crowd of people saw me off. Old women hoary with years being led by children, babies in mothers' arms, youths with a longing to venture into the great world beyond the village, reticent, curious men softly lingering in the background—all attended my departure. The setting sun bathed the village in a soft, hazy film, an image that stayed with me for days. I had to go back.

This book is a study of the economic life of a small peasant village named Teachive, of how the village's peasants derive wealth from their land and their work, how their land has supported them, and why it will ultimately fail them. Writing about the past and the present of a village with little recorded history requires a nearly total dependence on oral accounts. Archival records for the Masiaca *comunidad*, of which Teachive is a part, are scant. I was unable to locate any documents dating earlier than 1834. Historical references are equally scant, as I lament elsewhere in this book. When I reread *San Juan de Gracia*, Luis González's classic study of the history of a Michoacán village, I envied his fortune in studying a town with voluminous documented history and numerous residents of a historical bent. Most Mexican towns boast one or more prominent *cronistas*. Don Leocadio Piña Soto, an autodidact and the only prominent chronicler of the Masiaca community of which Teachive is a part, died before I undertook this study. His children burned nearly all of his books.

Teachive lies close to a larger town named Masiaca. Both sit on a populous plain near the lower Río Mayo in the Mexican state of Sonora.[5] In carrying out the research for this book, I made more than twenty trips to Teachive over a four-year period, between 1993 and 1997. My stays were usually for a week, occasionally longer. During that time I visited many other Mayo villages and met numerous individuals who were kind and generous enough to spend time with me, describe their life, and offer their opinions on how things are. On several occasions in 1993 and 1994, I was joined in the field by plant systematist Thomas R. Van Devender of the Arizona-Sonora Desert Museum, and at times by Rigoberto López of the University of Sonora. On those occasions, we engaged local people to help us identify plants and describe their uses.[6] More often, I arrived alone from the United States and would usually be accompanied in the field or in visiting other villages by Vicente Tajia Yocupicio of Teachive, who came to exert a strong influence on the observations and conclusions of the book. The repeated visits enabled me to become somewhat familiar to the people of Teachive and other villages in the comunidad of Masiaca, so that, gradually, the villagers relaxed their (justifiable) initial suspicions of a North American in their midst. After a while, people no longer viewed me as a police agent or government spy. They came to know that I was interested in how plants, or more accurately, the monte, *or bush, that surrounds Teachive, affected their community. My longstanding relationship with Vicente, his unending enthusiasm for his family, his village, and the surrounding forest, and his understanding of my desire to learn about them, have affected both of our perceptions of Teachive. Many of my observations and opinions reflect his opinions and suggestions. Other Mayos might offer differing opinions and conclusions.*

Teachive's peasants do not fit happily into most discussions of the peasantry. Their way of life has been altered as their region's economy has been transformed over the last fifty years from one of mostly small producers, peasant landholders, and grazers and gatherers, to one of corporate agribusinesses commanding vast tracts of irrigated farmland from which are manufactured fresh produce, vegetables, grains, animal feeds, and fiber crops.[7] In the seemingly endless fields of the Mayo Delta, computer assisted landowners and contractors employ the most up-to-date mechanical methods of agricultural production to extract wealth from the ground and distribute it internationally. Their planting strategies change daily as commodity prices fluctuate and production costs vary. Nearby dwell Mayos, hoping to endure, unchanged from years long past.

Teachive is an ancient peasant village. The ancestors of its residents have dwelt in the region for centuries, perhaps millennia. The natives of Teachive are, in one sense, minute cogs on a small gear in a peripheral apparatus in this gigantic capitalistic enterprise. In another sense they are apart, anchored to ancient cultural traditions and tied to the land by relations determined centuries ago. Teachive is small enough to afford personal glimpses into its people's individuality, yet closely enough related to the New World Order that the tensions between the ancient and modern, the traditional and the innovative, the culturally secure and the economically imperative, are visible. Its people have come alive for me as agents of an ancient regime and as tiny, quiescent witnesses of a contemporary economic juggernaut that threatens to obliterate the last traces of peasantry.

The 1990 Mexican census counted nearly 60,000 Mayos, making them northwest Mexico's largest indigenous group, more numerous than the better-known Yaquis. Their numbers are dispersed among dozens of hamlets and villages over an area exceeding three thousand square miles, extending southeastward into the state of Sinaloa and northwestward nearly to the Río Yaqui. Even prior to the arrival of the Spanish conquerors Mayos were involved in complex, though restricted interactions with the rest of the world. They had commodities that other people craved: salt, seashells, dried fish, fiery little chiles, and parrots (Hammond and Rey 1928). Also, their harvests of corn, beans, and squash, and the fruit of their immense forests of cacti were more reliable than those of peoples higher in the mountains, or in the cool, dry highlands on the eastern side of the continental divide. Usually, these crops were produced in surplus. Mayos won and lost battles, celebrated and mourned, intermarried, and traded with neighboring and distant peoples, by all accounts fiercely defending their autonomy. But with the arrival of the conquering Europeans, whom they accepted without organized resistance, they became ensnared in a skein of alien influences and control. Clergy, soldiers, miners, *hacendados*, merchants, Spaniards, *mestizos*, foreigners, and *latifundistas* settled in Mayo lands, superimposing themselves upon the Mayo culture and forever altering the Mayos' economic base. These outside forces waxed and waned over the centuries.

Today, the powerful centers of world commerce are inexorably reeling in those peoples on the fringes, even those who, like many Mayos, prefer to remain apart from the churnings of industry and the hum of computers. The women of Teachive now weave woolen rugs that may decorate an apartment in Tokyo. The men raise cows that may flavor soup in Hamburg; they weed fields of tomatoes and chiles that will grace tables in Santa Fe. The Mayos consume beans grown in Wisconsin and corn from Iowa. They wear clothing from Taiwan and listen to radios manufactured in Singapore. And so, in tiny Teachive, operating at the very margins of world commerce, some six hundred individuals influence and are influenced by affairs in Chicago, London, and Tokyo.[8]

CHAPTER ONE *The Land*

꙳ Teachive is an undistinguished hamlet forty-five kilometers south-east of the city of Navojoa in southern Sonora. It is one of ten villages along the banks of Arroyo Masiaca, whose small basin flows for fifty kilometers from the mountains southwestward to the sea. The village lies on the interrupted edge of a bajada (sloping alluvial plain) that spills out like a broad, velvet-brown river from inland mountains into wide, flat coastal plains. A kilometer to the north, not far from El Jitón, are modest volcanic hills rising out of the jito-studded lowlands like brown icebergs, and beyond them the larger mountains of the Sierra Batayaqui. Farther still to the northeast rise the steep sides of the Sierra de Alamos, a granitic mass torn and thrust upward during the basin-and-range geological period from twelve to five million years ago. Its pine-clad summit rises more than a mile above the plain. Beyond the Sierra de Alamos, north and east, rise the even higher mountains of Chihuahua—the real Sierra Madre and its immense canyons. East of the village is a more gently sloping bajada interspersed with rolling hills covered with low leguminous forest. This terrain flows for many miles into Sinaloa and extreme southwest Chihuahua, until it halts at the high ridges and convolutions of the great massifs and canyons of the Río Fuerte drainage.

West of Teachive, like a steep-sided island, lies the dark, lava-clad summit of Mesa Masiaca, two hundred meters above the plain. Atop the mesa, the Mexican government has commandeered a site for a microwave station. A cobblestone road leads up through the jumbled lava blocks to the summit. From its slopes, one can see far, across the vast checkerboard of irrigated fields of the delta of the Río Mayo and

MEXICO

Tepahui

Camoa

Tesia

Mocúzari

NAVOJOA

Cohuirimpo

ALAMOS

Etchojoa

HUATABAMPO

El Júpare

Teachive

Masiaca

Las Bocas

GULF OF

CALIFORNIA

The Río Mayo Region

finally, beyond them, to the Sea of Cortés. Across the flat, cactus-forested plains to the south are the shimmering sands and mazed estuaries of the Gulf.

The mesa's dark basaltic boulders are a welcome relief from the monotony of soils around the village west and south toward the sea. Powdery and soft when dry, a lumpy glue when wet, the soil is built from tiny windborne particles of clay. I have known them well since my first visit when the dust welled up in clouds and filtered into my pickup truck. Those choking sediments originated from multiple layers of mid-Tertiary volcanic rock, ash, and tuffs cemented together by heat and pressure in the great Sierra Madre to the northeast. This regional cap was deposited two kilometers deep, like icing on an elongated cake, atop a stout granitic batholith rent by catastrophic volcanic explosions and pyroclastic flows beginning more than forty million years ago and raging for another twenty million years (Thayer 1995). In that convulsive epoch calderas spewed forth more than 300,000 cubic kilometers of ash and ignumbrites. Even as it grew during those twenty thousand turbulent millennia, the great range was under attack, as it is today. The huge mass of mountains is gradually being leveled, the great works of Vulcan brought to naught by the relentless wearing down of its rocks, ever assaulted by wind, rain, hail, snow, lichens, mosses, and flowing water. Particle by tiny particle, grain by microscopic grain, the great mountains are being whittled, chiseled, and dissolved by a trillion cosmic toothpicks and transferred westward. Rain washes the particles into rivulets and creeks, streams and rivers, lifting and dropping them a thousand times until they arrive at the distant coast. Transported there by countless floodings, they have been deposited as fine silts, first here, then there, as the river channels meandered along the easiest route to the coast, or were forced into different directions by titanic geological forces—flows of lava or uplifts of whole mountains.

The journey of all this dirt, this finely ground rock, this partially digested cordillera, was hardly complete once it arrived at the sea. From there the particles piled into muddy mounds. Drying, they were blown into dunes, then whipped and buffeted along the coasts and inland by cyclones, squalls, and prevailing winds from the north, west, and south. A hundred million storms have ripped tiny bits of dune from the surface of the delta, flung the particles aloft, and dropped them on the Mayos' land, at the rate of an inch a century, ever so slowly filling up and leveling ancient gullies, canyons, and valleys, covering entire mountains, filling, filling, until today the old rough landscape has been buried under thousands of feet of finely packed dirt, a geological transfer from the Sierra Madre, its apology for such violent beginnings. The unending movement of fine silts seeps through every crack of human invention, inexorably burying every untended surface, a perpetual dust bowl. Now, just as a painter smooths over holes and cracks with putty and covers the surface with paint or a dammed river fills in a canyon reservoir, the land is flat. The crooked is made straight and the rough places plain.[1] Over the vast reaches of these great plains, one may wander for hours without encountering a single stone, much to the delight of the farmers who brought water to this dry land. Rocks are found only along the few watercourses that weave their way to the sea and where the few volcanic hills, the stoic inselbergs, managed to blast through the thick blanket of silt or, though themselves worn down, already were high enough to escape burial by the rising blankets of dust. Around Teachive may be found enough of these stones to warrant its ancient name.

Teachivans know well the landmark places: the Arroyo Masiaca, whose waters bring them life; Cerro Terúcuchi, a volcanic berg that rises five hundred feet above the surrounding alluvial plain about a kilometer to the north of the village; Mesa Masiaca (Masiacahui), the flat-topped basaltic mass to the west, some of whose ancient lava rocks sing like bells when struck; the Sierra de Alamos, called *nojme cahui* (the highest mountain)[2] by the Mayos, a mass large enough to capture moisture from air masses from the gulf and the south, intercepting their rain, storing it in its vast, porous network of seeps, and slowly releasing it into the valley below; El Jitón, the great tree, known to all who venture into the *monte*; and *la piedra bola*, a rock outcropping in the arroyo where water is always available and women come to launder clothing. The men of Teachive taught me about these places in my first days in the village, a sort of Teachive primer.

The climate of Teachive, at only fifty meters above the level of the Sea of Cortés, is arid and hot. Only on a few days each winter do the natives wear jackets during the day. Freezing temperatures are unknown. Some older folk know frost from other locations in the region, such as a killing frost in 1933 that decimated the tomato and pea crops of the delta. That freeze did not reach Teachive, however.[3] Snow is an object of conjecture and rumor, known only from photographs and the tales of travelers from afar. It has never been seen on the mountains visible from the Mayo country. Accounts of snow and below-zero temperatures are met with skepticism.[4]

Summer heat is oppressive, building up beginning in late April and continuing through October or early November, a period of sweat-filled days and, from late June through the interminable summer, muggy, insect-plagued nights. Temperatures above 35°C (97°F) are routine in these months, and they often exceed 40°C (104°F); rarely, they have reached 45°C (113°F). In Teachive only one home is equipped with evaporative cooling, which becomes ineffective in the high humidities of the summer rains. Eons ago, families incorporated into their daily lives the baking heat and drought that characterize much of the sun-drenched climate. Natives complain about the heat, but with little conviction.

During the months of heat each day begins with the first vague light of dawn. Light footsteps on the flat, dusty earth and the pat-pat of tortillas being shaped accompany the sounds of awakening birds, followed by greetings from roosters, burros, cows, goats, sheep, and dogs.[5] Beginning with one, but soon followed by another, and another, before long a hundred radios are blasting forth the relentless polka-style notes of *norteña* music.[6] Beasts of burden materialize, the motive force of local commerce that greatly outnumber motorized vehicles. Horse-drawn carts roll by, sounding their characteristic *clop-jingle-clop* as the trotting horses or slower burros are urged on by their drivers. The old reliable carts equal trucks in passenger-miles.

The early bustle takes an extended pause late in the morning, to resume only when the heat of the day begins to relent in the late afternoon. At times the heat is so intense that the mere act of sitting produces prodigious quantities of sweat. The natives utter only one lament, "¡Ay, que calor!" (Oh, what heat!). Waves of ascending heat distort the view across the open spaces of the village. The birds become still; livestock lie in shade and pant. Women who venture into the heat wear a towel or shawl over their heads to protect them from the sun.[7] Men wear mass-manufactured, Texas-style straw hats. Children seem oblivious to the throbbing heat.

In the shorter days of winter the village is rather noisier, as daylight work must be accomplished more quickly,[8] and the chatter of schoolchildren punctuates the midday stillness. The daytime temperatures are pleasant and more conducive to midday outdoor activity.

Rainfall averages about 350 millimeters, the same as Los Angeles, California, and only slightly more than Hermosillo, Sonora, in the hot desert to the north, but Teachive experiences greater humidity, thanks to meandering vapors from the Gulf of California and from the tropics. Residents assert that the rains are now fewer and less intense then they were in earlier times; this is perhaps nostalgia, perhaps fact. (Nearly everyone everywhere in the world believes the weather used to be better.) Summer rains, on which most vegetation depends, have generally failed in the last decade. According to published records

(Hastings and Humphrey 1969), most of the precipitation comes in July and August (August and September, in recent years), in the happy days known as *las aguas*. Then, if things are right (and they have not been right, natives complain, for a decade[9]), brief, heavy downpours occur, frequently accompanied by brilliant displays of lightning and resounding thunder, to the delight of all. Children burst with glee from their huts to revel in the water and mud. After the first such rain, the *monte* comes alive with creatures who have lain dormant awaiting this event, the myriad of lizards, toads, frogs, snakes, and many insects. After a heavy rain the night throbs with the thrummings of small animal life.

In December and January, and often later, gentler rains associated with cyclonic Pacific storms called *equipatas* often last for a day or more. These generally deposit smaller amounts of rainfall, the kind that sinks into the soil and does not run off. During these chilly, muddy days, children huddle under the roofs and in the portals, shivering (no home in the region has a heater) and hoping for entertainment by older folk who use the long nights and idle hours to describe how things were yesterday and long, long ago. Many crowd around radios to listen to episodes of *novelas* (soap operas). Some now watch television, which has slowly spread into the village, as electricity has become available.

In addition to *las aguas* and *las equipatas*, every few years autumnal storms lumber in from the tropical East Pacific to strafe the region. These *ciclones* drop heavy rains that flood the washes and drench the flat plain with sheets of water that mix with the silty clay soils to produce an impassable gumbo. Teachive mud, formed from the ancient wind-borne clays of volcanic origin, adheres to the passerby like the dung of Harpies. Villagers eye these storms with an uneasy hope, for the rain chases the heat, refreshes the air, cleanses the *monte*, and feeds the green leaves. The endless mud means no work, and an abysmal mess.

The vegetation of the region, the basis of local subsistence, consists primarily of coastal and foothills thornscrub (Yetman et al. 1995; see also Valenzuela 1984). To the south, southwest, and southeast of the village the thornscrub is a collection of low, thorny trees, spiny shrubs, thick-stemmed succulents, and several species of cacti of commanding size, including the great columnars, *pitahaya* (*Stenocereus thurberi*) and *etcho* (*Pachycereus pecten-aboriginum*). The canopy of this cactus-dominated coastal thornscrub is between fifteen and eighteen feet high (Gentry 1942), with occasional plants reaching over thirty feet. Hindered only by the profusion of spiny arms and branches, one can wander through this flat land and wonder at the many-armed giants and the profusion of other plants, easily becoming lost, so undifferentiated is the horizon. A few kilometers inland from the coast, *pitahayas* form dense forests, an unrecognized national treasure of Mexico. This vegetation, locally called *pitahayal*, is desertlike much of the year. With the summer rains it is transformed into a semi-jungle teeming with exploding plant growth, including vines of many species and biting and swarming insects in great numbers.

Inland—that is, east, north, and northeast of Teachive—the foothills thornscrub is more dense, with trees taller and occurring in greater variety. *Pitahayas*, fewer in number, taller and often with a hundred arms, great morning glory trees, acacias, mesquites, and a wide variety of tropical legumes populate the forest, whose canopy reaches more than twenty feet in height. Flocks of parrots frequent the trees and turkeylike *chachalacas* scurry and flit through the shrubbery.[10] The fortunate traveler who can spend the night alone in this open forest will look back on it as a most delectable experience, the moon illuminating the trees and the gigantic *pitahayas* and *etchos*, the night birds hooting and howling, the thick brush rustling with secretive creatures of the night. Rainy season growth in this habitat is even more spectacular and produces a jungle through which passage is difficult. A machete becomes a necessity.

In June, just prior to the onset of *las aguas*, trees begin to leaf out.[11] In late June or early July, if weather patterns cooperate, great thunderheads build over the mountains to the north and east. The great montane mass there may receive in excess of one meter (forty inches) of rain a year, most of it in July and August. Teachive averages hardly a third of that, fourteen inches. Slowly, as though with agonizing deliberation, sometimes teasing for tantalizing weeks, the billowing clouds spread into the adjacent valleys and the coastal plain, bringing with them the first rains, but not before kicking up clouds of stinging dust that sifts into houses like flour.

The rains are awaited with longing. Vicente and I have whiled away many evenings by dragging chairs into the open air, watching the lightning flashes far to the north, tracing their approach, and lamenting their failure to arrive. As villagers walk from here to there, they turn to the north in an often forlorn hope. Some women have their looms situated so that they can see storms approaching as they weave their blankets, keeping a watchful and hopeful eye on the far mountains. Often the storms build up over Nojme Cahui, a scant twenty-five kilometers away, flirting with the valleys, only occasionally bringing rain to Teachive.

Moisture and warm temperatures transform the usually dreary gray-brown landscape into a pandemonium of greens. Herbs, shrubs, and trees break into leaf within hours of the first sprinkles. Edible greens erupt from the soil and villagers scurry after them, racing against the goats, sheep, and cows for the most succulent harvest. Climbing vines explode, binding themselves to everything within grasp, jumping from tree to tree until the *monte* resembles one continuous plant of a hundred shades of green, saturating the countryside with luxurious growth. This metamorphosis endures for two to three months, depending upon the extent and duration of the summer rains. Gradually the rains taper off, the leaves on the trees and shrubs turn color and fall to the ground, the vines wither and die, and the herbs wilt and disappear or are consumed by herbivores. By late fall, if rains have not intervened, the landscape begins to appear silvery brown. By late spring all traces of green have disappeared except for the *pitahaya*, the *etcho*, the *jito*, and a few renegade trees such as the *saituna* (*Ziziphus amole*).

This forest is of immense consequence for the community of Teachive, as it is their most significant connection with a peasant life. The thornscrub of the hills and plains is home to more than two hundred plant species used by Mayos in one manner or another (Dunbier 1968, 232–34; Yetman et al. 1995; see also Appendix B). Ten kilometers to the north and east the thornscrub merges into tropical deciduous forest that supports an even greater variety of plants and taller trees, which Teachivans know and use to great advantage. Through the once unending forests the Mayos have passed for eons, gathering food, fiber, materials, medicines, and talismans for their very survival.

Even today Vicente teaches his grandsons what can be eaten and used in the vast *monte*. As the forest resource has been chewed by livestock, felled, and lopped, or has dried up in ongoing drought, and as foods from afar have supplanted the local, less convenient produce of the *monte*, gathering has dwindled. Still, no *campesino* (rural dweller) or *vaquero* (cowboy) passes through the forest without collecting something or other, a stone, a root, a fruit, a branch, a leaf, a flower, or some sap to take home. Herdsmen keep a constant watch for *panales*, hives of wild bees from which strong local honey is produced. They also watch for deer, which cross the *monte* from time to time, but in fewer numbers than only a decade ago due to heavy poaching and the loss of browse to domestic herbivores. The harvesting of a deer is a most special occasion for people who seldom are able to enjoy fresh meat. *Cholugo* (coatimundi), *mapache* (raccoon), *conejo* (cottontail rabbit), and *zorillo* (skunk) are also killed for their meat. The latter seems improbable, yet most men of the village insist that the meat is tasty. That anyone would eat skunk attests to a certain carnivorous desperation. Vicente reports, laughing, that one fellow killed a coyote and ground up the meat into meatballs.

Rattlesnakes are also common in the *monte*. Throughout the year, but mostly in the moist months of summer and fall, reports of sightings and killings arrive daily and are greeted with great interest. Don Rufino was bitten twice by the same snake in 1996 and suffered a lot of pain, but apparently no permanent injury despite his more than seventy years. A good deal of speculation circulated in the village as to how it was possible that someone could be bitten twice by the same snake. Most people agreed he must have been doing something weird, but they refused to discuss the matter in detail in a gringo's presence.

The snakes are killed and harvested in their entirety. Toño Gámez saves the meat and sells the skins. He collects the bile (*hiel*) in tiny bottles and renders the suet (*manteca*) into a liquid, dispensing both as cures for various ailments. He dries the skeleton and pulverizes it in a mortar, selling the powder to an eager Mexican public who sprinkle the ground bones on food as a virility fortifier.

Cactus fruits, which are dietary staples, are easily found within walking distance of the village, including *etcho* fruits in June and *pitahayas* in late July through September. Boys are often assigned the task of providing status reports. When the fruits are ripe, the word spreads quickly. Most of the fruits, which are covered with spines and *alguates* (glochids), grow high on the spiny arms of the cactus, well beyond human reach. Men and women prepare long poles of agave shoots, or, if these are not available, of *etcho* or *pitahaya* ribs and lash a sharpened stick to the end. With this simple tool (*bacote*), easily manufactured in the field, the harvesters impale the fruits, wiggle them carefully from the cactus, and lower them to the ground where they are grabbed and eaten by eager children or are popped into a bucket and carried home. With a few flicks of a knife the spines, which can produce a nasty puncture, are scraped off and the fruits are ready to eat. The more practiced gatherers handle the spiny fruits with consummate delicacy: they can carefully incise the point of attachment, peel away the skin, and without a single prick of the skin expose a golfball of delectable flesh.

Villagers have memorized the location of a myriad of individual plants, some of which Vicente pointed out to me. He knows which plants have long, stiff spines, which have spines with more venom, and which have spines easier to remove. He also remembers which plants are prolific producers, which have sweeter fruit, and which yield white (*zarca*) or rose-colored (*rosa*) fruits. The cactus fruits disappear rapidly, so that during the ripening of the *pitahayas*, villagers must compete for the harvest against each other and against a host of birds, insects, and lizards, which crowd around the ripe fruits. Competition is friendly, for there is plenty for everyone, as all know.

At harvest time mouths and hands are dyed red from frequent contact with the luscious fruits. Children eat dozens, spending entire mornings glutting themselves with the pulp. Adults are more discreet, matching the children's' intake, but more quietly. Even with this immense consumption, the harvesters return home with buckets of fruit. A steady trickle of older folk, mostly men with reddened mouths, can be seen returning from the *monte*, each with the long *bacote* draped over a shoulder, an overflowing bucket or bag of fruits swinging from the opposite hand. While *pitahayas* are eaten directly from the tree, they are also consumed in enormous numbers in homes (they are said to be easier to peel if left overnight in a bucket after harvesting), or are sun-dried into *pitahaya seca*, with a taste like a sweet dried fig, or made into a form of *tamal* (corn mixed with other ingredients and steamed in cornhusks).

A dry July, more common in recent decades than before, usually means smaller and fewer fruits on the *pitahayas*. Although the *pitahayas* (and to a lesser extent *tunas*, the fruits of the prickly pear) are sold in markets and supermarkets in Navojoa and Huatabampo, Teachive natives do not appear to harvest the fruits for sale. The highway and the markets are too distant. Natives of Chichibojoro and Las Bocas,

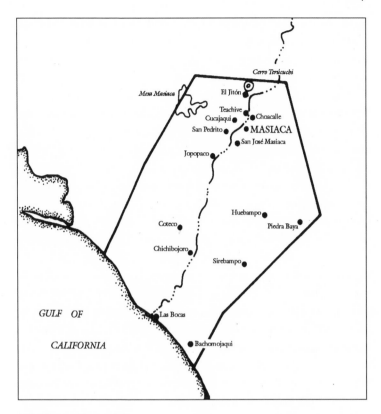

The Masiaca Comunidad

also villages in the Masiaca *comunidad*, collect fruit from the immense stands of *pitahayas* found nearby their villages and market them along the international highway that runs northwest to southeast, splitting the *comunidad* in half. Some *comuneros* also venture to the markets of Navojoa and Huatabampo and sell the cactus fruits there.

Among the villagers at Teachive, *etcho* fruits, which ripen in May and June, are also eaten, although they are less tasty than the *pitahayas*. A few women press the liquid from the *etcho* fruit, strain out the seed, and save both. The juice (*miel*) is boiled down to a powerfully sweet syrup that is relished by all. The women dry and grind the seeds, mix them with corn dough, and pat them into tortillas (with a taste that resembles blueberry pancakes) or stew them into *atole* (similar to cream of wheat). The intense labor requirements for producing *etcho* seeds limit production considerably. The seeds must be washed free of all pulp, strained, dried, then washed and dried once again, all the while protected from dust and dirt. Doña Victoria Acosta is one of the few women who now harvests *etcho* seeds. It takes her a full day to prepare a kilo of tiny seeds no larger than those of a poppy.

Teachive has developed in a narrow strip about a half-kilometer long on either side of the Arroyo Masiaca. The stream trickles quietly and faithfully through at least part of the village, to where the *bajada* nearly levels out, forming occasional pools where small fish (introduced talapia) swim fitfully in the meager flow. The streambed is wide and it grades gently enough that runoff flows and floods deposit silt from mountains and valleys above, like a tiny, unreliable Nile. These muddy waters nurture grasses in the riverbed and trees that line the streamside, providing fodder for livestock and shade and coolness for people.[12]

The floods are welcome for other reasons as well. Early one August morning don Vicente and I, accompanied by a host of barefoot boys, watched transfixed as raging flood waters brought on by a heavy tropical rain in the upper watershed, receded in the arroyo, leaving behind a nutritious muck. Vicente spotted a drifting branch and urged the boys to bring it in. The lads flowed down the bank like a cascade, plopped through the silty mud and in an instant had the snag in tow, quickly followed by another, then another and another still. Before long a month's supply of firewood, a gift of the rain god, was stacked alongside doña Teresa's kitchen.

Both banks of the river are lined with thick groves of mesquites and elegant, white-trunked *josos*, which also benefit from the floods.[13] Their dense shade offers relief from the blazing sun for men and beasts. In these great thickets, men, women, and animals who wish to may be concealed for whatever reason, even during the desiccating winds of late spring. Anonymity, not easily found in village life, is privately cherished in Teachive. For a good mile up the arroyo, the tangle of trees and shrubs on the banks is so thick one can become disoriented within—or hide with confidence. At the *aguaje*, a pool in the arroyo a few hundred yards north of the crossing, people bathe, usually at night, when their partial or total nudity will not be noticed. In late 1995 villagers cut down some of the great old mesquites along the arroyo. The explanation was that there was too much cover that might afford protection to thieves and rapists.

CHAPTER TWO *The People: A Brief History*

꙾ Historical references to Masiaca and Teachive are scant, yet considerable research has been done on the history of the Mayos (Pérez de Ribas 1645, Troncoso 1905, Sauer 1932, Spicer 1962, Acosta 1983, O'Connor 1989).[1] Prior to the Spanish conquest, the Mayos, who refer to themselves as *yoreme*, were an agricultural people loosely organized in settlements along the Río Mayo, a small regionally important river in southern Sonora originating in the deep canyons and lush coniferous forests of the Sierra Madre. Their language is classified as Uto-Aztecan, meaning that it manifests numerous cognates with Nahuatl, the language of the Aztecs, and that the two languages share considerable syntax. The language spoken by Mayos, Yaquis, and several extinct groups to the south is known as Cahita, meaning "there is nothing" in Cahita.[2] The Mayos lived far enough away from the Valley of Mexico—a thousand miles of mountains and canyons—that Aztec influence was limited to trading. The forty years of Aztec hegemony were not enough for the Aztecs to accomplish the military suppression of the far-flung Cahitas of the Chichimeca, the name Aztecs gave to the huge, vague area to the north and west of the Valley of Mexico.[3]

The Mayo economy was based upon corn, beans and squash, cotton, game, and a few other domesticated crops, which they raised in the fertile delta floodplain. They carried on limited trade with inland peoples. Though their languages were nearly identical, Mayos were frequently at war with Yaquis to the north, and intermittently with other Cahitan-speaking peoples to the south, and, in all probability, Guarijíos to the northeast.

Mayos did not leave a record of impressive architecture or social 19 organization. Perhaps they were relatively recent arrivals in the region. Perhaps the hot, dry climate along the river made construction of elaborate shelters unnecessary. Perhaps the region lacked the materials to make impressive monuments. For whatever reason, they did not construct large buildings, as did the Hohokam to the north, the Casas Grandes culture to the northeast, and the multiplicity of peoples in central and southern Mexico. Moreover, regular flooding of the Río Mayo made an elaborate system of irrigation ditches unnecessary, hence the archeological record does not reveal centers of agricultural production.

Because of this lack of physical evidence from earlier centuries, descriptions of the Mayos' social organization are scant, especially when compared with records from more architecturally oriented peoples in the New World. Likewise, the earliest Jesuit missionaries concentrated far more on conversions and military expeditions against the heathen than they did on describing the cultures of the peoples they encountered in northwest New Spain.[4] This absence of information about early Mayo culture is frustrating, not only to the historian but to contemporary Mayo as well.

The postcontact ethnographic record is little better. The invading Spaniards found little of interest to write home about; there was no gold or silver on Mayo farmlands (delta soils are thousands of feet deep, and any mineralization lay buried beneath the silt of the ages). The relative lack of riches may have been the Mayos' salvation, for the otherwise rapacious *conquistadores* found nothing worth pillaging among them, not even reports of gold upstream, as had tempted them in the adjacent region of Sinaloa, and no silver until nearly the end of the century.[5] Mayo lands were also sufficiently distant from the capital that taking Mayos back as slaves would have proved inconvenient, especially when there were so many other Indians living closer. On the other hand, the Indians themselves could work, and when silver was eventually discovered in 1679, seventy years after the arrival of the Jesuits, Mayo labor became indispensable for extracting the wealth from the ground. Moreover, Mayo farms were capable of producing much, a fact which would lead to the eviction of Mayos from their lands as agricultural trade developed and would be their downfall in the late nineteenth century, as the Industrial Revolution vastly expanded world agricultural markets.[6]

When the Jesuits entered Mayo lands in 1608, they introduced modest protections for the Indians against the exploitation of miners and *hacendados*. Limited as they were, they would have been the envy of millions of other Indians in the (then) wealthier southern provinces of Mexico, who staggered under the much heavier burdens of taxation and forced labor that the Spaniards imposed there.

Much of the early contact with Spaniards is well known. In the year 1533 Diego de Guzmán, nephew of Nuño de Guzman, the leader of a Spanish slave-gathering expedition, crossed the Mayo River, probably near present-day Mocúzari, while marching northward (Troncoso 1905, 37; Sauer 1932, 12). There, he found only an abandoned village, suggesting that the natives had received advance word of his expedition and fled. Guzmán's forward progress was turned back at the Río Yaqui, when Yaquis refused to allow him to cross their lands and a lively battle ensued. The Yaquis proved to be such valiant warriors that Guzmán lost his enthusiasm for proceeding farther north. He made note of the Yaquis' prowess as warriors, making no mention of any resistance by the Mayos, even though, given his family's slave-gathering tendencies, he must have enslaved any that he encountered. The Mayos' first contact with the Spanish, then, can hardly have made a favorable impression.

The early "Christianizing" (conquering) expeditions of the Spaniards into northwest Mexico were a disaster for the indigenous peoples there. After the first murderous expeditions, many groups resorted to flight rather than face cavalry, muskets, torture, and disease. In 1536 the shipwrecked wanderer Cabeza de Vaca encountered a group of Spaniards in southern Sonora or northern Sinaloa.[7] Later, he described what he found in what is now Sonora:

> We traveled over a great part of the country, and found it all
> deserted, as the people had fled to the mountains, leaving
> houses and fields out of fear of the Christians. This filled our
> hearts with sorrow, seeing the land so fertile and beautiful, so
> full of water and streams, but abandoned and the places
> burned down, and the people, so thin and wan, fleeing and
> hiding; and as they did not raise any crops their destitution
> had become so great that they ate bark and roots. . . . They
> brought us blankets, which they had been concealing from the

Christians, and gave them to us, and told us how the Christians had penetrated into the country before, and had destroyed and burnt the villages, taking with them half of the men and all the women and children, and those who could escaped by flight.
(Cabeza de Vaca 1972, 133–34)

Cabeza de Vaca wrote no names to associate with the peoples he described. His route, though, took him through Mayo lands (Sauer 1932, 20), so he could well have been describing the Mayos (among others).

Other early sources are singularly silent on Mayo resistance as well. At that time, numerous groups were identified by the rivers along which they lived, including the Sinaloa, the Zuaque (Fuerte), the Mayo, and the Yaqui (Sauer 1935). Although all these groups were united by a mutually intelligible language (Cahita), they viewed themselves as distinct peoples with distinct customs. Sinaloas and Zuaques, for example, are known to have offered tenacious resistance to the invading Spaniards, but Mayos are not among the resistors described (Pérez de Ribas 1645).

The next historical mention of the Mayos occurs in 1539 in connection with Coronado's unsuccessful expedition in search of the fabled seven cities of Cíbola (Acosta 1949). Coronado's route followed a northern tributary of the Mayo River (the Río Cedros, whose lower part is now an arm of Lake Mocúzari) into the higher mountains, skirting the Yaqui lands, quite possibly on the basis of Guzman's previous sobering experience. The fact that the expedition moved directly through Mayo lands indicates that Mayos were generally believed to lack hostility to Spaniards.

Another expedition into the same distant lands was undertaken in 1565 by one Francisco de Ibarra, a governor of the province of Nueva Vizcaya, who successfully traversed the Mayo country.[8] Baltasar de Obregón, who was part of the expedition, described the Mayos on the lower Río Cedros in his chronicle (Obregón 1988). The expedition proceeded only to a point near present-day Casas Grandes in Chihuahua, via the upper Río Sonora and Río Bavispe (Pérez de Ribas 1645, ch. 9; Sauer 1932; Acosta 1983). On his return, Ibarra spent some time among the Yaquis, long enough, at least, to use his troops to help the Yaquis defeat the Mayos in a skirmish and pillage and burn one of their villages. From his brief description, it is clear that the Mayos and Yaquis were enemies and had engaged in frequent warfare (Acosta 1983). The fact that the Yaquis recruited Ibarra's assistance suggests that there was a semblance of military equality between the two peoples.

Intermittent contacts with Spaniards occurred thereafter, mostly to the Mayos' detriment. One especially unfortunate episode resulted from a 1585 expedition led by Hernando de Bazán, an irascible governor of Nueva Viscaya. Angered by the deaths and mutilation of two of his soldiers at the hands of Indians (perhaps Sinaloans), Bazán went on a rampage in the region. Spurning Mayo gifts of food and supplies that were offered innocently and generously, he invaded Mayo lands, seized a few men, put them in chains, and dragged them back with him as slaves. For this, he was ultimately removed from office, for the Mayos even then were known for their peaceful, generous nature and Bazán's cruelty was considered excessive, even for those ruthless times (Pérez de Ribas 1645, ch. 10; Troncoso 1905).

In 1608, Spanish forces under the direction of Diego Martínez de Hurdaide entered Mayo lands and received the Indians' submission without bloodshed, an achievement that brought great satisfaction to Hurdaide and his Jesuit contemporaries (Pérez de Ribas 1645). The Mayos must have been impressed with the Spaniards' military efficiency and technological superiority, for they appear to have offered little resistance. For their part, the Spaniards were sufficiently impressed with the Mayos' military and provisioning skills that they recruited them by the thousands. The Mayos were described as "more than thirty thousand strong, and [they] could launch ten thousand warriors into battle" (Acosta 1983, 46).[9] That the Mayos were willing to provide warriors in such numbers suggests that they did not view themselves as a conquered people, but rather as allies of the Spaniards.

The Mayos' willingness to accept Spanish authority probably lay more in their hope for deliverance from disease and their respect for the Spaniards' superior armaments than in the self-evident truth of the Catholic faith. They hoped to escape the depredations of disease and enlist the new technology in battling their ancient enemies, the Yaquis, and, to a lesser extent, the Tahuecos and Zuaques to the south (Sauer 1934, Spicer 1962).[10] Indeed, the Mayos may simply have had the historic fortune or misfortune to have been the first of the Yaquis' opponents encountered by the Spaniards. The Mayos, seeing an opportunity to defeat their ancient enemy, allied themselves with the newcomers once and for all, especially with the memory of Francisco de Ibarra's military aid to the Yaquis only a generation away. Had the Yaqui lands been situated south of the Mayo, the tables might have been turned.

In 1609 Hurdaide recruited hordes of Mayos for an offensive against the Yaquis, who had incurred Hurdaide's wrath by granting asylum to two Tepehuanes accused of massacring two Spaniards. The Mayos approached the upcoming battle with enthusiasm (Pérez de Ribas 1645, ch. 10). The first and second allied attacks on the Yaquis failed miserably. The Yaquis inflicted resounding defeats on the combined forces of the Spaniards, Mayos, and other indigenous groups, nearly exterminating the Spanish forces in the process.[11] The Mayos must have been greatly relieved when the Yaquis approached Hurdaide in 1610 offering submission and requesting peace, much to the latter's surprise. One of the conditions of acceptance Hurdaide imposed was that the Yaquis cease their warring with the Mayos, a condition most acceptable to the latter (Acosta 1983, 58). The Mayos must also have marveled at the miraculous ability of the Spaniards, in the face of two nearly catastrophic military defeats, to extract apparent submission from the Yaquis.

The Mayos appear to have accepted the Spaniards and the Jesuits readily. Fray Pérez de Ribas professes to have been impressed indeed with the piety and devotion of the Mayo converts. He noted in 1614:

> I have never seen in any converts so clear a sign of the grace
> and presence of the Holy Spirit as among these [Mayos]. Even
> those still set in old customs, on being baptized, appear over-
> come with such extraordinary joy that the lame and aged seem
> to recover their feet and their youthful energy, and the mute
> recover their speech, so that they can run to the church and to
> their priest and give thanks for his merciful gift to them.[12]
> (Pérez de Ribas 1645, bk. 4, ch. 3, translation mine)

Pérez de Ribas assumes, naively along with nearly all of his contemporaries, that the Mayos received the Jesuits warmly due to the self-evident truth of the (European) Catholic way of life.[13] So confident was he of the obvious superiority of European culture that he and his colleagues were incapable of interpreting their own actions, or the Mayos' responses, except through the lens of their Eurocentric view. As we shall see, the Jesuits might have been a good deal less euphoric had they attempted to see events from a Mayo perspective.

Accounts like that of Pérez de Ribas may have established the reputation of the Mayos as a gentle and peace-loving people. Villa (1951, 31), writing in the 1930s, compared the Yaquis and Mayos: "As much as the Yaquis are characterized by their warlike and irascible temperament, the Mayos are of a peaceful nature, having shown themselves for some time to be submissive and obedient to the constituted powers." Vázquez (1955, 128) described them in a similar vein: "Mayos are of a gentle character and have shown themselves since long ago to be submissive to the Government. They have dedicated themselves to agriculture, to raising cattle and a few small industries, never reaching the level of resistance and political agility of the Yaquis." These are historical distortions that impugn Mayo integrity and their attachment to their land, as we shall see, yet the myth of Mayo submissiveness retains surprising acceptance.[14]

Five years passed after the Mayos' agreement with Hurdaide before priests became available to convert the Mayos and minister to their putative spiritual needs. When the clerics arrived, they worked tirelessly to make Europeanized Catholics out of the Indians. They "reduced" the Mayo population to seven or eight pueblos, herding all the Indians into religious centers where the clerics could more easily control and observe them.[15] The first Jesuits among the Mayos, padres Pedro Méndez and Diego de la Cruz, reported baptizing "around thirty thousand Christian souls" by the year 1620 without the least resistance, an average of about fifteen per day, year in and year out (Pérez de Ribas 1645, bk. 2, ch. 47; Nakamaya 1957, 73).[16] Sauer (1981, 169) estimates the aboriginal Mayo population to have been twenty-five thousand, suggesting that Fray Méndez inflated his figures. At any rate, these figures give a fair estimate of Mayo population at the time. Fray Méndez claimed to have founded seven Mayo pueblos, and in his first fifteen days to have baptized 3,100 children and 500 adults (Alegre 1888). Many of those who were baptized were ill and died soon thereafter, indicating that an epidemic was sweeping the Mayos at the time.[17] Neither Peréz de Ribas nor Francisco Alegre (writing two centuries later) describe the baptism ceremony, so it is impossible to know what the Mayos thought was actually taking place. What we do know is that the baptisms took place very quickly.

The early Jesuits in Sinaloa (which included the Mayo and Yaqui River basins at the time) were eager to please both their own superiors and the secular/military authorities with whom they had a close relationship, so they were apt to see the brightest possible side of any success and paint it in rosy colors. On the other hand, the Jesuits were stern disciplinarians with rigorous internal review procedures that discouraged exaggeration in the number of conversions and baptisms claimed. Still, the velocity of Méndez's baptisms precluded careful scrutiny. Double baptisms must have taken place. It should also be remembered that the Mayos had been bickering and jousting with the Yaquis (and others) for years, perhaps for centuries, and, if seventeenth-century testimony is any indication, they were decidedly second best militarily. Their ebullience at the arrival of the Jesuits, who promised, among other things, an end to hostilities with the Yaquis, is understandable from the standpoint of self-preservation. There is no evidence, however, apart from the descriptions of the clerics, that the Mayos recognized and accepted the inherent superiority of the "civilization" the Spaniards brought, including their religion. The Mayos may have interpreted the baptism ceremony as instilling a sort of protection against Yaquis and against disease, a magical mantle that would guard against injury. Baptisms were proffered as precursors to eternal life and so must have seemed to the Mayos a remarkable innovation indeed.

Pérez de Ribas does not mention the possibility of multiple baptisms of the same infant or child. While others dismiss the possibility of inaccurate tabulations (Polzer 1976), it can hardly be reasonably ruled out. Viewing the events of the early seventeenth century from a Mayo perspective, it is hard to imagine that Mayo parents did not line up with their children for repeated applications of whatever power the baptismal water would bring. It is equally hard to imagine the recently arrived Jesuits ferreting out from the naked or scantily clad throngs of milling natives those souls who were requesting inoculation for a second, third, or even fourth time.

Jesuits exhibited the dominant European view toward New World natives as savage, nonrational barbarians. They characterized the

Mayos, young and old alike, as childlike. The Jesuit Pfefferkorn's characterization (of Sonoran Indians) is most revealing:

> Imagine a person who possesses all the customary qualities
> which make one disgusting, base, and contemptible; a person
> who proceeds in all of his actions blindly, without considera-
> tion or deliberation; a person who is untouched by kindness,
> unmoved by sympathy, unshamed by disgrace, not troubled by
> care; a person who loves neither faith nor truth and who has no
> firm will on any occasion; a person not charmed by honor, not
> gladdened by fortune, or sorrowed by misfortune; finally, a
> person who looks only at the present and the sensual, who has
> only animal instincts, who lives indifferently, and who dies in-
> differently. Such a person is the true picture of a Sonoran.[18]
> (Pfefferkorn 1949, 166)

Pfefferkorn goes on to lament the Sonorans' "natural stupidity, their complete neglect of themselves, the baseness of their spirits ..." (1949, 172) He did not like chiles, either. A Jesuit contemporary of Pfefferkorn, Juan Nentvig, made a similar pronouncement:

> The disposition of the [Sonoran] Indian rests on four founda-
> tions, each one worse than the other, and they are: ignorance,
> ingratitude, inconstancy, and laziness. Such in truth is the
> pivot on which the life of the Indian turns and moves. (Nent-
> vig 1951, 54)

The Father Visitor Roderigo de Cabredo wrote in 1610 concerning Sonoran Indians that "experience teaches that the natives who apply themselves more readily to work are less prone to uprisings and distur-bances among themselves." This meant, of course, that work should be piled on (Polzer 1976, 64).

The Mayos' rationale for acceptance of the Spaniards was surely as carefully calculated as the Europeans' plans for the Mayos. Jesuit docu-ments suggest that the black robes did not contemplate the lengthy discussions that undoubtedly took place among Mayo leaders weigh-ing the pros and cons of policies toward the newcomers. From the Jesuit viewpoint, their mere appearance was the cause of spontaneous

rejoicing and long parades of welcome. Although we can only speculate on the Mayo standpoint, their response must have been arrived at
after long deliberations and interminable meetings among villages and
families, including rumors and gossip based on reports from the south,
where the Spaniards were already well established.[19] If we are to believe
Jesuit accounts, Mayo sorcerers envied the Jesuits' powers and sought
unsuccessfully to dissuade the Indians from accepting the Europeans.
The polemics of these Mayo clerics are described for us only by
Europeans, few of whom were fluent in Cahita, and who made little if
any effort to portray or understand the context in which the native
practitioners attempted their persuasions. The Mayos' eventual acceptance of the Jesuits can hardly have been the univocally positive response Pérez de Ribas describes.

Even more important in understanding the Mayos' enthusiasm for
the Jesuits is the fact that diseases were already rampant in the region
by the time the Jesuits arrived. At least two epidemics, one in 1602 and
one in 1606–07, decimated populations among Cahitas, probably including Mayos (Reff 1991). Previous epidemics to the south were undoubtedly well known to the Mayos, including one in 1593 which may
have affected them as well. These were among dozens of epidemics
that reduced the indigenous population of New Spain by as much as
90 percent in the first one hundred years of Spanish occupation. Natives, noting that the Jesuits seemed far less prone to infection than
themselves, concluded logically that the priests' immunity had something to do with the faith the Spaniards were promoting, and signed
up in droves, hoping to be granted the same relative freedom from
disease as the black robes. Reff cites contemporary sources telling of
natives who traveled great distances seeking blessings from the Jesuits
in the hope that they could ward off or cure the new plagues that
rained down on indigenous peoples. The Jesuit's were concerned that
the natives would misconstrue the spiritual intent of baptism as a
medical procedure.

Whatever the reasons, the Mayos do appear to have welcomed the
arrival of the Jesuits, if not of the Spanish in general. Their enthusiasm
for the new faith and the benefits of baptism must have diminished
somewhat in ensuing years, for in the next three decades, in spite of
their adoption of the European religion, their numbers continued to
be ravaged by diseases introduced by the same forces that brought

them the new religion. Jesuits have been nearly universally praised for the "civilizing" benefits of the mission system and the introduction of European technology and commodities (Dunbier 1968, 124). These "benefits" are seldom spelled out, however, and when examined closely, they usually fail to represent much more than a covert depreciation of native American cultures.[20] One thing is clear: the mission system brought people into crowded conditions, greatly assisting the spread of such diseases as dysentery, influenza, leprosy, malaria, measles, plague, smallpox, typhoid, and typhus.[21] The Mayos' numbers had probably been greatly diminished by disease in the previous seventy-five years since contact with early Spanish explorers; at least half of those remaining died horrible deaths from smallpox and other epidemics following the Jesuits' arrival (Pérez de Ribas 1645, bk. 2, ch. 48).[22] The warm embraces with which the Mayos received the Europeans were the Indians' downfall, for the close contact with Spaniards and the native Americans' lack of resistance to alien disease left them frightfully vulnerable.

By contrast, Yaquis to the north stoutly and successfully resisted the Spanish invasion and accepted missionaries only on their own terms—in small numbers and unaccompanied by soldiery and civilians. This proscription undoubtedly decreased the pool of pestilential inoculum and shielded them from the worst initial epidemics of smallpox and measles, a lesson that was surely not lost on the ever-vigilant Yaquis (Spicer 1982). Even though they were to suffer deeply from later pestilences, for example, that of 1616–17 (Reff 1991, 158), homeopathic doses of European plagues were surely sufficient to convince the Yaquis to reinforce their historic xenophobia against non-Yaquis, especially Europeans.

The Yaquis, sending a woman *cacique* as an ambassador, convinced two Mayos to act as go-betweens in their negotiations for missionaries with the twice-defeated Captain Hurdaide (Pérez de Ribas 1645, bk. 2, ch. 53). From the standpoint of history, one might view the Yaquis as successfully using the Mayos as cannon fodder, or in the light of Reff's analysis, as rubber gloves.[23]

For nearly seventy years after the arrival of the Jesuits, the Mayos lived in relative tranquillity. That is to say, apart from the diseases that decimated their numbers and the regimentation imposed by the Jesuits as a price for their ministrations, both spiritual and administrative, no major rebellions stand out in the historical record.[24] Whether the Mayos felt this was a peaceful time or not, the Jesuits seem to have considered it such. While they must have benefited from the end to regional hostilities, the Mayos can hardly have enthusiastically accepted the judgments of the Inquisition and the imposition of harsh religious requirements, including whippings and other corporal punishments for petty infractions such as failure to attend mass, recite incantations, or supply the required labor to the mission. Nor can they have accepted gracefully denunciation, punishment, and the labeling as a sorcerer of anyone who questioned the correctness and rationality of the Catholic faith. Pérez de Ribas dismisses the objections to the Jesuits' message and practices by various Mayos as the work of resentful sorcerers whose power was diminished by the truth of the Catholic faith.[25] His pious rejoicing on the defeat of such "sorcerers" appears today as a patronizing and arrogant dismissal of legitimate objections by Mayos to the imposition of a foreign way of life upon them.[26]

Life under the Jesuits can hardly have been idyllic. Arbelaez describes the Jesuits' demands:

A strict sedentary life and Catholic chastity, indoctrination, and social norms were introduced. Autochthonous religious practices were prohibited and hunting and gathering banned unless directed and supervised by the priest. Monogamy, strict control of sexual relations, and discipline were harshly implemented. (Arbelaez 1991, 369)

As one of the missionaries wrote in a letter in 1752: "Every missionary must accomplish three main points in the reduction of the Indians: (1) they must not have more wives than the ones given by God, the Church and the Priest; (2) there must not be any drunkenness or the Indians allowed to have wine, and (3) there must not be any thieves or burglars" (1991, 369).

The Mayos can hardly have accepted happily these proscriptions on what must have previously been a free-spirited existence. Just why the priests, and not the Indians, should have been allowed to indulge in wine, must have perplexed and rankled their sensitivities. Furthermore, hunters the world over dislike being told that their activities will be curtailed or subject to magisterial supervision. Even today, the Mayo men of Teachive while in the *monte* keep a constant eye out for *venaditos* (deer) that might supplement their simple diet.

Note the carefully worded orders from Father Visitor Roderigo de Cabredo for the operation of the *cabecera* of Tecoripa:

> Whenever a *reducción* has to be undertaken to improve indoc-trination, i.e., when Indians must be physicially moved and brought into pueblos, it is fitting that this be done with utmost ease and the least violence possible. The Indians are *first* to be invited with prayer and kindness, especially those to whose pueblo the others will be joined [italics mine]. (Polzer 1976, 61)

The priest could easily have been writing orders for the operation of a day-care center.

The Jesuits were absolute rulers—lawmakers, judges, and jury on all matters.[27] In addition to stern religious requirements, the Mayos were required to provide a minimum of two days free labor to the church's fields each week, a practice they can hardly have endorsed with much enthusiasm. Nevertheless, in spite of these negative aspects, the Mayos, reeling from the depredations of disease, experienced several decades of relative peace with the Yaquis following the arrival of the Jesuits, an overall favorable development for them. If regimentation was the price they had to pay for security from attacks and depredations by other tribes, well, then, so be it. Protection from threats of external enemies is frequently the justification for the imposition of authoritarian mea-sures. Communities often endorse that rationale, however tenuous.

In the 1680s, events that were to change forever the Mayo way of life began with the discovery of silver at Promontorios near present-day Alamos, some thirty kilometers from the Mayo River. Within only a few years, more than forty mines were operating in the region (Bolton 1936). Less than twenty years later, an additional lode was discovered at Baroyeca to the west of the Río Mayo, which brought a further on-slaught of wealth-seekers to the region. By 1781 the town of La Aduana, ten kilometers west of Alamos had "four thousand souls . . . , a dry arroyo, a fine plaza, two royal officials, and a lieutenant governor" (Morfi 1967, 354). The silver had to be dug from the ground and, unless it was in metallic form, smelted to obtain the pure metal. To accumulate this treasure, the colonists needed labor and lots of it. The

Mayos were available. The mine owners swept down on villages and virtually kidnapped men, forcing them to work in the mines as part of a *repartamiento*, or system whereby villages were required to provide men to work in the mines (West 1993, 62). The Jesuits protested, and eventually laws were passed limiting, but not eliminating, the number of months in which the Indians could be required to work (West 1993, 64).[28] For the most part, these laws were ignored and the Mayos were semivoluntary slaves to the mines.[29] The work was dangerous and punishingly hard, the hours interminable, the living conditions deplorable, the pay scandalously low.

As more mines opened and the demand for Indian labor increased, mine owners, competing for scarce labor, offered better pay and working conditions (Brading 1971). Other mines, some producing gold as well, appeared in the region and east of the Sierra Madre in Chihuahua, especially the mines at Santa Barbara and Batopilas. Mayos went to work at those distant excavations. Some left their villages voluntarily, perhaps lured by tales of good pay, loose life, and freedom from the religious dictates of the priests.[30] West (1993, 63) suggests that many of the expatriates returned to their fields during the planting season to assist with the planting and harvesting, only to return thereafter to the mines, a source of dissatisfaction to both the clergy and the mine owners. In addition to offering freedom and affluence to Indians, work in the mines provided them with cosmopolitan camaraderie, access to ideas of rebellion and, quite probably, opportunities to learn the use of firearms and military tactics. These ideas of freedom, wage labor, and resistance, gleaned from the companionship that the free life bred, ultimately made their way back to the towns in the Yaqui and Mayo Deltas.

The mining enterprises initiated an almost unbroken history during which Spanish colonists and, later, European and North American entrepreneurs, found exploitable natural resources in the Mayo region.[31] The Mayos who live in the vicinity of Alamos today are probably there because their ancestors labored in the mines, for the mountainous terrain lacks arable land that would have been capable of sustaining them agriculturally prior to the conquest. Alamos itself, in its day the wealthiest city in northwestern New Spain, owed its riches and its colonial monuments to the labor, some free, some indentured, of Mayo Indians. The Alamos mines yielded riches well into the twentieth century, the gleaming bars and coins bringing wealth to the Crown and the mine owners, wealth that was torn from the earth by the arms and the backs of the Mayos.

Even as the veins yielded less, the value of the Mayo lands toward the coast was increasing, and entrepreneurs realized that the delta soils under irrigation were capable of producing several crops a year, all in great abundance, while the vast foothills could become home to thousands of head of cattle. Jesuits had recognized almost immediately the potential of Mayo (and Yaqui) lands to produce an agricultural surplus. Indeed, the expansion of Jesuit missions into Baja California was possible only because they could be supplied with crop surpluses from the Cahitas (Crosby 1994). The wisdom of the policy of reduction as a gathering of an agriculture workforce should not be underestimated.

However agricultural production may have risen, it remained regional and not international. Transportation to the populous center of the country was monumentally difficult, so basic food crops seldom made their way into the far interior. (As late as the early twentieth century a trip to Mexico City from Alamos [one thousand miles] required at least a week, usually more.) Certainly there was no hope for producing crops for export to Europe, such as cotton, tobacco, or sugar cane.

Commercial production of cane was not introduced into the northwest coast of Mexico until after World War II, and has been confined to the Río Fuerte and south, where climate and available irrigation make production profitable. It is not an economically significant crop in Sonora, even though some areas (Ures, Alamos) are known for cottage production of brown sugar. Even the development of cochineal dye was never highly encouraged among the Mayos. Had their lands lain instead on the east coast of Mexico, the Mayos would have been reduced to slavery, and African slaves would have been introduced as well (Frank, 1972). The Mayos (and Yaquis) and their lands were too far removed from European commerce for their agriculture to have produced an economic surplus capable of supporting international trade.

Production of crops for local consumption was a different story. Jesuits saw the benefit to their order and to the Indians of a reliable crop surplus and subsequently made food available to mines throughout the region, creating thus a bustling trade and undercutting the prices charged by merchants who brought food supplies from Mexico City along laborious trade routes.

Those whose financial accounts were thus diminished by Jesuit competition and other would-be importers from the hinterland formed a chorus of critics who lambasted the Jesuits for this practice. These adversaries invented all manner of stories about supposed accumulated treasures hoarded by the black robes as a result of their parleying their missions' agricultural surpluses into precious metals. Rumors flew that Jesuits hid their riches and left them behind when they were expelled. These yarns continue to inspire. Treasure hunters still snoop around towns in the Sierra Madre hoping to find tons of buried silver. To this day, Mayos speak mysteriously of hidden treasures and lodes of precious metals waiting to be uncovered.

As the mines expanded, so did the number of colonists seeking to find their fortune in Mexico's northwest, a trend which continues to the present day.[32] These were hardly a sympathetic lot, staking out claims for mines and lands and gradually encroaching on Mayo territory with their livestock, building homes where they wished, and refusing to recognize any historical right of an Indian to any land whatsoever. The colonists dismissed Indians as subhuman savages.[33]

While the increasing numbers of colonists added to the prosperity of Jesuit missions, which benefited by sale of commodities to the miners, the increased numbers of non-Indians posed a continuing threat to the security of indigenous people. To the colonists, Indians were a nuisance blocking the colonists' acquisitive drives, a theme with a familiar ring to those who have studied the history of the United States. When land disputes arose, it was the colonists, not the Mayos, who had the ear of the Crown. Only the Jesuits acted as advocates for the Indians, with varying degrees of zeal, and with religious orthodoxy as the price of their advocacy. They feared the colonists would contaminate the natives with worldly notions as well.

Mayo frustrations mounted as they saw their lands invaded and claimed by a new brand of ruthless occupier who brought new strains of disease, violated women, dragged men off into forced labor, and let cattle destroy their crops. In spite of Jesuit pleas, Mayo rights were ignored. Finally, in 1740, over the protests of the clerics, many Mayos joined in a rebellion fomented by a shadowy Yaqui named Muni, who sought leadership over all Cahitans (Spicer 1980). That the Mayos responded enthusiastically to Muni indicates that by then the historic animosities between Mayos and Yaquis had been left behind, a Cahita consensus had begun to emerge, and that the Indians had had enough of the Jesuits' teaching and authoritarianism. During this period, other Indians in northwestern Mexico also rebelled. They had evaluated Spanish-imposed institutions for more than one hundred years and realized that, far from the promises of a better life offered by the Jesuits, the real offerings were disease, exploitation of labor, theft of lands, brutality, and disrespect for native institutions.

Muni appears to have been a charismatic master of intrigue, playing the Jesuits off against the civil authorities. While he was visiting Mexico City (purportedly protesting Jesuit treatment of the Yaquis), a follower named Juan Calixto (whether Calixto was Yaqui or Mayo is unclear, a significant fact in itself) led an insurrection among the Mayo villages.

The rebellion led to the death or expulsion of all non-Cahitas from the region. All Spanish settlements were sacked and burned, including the mining town of Baroyeca, and all non-Indian property was destroyed (Acosta 1983). The Mayo lands were free of foreigners. So much for the reputation of the Mayos as peaceful and passive. Once the shaken Spaniards had regrouped, the revolt, of course, was broken, even though the Crown could not claim that Mayos or Yaquis had been defeated.[34] A repressive period ensued, as the Crown tightened its grip on the Indians. The Crown blamed the Jesuits and called for better strategy for treating the Indians, not for an overhaul of its colonial policies.

Following the revolt, the Mayo population declined drastically, and at the time of the expulsion of the Jesuits in 1767, fewer than six thousand Mayos lived in the villages along the Río Mayo (Spicer 1962). Spicer suggests that a diaspora of Mayos and Yaquis (who had also by now experienced drastic population decline) may have accounted for part of the population decrease. Cahitas moved to the various mining towns up and down the Sierra Madre and to distant *haciendas* as well, where they were eagerly hired as cowhands. From this time forward, Yaquis and Mayos formed the backbone of the mining industry in Sonora. It may be that Masiaca and Teachive also experienced an increase in population, as Mayos, seeking refuge from Spanish revenge over the uprising, took up residence outside the Mayo

River valley, associating with people who, though of different identity, spoke their language and observed the same general customs.

After the expulsion of the Jesuits in 1767, a secular priest, Francisco Joaquín Valdez was assigned to the Yaquis, and a happy assignment it was, for during his twenty-three years among them, he gained their confidence and encouraged them to establish cottage industries, including sheep-raising and the weaving of woolen blankets (Spicer 1962, 54–55). It is almost surely from this period that Mayos took up sheep husbandry and blanket weaving from wool. Sonoran natives had for centuries woven fine textiles from cotton (Cabeza de Vaca 1972), quite superior to any available in Europe at the time, so weaving was nothing new.[35] Woolen clothing and blankets in the hot climate of southern Sonora are useful only in three winter months. Wool, though, with its greater insulating power and durability was also easier to harvest and work. Ironically, the Yaquis lost the craft, perhaps during the extreme persecution they suffered in the late nineteenth and early twentieth century, while the Mayos not only retained weaving, they imprinted it with their own special designs and styles and practice it to this day, the only Sonoran indigenous group that continues to weave.[36]

The Jesuits left their missions abruptly in 1767, in chains and under arrest. After their departure, a scramble took place among Spanish officials and colonists to appropriate the lands and possessions the Jesuits had left behind (Calderón Valdéz 1985, 2: 261–69). Over the strident objections of the Mayos, surveying of the Mayo Delta was completed by 1790 and much of it allocated to non-Mayos. Only the ongoing fear that the Mayos and Yaquis would be incited once again into revolt prevented all their lands from being appropriated. Nevertheless, little by little, settlers and squatters whittled away at the ancestral holdings. To protect their holdings, members of indigenous communities petitioned the crown and, after independence, the Mexican government, to provide them with titles for lands they had historically occupied. Such was the basis for the survey of the lands of the Masiaca *comunidad* (see chapter 4).

Attacks by Apaches, and the Spanish preoccupation with defending against these whirlwind invaders from the north, gave the Mayos some breathing time. Spain poured money and troops into dealing with the Apaches, who raided as far south as the Río Mayo. As the Spanish rule of Mexico slowly deteriorated, Mayos and Yaquis watched from the sidelines, hardly comprehending the internecine struggles and, thereafter, the war of independence. They could scarcely have objected, since they, at least, were not being plundered systematically at the time.

Shortly after the Mexican government was formed, issues became clear indeed. It became the policy of Mexico (as it is today) to assimilate Indians into Mexican society, that is, to make them into proper Mexicans. La Ley Almada, decreed in Sonora in 1828, ordered that lands illegally seized be returned to indigenous people and that these lands be divided and individually allocated for purposes of taxation. Benito Juárez himself sought an end to the traditional Indian communal farm, believing that a more efficient system of private ownership would increase production and overcome historic blockages to a modern industrial economy in Mexico. Thus, the Mexican government assumed that communally held lands would be divided up among individual Yaquis and Mayos, who would then become individual peasant farmers and ranchers and thus be taxed. Since the Indians were to be treated like everyone else, they should be taxed as everyone else. The Cahitas begged to differ. Neither tribe recalled having been conquered by Mexicans. The Spanish clerics had resided in their lands by invitation only. The natives had never paid land taxes to Spain for the land which was, after all, theirs, and they saw no reason to begin offering tribute now. They also found the notion of individual land ownership to be contrary to nature, explaining, "Diós dió a todos la tierra y no un pedazo a cada uno" (God gave the land to all, not a piece to each) (Calderón Valdés 1985, 4:370). Thus began a period of resistance to Mexican control of Cahita lands that was to continue off and on for a hundred years. To some extent, it continues today.[37]

By the year 1800, two-thirds of the Sonoran population was *mestizo*. Forty years earlier, the figure had been less than one-third (Gerhard 1982, 285). Indians were now a minority, and threats to their traditional lands increased each year. Sonoran Indians, in general, were besieged by outsiders greedy for their lands. The Cahitas, whose lands were most suitable for irrigation and of almost legendary fertility, were the most vulnerable. Mexican independence removed the power of the Spanish Crown to protect communal lands from invaders, uneven though that protection had been. When *mestizos* threatened to overrun the Mayo and Yaqui lands, armed response became inevitable. In 1824 government authorities announced their intention to survey and measure the

Mayo and Yaqui lands in order to establish a basis for taxation. Taxation, the Cahitas understood, was a preliminary step toward alienation of their lands.

The leader of the first sustained rebellion against Mexican intrusion was a Yaqui named Juan Banderas (Zuñiga 1835). In 1825 he recruited Mayos and other native groups in Sonora to his cause of driving *mestizos* from indigenous lands.[38] He nearly succeeded, and it took the rather disorganized Mexican government nearly eight years before they managed to capture and execute him. By this time, both Mayos and Yaquis realized that if they were to preserve their ancestral lands, they would have to be prepared for constant battle with the new Mexican government. They also divined that they possessed the military ability to harass the Mexicans and keep them off balance. Although the leadership of the resistance was more often than not Yaqui, Mayos certainly took an active role.

For the next fifty years, following Banderas's death, Mayos and Yaquis fomented insurrections and rebellions repeatedly.[39] In their struggles against the government, the Indians aligned themselves with the forces of Manuel Gándara (an opportunistic federalist) against those of Ignacio Pesquiera (an equally opportunistic centralist), since Gándara appeared to support their claims to their lands.[40] In these epic political struggles of the nineteenth century, Gándara lost. In 1865, the French invaded Sonora.[41] The Mayos allied themselves with the foreigners because they believed French promises to return their lands to them. The French promises may have been real, for French monarchic institutions respected the rights of the clergy to own great tracts of land. They also recognized communal lands occupied by indigenous peoples. Mayos were instrumental in helping the French invaders take Alamos. Ultimately, the French lost, and with the defeat the Mayos were once again subjugated.

This time the Mayos were scourged by one Ignacio Pesquiera, a Sonoran strongman and politician whose enmity the Cahitas had aroused because of their loyalty to Gándara, who had lost to Pesquiera (Almada 1959). Pesquiera had led the Sonoran resistance to the French occupation in a most clumsy fashion, and once the foreigners were driven from Sonoran soil, he had vowed revenge on all those who had aided and abetted the enemy, except for the wealthy, whom he found easier to forgive. Pesquiera swore that he would end the Cahitas' belligerence once and for all, and he had managed to pacify the Mayos by the end of 1868, though not without difficulty, and not without a campaign of bloody violence.[42] After inflicting a resounding defeat on the Mayos at Santa Cruz, he lost interest in his campaign of submission, turning over the chore to his assistant, General Jesús María Morales, who maintained a reign of terror over the Cahitas, especially the Yaquis (Spicer 1962, 66).

Under the dictatorship of Porfirio Díaz, Juárez's successor, the alienation of communal lands regained momentum. The establishment of modern agriculture in the deltas could only be accomplished by first securing the lands from the constant and irritating skirmishes fought with the government and with settlers by the land's aboriginal inhabitants. Garrisons were manned in both deltas to maintain the peace and permit peaceful development of the lands, which meant that resistance by indigenous people would not be tolerated. The movement to turn over productive lands to landed elites and foreigners gathered momentum and drew the wrath of Mayos and Yaquis.

The 1870s saw rapid penetration of capital into the valleys. It also saw the rise of the greatest Yaqui leader of all, José María Leyva, better known as Cajeme (Caa ja'eme = he who drinks no water), who united the Yaquis and Mayos in a rebellion that nearly established a permanent indigenous nation of Yaquis and Mayos. The cause was much the same as before, the theft of native lands by outsiders, who, in this case were encouraged by don Porfirio. Under his dictatorship, and guided by principles of liberal reform, foreign investors were encouraged to establish modern systems of agriculture in Mexico. Yaqui and Mayo lands were the most fertile in the country and the most ripe for the plucking. The government assisted private interests in constructing canals and irrigation works to bring water from the Río Mayo and Río Yaqui and exploit the fertility of the land. The Cahitas objected and rebelled. Cajeme was the leader.

As was the case with Juan Banderas, Cajeme came close to winning the rebellion and establishing a separate Cahita state. In 1882 a force of Mayos and Yaquis under Cajeme's leadership managed to defeat government troops at Capetemaya near Navojoa, after which the rebellion in the Mayo region heated up considerably. Mexicans fled the villages or armed themselves heavily and called on the government to protect them. All of Sonora panicked, fearing a Cahita victory.

The government responded to the Mayos' insurrection by capturing and executing anyone who might pass for a Mayo leader or warrior. In 1884 the Mayos were decisively defeated near Navojoa and ceased to be a factor in Cajeme's rebellion. The Yaquis provided little assistance to the Mayos during the critical months before the battle, and the Mayos' resistance to the government waned. Many of them were demoralized and weary of fighting; Mayos were deeply divided between rebels and those who wanted peace on the Mexicans' terms. With the defeat and execution of Cajeme in 1887, the widespread Mayo rebellions, after one brief flare-up, came to an end (Troncoso 1905). Cajeme had lost. Lost as well were Mayo dreams of maintaining their lands free of non-Mayos.

Still, Mayos were not yet finished protesting the Mexican appropriation of their lands and the destruction of their culture. In September 1888 Mexican military officials reported that large numbers of Mayos were abandoning their work as peons on landed estates and converging on villages, where they listened to a wave of prophets, men and women, who preached the end of the world by flood. The most notable of these gatherings took place in a village near Masiaca, where a sixteen-year-old Mayo named Damian Quijano drew large crowds as he spoke of impending doom to those who had usurped Mayo lands. Quijano was arrested, along with sixty of his followers and protectors, as a threat to the peace and tranquillity of the land (Troncoso 1905).

Mexican military authorities were touchy about these large gatherings, seeing in every group of more than three or four people another incipient rebellion (Troncoso 1905). They were especially concerned about Damian, since he was said to be a nephew of one of Cajeme's close associates. Soldiers found suspicious-looking saints and images in nearly every Río Mayo village and sensed an imminent insurrection. The worst threat of all was posed by one Teresa Urrea, known as La Santa de Cabora. The daughter of *mestizo* parents, she became a charismatic prophetess who reportedly had influenced Damián and became enormously popular in her own right among the Mayos. She purportedly performed miraculous cures at her father's ranch in the Mayo country.[43] Subsequently, she had uttered vague and mysterious prophecies calling on the Mayos to beware of floods that would inundate all gentiles. Prophetic followers of Teresa sprang up throughout Mayo country. Mexican authorities, though uneasy with the undercurrents in the prophetic movement, took little action, reluctant to spark a new rebellion by interfering with charismatic leaders who appeared harmless.

Teresa's words acted as a slow-moving catalyst on many Mayos. In 1892, to the complete surprise of Mexican authorities, a large band of Mayos rallied behind the cry "Viva la Santa de Cabora" and descended upon Navojoa, sacking the city, executing the municipal president, and seizing some money and arms in the process. Elsewhere, small bands of Mayos attacked *mestizo* settlements, then rushed to Cabora to be blessed by Teresa. Though the rebels were apparently armed primarily with bows and arrows and only a few assorted modern weapons, the military authorities quickly acted to put down the rebellion, executing all the leaders and participants they could find. Teresa Urrea was arrested, along with her father, and taken to Cócorit, a former Yaqui village, where both were incarcerated. Eventually, both were exiled to the United States, even though Teresa's father was a prominent and wealthy member of Alamos society.

The prompt and ruthless military action made this prophet-inspired rebellion short-lived.[44] Mexican soldiers hunted down any Mayos who appeared capable of complicity in the supposed uprising and either executed them on the spot or dragged them off to be shipped south to slave plantations.[45] Bands of soldiers combed the Mayo Valley for signs of rebellion. The slightest resistance provided grounds for assassination. Military authorities exhorted the Mayos to return to their fields, by which they meant, get back to their masters. The government's main concern was the fact that the prophets' followers abandoned their *pueblos* and their peonage, leaving the *hacendados* with no one to watch over their livestock and tend their crops. The Mayos had a job to do: provide cheap labor for the rich. In Sonora, "the Yaqui problem" was how to maintain *mestizo* control of Yaqui lands and keep the Yaquis peaceful. The "Mayo problem" was how best to keep the Indians on the *haciendas*, so as to maintain the farms' productivity for their *mestizo* owners.

By the mid-1890s most traditional Mayo village organization had been disbanded by order of the military authorities. Never as tightly organized in related villages as Yaquis, the obliteration of the Mayos traditional governmental structure dealt a severe blow to whatever hopes they might have had for establishing a pan-Mayo organization. Many villages ceased to function, as families became virtual slaves on

haciendas (Crumrine 1983). While prophets continued to appear sporadically, responses to them were more and more fragmentary. As
modern agriculture spread across the delta, more and more villages
were swept aside and relocated.[46] A diaspora of Mayos set in and the
close community necessary for maintaining ancient cultural ties was
gradually eroded.[47]

The two decades from 1910 to 1930 were terrible for the Mayos. As
armed rebellions faded, militant Mayos turned instead to more political strategies.[48] They saw in the turmoil of the Mexican Revolution an
opportunity to gain support for their ancient struggle to maintain
control over their lands. They were all too easily persuaded by various
warlords to join their forces, believing the fake promises of men with
no principles. They sided with the constitutionalists in their campaign
against the remnants of Porfirism and against the conventionalists,
namely, Francisco Villa and Emiliano Zapata. The constitutionalists
soon began to bicker among themselves, separating into several factions. The Mayos chose to side with the faction led by José María
Maytorena, who was opposed by the forces of Plutarcho Elías Calles.
Maytorena lost. Calles went on to become president and never forgave
the Mayos.

Many Mayos joined the constitutionalist forces of Alvaro Obregón
(himself a grower of garbanzo beans in the Mayo Delta on lands
his family, the Salidos from Alamos, had appropriated from historic
Mayo occupancy) in great numbers, accepting his promise that once
the constitution was restored, he would support them in their land
claims. They formed a solid though small bloc in Obregón's forces
(Hall 1981). Obregón freely acknowledged the military presence of his
Mayo friends:

"This happened on the last days of March, 1912, and by the 14th of
April I had gathered three hundred men, mostly natives of the region,
of indigenous stock, most of them land owners, including me, who had
been cultivating garbanzo beans on my little hacienda that I owned on
the left bank of the Río Mayo, which bore the name Quinta Chilla."
(Obregón 1959, 8)

A photograph in the municipal museum of Huatabampo shows the
young Obregón, then president of the *municipio* of Huatabampo (elected by a strong Mayo vote), surrounded by his "landowners." They are
a host of Mayos, dressed in traditional muslin *calzones*, heads covered

by straw hats and brandishing machetes and bows and arrows. On April 14, 1912, they strode off to battle in full dress, including their bows and arrows. The Mayos mounted a train in Navojoa and arrived the next day in Hermosillo. Sonoran officials there bestowed on Obregón and his Mayo followers the title of the Fourth Sonoran Irregular Battalion. A month later Obregón had consolidated forces, including "at Navojoa . . . a large number of Indians armed with arrows" (Obregón 1959, 34).

Fight bravely and mightily they did, joined by many Yaquis and following Obregón throughout central Mexico in his victorious campaigns.[49] Ironically, they probably participated in the battle of Puebla on June 5, 1915, where they would have engaged, if only on a small scale, with the forces of Emiliano Zapata, who was fighting for precisely the same cause—the right of people to retain their aboriginal lands. Zapata lost the battle and thereafter his military initiative and his agrarian movement declined (Brunk 1995).

The Mayos' decision to align themselves with Obregón was an unhappy one. Obregón originally supported the presidency of Venustiano Carranza, a patrician *hacendado* philosophically and personally opposed to the land reform sought by the Mayos (and an implacable opponent of Zapata's Plan de Ayala, which would have granted the Mayos all their wishes). Obregón himself, though hardly a *latifundista*, was of *hacendado* blood and owned a medium-sized farm. He could hardly have been expected to prove himself a champion of the land claims of indigenous peoples. In the words of Paul Friedrich, Obregón, "himself a big landowner, exploited a nominal liberalism to mask the slowdown or stoppage of agrarian and other reform measures" (1970, 105). Indeed, he was committed to the capitalist transformation of Mexico, including the "opening up" of Mayo and Yaqui lands to "development."

The Mayos' support of Obregón and their great personal sacrifice gained them nothing. After Carranza's assassination and Obregón's victory they returned to Sonora, the revolutionary battle won, believing they had ensured a new future for the indigenous people, and hoping to be viewed as heroes and rewarded with the return of their lands. What they found was even greater control of their lands by *mestizos*. Many found their towns depopulated, their families missing, their homes leveled. When they did have land, no water for irrigation was available. Obregón turned out to be an even worse traitor than the others. He went on to become president of Mexico, and he was characterized as one of Sonora's favorite sons, at least among wealthy Sonorans. They benefited from Obregón's coziness with the same *hacendados* against whom he had battled, and his willingness to interpet the Mexican constitution favorably for *mestizos* who had acquired Mayo lands (Hall 1981). The Mayos looked on with silence and dismay.

Their troubles were not over. Obregón was succeeded by his fellow Sonoran and close associate, the rabidly anticlerical Plutarcho Elías Calles, whose troops and appointees demonstrated to the Mayos in 1926 just how long a memory Calles had and how vicious he could be.[50] During Calles' campaign against the Catholic Church, most of the Mayos' churches were burned and their saints and images were destroyed by *mestizos*, whose own sanctuaries were often spared. Calles was getting revenge for the Mayos' early support of Maytorena.[51] With the vision of burning churches, desecrated shrines, and defiled saints fresh in their minds, some Mayos renounced their faith and their traditions (Erasmus 1967). If their saints failed so miserably to protect them, what good were they, and why waste time with them?

By 1930 the Mexican Revolution was over and organized rebellions had ended. Even so, sporadic outbreaks of organized and armed resistance to Mexican policy continued. In 1940, for example, government (military) sources learned through informants of a gathering of dissident Mayos near Macoyahui on the Río Mayo. The conspirators were allegedly en route to a purported rendezvous in Chihuahua with representatives of other indigenous groups. The supposed purpose was to plan armed struggle against the government for its ongoing refusal to provide the water necessary for irrigating their lands. Word of the movement reached military authorities, and before it could develop further the group was dispersed by the army and its leaders were detained (Calderón Valdés 1985).

Mayos' sympathy with eschatological prophets continues to this day. Mayos are far more open to conversion to evangelical and messianic Protestantism than are Yaquis. Every Mayo village sports an evangelical church, where *hermanos de la fe* (brothers of the faith) gather to hear predictions of the end of the world.[52] Gone from these fiery preachers, however, is the message that Mayos alone will be spared or saved. Instead, they preach the abandonment of traditional Mayo ways and the adoption of puritanical capitalism (O'Connor, pers. comm.). Authorities no longer view Mayo evangelism with concern.

The highly touted Mexican Revolution left the Mayos no better off than they had been under the *porfiriato*, perhaps worse. Their military alliances failed, since warlords like Obregón had managed to strengthen their own landowning hands, while their wealthy friends had helped themselves to the rich lands of the Mayo Delta. The prophets' words had been proved wrong. Their cherished holy objects had been vandalized. And they had little or no land. Although some communal lands were later returned to the Mayos, and some ejidos created, most of the best lands remained in the hands of *mestizos*, as they do today.[53] The community of Masiaca, for example, while large, contains only a few hectares of irrigable land, the source of most wealth in the region. The system of canals that move irrigation water from the lake at Mocúzari (built in 1951) to the fields was constructed with powerful *mestizos*, not Mayos, in mind. In 1996 the Masiaca community had been promised sufficient water from the newly created Huites Dam on the Río Fuerte in Sinaloa to irrigate 3,500 hectares. The arrangements for delivery and the location had not been completed. Acceptance of the water by the community will put them in a position of moral compromise: the construction of Huites Dam caused the flooding of the ancient Mayo town of Huites, its mission church, its revered petroglyphs, and its sacred ceremonial sites. Furthermore, the government appears to have substantially reneged on promised relocation moneys, leaving many of the Huites Mayos with decidedly inferior housing and living conditions (López et al. 1995). The Masiaca community's gain will be the Huites community's loss. The severe drought of 1996 left the newly constructed dam empty. The shiny new turbine generators remained silent a year after their installation. Persistent rumors declare that the waters of Huites will remain in Sinaloa and will not reach Sonora.

MAYOS IN MASIACA AND TEACHIVE

The recorded history of the people called Mayos took place along the Río Mayo, some forty kilometers north of Teachive. The historical connection between the riverine Mayos and those who now inhabit lands to the south, including Teachive, is murky. Apart from a concentration of towns on the coastal plain in the Mayo Delta region, it is hard to define which pueblos were Mayo and which were not. As late as the 1930s, Gentry found the Río Mayo village of Macoyahui, some fifty kilometers northeast of Navojoa, to be of ambiguous ethnicity, perhaps belonging to a distinct Cahita-speaking group known as Macoyahuis, perhaps merely Mayos with a certain nationalistic pride in their village (Gentry 1942). As Sauer has pointed out, a good dozen Cahitan-speaking peoples populated the region from well north of the Río Yaqui to nearly mid-Sinaloa. The Basiroans, whom he classifies as a separate group, lived on the Río Cuchujaqui no more than thirty kilometers east of Masiaca, in a village now viewed vaguely as Mayo (Sauer 1934). The village of Tapizuelas, south of Basiroa, also of pre-Columbian origin, supplies pascola dancers for Mayo fiestas throughout the region. It seems quite possible that the pre-Columbian Cahitans of the Masiaca area also viewed themselves as distinct from the riverine Mayos.[54] (At the other extreme, one early Sonoran historian goes so far as to remark that Yaquis and Mayos are really one "nation" [Zuñiga 1835].) It seems highly unlikely that any group living along the Arroyo Masiaca would ethnically identify itself with Mayos, a people forty kilometers away who themselves are clearly distinguished as a separate people by every observer who left historical records.

Tracking archival records is a challenge in this region. Masiaca (as well as the region between the Río Mayo and the present-day boundary of Sinaloa) was included in the province of Sinaloa until 1830, when it was added to Sonora (Gerhard 1982, 273). Prior to that time, records would have been stored at El Fuerte, and after that, either in Alamos or Hermosillo. Emotions ran high around the question of where to place Alamos: Sinaloan officials undoubtedly had little incentive to provide Sonoran officials with archival records, and Sonorans probably had little desire to have truck with the Sinaloans. The move worked a further hardship on the historian.

Sonoran state documents from 1835 onward refer to "the natives of Masiaca of the Río Mayo." This particular geographical finding is peculiar, since the Arroyo Masiaca forms its own basin and the town is a good forty kilometers from the nearest Río Mayo town. In fact, the Masiacans in all probability tended more toward the Río Fuerte groups than toward those of the Río Mayo, since Cahitan-speaking non-Mayo peoples were found at regular intervals south to the Fuerte and beyond.[55] Water is more abundant to the south, and villages are more plentiful.

My friend and guide don Vicente is intrigued by this practice of classifying Masiaca as pertaining to the Río Mayo. He owned that it was geographically confused, all right, but thought it not at all strange. For, as long as he could remember, all the villages south of the Mayo to the Fuerte itself were considered as belonging to the Río Mayo.

Official documents shortly after the end of the rebellion of Juan Banderas suggest that at least some inhabitants of Masiaca had come from other villages, including Santa Cruz (now Júpare) and Etchojoa, both Mayo settlements on the Río Mayo. Perhaps official population accounts took into consideration a resettlement of Mayos away from the river and added the phrase "del Río Mayo" as a footnote.

What became of the many other Cahitan groups (e.g., the Basiroas, Macoyahuis, and Tapizuelas) is not clear. Sauer notes that they were considered separate nations (1934, 31). Basiroans moved to some 4 leagues from Conicárit (Sauer 1934). Some of them were suppressed militarily in the early years of Spanish occupation, either because of their belligerence, because they withheld submission to Crown, or because they were insufficiently open to the rigors of the Catholic faith. Others were exterminated by disease, reduced to such small numbers that they joined other peoples out of necessity. Still others were forced by the Spaniards to settle in mission towns with peoples from different groups in carrying out the Spanish and Jesuit policy of "reduction," or relocation to the immediate vicinity of a mission.

The determination of which groups should be "reduced," and to which site, was made by the Jesuits according to their own logistical convenience, and not by consulting the native peoples or according to their convenience (see, for example, Dunbier 1968). This practice had several rationales. It kept new converts well within the sphere of priestly influence and less subject to the temptations of pagan and/or insurrectionary influences. It also shielded them from the corrupting lowlife habits of Spanish miners and colonists whose lives were often given over to debauchery. Further, it provided the Indians some protection from the predatory desires of settlers and miners, who saw in them an inexhaustible source of nearly free labor for their mines or their estates. It also amassed a convenient workforce capable of producing a marketable agricultural surplus. Finally, it had produced a forced mixing of peoples who viewed themselves as ethnically distinct from each other, merging them into a more homogeneous mass, although still indigenous, and tending to reduce nationalistic impulses. At Masiaca we may be dealing with a people whose ancestors came from a variety of different peoples.

Given the restricted flows of the Arroyo Masiaca, it is doubtful that a large population could have subsisted on flood farming alone, as did the Mayos of the Río Mayo. The Masiacans would have had to supplement crops with hunting and gathering, which, in turn, would have made them a less sedentary people and less inclined to accept reduction by the missionaries.

CHAPTER THREE *The Town*

🌢 A hundred meters from the east bank of Arroyo Masiaca sits a dark rock, solitary, as though it had dropped from the sky into the treeless, baked clay flats of Teachive.[1] It is smoothed and rounded after eons of being sprayed and shoved by currents of water. Its surface is engraved with inscriptions and designs, figures from a mythical and lost people. How and when the rock got there, no one is certain. Older folk say that many years ago, at least a hundred years,[2] the town of Teachive was located upstream in more hilly environs. The stream meandered, the channel widened, and the waters dried up as miners upstream cut down the trees and ranchers allowed cows to trample the watershed. The villagers then moved downstream to where bedrock forced the underground waters to the surface, and where the waters never failed. After houses had been built for all, the men banded together and with mules and horses transported the rock, which weighs at least a ton, to its present site. If this story is accurate, the relocation would have to have taken place more than a hundred years ago, for some of the houses in Teachive are nearly that old.

Doña Buenaventura Mendoza of Teachive, born in 1905, reports that the old village was moved because Yaquis attacked the upper hamlet before 1900, burning the houses and robbing and killing some of the inhabitants.[3] Perhaps the combination of Yaqui attacks and the drying up of the stream produced the relocation to the present site. A visit to the old site today suggests that the stream's meandering has continued and that further movement of the channel to the southeast seems inevitable. By contrast, the present site of the village provides for a more stable channel.[4]

49

Among the glyphs on the smooth surface of the rock that marks the new town of Teachive are two inscribed crosses, sacred to the community. The villagers assume they are Christian crosses, although they are probably preconquest artifacts (German E. 1987). Children clamber over the rock and proudly trace the interstices with their fingers. For as many years as anyone can recall, villagers have erected a ramada around and over the great rock. Each year during the *fiesta* of the Santa Cruz the ramada is rebuilt and festooned with freshly cut leafy branches, a nave for the shrine. Three families have taken on the responsibility for the annual refurbishing of the ramada over the *"piedra de la santa cruz."*

The name Teachive means "scattered round stones" in the Mayo language.[5] The village lies about two kilometers north of the ancient town of Masiaca,[6] in the *municipio* (county) of Navojoa (it was part of the *municipio* of Alamos until 1934). Teachive sits on the edge of the broad coastal plain of southern Sonora, a level expanse extending from just south of Guaymas, Sonora, to some fifty miles south of Culiacán, the capital of Sinaloa. The plain is interrupted only by a few low hills. Today much of it has been cleared of its scrub forests and leveled for irrigated agriculture or planted with buffelgrass for pasture.

According to the 1990 census, approximately six hundred people live in Teachive, some ninety families. All are said to be Mayos, except for a few *mestizos* who have married into the community.[7] Most of the families have resided in the village (or adjacent villages) for several generations. Typical is the family of doña María Gonzales, who was born in 1904 in a house fifty feet from her current home. Her mother was also born in Teachive. The village's common surnames are Moroyoqui and Yocupicio (the most common), Alcaraz, Buitimea, Féliz, Gámez, Leyva, Matus, Nieblas, Piña, Tajia, Valenzuela, and Zazueta. Although scores of individuals have emigrated, the families remain and a smattering of new houses appears each year in Teachive. The population is growing as families expand, contrary to the decrease in population experienced by many other rural towns in the region.

Mayos are not distinguishable by their clothing. Women in the village dress in conservative, rural fashion, the older ones wearing long cotton print dresses or skirts and blouses, with nothing in their dress to suggest that they are Mayo.[8] When they venture from their houses, they often wear scarves or towels over their heads. They say it protects them from the powerful sun. It is surely a remnant of the long *rebozo* that Indian women throughout Mexico once wore. Younger women occasionally don pants or even shorts, though they reserve the more daring fashions for the anonymity of Masiaca during the fiesta of San Miguel.

Men as well wear *mestizo*-type clothing. They prefer light-colored, long-sleeve shirts, darker-colored slacks, and a mass-produced straw hat. The older men seldom have more than one or two changes of clothes. Young men adorn themselves with Levi's and ornate cowboy shirts. Most men wear *huaraches* when they work. They also generally own a second pair of shoes that they wear when visiting a store or on more special occasions. Younger men wear cowboy boots, preferably US-made, when they can. Children wear what children wear everywhere, clothes made in factories in Mexico, Manila, or Singapore. It is not by dress that Mayos can be distinguished from non-Mayos.

I first came upon the village of Teachive in 1990, urged on by rumors of handmade blankets, a traditional village, and diverse and unfamiliar vegetation. I went from house to house, inquiring about weavers. When I finally found one, I spent several hours chatting with her and her family, completely losing track of the time. When I noticed the sun was setting, I rushed off to the east to find a camping place, assuring the small crowd that I would be back, a promise that has been rather easy to keep.

The community has the appearance of a traditional Mayo village. Most dwellings are of Mayo construction and design, with adobe walls and roofs of stout poles with a cross-hatching of *latas* (slats) which are in turn covered with plaster or dried hanks of grass. On top of all this are layers of mud. The dense mass is supported by solid timbers, heavy *vigas* (beams), and upright *horcones* (forked, stout trunks into which the *vigas* fit neatly). Some houses are of older design, purely adobe with some walls of wattle-and-daub, a common style of Mayos a hundred years ago, when metal shovels for mixing mud for adobes were a luxury few could afford.[9] A few of the newer homes have concrete pillars and bond beams filled in with fired bricks, *mestizo*-style. All houses have extensive *portales*, or porches, which provide shade and living space for most of the year. *Portales* face east, providing shade for the burning afternoons of the warm months. The *portales* of older homes consist of posts of thick trunks of *amapa*, *mauto*, or *mezquite*, and beams of the same, with roof beams of *mauto* or *palo colorado*.[10] In the center of a room of one old house, a *mezquite* trunk half a meter thick bears the weight of the roof. The roots of the dead trunk are still in the ground.

The interior rooms are furnished sparsely, if at all. Mayos use their houses more for storage and protection from rain and cold winter nights (and increasingly for watching television) than for living. Except in cold months and during rain, they sleep outdoors—in the *portal* when dew is likely, or under the stars when it is not. All homes have several simple folding cots (*catres*) which are cross-pieces of wood connected by two-by-fours bolted in the center so that they will open and fold shut. This frame is covered by *ixtle* (burlap). At night the cots are unfolded and a blanket put down for a mattress. In summer a nighttime aerial photograph would show much ground covered with sleeping Mayos. When the sleepers rise in the morning, they immediately fold the blankets and cots and lean the latter against the house or store them inside the building. The signs of sleep have vanished. In my early visits I camped in the nearby *monte* and never arrived at the village before mid-morning. I began to wonder if the Mayos slept at all.

Most homes have a separate or even detached cooking area made of wattle-and-daub, brick, or adobe, with a roof of *latas* covered with mud, so that cooking can be done during inclement weather and so that smoke will not permeate the house proper. The women heat tortillas on *comales*, usually a discarded tractor disc positioned over the flames, a most satisfactory recent innovation.[11] A metal or clay pot of beans is usually simmering in the kitchens. Many houses have propane gas stoves as well (propane gas tanks are purchased in Masiaca). Most women still cook tortillas and beans over wood fires, for propane is expensive and stoves are too small for the large bean pots cooking beans or for the *comales*. Most important, their men like the taste of tortillas cooked over fire, they say. The stove is useful, for water boils quickly on the stove and the burners are available for morning coffee and eggs, potatoes, and other delicacies that can be quickly cooked and served. A daughter of Vicente and his wife María Teresa explained to me proudly that her mother seldom uses the gas stove. "She is very economical," she said. Teresa later informed me that it was her duty to be economical and not waste money on gas when she could get firewood for free, so she seldom used her stove.

Unless the weather is stormy, meals are served in the *portal*, where the family table is located. Usually only the men of the house gather around the table, while the women wait on them. Women and children eat standing or seated in other background locations. Around puberty or a couple of years later, boys are accorded the honor of admission to the table. I was uncomfortable with this inegalitarian custom while eating at don Vicente's home. After suggesting to doña Teresa that she join don Vicente and me at our meal, I relaxed, realizing it was inconceivable to her to do such a thing. After the guests, Vicente is served first. He gets the best food, and, I suspect, in the case of foods which must be rationed, the most. He is most solicitous of his grandchildren, making sure that they eat properly and have ample food. Occasionally, guests or relatives from out of town stop by. The women serve them a large meal as a sign of hospitality.

Each home has a privy situated as far away from the house as possible. The seat is typically a rough concrete cylinder placed over a pit. A simple roofless ramada, disturbingly short, provides privacy of sorts. The enclosures' sides are shielded with boards, brush, asphalt-impregnated cardboard, or simply old sheets and blankets, which whip and blow in the wind. These facilities are kept most clean and usually do not generate obnoxious odors.

The neighborhood on the east bank of the arroyo is older and has a more traditional appearance than the newer neighborhood on the west bank, where don Vicente lives. The houses are also farther apart (fifty meters is not unusual) and are not attended by an identifiable roadway. Nearly all were constructed long before the need for motor roads, so there is no recognizable layout to the neighborhood. Indeed, the houses appear to be randomly placed, large open spaces separating many of them. This configuration marks the town as non-*mestizo* in origin, for it deviates from the plan of towns universally seen in Mexico, founded on the basis of the Laws of the Indies (Varegge 1993). To approach with a vehicle one simply drives cross-country to a convenient place, follows a track, if one exists, and parks near the house. While this detracts from any obvious sense of community structure (Teachive is so spread out that when one first arrives, it is uncertain where the town actually is), it gives a sense of openness to the town. It also reinforces the Mayos' desire to avoid excessive togetherness, a striking contrast to *mestizo* towns and cities in which people live in the closest possible proximity, avoiding isolation at any cost.

The unbuilt areas on the east side are kept free of most vegetation, so that the village has a stark appearance. This lack of plants in the inhabited area (contrasting sharply with the rich variety of thornscrub that surrounds the town and lines the arroyo) has several explanations. First, livestock, close to home and attention, constantly roam the area, trampling and eating anything that might grow. The shade of a huge ironwood tree in the middle of the village is a popular sleeping place for a herd of fifteen cows, a place Vicente jokingly calls "el jardín de las vacas" (the cow garden). Second, Mexican public health authorities exhort the villages to keep bushes cut at ground level to prevent infestations of mosquitoes (the empirical basis for this exhortation has not been specified), and volunteers steadfastly comply. Third, Mayos like it that way and go out of their way to preserve the clean, open appearance, reserving shrubs and trees for the immediate vicinity of their houses. They feel that absence of unmaintained vegetation tells outsiders that the village is *limpio* (clean), and that they work hard to maintain the *limpieza*, a message they are anxious to convey. Some homes on the (older) east side of the arroyo have no fences. Even so, all have some means of keeping livestock out of the living area, one strategy being to keep the vicinity of the house free of any plant that might be attractive to a wandering herbivore. From time to time, work parties clean up brush and small trees and burn the mass in a huge pyre as a community service.

Finally, and most telling, in recent years villagers have become alarmed at what they perceive to be increasing levels of violence. They have taken to cutting down small trees and large bushes, so that would-be attackers have fewer places to conceal themselves.

On the (younger) west bank, houses are somewhat closer together, though still on large lots. The properties are delineated by fences, often of barbed wire, ostensibly to keep out livestock. Vicente's yard is fastidiously fenced. He leaves a gate open during the day and closes it each night before retiring to make sure that burros do not wander inside to wreak havoc on the garden and the house. Still, burros manage to sneak in from time to time and damage the trees or even the furniture. Vicente, unlike most men, does not own a burro.

The main roads of Teachive are dirt and are lined with whitewashed rocks. These markers serve as part of an important sign to outsiders that the village is clean, and they also provide visible markers for the myriad of people who walk up and down the roads at night and might be temporarily blinded by the few outdoor lights. A dirt road running parallel to the arroyo on the west side connects from Masiaca. It runs between rows of houses, for most were built after the advent of automobiles.

It is down this route that buses pass throughout the day, departing for and arriving from the cities of Huatabampo and Navojoa, both about 30 miles away. Another roadway to the south passes through Cucajaqui and joins an improved dirt road that connects Masiaca with Mexico Highway 15, four miles away.

The yards of the houses are swept clean several times daily, and often sprinkled with water to suppress the ever-present dust. Mayos everywhere are recognized for their cleanliness. Passing through the village in the early morning when the yards are freshly swept and the rocks freshly painted is an agreeable experience. The sweeping is necessary. All dwellings are home to dogs, chickens, and goats, and many others to sheep, pigs, cows, burros, and horses, whose leavings in the absence of regular and frequent sweepings, would quickly accumulate and add to an already burdensome fly problem. The detritus aggregated from sweeping, an accumulation of manures, paper, tin cans, glass jars, plastic, and inedible vegetable residues, is dumped in piles near the arroyo. There is nowhere else to take the garbage, and no landfill or refuse service is provided by the municipal government— unless, that is, the residents wish to carry their trash on a bus to Navojoa, whose dump is some 35 miles away.

Apart from the shrinelike *santa cruz*, Teachive has no chapel, no plaza, no village square, no center where people gather on special occasions.[12] This is in marked contrast to San José, Las Bocas, and Jopopaco, other villages of the community, which have both a village square and a church. (Only the Las Bocas church, built by *mestizos*, has a *fiesta*). For traditional Teachivans all formal religious activities, including Mayo cultural celebrations (except for some processions, e.g., the wanderings of the *fariseos* during Holy Week), take place in the town of Masiaca. The church there is viewed by Mayos of Teachive and the surrounding region as *their* church and the adjacent plaza part of *their* social life.[13]

The handsome church and its plaza are 2 kilometers from Teachive. Without a public building, no formal community activities take place in the village. A priest lives in Masiaca. He also performs masses in San

José and Jopopaco, but not in Teachive, which has no church, chapel, or Catholic shrine. Only the semi-pagan *santa cruz*, the arroyo rock outcrop called *la piedra bola*, the *aguaje* on the arroyo above the village, and the school serve as community focal points.

A kindergarten and a primary school are on the south of the east side, and these buildings are objects of some considerable pride to the villagers. They were built using community labor. Tiny and generally austere, their outsides are decorated with gaily painted murals. A *pila*, or *tinaco* (elevated water tank), that might serve to demark the village is located instead in Choacalle to the south. It bears the broadly painted names of both villages below the bright banner of former Mexican President Salinas de Gortari's Solidarity organization. Someone in Choacalle apparently had more political pull than anyone in Teachive.

No shops or stores are to be found in the village, either, apart from three houses that sell soda pop, fruit ices, and a limited supply of tinned foods and matches. Teachivans shop in Masiaca or in the large cities of Navojoa and Huatabampo. Even stores in Masiaca sell only basic foods and goods—except for *huaraches*, which are readily available and are made for shipment all over the region, and honey, which is also produced in Masiaca. For other than day-to-day items, residents travel to the larger cities.

In short, the village is a village because of its inhabitants' sense of a shared historic place and because of the deeply shared relationships of the families, not because of any structural signs of community or industrial base. Other than its collection of dwellings, nothing indicates to the outsider that Teachive is a village. Yet, for Teachivans the village identity is strong, strong enough for boys to have formed a baseball team that plays against other villages, strong enough for natives to express a mildly chauvinistic pride.

Teachive is viewed as backward by residents of other villages in the *comunidad*. Don Benito Alcaraz, a Mayo resident of Choacalle born in Teachive, asserted that Teachive was not *inteligente*. By this he meant that it lacks important community institutions such as a church (Choacalle has no need for one, since it is immediately adjacent to Masiaca, which has a church), a center for adult studies, a center for families and children, and a water storage tank, all of which are present in Choacalle. While there may be good reasons why all of these are absent, to Benito their absence indicates that Teachive is lacking in progress. When there is no church, he says, people lack *respeto* (respect). Because of this lack, men in Teachive drink too much and lack moral strength. When pressed on this issue, though, Benito backed off, lamenting that all the villages, towns, and cities that he knew were in moral decline. When I asked him just what he meant by *respeto*, he answered with an example:

> Until a couple of years ago I worked near a hospital in Navojoa and saw all the ambulances that came in. One night two youths were killed in an automobile accident, a girl and a boy. Another girl, a sister of the dead girl, and another boy were in the car, too. They had all gone to Alamos to drink. Driving home, they crashed near Navojoa and two were killed, the other two hospitalized. When the authorities informed the father of the girls that one of his daughters had been killed, he [the father] heatedly denied it. "My girls aren't allowed outside. They are here in bed. You have them confused with some others." It was an insult to his honor that anyone would suggest such a thing. When the authority replied that one was dead, another in the hospital, the father became abusive and angry. "Look," said the authority, "Just check, will you?" And, of course, the girls were not there. Both they and the father lacked *respeto*, they for sneaking out, he for not checking to make sure that his daughters were home.

Don Benito and Juan Ortega, another former *comisariado* (roughly, the commissioner or president of the *comunidad*)[14] believe this lack of respect stems from two areas: excessive drunkenness in public and parents' failure to discipline and control their daughters. In the old days, they lament, women watched their daughters better, taught them respect, and thereby molded them into good women. Nowadays, girls do what they want, without the benevolent despotism of the mother and father to guide them along the true path. They wear provocative clothing. Sometimes their parents don't even know where they are. And too many men now spend all their money on beer and neglect their families. Even boys get drunk on Tecate beer. Then they disrupt church activities. It's worse in Teachive than elsewhere, they say.

Vicente shares a similar view, expanding the analysis to include boys as well (although he denies that Teachive is worse than other places;

there is less crime in Teachive, he notes). Boys are no longer taught to obey, he fumes. When one of his grandsons failed to respond quickly to an order to drive a marauding goat from the garden, he pointed it out to me. "Look, David, these boys don't have respect the way they should. They aren't attentive to orders from their elders. They don't work hard. They disobey orders." Why is this, I asked? Lack of *respeto*, he responded. They spend too much money on fancy clothing, he added.

In general, though, the men of the *comunidad* tend to lay the blame for lapsing morality on the loosening of controls over women. Boys will be boys. Girls must be watched over with care. They must not go anywhere alone, even when they are grown up. They should work hard and learn how to organize the household. In Teachive, some say, the girls have less *respeto* than in other villages. There, the girls don't show any interest in weaving or hard work. All they think about are the *fiestas* and loud music and movie stars. Loose girls will cause moral weakening in boys.

Most Teachivans have lived in the village all their lives and assume their children will also stay nearby. The Mayo language (*la lengua*) is still commonly spoken among adults, but it is not spoken among children, few of whom understand it. I found only one adult who was unable to speak the Mayo language, and one other adult male who could barely speak Spanish.[15] Mayo is seldom spoken between older people and children. The only child under fifteen in the village known to speak Mayo is the son of an eccentric, single woman whose bizarre behavior is the object of considerable local gossip, most of it carried on without malice. The lad is treated with sympathy and a certain degree of admiration for his linguistic ability. Vicente enjoys engaging him in conversation for the sheer joy of hearing a youthful voice speaking Mayo. Most children, while not conversant in Mayo, have heard it spoken so frequently that they are able to imitate the sounds and, with sufficient incentives, they will learn phrases quickly.

There is little economic difference among Teachivans. All are poor by North American standards. The richest among them lives little differently from the poorest. No one has fancy furniture or a pretty car. The poorest may be pitied because they are on the verge of destitution, but no one else is very far removed from economic desperation, either. The young people of Teachive do not aspire to important jobs or positions. There is little competition. The boys learn to care for livestock while young, to glean food and wood from the *monte*. They go to the *fiestas* and to round-ups. When they reach their early teens, they generally go to work as *jornaleros* in the fields of the delta. The girls may do so as well. They are also expected to help with housework and learn to cook, sew, and process foods gleaned from the *monte*. Young people are early classified as *flojos* (lazy) or *trabajadores* (industrious).

The townsfolk define each year in terms of *fiestas* and rains and the harvests of *pitahayas*. The soap operas on the radio, and occasional family *fiestas* and dances are their entertainment. No one in the village is viewed as a leader. A few people are considered to have serious vices, such as drunkenness, promiscuity, or neglect of children. No one is ostracized for their weaknesses, however. No one can think of any significant events in Teachive in modern times. Young people think the village is a boring place. Most are expected to marry inside the village and take up residence there. If they marry outside, however, no fuss is usually made. An equal number of young people leave, temporarily at first, then, as the months pass, their absence becomes permanent.

TEACHIVE AND FIESTAS

Vicente casually mentioned to me one day as we plodded through the *monte* that it was his birthday. No one in the home had observed the occasion, and he seemed to expect no fuss to be made. I realized, then, that in spite of the dozen or so people who frequented don Vicente's home, I had never heard mention of a single birthday or anniversary. Mayos, it seems, place little emphasis on such rites of passage, which are celebrated in more traditional Catholic societies. Some older folks are not even certain of how old they are.[16] Some men claim to be younger than they could possibly be. *Fiestas*, on the other hand, *are* significant and everyone is aware of their dates and can recall past *fiestas* with fondness. Nearly all Teachive men and most women attend these festivals.[17] Individuals and individual celebrations are less important to Teachivans than the community of which they are all a part and its celebrations.

The Masiaca community (and, by inclusion, Teachive) hosts three major *fiestas* each year: (1) Lent and Holy Week (*cuaresma* and *semana santa*); (2) Flag Day (*día de la exaltación de la bandera*), on or around

February 28;[18] and (3) the Festival of Saint Michael (*fiesta de San Miguel Arcángel*), the patron saint of Masiaca, which is held on September 28 and 29. These are purely Mayo celebrations taking place in a town that was aboriginally Mayo and is now *mestizo*. Except for the village of Las Bocas, which celebrates the *fiesta* of San Pedro on June 28, none of the villages in the *comunidad* has its own *fiesta*.[19]

O'Connor (1989) argues forcefully that one test of whether an individual is Mayo is the degree to which he or she participates in Mayo *fiestas*.[20] Indeed, the *fiestas* still define the Mayo year—and the year in Teachive as well. Holy Week is still the pivotal time of the year, but Christmas is gaining ground (a couple of families now have Christmas trees and one even has lights). In terms of community excitement, the *fiesta de la exaltación de la bandera* has more ceremonial importance than Christmas, and the *fiesta* of San Miguel Arcángel is the year's highlight. Doña Teresa Moroyoqui, an excellent source for such matters, told me that without a doubt the year's most important days are Good Friday and St. Michael's Day.

If O'Connor's test is applied to Teachive, one might conclude that it is not a typical or strongly Mayo village. The inhabitants of Teachive participate in Mayo religious ceremonies and support them to varying degrees. Overall participation in the *fiestas* is not vigorous, and attendance is uneven, perhaps even apathetic. Teachive has not produced any *pascolas* (ritual dancers) or *venados* (deer dancers) in nearly a generation, which suggests the absence of a strongly reinforcing cultural atmosphere in the community. Several families have a member or relative who has been a *pascola* or *fiestero* (*fiesta* sponsor) for ceremonies that take place in Masiaca; but Teachive has proportionally fewer *fiesteros* than other villages. No Teachivan was a *fiestero* in 1995–97.[21]

A successful *fiesta* that people will remember fondly and that will bring prestige to the *fiesteros* requires intricate planning, immense amounts of work, and considerable funds. *Fiesteros* form a self-perpetuating board of women and men who oversee the festivals and call upon villagers to participate. To a great extent the *fiesteros* are the cultural backbone of the community. Without them, traditions would decline and the community would be left with no focal points. The *fiesteros* are in charge of all of the *fiestas* in Masiaca.[22]

The organization of the *fiesteros* is hierarchical. In charge of all is the *alpez*,[23] or *fiestero mayor*, the director of the *fiesta*, who has an assistant, the *alpez menor*. The *alpez* chooses the musicians, *pascolas*, and *venado* and orders the arrangement of the *cocina* (kitchen). The *alpez* gives orders to the second in command, the *alaguássim* and his or her assistant, who act as messengers for the *alpez*. The *alaguássim* have the honor of wearing the skin of a fox draped over a shoulder or over a belt throughout the *fiesta*, a decoration which they display proudly and from which they derive much esteem. They work unceasingly throughout the celebration, assuring that the *pascolas*, musicians, deer dancer, and *matachines* (a group of men wearing brightly colored headdresses who dance a ritual dance) are supplied with all the coffee, water, cigarettes, and food they need.

A third set of officials are *parinas*, whose function is to carry out the multitude of details necessary for the smooth operation of the *fiesta*. While the *alpez* and the *parina* may be a woman or a man, it appears that the *alaguássim mayores* (the principals, not necessarily the assistant) are always or nearly always men, perhaps because of their intimate interaction with the musicians and dancers, all of whom are male. Furthermore, they must journey afar, to other towns or ranches, to retain the services of dancers and musicians, a task that would be considered inappropriate or dangerous for women.

The first task of the *alaguássim* is to contact the best possible musician, recommended by the *alpez*, and retain him for the *fiesta*.[24] This musician is then denoted *músico mayor* and is in charge of all other musicians and is charged with retaining the best available *pascola* dancer, who will be dubbed the *pascola mayor*. This *pascola mayor* invites other *pascolas* to participate as well. At the Fiesta de San Miguel in 1996, twelve *pascolas* performed. A *pascola* (translated "old man of the *fiesta*," but who may be quite young) wears a fantastic, carved wooden mask that covers the face only, cocoon rattles (*téneborim*) on his legs, and a belt of many small *coyoles* (bronze bells or deer or goat hooves) around his waist. He (nearly all are men, though occasionally one is a woman) is judged by the rapidity with which he can beat his feet, by his ability to match the pounding of his feet with the syllables and meters of the hundreds of *sones* (traditional songs), and by his skill in making the crowd laugh. The *alaguássim* next locates a deer dancer (*maaso* [Mayo], or *venado*), who must be athletic, nimble, and intimately familiar with a different series of *sones*, and so on, until the *fiesta* professionals are all recruited. It is the task of other *fiesteros* to assist the six officials (*alpez mayor* and *menor*, *alaguássim mayor* and *menor*, and *parina mayor* and *menor*) in accomplishing a *fiesta* where all will enjoy themselves and yet be spiritually fulfilled by the power of the rituals and traditions.

In 1995 there were twelve *fiesteros* for Masiaca, each with different duties. Some were *fiesteros* in name only, and did little or nothing for the *fiesta*.[25] Some came from different towns outside the community, and as far away as Huatabampo. In that year, none were from Teachive. Villagers usually feel called upon to become *fiesteros* after a promise is made to Saint Mary or another saint during a personal or family crisis. These are of the form, "Saint so-and-so, you get me out of this mess and I'll help put on a great *fiesta*." An aspiring *fiestero* submits his or her request to the *alpez*, who must determine if the applicant is serious and capable of carrying out the rigorous demands of the office. One of Vicente's sons recently showed an interest in committing himself to the office of *fiestero*. He doubted that he could afford the great monetary expense and the time obligations, however. Vicente encouraged him to do so, offering him financial and moral assistance. He wanted his son to gain the public esteem associated with being a *fiestero*.

Some *fiesteros* are recruited by current sponsors, especially if it appears there are insufficient volunteers to form a full complement and more are needed to guarantee the production of the *fiesta*. In Masiaca, this is seldom the case.

Accepting the role of *fiestero* is a solemn, burdensome undertaking, not to be entered into lightly.[26] *Fiesteros* serve for three years and act as advisors for a fourth. They can expect to contribute between three hundred and five hundred dollars of their own or their family's funds each year, a fact which precludes participation by the very poorest of Mayos unless they have strong family associations. A very poor widow in Choacalle committed to being a *fiestera* and became mentally depressed because of the financial burden, which she was unable to meet. She sought and received limited assistance from relatives to fulfill her promise. Still, she was forced to go deeply into debt. At one point she was sick, with no money to buy food or medicine. A kindly shopkeeper in Masiaca extended credit to her, knowing that the prospects of complete repayment were not bright.

Fiesteros meet monthly on Sundays at the Masiaca church for a church service (usually presided over by a *maestro*, or lay catechist). The service is followed by often lengthy meetings, which are conducted in the Mayo language. The *fiesteros* eat a simple meal together, then take up the planning of the next *fiesta*. Every detail of the three *fiestas* is discussed, each person's role is delineated, and schedules are detailed.

The *fiestas* last for at least two days, sometimes three, and, once begun, they continue nonstop until the end, persisting throughout the night. During the *fiesta* days, the dancers rest. The *fiesteros* get very little, if any, sleep. They work constantly to maintain the pace and vitality of the *fiesta*. Contacting and hiring the four or more *pascolas* (without whom there can be no *fiesta*), the ten to twelve musicians (specialists in Mayo music, these include a drummer-flautist, harpists, and violinists), and the deer dancer, without whom the *fiesta* suffers greatly, is expensive and time-consuming.[27] All these performers must eat, and the great quantities of food required demand a *cocina*, whose location and construction is ordered by the *alpez*.

The *cocina* is actually a semicircle of side-by-side ramadas at the edge of the plaza, hardly twenty yards from the *ramadón* (the *pascola* ramada). *Fiesteros* from different villages maintain their own cooking area and tend to their village's own participants. Their ramada becomes a shelter and gathering place during the *fiesta*. The *cocina* is an integral part of the *fiesta*, and the appearance of women cooking great vats of beans and *huacabaqui* (beef-based vegetable soup) over wood fires and preparing tortillas precedes the beginning of the ceremonies by many hours. Indeed, the smell of smoke from the many great cooking fires is a welcome harbinger of a *fiesta*. The *fiesteros* organize these kitchens and provide food for the entire *fiesta*. The row of booths, each with a simple table and chairs in the shade of a ramada, is the locus of great and extended socializing for the duration of the *fiesta*. Indians from scattered villages exchange gossip and more enduring information, even forming new and tighter social ties, during the long nights of the *fiesta*. All through the *fiestas*, especially throughout the often chilly nights, the *cocinas* remain active, a constant murmuring of gentle Mayo sounds issuing from them.

When acquaintances meet, the first question to be asked after introductory greetings is *¿Vas a amanecer?* (Are you going to stay up all night?). An affirmative answer is proof of dedication to the *fiesta* and the Mayo way. Each village in the region maintains its own *cocina* and serves people from the village without charge. Acquaintances from other pueblos are welcome at the rustic tables under the ramada and at all hours people chat away. The fires never die down, except for a quiescent period in mid-morning when the plaza tends to be deserted and *fiesta*-goers snatch a few moments of sleep.

The *fiesteros* also prepare the *fiesta* site, sweeping the grounds, picking up trash, putting up ribbons and colored-paper decorations, lopping off the necessary tree poles and branches of greenery in the *monte* and bringing them in by burro, and constructing the *ramadón* and the ramadas for the *cocinas*. As if this were not enough, *fiesteros* also haul and store water in large drums for the participants and gather and stockpile firewood in great mounds for the cooks, and attend to a hundred other small details. The work has its immediate rewards. During Holy Week processions, the *fiesteros* march in a privileged and conspicuous place, where they are admired by all onlookers. The biggest reward for being a *fiestero*, in addition to the *promesa* (spiritual commitment) fulfilled, is the esteem gained from family and neighbors who look back fondly on a well-organized *fiesta* as a time of fun and fulfillment. "The most important thing you get from being a *fiestero*," said an older Mayo man and former *fiestero*, "is that afterwards people will say, 'That was a fine *fiesta*.'"

Current and former *fiesteros* also earn prestige in the community. They are regarded with esteem by many, and when others talk about them, the description usually includes the fact that they are a current or former *fiestero*. Sometimes, especially in less traditional Mayo towns, they are viewed with scorn, as having wasted their money and time, or as being fools (Erasmus 1967). Except among evangelicals, this reaction is uncommon in Teachive. Vicente, never a *fiestero* himself, has taken pride in introducing me to *fiesteros*, exhibiting the same level of respect that we might exhibit when introducing the recipient of some important honor.

The activity of a Mayo *fiesta* is typically centered around the *pascola* ramada, where dances take place nearly nonstop from dusk through dawn throughout the festival. The *pascolas*, wearing traditional costumes of tight, white cotton knitted cloth with bold red sashes and bandannas, take turns with each other and with the deer dancer, who wears a similar, slightly different costume. The dancers mark complex rhythms and choreography to the music of violin and harp (for *pascolas*), or drum, water drum, and flute (for deer dancers). The deer dancer's musicians also sing, often in loud voices, for the *pascolas* and deer dancers may perform at the same time only ten feet apart, and each wishes to drown out the others' sounds.[28] The dancers are for the most part highly skilled professionals who have passed through an apprenticeship and are recognized for their talents. Most of them are hired from towns in the delta. They are well-paid for their efforts.[29]

Having skilled *pascolas* and a deer dancer is the mark of a good *fiesta*, and the dancers are watched closely by all participants, especially the men, who have developed over the years a highly critical appraisal of the talents of a *pascola* and a *venado*. Onlookers crowd around the *ramadón* five or six deep, straining to get a glimpse of the show, while children sneak inside to sit on the dirt floor as near to the dancers as possible. Even in the wee hours of the morning the *ramadón* is crowded with onlookers. Children sometimes fall asleep on the floor, and some men pass out from intoxication. Drunks sometimes join the dancers and attempt to demonstrate their skill. The *alaguássim* tolerates them for a short time, then gently and tactfully escort these fellows from the *ramadón*. From time to time an older women (and, rarely, a little girl) will take to the floor and dance a *pascola*, usually to the delight and approval of the onlookers.

A town that produces accomplished *pascolas* or deer dancers has a certain prestige, as is the case with musicians as well. The hamlet of San Pedrito, just south of Masiaca, is renowned for being home to a superb harpist and instrument builder. Yavaritos, a nearby hamlet outside the community, is famous for skilled *pascolas*. The dancers become well known in the region and develop reputations for their personalities as well as for their talents as dancers. Vicente once whispered to me as we strolled down the street of a village outside the community, "David, that fellow we just passed is a deer dancer." It was as though we had just passed a movie star.

Of late, the *fiestas* have been heavily penetrated by commercial enterprises, especially by beer companies.[30] Whereas in the past *fiesteros* have constructed ramadas (or roofs of leafy branches for the *ramadón*) for the *pascolas* and for the *cocinas*, nowadays the brewing giant Tecate (and, to a lesser extent, Modelo) relieves them of this chore. Tecate's trademark now dominates the *fiestas*. Formerly, the *ramadón* was constructed of timbers for posts and a dense roof of branches and greenery gathered from the *monte*. Now it is framed by a red tarpaulin canopy with a blazing Tecate emblem clearly identifying the company. All the participants agree that it is hotter inside the new Tecate-sponsored *ramadón* than under the old hand-made one. Some of the participants complain that the *cocinas* were cooler and more attractive when the Mayos built them from shrubbery than they are with the commercial galvanized sheet metal siding provided by the beer company.

Those uneasy with the beer companies' intrusion into the *fiestas* recall the warning by a previous leader of the *fiesteros* that they should never allow the *ramadón* in the Masiaca plaza to be taken down. When he died in the early 1980s, his great prestige and his advice died with him. According to local Mayos, Masiaca *mestizos* tore down the old, permanent *ramadón* to have more space in the plaza for their dances and programs. Now, the *ramadón* must be erected anew each year, to the advantage of the beer companies who, the Mayos say, are typical *yoris* lacking in respect for the religion and customs of the Mayos. The dominant landmark of the *fiesta*, now, is the enormous beer tent (complete with loudspeakers that blast *norteña* music at the crowd, drowning out the music in the *ramadón*). Here, natives, Mayo and *mestizo* alike, purchase Tecate in vast quantities, and the younger men drink with practiced ostentation to exhibit their manliness.

Tecate's success at taking over the *fiestas* is a commercial coup for them (more than five hundred cases of beer were sold at one *fiesta* in 1995, according to a *fiestero*, more yet in 1996). In the past, alcohol was also consumed at the *fiestas*, and often in great quantities. It was of local manufacture, however, consisting primarily of a potent mescal brewed commercially at nearby Yocogigua, or of moonshine agave liquor brewed in other towns.[31] Participants in the *fiesta* would ceremonially pass around a bottle of the fiery liquid and take a considerable pull. It was an act of brotherhood. Tecate's sponsorship of the *fiesta* not only brings a powerful element of commercialism and market brainwashing into the *fiestas*, it also represents a sizable drain on the local economy.

This "alcoholization" of the *fiestas*, of Mayos, and of the Mexican poorer population in general, is hardly a new phenomenon. Wallerstein noted the same dynamic in the seventeenth and eighteenth centuries:

> The most successful industry was unquestionably that which produced the perpetual standby of the poor who get poorer—alcohol. We associate gin with the new urban factories of England in the late eighteenth century, and whiskey with the uprooted indigenous populations of nineteenth-century frontier areas. Similarly, it was vodka and beer in Poland and wine

in Hungary for the pauperized peasantry of the seventeenth century. The key institution was called the *propinatio*, the "invitation to drink," which meant in fact the monopoly of the seignior in the production and sale of alcoholic beverages. In the period from 1650 to 1750, the *propinatio* often became the nobles' main source of income. (1980, 141)

Due to saturation marketing, Tecate's nobles, its corporate directors, have an enviable record of corporate accomplishments. Tecate has single-handedly replaced locally brewed *pisto* (moonshine liquor) or *mescal* as the booze of choice, and in so doing has carved its way into the consciousness of every Mexican in Sonora. According to all testimony, men drink far more now than they did two decades ago, and spend far more money on their brews. A woman noted bitterly to me that the men will work a few days just to have money to buy beer at the *fiesta*, nearly exclusively Tecate, which they must have to achieve social prestige. Boys as young as ten years of age purchase beer openly and practice the art of ostentatiously holding the red can.

In addition to the individual and family demoralization produced by the huge expenditures on beer, money spent on Tecate leaves the community for good. The traditional alcoholic products, manufactured and sold locally or regionally, were of considerable local economic importance. Tecate's intrusion into the market has altered those old relations. Neighboring Yocogigua was a relatively prosperous community as long as its *fabrica de mescal* (mescal production plant) was operating. Since the closing of the still in the mid-1970s, the village's economy has slid into disaster and the village has experienced a cultural and social decline. Tecate's enrichment represents a further impoverishment of Masiaca and Teachive. It is also a *mestizo* institution effectively eroding the most enduring Mayo tradition, the *fiesta*.

Still, the *fiesta* is a conservative institution. The *fiesteros* are Mayos and only undertake the obligations incurred by being a *fiestero* because of a strong feeling of Mayo-ness. Psychologically, a promise to become a *fiestero*, arising out of a family crisis or aspiration, is a commitment made to the community, which, in turn, can provide miracles as well as care and understanding. I asked María Teresa Moroyoqui, Vicente's wife, if I could possibly be a *fiestero*. She might well have laughed. She is of a gentle and kindly nature, however, and she looked at me thoughtfully and remarked, with consummate diplomacy, "Well, David, a few *fiesteros* are not fluent Mayo speakers." She owned, however, that all the proceedings transpire in the Mayo language, so one who did not speak the language might find it difficult to follow the proceedings. In other words, of course, she was reminding me that I would be utterly goofy to attempt to become a *fiestero*. It is for Mayos only.

The institution of the *fiestero* binds the individual *fiestero* and the individual's family tightly into the festival organization. Since, in the case of Teachive, the festivals are held in Masiaca, acceptance of the role of *fiestero* also binds the *fiestero* to Masiaca and the other pueblos connected with the larger town. Teachive's rather low rate of participation, as indicated by low numbers of *fiesteros* and the townspeople's apparent indifferent attendance at the *fiestas* demonstrates here and in other institutions as well, that Teachive, while a traditional community, is by no means a conservative Mayo community.

The *fiesta* has played an historic role as a leveling mechanism, serving to plow some of the community's riches back into the community, with the expectation that the rich provide a larger share than the poor (Netting 1993, 181). Ideally, such an egalitarian arrangement serves to smooth over differences in wealth, a goal that older Mayos keenly endorse. It is doubtful, however, that the economic burden on the *fiesteros* any longer serves a socially leveling function, as in the past. It appears, rather, to place a heavier burden on the poor, who are driven to the verge of destitution by exactions for the *fiesta*. Still, the individual contributions are made quietly, so that one *fiestero* does not stand out above the others, even though their relative prosperity and poverty are well known in the community.[32] *Mestizo* culture, in contrast, places a far stronger emphasis on individual (rather than corporate, e.g., *fiestero*) sponsorship of *fiestas*, and on competition and accumulation of material goods (Crumrine 1977). This undermines the old Mayo way, and, in the long run, undoubtedly undermines the economic basis of the *fiesta* as well. *Mestizo fiestas* typically take the form of Catholic rites of passage, and are a celebration of individual and family rather than community strength.

TEACHIVE'S NATURAL ADVANTAGES

Teachive has several advantages over other villages in the community. First, its easy access to water from the arroyo is of great benefit to the natives, making life easier by relieving the burden of transporting water for domestic use across long distances or from deep wells, and providing better forage for livestock, a natural enrichment available to very few other Mayo settlements. An *aguaje* (natural pool) in the arroyo at the north end of the village is routinely used by villagers for bathing and cooling off, an amenity shared by no other village in the region. The *aguaje* is also indispensable as a watering hole for livestock.

While all villages in the *comunidad* have systems to deliver potable water, Teachive's is the simplest and the water is most abundant.[33] In the arroyo, toward the northern end of the village, a community well was sunk and a pump and pumphouse were installed in the 1970s. A distribution system was then installed, so that homes would have a faucet delivering running water. For many years the pump was operated by a diesel engine. The bothersome noise, the maintenance demands of the engine, the unsightliness of barrels of diesel oil, and oil spills were ongoing problems. Sometime around 1990, an electric pressure pump was installed with the help of the municipal government. It is maintained by the people of the village, who are expected to bear all the costs involved. A committee was established and an individual designated to watch over the pump and keep it running. Repairs are the responsibility of the community.[34] In 1996 Juan Féliz was president of the committee.

Most homes now have a water spigot nearby. Because of the high water table, pumping costs are minimal, and each family contributes no more than a few dollars a month for the right to unlimited use of water. With the piped water, many new fruit and shade trees are now growing in the village, especially on the newer west bank, where residents appear to be more heavily into horticulture. In another few years these will give a more shaded, lush appearance to the neighborhood on the west side of the arroyo than it now has.[35]

In June 1996 the pump broke down. Attempts were made to have it repaired. It was difficult to arrange for a repairman to come out from Navojoa, and, when he finally did, in mid-July, he said the repairs would be expensive. The severity of the 1996 drought was such that most families claimed they could not contribute to the repairs and the pump remained shut down. In August, another estimate was made, this one for ten thousand pesos, but the pump committee was able to raise only one-half that amount by levying assessments on users. As of

October 1996, the pump was still broken and villagers were being forced to carry water in buckets from the arroyo. Fortunately for them, the arroyo had plenty of water.

Villages downstream from Teachive are at a comparative disadvantage. In 1995 the village of San José, one kilometer south of Masiaca, was without water for more than three months. Don Modesto Soto found it necessary to dig a new well by hand. It was a huge hole, eight feet wide and quite nicely cylindrical. He struck water at ten meters and decided to go down two meters more. The work took three men two months to finish. Bringing the water to the surface via rope, pulley, and bucket is a tough job.

Nearby San Pedrito is inured to pump failures, as is Huebampo. At Yocogigua, a Mayo *ejido* twenty kilometers to the east, the pump broke in early 1995 and eighteen months later still had not been repaired. Residents have had to lift water from the community well and carry it more than two hundred meters to their homes. Some villages have elevated water towers built by Solidaridad. The pumps for these reputedly break down, and the tanks leak and rust. Few of these prominent tanks (*tinacos*) actually provide water to the communities.[36]

While Teachive benefits from ready access to water, it suffers from a lack of irrigable land. None of the land near the village is flat enough or has rich enough soil to permit flood irrigation. Teachive's name means scattered round stones, and the area has plenty of them. San José and Jopopaco, both downstream, have extensive floodplain areas with better soil, which is planted when the wash floods.

Teachive's location at the upper end of the arroyo and near permanent water is one advantage. Another is the village's location in an area with sufficient gradient to provide a marketable supply of gravel, an immediate source of wealth for the men of Teachive. The quality is better than that found farther downstream, where aggregates are more finely divided. (The sand and gravel are available to all, but no one from other villages makes the long walk to Teachive to work the deposits. Some work deposits downstream.)

Teachivans also benefit from being nearest to the hills that rise from the coastal plain. These small mountains yield a more varied vegetation and a more interesting landscape as well. An old man from the village of Sirebampo mentioned to me that the *monte* near Teachive was richer in plants. Cerro Terúcuchi, while not a large mountain, is big enough to house many thousands of small trees and shrubs, some not found elsewhere in the *comunidad*. The *bajada* that flows to the west is rich in leguminous trees that villagers exploit. Deer are also more plentiful in the mountain habitat than in the flatter plain. Firewood, poles for construction, and fenceposts are also more abundant near Teachive than other villages in the community.

Finally, Teachive, more than any other Mayo village, has a wide-spread reputation as a center for production of native arts and crafts. At least ten women in the village weave traditional woolen blankets (*jinyam* [Mayo], *cobijas*) of various sizes and colors, many of high quality. These are a source of revenue not available to most villages.[37] Furthermore, at least three families produce other *artesanias* which are purchased by tourists in the village or in nearby Alamos or Navojoa. Revenues from these manufactures are important for the economic base of the community.

These natural advantages make Teachive somewhat more affluent than other Mayo villages nearby. In the *comunidad*, only Jopopaco and Las Bocas are considered wealthier, the former because it has fields more capable of producing crops, the latter because of the wealth from the sea and from Mexican tourists. In spite of its relative affluence, Teachive is not the most united village. Most people agree that both San José and Jopopaco have a stronger sense of unity and industry among their residents.[38] It is not coincidental that both villages also boast churches and plazas, while Teachive has neither. In these two towns the houses are also built more closely together as well. They are notably less Mayo.

Teachive's principal natural disadvantage is that it is the village farthest from the sea in the *comunidad*. Distance is a relative term here, since Teachive's *actual* distance from the sea is a scant twenty kilometers. Still, I have not seen seafood eaten in any of the homes in Teachive, which stands in sharp contrast to the residents of Las Bocas and Chichibojoro, who regularly consume the high-protein marine life. As of 1995 few Teachivans had even seen the ocean or visited Las Bocas. On several occasions I have driven carloads of young people to the beach, where they are transfixed by their first glimpse of the ocean. The children find the surf mystifying and confusing, though enchanting. All of their shoes or *huaraches* are soaked by the first wave. They then scatter with gales of laughter as tongues of salt water sweep toward them on the beach. Doña Teresa Moroyoqui was hypnotized by the water. At my urging she finally removed her shoes and walked with the children at the edge of the waves. When the time came for us to depart, she scooped up a handful of sand and sifted it into her pocket. "It will remind me of this dream," she said in a voice hardly above a whisper.

Teachive is also at the end of the road, the last village before the fences of the *latifundista* to the north bar entry to the Mayos. Apart from those few tourists who come to purchase arts and crafts, hardly anyone without business drives up the road to the village. There is nothing to see in Teachive: no one known to have a special talent, no industry, no meeting place. There is no place to buy food, no place to purchase a meal. Teachive is isolated, even within the community, by its location. Apart from the men who attend *fiestas* outside the village, its residents seldom venture much beyond Masiaca, three kilometers away, except as they are transported to the fields of the delta, where they work as *jornaleros*, or to the Ley department store in Huatabampo.[39]

Teachivan peasants, then, have advantages and disadvantages over peasants from other villages inside and outside the community. Some resources are freely available to them that are not available in other parts of the *comunidad*. They lack some resources available to other villages. On balance, Teachivans believe they are ahead of other towns, and far ahead of Mayo peasants who live on *ejidos* in the delta. Their advantages are of great significance to them, and they are most aware of them. Teachivans are peasants with restricted subsistence, laborers who have their own land.

RELIGION IN TEACHIVE

Teachive is primarily, though only nominally, Catholic. Few of the villagers attend mass with any regularity at the church two kilometers away. Still, they universally cross themselves when entering the church during *fiestas* or on holy days. Their lack of religious zeal is apparently more related to the current priest than to religious scruples. Indeed, many are hostile to the *mestizo* priest, who from the pulpit has denounced Mayo festivals as pagan. (During the 1995 Easter festivities he posted a schedule of Holy Week events, omitting any reference to the numerous Mayo ceremonial activities which took place in and around the church.) He is also said to have forbidden the entrance of *matachines* into the church, even though, critics claim, the building does not belong to him. He is described by one resident as "crazy" because of his antipathy to Mayo ceremonials. He is not crazy (he has the loyalty of many *mestizos* and some Mayos in the community). He is dead set against the Mayos' traditional activities and determined to weed them out. Among Mayos in Jopopaco, San Pedrito, and Teachive, he is criticized. Some complain that he charges high fees for performing religious rites.

The priest, Padre Ramón, is a congenial fellow, quite traditional and amiable. He finds the Mayo ceremonials to be pagan and blasphemous and inappropriate in the church. He is correct about the paganism of the ceremonials, for they retain much of their pre-Columbian content. The *pascola* dance, the *venado*, and possibly elements of the *matachines* are all ancient fixtures of Mayo culture, old when the Spanish arrived (see, for example, Griffith 1967).[40] The Mayos long ago achieved a syncretism between aboriginal rituals and Catholic ceremony and are not about to give these up simply because some priest denounces them. After all, priests come and go and their social pronouncements vary.[41] As a result, Mayos tend to shy away from the padre's services (some still attend mass regularly and ask him to officiate at funerals), and he is not often seen in the village. Padre Ramón is not alone in his aversion to Mayo cultural practices, for clerics from the church of Huatabampo and others in the region as well have reportedly made attacks on historic Mayo cultural practices. Whatever the basis for the priests' reported antipathy, Teachivans feel it sharply.

Don Modesto Soto is a former *comisariado* of Masiaca who, although a very poor Mayo, is also a devout Catholic and often reflects a conservative position. Don Modesto no longer attends the *fiestas*. He explains the Masiaca priest's intransigence from a different perspective. Soto observes a decline of the *fiestas*, reflecting an ongoing decrease in the strength of the community, all due to a lack of *respeto* (respect). The increase in the consumption of beer and the commercialism of the *fiestas*, the lack of modesty in young women and politeness in young men, the failure of younger Mayos to take the *fiestas* seriously, all are a sign of lack of *respeto*. Children do not immediately do as they are told. They go places without permission of their parents. They are flippant about their catechism. They do not automatically defer to adults on all matters. Soto views the priest's refusal to acknowledged the *matachines* in the church as a reasonable edict in the face of the rowdyism and license which he sees with increasing frequency.

"The priest demands that people show *respeto* in the church. He doesn't reject Mayo customs, he just won't stand for the drinking and carrying on going on in the church. Right now we don't have a *fiesta* of order, we have a *fiesta* of disorder. As soon as the people show *respeto*, they will be allowed back in the church, I'm sure." "Respect," for Soto, is a group of behaviors centering around (1) the acknowledgment that older people (especially men and, above all, priests) should be heard and obeyed, and (2) young people should not stray from those activities sanctioned by the church and its priests.

Soto's observations are not difficult to verify. Immense amounts of alcohol are consumed during the *fiestas*, producing a rowdyism that would dismay even the most liberal-minded cleric. Drunks stagger into the church. Young, unmarried women dressed as scantily as possible approach the altar, while young men strut in a macho gait, flaunting expensive cowboy clothing. The public displays of affection among youth, even inside the church, cause consternation among older folks and are mortifying to the clergy and older, more conservative Mayos alike. Nearly everyone agrees that at the *fiestas* money that should go to maintaining the family is squandered on drink. A Masiaca *mestiza* lamented to me that almost no young people attend mass and complete their cathechism.

Don Benito Alcaraz, a Mayo, and Don Juan Crisóstomo Ortega de Contreras, a Masiaca *mestizo*, share Soto's complaints. Both are former officials of the *comunidad*. Alcaraz was the *consejo de vigilancia* (a watchdog official), and Ortega a former *comisariado*.[42] Both believe that the priest tried to involve the *fiesteros* in the Catholic rituals. According to them, the *fiesteros* refused. Ortega, speaking from the viewpoint of a non-Mayo (he speaks *la lengua* but is of *mestizo* background), says the traditional Mayos are ignorant. They behave badly in church and show no *respeto*. The Indians say the church is theirs, he complains, and that they can order anyone around concerning the church. Ortega thinks the priests should have control over the church. The priests have only the best interests of the people at heart. Both feel that young people are no longer taught to recognize the authority of the priest.

The lack of specificity from the priest as to what must be done to extend the services of the church to all the Mayos, and his perceived

antipathy to the Mayo culture, seem to go far deeper than mere discom-
fiture at lack of *respeto*. Some Protestants in Teachive felt that he treated
them as though they did not exist.[43] Other Mayos feel that he cares only
about the *mestizos* in his parish, and looks down on poor Mayos.[44] These
are the perceptions from various parts of the community.

Teachivan Luis Tajia, a prospective *fiestero*, gives this perspective on
the priest and the general atmosphere of dissolution surrounding the
fiesta:

> There is a lot of drinking and carousing at the *fiestas*. It is a bad
> thing, all the money people spend and all the while their fami-
> lies are suffering. There is too much disrespect. But it is wrong
> to blame this on the *fiesta*. The *fiesteros* take a vow to keep their
> respect and not drink alcohol during the ceremonies. They
> obey their vows faithfully. They do not want the drinking and
> disrespect to continue, but what can they do about it? They
> don't want all the beer and the secular dances, either, but it is
> wrong to blame the *fiesteros* for all that when they are doing
> their best to keep the ceremonies pure and religious.

A fundamental divide separates the folk-Catholic religion of the
Mayos from the modern *mestizo*-Catholic clergy. The former reflects a
fiesta-based community ethos originating in shared values, tradition,
language, and cooperation, which historically has incorporated an
alien religion into its culture, modifying, accommodating, and interpreting as necessary. The latter represents an individualistic, competitive society and a church historically and currently dominated by the
interests of the oligarchy. The rituals performed by the priest in the
church in Masiaca are not substantially different from those performed in Spain.[45] The Mayos of Masiaca (and in most traditional
villages) respond to this tension, this irreconcilable gulf, with a general
lack of enthusiasm for formal participation in Catholic hierarchical
functions, especially those presided over by *mestizo* priests.[46]

An example of this deep division can be seen in the traditional
Mayo ceremonies. The Mayo *fiestas* involve far more lay and community control than do Catholic-sponsored festivities. Even though
priests are welcomed at the Mayo ceremonies, Mayos organize, fund,
and direct their *fiestas* themselves, including the Easter rites, without

the participation of a priest (and often in spite of clerical opposition). The Mayos view involvement of the Catholic hierarchy as optional in such community-based traditional celebrations. It is as though the community were saying to the clergy: "You are welcome to attend the ceremonies as our guest, in fact, we would love for you to attend and bring your prestige and power. It is, however, *our* show, not yours." This is in sharp contrast to *mestizo* festivities, especially those occurring during Lent, which are typically organized, funded, and directed by the clergy. This autonomy of the Mayo ceremonials from clerical control is a source of irritation to hierarchical-oriented clerics. Indeed, the community sponsorship of the *fiestas* in general runs counter to the *mestizo* practice of individual or family sponsorship.[47]

In an atmosphere of priestly neglect, however benign, and a gradient of hostility to native customs, it is not surprising that evangelical Protestants have made considerable inroads in Teachive,[48] more yet in the neighboring, poorer village of Cucajaqui.[49] One Mayo estimates that fifty residents of Teachive are now "*hermanos de la fe*" (brothers of the faith) or *aleluias*, a high percentage in a nation where to be viewed as Protestant is an almost certain invitation to be ridiculed or ostracized.[50]

The Teachive Full Gospel Church of God, a ramada with benches for pews, began in 1996 with a pastor of its own and thirty-three members. They had held services in homes for years before. The evangelicals are known primarily for their condemnation of "worldly" pleasures, especially drinking, smoking, dancing, and general carousing. They meet several times a week, sometimes nightly, and their singing and exclamations can become quite noisy. A pastor is assigned to the church by the director of a centralized district consisting of ten churches. The pastors remain for only two years and are then moved to a different congregation.

These churches are run quasi-democratically, in that all *hermanos* are viewed as equals, including the pastor. Even though the district director decides who will be pastor, the congregation is consulted and involved in the decision. This new model, brought in by the evangelicals, with its absence of a strong central authority, is puzzling to traditional Mayos. Although the *fiestero* society is similarly democratic, centuries of association of religion with Catholic authoritarianism have embedded in the Mayo consciousness the assumption that all religion is based on male authority that must be unquestioningly accepted. In contrast, the *evangelistas* refer to each other as "brother" and "sister," intentionally blurring the distinction between Mayos and non-Mayos, men and women,[51] clerics and laypeople, and thus breaking down the cultural lines which Mayos have traditionally drawn between themselves and *mestizos*.

The evangelicals condemn the traditional *fiestas* and everything surrounding them.[52] They denounce the *pascolas*, deer dancers, and *matachines* as the work of the Devil. The *fiestas* are worldly, idolatrous, blasphemous, and, above all, wasteful, they say. The atmosphere of celebration encourages drunkenness, idolatry, harlotry, and fornication.[53] Worst of all, they seduce men in particular to dissipate their meager earnings and leave their families without a leader and provider. A member of the Teachive congregation told me bluntly, "The *fiesta* is prohibited by the Bible." During the *fiestas*, the *evangelistas* increase the number and duration of their services, competing with the Devil for human souls. Some villagers have joined the evangelical church, then left it. Others are staunch adherents.

If evangelical Protestantism proliferates, the *fiestas* may be irretrievably eroded. *Evangelistas* carry on their own *fiestas*, frequently noisy, emotional meetings and revivals that feature loud singing, praying, "speaking with tongues," and public emotional releases—weeping and rejoicing aloud. They eschew political involvement, preaching the impending arrival of the day of judgment and the inexorable consequences for those who do not heed. They emphasize individual salvation and, according to critics, they seldom address issues of communal or broadly social concern. They admire U.S. capitalism and view it as their goal to be Calvinistic entrepreneurs (M. O'Connor, pers. comm.) Their morality is based on free enterprise and the individualistic morality preached by evangelists. One Teachivan complained that while he doesn't object to the beliefs of the *evangelistas*, he is uncomfortable with their apparent lack of concern about the community. They worry only about their own salvation, he thought.

I asked some members of the Teachive congregation about this criticism. They found it confusing and responded with indignation. One couple pointed to the husband's involvement in the water pump committee, of which he is president.[54] He is also an active member of the dominant PRI political party. Not long ago, he headed a small delegation to Masiaca to demand assistance with the pump from the *municipio*, much, he says, to the astonishment of *mestizo* Masiacans, who assumed that the *indios* of Teachive could never organize themselves for anything. I learned also that after the village pump broke down, when all of the natives were forced to venture to the arroyo and carry buckets of water to their homes, his wife had taken it upon herself to assist all those who had to haul water, which often became contaminated with mud and was in danger of containing livestock feces and urine. She sculpted a small well from clean sand and imbedded a perforated galvanized tub deep into the conglomerate. The water that trickled in was well filtered and clear and villagers could easily scoop out the water and fill their buckets.

The husband relates his conversion with enthusiasm. "I was a railroad worker before I was converted," he confesses. "I left my family in Teachive when I was working. I would throw away most of my pay on liquor and other things. I did it for years. My family suffered. A couple of times I was robbed when I was drunk. Then one day in 1973 a preacher came by and spoke in the home of a friend of mine. I took to the preacher's words and three days later I found myself converted. My wife soon joined me. We have been *evangelistas* ever since. My life is much better, now. We have the Bible and a strong family."

Traditional villagers are still unquestioningly Catholic, assuming the general correctness of the Catholic ideology they have retained. Vicente once expressed wonderingly the fact that some people do not believe in God. Such traditionalists view the converts to Protestantism with a mixture of curiosity and scorn. They find it most remarkable that my heritage is Protestant and that the United States is predominantly Protestant.

Religious trappings are found in nearly all Catholic homes in Teachive, usually a print of Our Lady of Guadalupe, of a Madonna and the child Jesus, or of a classical religious scene. In general, these are relegated to less conspicuous parts of the house. Few villagers regularly attend mass. Furthermore, only three homes prominently display the house cross, a conservative Mayo custom (O'Connor 1989, 54). Still, nearly all adults refuse to work during Holy Week and other *fiestas*, reserving that time for renewing community ties. That time belongs to the *fiestas*. In general, they view the *fiestas* as the most important times of the year and, even in the atmosphere of commercialism and heavy beer consumption, they look forward to *fiestas* more than any other period. If there is any one activity which brings all older Mayos pleasure, it is gathering with other Mayos and speaking the Mayo language with no heed to time or topic. Chatting in *la lengua* is what they do when they take off their shoes, or, more properly, their *huaraches*.

MEDICINE AND CURING

Teachivans discuss their medical problems openly and in detail. Whatever the ailment, a myriad of lay prescriptions is always forthcoming. Everyone has a stash of anecdotes about people, usually relatives (often distant relatives) who had such-and-such a condition and were cured by so-and-so. Especially abundant are cures for diabetes, rheumatism, prostatitis, hemorrhoids, hypertension, parasites, and kidney problems. In general, people are more prone to dispense medical advice than to accept it.

For minor medical problems, some Teachivans visit first a modest clinic in Masiaca, staffed by a Mayo nurse who will take pulse and blood pressure and dispense simple medical advice. For more serious complaints villagers visit a clinic in San José, where in 1996 a young couple, both doctors, were stationed for their required year of government service.[55] The clinic is usually busy and it is common to see tethered horses and horse- or burro-drawn carts in front, the beasts of burden patiently waiting their drivers. Patients are charged a minimum fee, which many cannot pay immediately. If the local diagnosis is unsatisfactory or if further treatment is recommended, most patients travel to Navojoa, where a minimal level of free health care is available. The waits at the crowded clinics in the city are interminable. Most medicines must be purchased and are expensive. (For example, an asthma inhaler costs seventy pesos, roughly twice the average daily wage for a *jornalero*.) Elective surgery must be paid for, usually in advance. Dental care must also be paid for. Comprehensive health care is beyond the means of the vast majority of people of the *comunidad*. A majority of older Teachivans suffer from malformed or poor teeth, which could be improved by simple dental procedures. They cannot afford the fees.

Most people at one time or another resort to the herbal or folk remedies, which are effective in many cases. For serious infections and

illnesses, though, they consult the clinic first and use traditional remedies, if at all, as a supplement to modern medicine. There is a certain
prestige in being attended to by a *mestizo* doctor who practices the
medicine of the wealthy classes. Nearly all older people use traditional
remedies for common ailments. No household is without a bundle of
curing herbs hanging from the ceiling. Though Teachivans recom-
mend herbal cures with enthusiasm, they accept their limitations and
usually prefer modern medicine as quicker and more effective.

No one in Teachive is recognized as a *curandero* (curer), a practitioner who combines herbal medicines and mystical rites. Vicente's
familiarity with plants and medicinal cures is widely known and villagers consult with him. He also consults with other people known to
be knowledgeable in medicinal plants and remedies. He is not considered a *curandero*, however. No person is known to be able routinely to
cure ailments such as *pasmo*, *empacho*, or *susto* (what we might call folk
illnesses).[56] No one prepares special mixes of herbs in response to
specific pathology. No one is recognized for the ability to massage or
manipulate a part of the body to reassert the proper balance of hot and
cold. Instead, most natives visit the clinic in San José or in Navojoa.
Very poor folk with chronic illnesses may visit *curanderos* in other
towns. A relative of Vicente's experienced ongoing gynecological
problems. She visited both the local physician and a *curandera* in Huebampo. She appeared to have more confidence in the *curandera* than in
the physician and pronounced herself cured by the practitioner.

Most natives of the region believe that *brujos* (witches) and *hechiceros*
(sorcerers or evildoers) are active in the community. No one knows for
certain who they are. Villagers have their suspicions, and rumors to
this effect can be powerful. Practitioners of dark arts are believed to be
capable of inflicting spells that produce a physical condition referred
to as *mal puesto*, characterized by aches and pains, general malaise, or
sudden injuries and death. Their motivation is said to be pure vindic-
tiveness or jealousy, because someone insults them or because they
covet something or some ability possessed by another. The only cure is
to seek out a *curandero* who can cure the condition by producing a cure
with a contrary effect and identify the offending sorcerer. Nowadays,
villagers say, few *curanderos* remain.

Teachivans identify a woman from Huebampo as a *curandera*. Huebampo is a poor hamlet a half-hour drive from Teachive. If an ailment

has not responded to a doctor's care, or if it is diagnosed by one's family or friends as *mal puesto*, the sufferer will often make the long trip to the curer. She will identify the pathological condition and the perpetrators, and with herbs and spells correct the condition. She (as most *curanderas*) operates without instruments or medicine, using many herbs, bones, hair, or other common substance in her rituals. The cure for *mal puesto* is primarily spiritual (i.e., it involves ritual manipulations and spells), just as the cause is spiritual. This curandera does not charge a fee for her services. Such is her influence that her clients reimburse her well with money or gifts.

Most villagers appear to accept this cosmology of healing unques-tioningly. One curer informed Vicente that the injury caused by a plant spine that penetrated his eye in 1964 and caused him to lose it, was inflicted by a man from a nearby village. Vicente appears to be undecided still whether to believe the allegation or not. He prefers to seek medical attention for his ailments. In spite of his ambivalence to-ward the practice of *curanderismo*, he enthusiastically related the widely believed story of a contemporary Yaqui *brujo* whose evil powers led to many sicknesses, injuries, and deaths. According to Vicente, the Yaquis complained to the governor of the state, to no avail, that this man was killing many people. (The tone of Vicente's delivery contained a hint of condemnation of the governor for not taking action.) Finally, he says, the Yaquis took matters into their own hands. They seized the witch, bound him, dragged him through the streets, doused him with gasoline and placed him on a pyre of firewood and set him on fire. The killings and deaths then ceased, he reports.

Villagers also are wary of owls and persecute them. Owls are used by witches to kill people, they say. They fear snakes as well. They kill rattlesnakes and use every part. Other serpents are attacked and killed. No one is willing to touch a live snake except for the *corua* (Boa constrictor), which is the object of considerable mythology, largely favorable. Also respected is the *babatuco* (indigo snake), said to have helpful powers as well.

VILLAGE LIFE

Teachivans pay little attention to national and international affairs. They will discuss the assassination of Luis Donaldo Colosio in 1994, and they deplore what they see as the probable involvement of former president Carlos Salinas de Gortari, on whom they blame all the nation's ills. They applaud the arrest of *mafiosos* and denounce those who elude arrest. Few support the ruling PRI party; far more support the left-of-center PRD. Teachivans exalt or rail against very famous singers and soap opera stars. They are shocked by violence against illegal immigrants in the United States. They still hope some relative or other will make it there. They are little moved by hardships in other villages, are fascinated by disasters, and indignant about well-publicized corruption.

In general their conversations devolve on the day-to-day life in the village. Villagers crane their necks and prick their ears to overhear the latest price of *maseca* and beans, or who has new *huaraches* or a new flashlight. If Pancho has a prostate problem or Concha has a dropped uterus, no one is shielded from the news. When Zaragoza was repeatedly stabbed, stories flew: everything he owned had been stolen; his bicycle was still there. He had been beaten while passed out drunk; he saw his attackers clearly. He lost all his money; he lost not a cent. He was dead; he was badly wounded in a hospital. When Poli, age ten, went to work in the fields, everyone pitied him, son of a demented mother who feeds him only crackers. Such news involving death, a sudden illness, a pregnancy, or a love affair travels fast. Even children know all the details within hours.

Nearly everyone in the village has plenty to do. Except in the hottest months, children go off to school carrying their little backpacks, even if they have nothing to carry in them. The school is crowded, so shifts are split between morning and afternoon. Women watch babies and young children as they cook, clean, iron, wash, tend livestock, sew, chitchat, and weave. Men depart for the fields by truck or bus, or plod off into the *monte* with a burro, a ritual they perform even if it is only to sleep for a while. Some stretch, pack a canteen and a bag of tortillas, and head for the arroyo to shovel gravel. Few young men are to be found in the village during the day. They have mostly departed for work or for good. The bigger, faster world of business, diplomacy, and government seems remote and other-worldly. Few newspapers and even fewer books supplement radio music, soap operas, and brief news stories. A few comic books and *novelas* (photographic novels) are seen here and there. The few televisions in the village are popular. Their productive life is ephemeral, coming in and out of existence as the heavy dust, irregular power surges, and difficult reception take their toll. In the homes of Protestants, bibles are usually to be found, as bible-reading is part of daily activity.

Transportation

Only one individual or family owns an automobile in the village, the schoolteacher, whose house also features the only evaporative cooler. One man is part-owner of a truck used for hauling bricks, and another truck is claimed by a Teachivan. Others assert he doesn't own it, how-ever, but merely keeps it for the absentee owner. For transportation the entire village relies on the buses that regularly ply their way through the streets, or on bicycles, which are commonly used by men as well as boys (women do not ride bicycles), or on burros, mules, horses, or animal-drawn carts (all for men only). Occasionally, only occasionally, a woman drives a cart. The buses are owned by a Masiacan, who is viewed as rich and ambitious and is said to own a two-storied house in Navojoa. He charges more than one dollar for the trip to Huata-bampo, the same for Navojoa.

The first bus arrives in Teachive at 5:30 A.M., announcing its arrival with regular blasts of its horn designed to alert all the village of its imminent arrival, and all late sleepers to its presence as well. The bus originates in Masiaca and arrives at Huatabampo at 7 A.M., stopping in innumerable villages en route. Sleep in Teachive becomes impossible after this hour, for the next bus comes fifteen minutes later, its destina-tion Navojoa, its arrival also announced by the earth-shaking blast. Several more buses depart for the cities in the early morning, all blasting their way through the village. Everyone knows which bus is which by its mere sound. By mid-morning, the same buses return. On these, village residents are able to ride into Masiaca for a pittance and spare themselves the long walk.

On weekends, Ley, a major department and grocery store in Huata-bampo, sends a bus through all the pueblos, providing free transporta-tion to and from the huge store, nearly twenty-five miles away. Many residents take advantage of this service, viewing it also as recreation. The Ley bus is often crowded with women dressed in their Sunday best, as though they were attending a social event. The supermarket is crowded on weekends with villagers from throughout the lower Río Mayo, shuttled to the store by its small fleet of courtesy buses.

The convenience of the Ley bus has increased shopping and social opportunities for Teachivans, especially women, who otherwise would seldom have the opportunity to leave the village. It regularly exposes them to the more cosmopolitan atmosphere of the larger city, and affords an opportunity to communicate with other Mayos from the region. It probably also has increased their long-term inconvenience. The shift of the villagers' individually small but collectively substantial purchasing power from shops in Masiaca to the department store Ley in Huatabampo has worked to the detriment of the former, significantly decreasing the range of goods available in Masiaca's stores. In all probability one or two of the four retail general stores in Masiaca will be forced to close for lack of business, and the remaining two will carry a smaller range of merchandise. This in turn means that fewer items will be readily available in Masiaca compared with the past. The villagers will have to wait for weekends and the Ley bus to purchase these items, or simply do without. At the same time, a small diminution in the economy of Masiaca will have taken place, which is bound to have a negative ripple effect on the entire community.

Electricity

Electricity arrived in the village in the mid-1980s. Teachive was not the first pueblo to be wired, nor the last. Only about one-half of the houses are wired. The costs of hooking up to the line and the monthly bills (usually around eight dollars, roughly two days' pay in the fields) are a deterrent. The villagers figured out quickly that along with the blessing of electricity come the additional expenses of purchasing appliances and an unending variety of light bulbs, cords, fans, and so on. Vicente pointed out one family who is without electricity. He thinks it is because the husband is a known cheapskate who gives nothing to his family. Perhaps he is right. Perhaps the husband is smart enough not to get his family hooked into heavy expenses. (His wife lamented the absence of a fan that might enable her to continue weaving in the hottest days of summer.) Some who have electricity enjoy outdoor lighting, which is a clear sign to everyone that their place is wired and that they can afford the electricity. Failure to pay the electric company for the electricity to run the community water pump has caused it to be shut down on occasion. No permanent solution to this problem has been found, even though the village has a committee to oversee the pump.

Alcohol

One individual is known as the town drunk. Always willing to join a party and perform a *pascola* dance, even in the middle of the day, he is viewed as incapable of sustained work and prolonged conversation. He wanders about the *monte* drinking cheap *mescal*, which is said to produce a quick drunkenness and a throbbing *cruda* (hangover). His family is pitied by other villagers, for he is an economic burden to them.[57] Another family is known to be plagued with alcoholism. They somehow manage to stay afloat by hard work and by recruiting their many sons into the family business.

Other men are notorious for excessive drinking. They also manage to work, some of them very hard. It does not appear that the rate of alcoholism is as high as in other Mexican towns.[58] During the *fiestas* it is expected that men will get drunk, and no particular stigma is attached to drunkenness at that time. Men frequently announce (with a degree of pride) that they intend to *pistear y emborracharse* (go drinking and get drunk). Drunkeness in Teachive is viewed with opprobrium only if and when the drunk's family suffers as a result. Given the poverty of the village, it is hard to imagine any drinking that does not have an adverse effect on a family. Beer costs about three dollars a six-pack, nearly the daily wage of many *jornaleros*. One can of beer costs more than a kilogram of corn flour or a pound of beans.[59] The price of a six-pack of beer will feed a family of four for a day. Beer drinking is a *mestizo*, not Mayo custom, and to the extent that men now find drinking beer to be an acceptable pastime, they have been pulled away from the Mayo culture.

Women do not appear to drink, and their tolerance for the men's indulgence does not appear to have been widely tested. Whatever their feelings about men's expensive habits, they disguise them well. The fact is that women are never seen near the beer tent at *fiestas*. Whether this is a male fiat or a self-imposed prohibition is unclear. The message is clear, though: having fun with booze is a man's right and his only.

Women could not possibly be trusted to handle the volatile liquid. Vicente states that a woman seen holding a beer in public would be viewed as crazy or worse.

One man complained that his son was getting fat on beer and that it interfered with his taking care of his family, which includes two young children. The son visits one bar in Masiaca and another on the international highway south of Jopopaco. He forbids his young wife to leave the house in his absence, which is most of the time. The father does not approve of his son's treatment of his daughter-in-law. In fairness, he acknowledges having gotten roaring drunk himself when he was younger; now he seldom drinks.

The pressures on young men in Mexican society to drink alcohol are enormous. Not only is drinking expected of them, it is demanded.[60] A former Sonoran governor told me indignantly that Mexican mothers urge their young sons to drink so that they will not be suspected of being sissies, or, worse, homosexuals. Beer companies have mounted highly successful marketing campaigns aimed at increasing consumption and at getting younger people to associate social success with beer drinking. Older men are more content to drink tequila or mescal. Young men must have the highly promoted beer. A few hours before a Masiaca *fiesta* was to begin, several young men who had been employed to set up *fiesta* props were taking their ease on the curb. They drank Tecate while they rested, taking care to make the red color as visible as possible. One held up his bright red can of Tecate. "*Colorada* [red]," he proclaimed, holding the can high. Beer industry investment in advertising has paid off handsomely.

Smoking is uncommon, perhaps because it is a conspicuous and ongoing cost (not a binge cost like beer). Most men will smoke if a cigarette is offered. Almost no one chain smokes. Women do not smoke, and children do not begin the habit young. In cities such as Navojoa, however, almost all men and most boys smoke in varying degrees.

Marriage, baptism, and death

Part of Teachive's strength lies in its long history of shared relationships, through bloodlines (intermarriage is widespread), *compadrazco* (godparenting), and through physical closeness. Nearly all the older people in town married someone local, at least from within the

Masiaca community, thus reinforcing already close kinship ties. The institution of *compadrazco* does not appear to be as important or as highly developed among Mayos as among *mestizos*. Still, most grown men and women are godfather and godmother once or twice, which further strengthens and complicates the social relations of the village. Throughout the day, a parade of neighbors and relatives pass through the Tajia-Moroyoqui household. Neighbor children and their parents drop by to chat, although it seems to me that nonfamily adults usually have a specific purpose in mind when they stop by (it may even be their curiosity about a gringo living in a Mayo household).

The village holds few secrets from its members. Vicente and one of his granddaughters sat down with me and named every member of every household in the village, what they did for work, and how old they were. It is nearly impossible for someone to enter or leave a house without someone else observing their arrival or departure. Children are so numerous, and life is so oriented to the outside, that someone is nearly always observing the street. Each house retains the services of dogs (mostly mistreated, mangy curs) whose primary duty is to bark at strangers. For the gringo who frequently goes on walks into the *monte* at night, its mysterious sounds, its stillness, and its wildness prove most attractive. Seldom does such an outsider pass unnoticed, even though the night is dense. The same is true for everyone. Dalliances occur and sinister plans are carried out, and there is ample bush country nearby. Those who dare such liaisons or schemes run the risk of being found out. Usually everybody's whereabouts is known to somebody.

Many, if not most, older Teachivan couples have never been formally married. They simply carried out the Mayo custom and took up a joint household. Numerous Teachivans are "divorced" and "remarried," or at least living with a second mate. In several cases, men have left their wives for other women. Their whereabouts is usually known. An older woman related with grave secrecy that a particular single woman had had a child by a married man who lives in the village. She exhorted me not to tell a soul, in spite of the fact that everybody knows what has happened. In another case, one mother is known to have had children by several fathers. She is not ostracized, and is rather well-liked. Men lust after women. They denounce the more revealing clothing of modern young women, loving it the whole time. Dubious paternity is rumored of this or that child or adult. Families are large and pregnancies frequent. Family honor is not a matter of life and death, as it is among more Iberian-oriented peoples.

Younger parents are usually married, for their children cannot be registered if the parents are unmarried. Most children are born at home, so the issuing of a birth certificate is not automatic. Baptisms are performed strictly according to Catholic traditions, usually in Navojoa, sometimes in the church in Masiaca. Parents are diligent about seeing that their children's names are noted in the official registry, found in the home of Jocha, the justice of the peace in San José, who registers them in the official birth lists, usually before they are three. An unregistered child may not attend school and will have difficulty later in life in voting, proving residence, and collecting whatever government benefits may exist.

One must prove residence to obtain a voter identification card, without which one is subject to harassment and arrest by federal authorities. One Indian from a Mayo village was denied passage on a bus and detained when he could not produce his identification. When I drive Teachivans to other towns or cities outside the *comunidad*, passengers always carry their identification card, for they subject themselves to the risk of being stopped and searched by *federales* and soldiers, who will also demand their documents. All parents thus understand the importance of having children registered.

Funerals are strictly Roman Catholic ceremonies. A mass is held in the church, and sometimes in the home as well. The dead are usually buried in the Masiaca cemetery located at the northeast end of town. When Juan was murdered, his family made a monument of heaped stones near the house

Credit
For a villager needing credit, resources are slim. There is no bank in Masiaca, and no Teachivan owned up to having a bank account anywhere.[61] A Sinaloan who lived for years in Masiaca would lend money for little or no interest, trusting that people could pay him back, which they almost always did, most say. For loans, villagers usually resort to relatives and friends, or, for those who own cows, an advance on the retail value of the cow. The Masiaca livestock buyer knows the suppli-

cants well enough that he will determine the weight of the cow and loan a percentage of the current weight, without interest, he says. When the calf or cow is sold, he will deduct the amount advanced. While he claims not to charge interest, he alone determines, at sale time, the quality of the cow, and pays according to his judgment. The buyer lives in a modest house in Masiaca and professes to make only a tiny profit on each cow. Villagers mumble that he has many enterprises and much money, and only appears to be poor because he lives in perpetual fear of being robbed.

Itinerant salesmen will sell furniture and appliances on credit, usually at high interest rates. They run a cursory credit check and then deliver the appliance, knowing they can repossess the item if necessary, with the full backing of the police.

Salesmen

The rather predictable life of the village is made less monotonous by the frequent passing of these itinerant salesmen. Hardy peddlers (sometimes with their families) wind their way slowly through the neighborhoods of even the most remote villages of Mexico, hawking a huge variety of wares.[62] Their vehicles—ancient trucks, battered pickups, even old sedans—are equipped with public-address systems, usually with speakers cracked just enough to distort their announcement and add to their mystique. These mobile marketers announce themselves well in advance of arriving and idle through the village so that the prospective buyers have ample time to collect their widows' mites. The pronouncements are blared out with fake excitement in the tone of circus roustabouts. The salesmen have perfected the sales pitch in the tradition of Mexican radio announcers who turn any old drab announcement into a melodrama, hoping to seduce the most parsimonious of housekeepers. Some salesmen peddle fruits and vegetables, others, only herbs, vitamins, and elixirs; some hawk household furniture such as sofas, tables, and chairs; others offer electric appliances from blenders to fans to refrigerators. Some specialize in a huge variety of knick-knacks ranging from jewelry to watches to sewing notions. From time to time a truck will appear, bulging with merchandise, that sells all of the above. Every household has some item or other that was purchased from a traveling salesman. As the vendors cruise by, natives stream from their houses to examine the wares and, more often than not, purchase something or other. Thus is the world brought to those who cannot go to the world.

In March 1995 a huge pickup truckload of citrus ambled through the village. The loudspeaker urged housewives to "buy juicy oranges to make juice and protect the health of their family." In April a truck carrying *elotes* (roasting ears of corn) cruised by. These were billed as "the perfect corn for making a tasty and nutritious stew for your family." Just prior to St. John's Day in June, watermelons, traditionally eaten on that day of celebration, appeared. These needed little promotion. They were gobbled up almost instantly by crowds of purchasers. With the advent of the bus provided by the giant Ley supermarket chain, business is off, for the villagers have better access to a huge department store where prices are lower than the itinerant salesmen can afford to sell. The days of the roving peddlers are numbered.

Police and crime

Law enforcement in Teachive is provided by the municipal police stationed in Masiaca. State judicial police also roam the area and often become involved in local criminal cases. They assume jurisdiction of felonies. The local police are known to all and related to many. The police commissioner of Masiaca is elected; it is the only local office for which all adults may vote. Vicente's eldest son Bernardino has been commissioner (*comisario*) in recent years. He seldom visits Teachive, for he has six villages plus Masiaca to supervise. He knows the secrets of the town and the villages, knows who hates and who loves, and, usually, why. Officers like Bernardino are neither well-trained nor heavily armed and are at a disadvantage in the case of armed robberies or shootings, where the perpetrators are often better armed than the police. Even state and federal police shy away from some notorious criminals, drug *mafiosos* whose armaments are technically superior to their own.

The state judicial police are viewed with mixed emotions by locals. *Judiciales* have a reputation for being cruel and corrupt (though not as bad as the despised federal judicial police, the *federales*). They are generally not viewed as protectors of the people. They are seen as a lawless force that metes out punishment to the poor. They are summoned only in desperate cases. Their appearance in the town usually causes the suspension of most human activity.

In recent years the presence of the *judiciales* and municipal police in Teachive has increased, as the force has obtained more vehicles. Still, police presence is defined by occasional passes of the small pickup truck driven by a municipal policeman. Violent crimes are usually investigated by the state police, often with surprising thoroughness and efficiency. Vicente observes that neighborhood disputes are taken before the *comisariado* in Masiaca for adjudication. He or she attempts to settle the dispute in a way that diffuses the situation, helping parties to save face and thereby preventing further escalation. Technically, only civil cases, those involving land disputes and related questions are under the jurisdiction of the *comisariado*. If a felony is involved and the police are summoned, the situation leaves community hands and becomes more serious, usually involving jail, lawyers, and politicians. Cases that involve the police subject Mayos to *mestizo* justice (usually entailing the intrusion of the *judiciales*), which they neither understand nor trust. They believe that the Indian is constantly at a disadvantage in the government system. Vicente is also convinced that the *yori* (*mestizo*)-influenced leadership of the *comunidad* is in cahoots with the *mestizo* politicians and the state police to weasel the Mayos out of their land, resources, and rights. In general, then, whenever possible, village disputes are settled by the villagers themselves with the wise judgment of the elected *comisariado*. The state and federal police are viewed as outsiders whose role is to watch for illegal activities by other outsiders or especially serious crimes.

The people of Teachive speak often of the increased crime and violence that is perceived to be sweeping Mexico, and they express fear for their security. All are acquainted with someone involved in drug traffic and know the dangers in that enterprise (no one in Teachive is acknowledged as regularly receiving income from working with the drug traffickers). One knowledgeable fellow expressed doubt that much drug trafficking occurred in the community. The land isn't mountainous enough and there is insufficient water, he assured me. Still, there is a heightened suspicion of outsiders and strangers and an increased reluctance to walk or ride alone in the *monte*. The villagers' reluctance to discuss the matter of local drug traffic in any detail leads me to believe that some men, probably younger men, have dubious connections to the industrialization of marijuana.

Whether the increased hazard of crime is real or perceived, it has become a routine matter of discussion and is forcing all villagers to reconsider their previously innocent wanderings. My colleagues and I camped several times near the village during the early stages of my studies. On the advice of one *comunero*, we decided never to camp more than two consecutive nights in one place, a policy enthusiastically endorsed by Vicente and other men to whom we spoke.

The crime "wave" is well documented in the minds of the natives. In 1995 a villager from nearby Choacalle robbed a truck and was killed in the attempt. A gas truck was robbed four weeks later a few kilometers away. A bus was held up at gunpoint on the same day. In Sirebampo, part of the Masiaca community, the two village stores were robbed in the space of two months by thieves who came on foot to the village. As reports of these crimes came into the village, Vicente suggested that I hide my vehicle in his yard so it couldn't easily be seen from the roadway.

Teachivans are less obsessed by defense of family and personal honor than is the case in many other Mexican towns.[63] Families, perhaps because of complex intermarriages, seem not to harbor long-time grudges against other families, and insults are not often interpreted as challenges to manhood that must be avenged at all costs. Still, villagers were stunned by news in 1996 that Zaragosa, age sixty-three, had been stabbed repeatedly and left for dead. At first the rumor was that he was drunk at the time and had no idea who had assaulted him or why. Robbery was the presumed motive. For days the poor fellow lay on the edge of death in a Navojoa hospital. Then police revealed that the crime had been committed by Victor, from San José. Victor bragged to a policeman that he had stabbed Zaragoza. It was vengeance, pure and simple. Years ago, Zaragoza had allegedly assaulted Victor's brother and stabbed him. The family's honor was reclaimed when Victor returned the favor. Teachivans shook their heads in wonder and sadness. Zaragoza survived. Some Teachivans thought it was simply personal *venganza*, others that it was a family matter.

Vicente has thought much about the causes of the apparent increase in major crimes. He observes that robberies happen more frequently close to *fiestas*, particularly the Fiesta of San Miguel at Masiaca at the end of September. "People want to have money for the *fiesta*, to buy beer and food and have fun. They are poor, so they rob buses and trucks when they know the drivers have money. Beer is expensive, so they need money, a lot of money to buy it." This was not sufficient to explain all the increase in crime, he realized. After thinking for a while, he added, "I think there are just too many poor people. They have nothing, so if they can get a little by robbing, they will rob, even if it means they may go to prison or even be killed."

The threat of crime has a remoteness to it, in spite of the many examples known to the villagers. No one in Teachive has enough money or valuables to warrant major theft. The wealthiest Teachivan is very poor by U.S. standards. When Teachivans speak with resentment about "*los ricos*" (the rich), they are referring vaguely to more or less anonymous folk who live in the cities. They consider a few *mestizos* in Masiaca to be rich. Even they would be considered poor in the United States.

CHAPTER FOUR

The Community

ᔐ Teachive is a village in *la comunidad indígena* (the indigenous community) de Masiaca; it is 46,400 hectares (nearly 200 square miles) in size. While its historic roots can be traced back for centuries, the community was formally created in 1941 under President Manuel Avila Camacho, when the Mexican government recognized the Mayos' long and continuing occupation of the lands. The community's legal status was further endorsed in 1946 on the basis of surveys done in 1834. A formal survey using modern techniques was completed in 1951, and signed by President Miguel Alemán.[1] The final boundaries are still in question, for, according to some, the current community limits omit roughly six thousand hectares of lands from what was originally promised and some inholdings now in private hands are disputed by the community.

The community of Masiaca extends from roughly twenty kilometers inland to the Gulf of California. It runs for twenty-three kilometers along the coast. From the town of Teachive in the north to Sirebampo in the southeast, the distance is nearly thirty kilometers. The *comunidad* includes the villages of Las Animas, Bachomojaqui ("seepwillow in the wash"), Las Bocas,[2] Chichibojoro ("ragweed hole"), Choacalle ("cholla cactus in the road"), Coteco ("pile of broken sticks"), Cucajaqui ("arroyo of sweet acacia"), Huebampo ("amaranth in the water"), Jopopaco (*"palo blanco* out there"), Masiaca ("centipede hill"), Piedra Baya ("squash-colored stone"), San José,[3] San Pedrito, Sirebampo (*"granadilla* in the water"), and Teachive ("scattered round stones").[4] Except to the north of Teachive, the lands are mostly flat or gently undulating. The vegetation consists almost entirely of coastal scrub and low foothills thorn forest. 95

In addition to being the largest town of the *comunidad*, Masiaca is also the *comisariaría*, the seat of the government of the community. Residents of eight of the villages (those in the *municipio* of Navojoa, as opposed to the *municipio* of Huatabampo, in which the other villages are found) vote in elections for Masiaca officials. Government village programs are administered from Masiaca.[5] Police of the *municipio* are also stationed in Masiaca. Their jurisdiction ceases at the international highway. From there southward, communal lands are in the *municipio* of Huatabampo. Some Huatabampo municipal police are stationed in Las Bocas.

The *comunidad* of Masiaca, which exists within the *municipios* of Navojoa and Huatabampo, is a closed corporate community (Wolf 1966) in that it is closed to new members, and in that corporate or group decisions determine the major questions of land use and tenure.[6] It has its own governing body and its membership is limited to a fixed number of members, 971, whose eligibility is established by the historical presence of their ancestors. According to Wolf, such communities represent "an enduring organization of rights and duties held by a stable membership." Wolf's definition strains the actual nature of the Masiaca community somewhat. It is more accurately characterized by Sheridan's description of "an organization of peasant households that controls certain basic natural resources, and that preserves its corporate identity through time" (Sheridan 1988).[7]

The *comuneros* constitute the *asamblea* (assembly). All are eligible to elect the officers of the *comunidad indígena*, who are elected for three-year terms, a *comisariado* (chairman),[8] and a *consejo de vigilancia*, a watchdog whose job it is to keep an eye on the president. The latter is often, if not always, the loser in the election for *comisariado*, head official of the *comunidad*. It is as though there were two presidents, one to govern and the other to make sure that the president governs honestly. In 1996 an extremely poor man from Huebampo was elected *comisariado*.[9] The two officers appear to work in harmony, and the competition of election appears to have dissolved once the vote was taken.

Of the numerous villages in the community, Masiaca (the town, not the *comunidad*) is by far the largest with about 1,100 permanent inhabitants. It also contains by far the smallest percentages of Mayos; it is a *mestizo* town. None of the other villages, which, except for Las Bocas, are overwhelmingly Mayo, is much more than half as large.[10] The total

community population is roughly 5,000. Teachive, Choacalle, Cucajaqui, San José, and San Pedrito are very nearly contiguous with Masiaca.
Nevertheless, they have sufficient demographic and historical autonomy to be considered as separate villages. The residents of Teachive,
for example, view themselves as residents of a distinct village, and
clearly demark the boundaries that separate their village from the
others. Teachive and Choacalle are both rather dispersed villages, each
lacking a central square, and they merge into one another. The boundary between them is an undistinguished-looking arroyo that would
hardly be noticed by outsiders. It is well known to residents, however.
Houses of Choacalle are hardly a stone's throw from dwellings that
pertain to Masiaca. Still, in the minds of the inhabitants, Choacalle is
as distinct from Teachive as Los Angeles is from San Francisco, and
both are equally distinct from Masiaca. Likewise, the boundary between Masiaca and San José is marked by an undistinguished fence-
post and a field, identifiable as boundaries only to one thoroughly
familiar with the area. The marker has great local importance, demark-
ing the limits of two villages with distinct loyalties and histories. San
José is a Mayo village; Masiaca is a *yori* town.[11]

Documents describing the community before 1835 are sorely lacking. I can only speculate that prior to Mexican Independence the
Masiaca *comunidad* lay within the sphere of influence of one or more
powerful *hacendados*, who received tribute, or *corvee*, from the *comuneros*.
The *comunidad* as an entity has its origin in Spanish colonial administration, which found it convenient under the system of *haciendas* to
leave Indian communities more or less intact. Wolf notes:

> The Spaniards had reinforced the cohesion of the Indian com-
> munities by granting them a measure of land and demanding
> that they make themselves responsible collectively for pay-
> ments of dues and for the maintenance of social order. The
> communities had responded by developing, within the frame-
> work of such corporate organization, their own internal system
> of political organization, strongly tied to religious worship.
> Nearly everywhere, sponsorship of a sequence of religious fes-
> tivities qualified a man [sic] to become one of the decision
> makers for the community as a whole. A man who sought
> power, therefore, had to do it largely by meeting criteria laid

down by the community. . . . Power was thus less individual
than communal. (Wolf 1969, 17)

The Spanish colonial system "usually subordinated a corporate peasant community to a dominant domain owner in the vicinity" (Wolf
1969, 4–5). According to Wolf,

> Each [Indian] community retained its own custom and lan-
> guage, and ringed itself about with a wall of distrust and hos-
> tility against outsiders. A set of such communities might be
> subservient to a *hacienda* down-valley from them, but they also
> retained a strong sense of their cultural and social separateness
> from the *hacienda* population. Thus Mexico emerged into its
> period of independence with its rural landscape polarized
> between large estates on the one hand and Indian communities
> on the other—units, moreover, which might be linked econom-
> ically, but which remained set off against each other socially
> and politically. Seen from the perspective of the larger social
> order, each *hacienda* constituted a state within a state; each In-
> dian community represented a small "republic of Indians"
> among other "republics of Indians." (Wolf 1969, 4–5)

Almost certainly the Masiaca community served as a source of ranch
labor, quite possibly for the Almada family of Alamos, who owned
numerous ranches and mines in the region, providing beef for the large
mining town of Alamos. So great was the power of the Almada family
from the eighteenth century on that one scion could, in 1835, dictate
the conditions of the Masiaca boundary survey (Archivos del Estado
de Sonora [hereafter cited as AES], Tomo 135).[12]

EJIDOS, ETHNICITY, AND THE COMMUNITY

Masiaca is a *comunidad*. The Mayo village of Yocogigua, fifteen kilometers to the north, is an *ejido*. When I asked don Vicente how a *comunidad*
differed from an *ejido*, he confessed that he felt inadequate to the task
of explaining the difference, ever despairing of his inability to read and
write. He suggested instead that I visit Jesús Moroyoqui, who lived
three kilometers away in San Pedrito, or, more correctly, in a tiny part

of the small village of San Pedrito which they used to call Huírivis before floods came and washed it away. In fact, Jesús lives in the only remaining house in Huírivis and is often referred to merely as "El Huírivis." Don Jesús, Vicente thought, would be especially helpful because he speaks both Spanish and *la lengua* (Mayo) and he reads and understands complicated legal issues.

Moroyoqui's house is a Mayo structure, which was brimming on that particular day with relatives from various pueblos in the area. Widowed, don Jesús has sometimes shared the house with his son, but now he was alone. In hot weather he sits, shirtless, in the *portal* of his house watching the traffic pass by on the graded road from Masiaca to the international highway.

Vicente was right. Jesús, who is in his early seventies, greeted Vicente in Mayo and was more than eager to supply details and analysis of the recent history of the community. Chairs were magically produced, as they always are in Mayo households, and were set rather close together so as not to interfere with the variety of human activities that were taking place in the household—clothes being washed on a scrub board, tortillas cooking, children playing, a broken-down truck being repaired, the dirt floor and yard being swept, and a radio playing *norteña* music rather loudly. Without any further introduction, Jesús began to expostulate on the nature and workings of the community. He began by assuming a rather exaggerated posture and the air of an orator, speaking in a loud, pedagogic voice.

"One important difference," he began, rapping me on the arm repeatedly for emphasis and to guarantee my continuous attention (a *mestizo*, not a Mayo custom), "is that anyone at all can become a member of an *ejido*, while only a descendant of an original member of the community, an *indígena*, can belong to a *comunidad*." I nodded in understanding. As he spoke, don Jesús found it troubling that a *comunero* had to have been an *indígena* if, by *indígena* was meant one with precolumbian New World ancestry. The Masiaca *comunidad*, we both knew, includes nonindigenous people as *comuneros*, and Jesús himself is *mestizo*.

He continued undaunted. A second difference, he said, is that community members have more control over their lands than *ejidatarios* do over theirs. At the same time, the governing body has more power over *comuneros* than the *ejido* government has over *ejidatarios*.[13] Both *ejidos* and *comunidades* are governed by assemblies. (The Masiaca *asemblea* meets in Masiaca every month and takes up community questions and attempts to resolve them. *Ejido* assemblies must meet at least quarterly.) *Comuneros* have more power over their lands than do *ejidatarios*, Jesús claims. "*Comuneros* have more independence," he thought. "We are less controlled by the government." But, then, he recalled, the Masiaca assembly can take away a right to use land, so the independence wasn't as comprehensive as he thought after all.

"And even now," he went on, "lands of the *comunidad* may not be sold. The new changes in Article 27 of the Mexican Constitution allows *ejidatarios* to sell their parcels. *Comuneros* may never sell theirs."[14]

Those were the differences, he said. He showed me letters, documents, and maps that he kept carefully stored in a plastic bag hidden in the recesses of his house. He handled the documents with great pride. He was not entirely satisfied with the results of his teaching, for he realized by my hesitation and further questions that the distinction between a *comunidad* and an *ejido* was muddy to him, as it was to me and Vicente, for we all knew that the Masiaca *comunidad* includes non-Mayo members, and that some *comuneros* treat their land as though it were their private property.

I journeyed to Hermosillo to talk about *comunidades* with an official of the Mexican Department of Agrarian Reform. He owned that some fine points about *comunidades* are unresolved and cause ongoing problems in the thirty-some *comunidades* in Sonora.[15]

Gradually, though the differences became clear. Ejidos are made up of members whose origin may be anywhere at all. The decision to add new *ejidatarios* or not is entirely up to the assembly. In contrast, the membership of *comunidades* is fixed, limited to those who have historic tenancy. The assembly may not add members to the roll except through a seldom-used and elaborate appeal process whereby an applicant may demonstrate historic land tenancy, and then only with explicit permission of the federal government.[16]

Yet within La Comunidad Indígena de Masiaca, as it is officially known, there are *comuneros* who are not Indians, not indigenous, not even partly so. Some non-Mayos who long ago succeeded in insinuating themselves into the community became *comuneros*. These *mestizos* view the community in historic and economic terms, as a land-grant reserved for those who can trace their personal and family histories to that land. Mayos, on the other hand, tend to view the community in ethnic terms, as a Mayo institution whose members should be able to demonstrate not only physical roots but cultural roots as well. They perceive the non-Mayos as outsiders who have moved in and have gradually increased their domination of community affairs. As a half-Mayo, half-*mestizo*, Jesús was caught between these two worlds. He views himself more as a Mayo than a *mestizo*, and his loyalties are to the Mayos.

From the government's standpoint, recognition of the community and limitation of membership to native sons and daughters represents an acknowledgment of a historic occupation and vested right of use. It is not, however, an acknowledgment of Mayo culture as unique or a paternalistic instrument to shield Mayos from *mestizo* culture and institutions. The *comunidad* is not a Mayo Indian Reservation, even though the National Indigenous Institute, Mexico's Bureau of Indian Affairs, charged with hispanicizing Mexico's Indians while acting as advocate for them, is active in the community. Mexican government policy, after all, has been to integrate all Indians into the mainstream of Mexican society. Small wonder, then, that the full distinction between the *comunidad* and the *ejido* is not completely clear to many Mayo community members, including Jesús.[17]

Even though its historical foundation lies in Mayo natives, and even though Mayos still tend to occupy the most important elected posts, over the last few decades *yoris* have indeed taken over the power in the community.

How did this state of affairs come to be? How did a Mayo community come to be dominated, as it appears to be, by *mestizos*? How did *mestizos* come to be members and increasingly dominate the community decisions that are of great concern to many of the Mayos? I asked this question of two Mayo *comuneros* from Jopopaco. "That's exactly what we would like to know," they fumed, knowing full well that Masiaca, as a *comunidad indígena*, could only exist because of its long history and generations of residence by Mayos.

The *comunidad indígena* was created by order of the federal government through the national Department of Bienes Comunales (Department of Communal Lands), which is part of the Secretaria de Reforma Agraria (Secretary of Agrarian Reform).[18] In the years 1951 and 1995, membership in the community assembly stood at 971 individuals, most of them Mayos (*yoremem*), in that they bear Mayo names, speak the Mayo language, participate in Mayo *fiestas*, and observe, or at least respect, the use of the house cross (O'Connor 1989).[19] Membership in the community is closed. Barring an act of the federal government, the number will never exceed the original 971, as Jesús pointed out.[20] Jesús and Vicente are both *comuneros*. Jesús's deceased wife was not; Vicente's wife is not. In order to have been named a *comunero*, one must have demonstrated continuity with the historical community and have been listed as a historic resident in the official census which took place by government order when the *comunidad* was established. Only a direct descendent of the original 971 can become a *comunero* and then only when the original enrollee dies. The *comunero* designates his or her successor. The remaining 4,000 or so souls in the community have no participatory rights in decisions concerning the disposition of communal lands.

According to Modesto Soto Ortega of San José, himself a Mayo and former *comisariado*, who views the *mestizo* presence more favorably than many other Mayos, early in the twentieth century community members allowed non-Mayo outsiders, at least six of whose names are now prominent in the community power structure, to build houses and live in the Mayo community. The "takeover," he says, happened roughly as follows: At the time of charter formation of the community in 1941, Mexican laws (in accordance with the government's stated desire to make all citizens Mexicans) precluded any "test" that would actually have excluded non-Mayos from belonging to the community.[21] Prior to official creation of the *comunidad*, these *mestizos*, welcome or unwelcome, had already moved onto traditional lands and claimed legitimacy by satisfying the government's minimal criteria for recognition of an individual as a member of the community. Some *comuneros* claim they did this merely by learning a few words of the Mayo language and in the process ostensibly proving that they could trace their ancestry to the community, or by partaking of community customs (mere attendance at a *fiesta* or watching Holy Week ceremonies would suffice), or by claiming to be *indígenas*, whatever that meant.

Why did the Mayos allow non-Mayos into the community? Because, Modesto Soto says, they were viewed as an asset to the community. "They had a certain *visión* (vision) for developing our economy," he notes. "They knew the business of raising cattle and farming and selling the products. They also knew the laws and could read and we didn't. So we let them join. They would be a benefit to us."

When the community was delineated, he recalls, all who had houses were defined as *comuneros*, including the non-Mayos, who, just to be safe, learned a little Mayo. They were "grandfathered" into the community, considered as *indígenas* by the government. Soto acknowledges that these families have now come to dominate the political and economic affairs of the community. Many Mayos believe the *mestizo* domination works to the detriment of Mayos. Soto is not among them.

Jesús Moroyoqui snorts at Soto's explanation. The *yoris* are there, he says, quite simply because they bribed the official (*mediador*) who was compiling the census, the official list of *comuneros*, offering him cash to include their names. He singles out the Verdugo family, owners of many cows and much land, as an example. "We never invited them, we never welcomed them. They bribed the *mediador*. That's what happened."

Whatever the real history, the *mestizo comuneros* have made Masiaca into a *mestizo*, rather than a Mayo, town. Although they constitute hardly more than ten *comuneros*, with their greater wealth and better knowledge, education, and sophistication, they have come to control the assembly and orient its policies toward their own ends, which frequently conflict with those of more legitimate Mayo ancestry and Mayo cultural values.[22] The most important issues are those involving land and who gets to use it, and the running of cows on communal lands. *Mestizos* and what Teachivans view as *mestizo*-ized Mayos control the best lands. They live in Masiaca. They are the wealthiest and most prominent members of the town. According to many Mayos, they seem to run things the way they wish. Their cultural background is *mestizo*, and their values are hardly compatible with those of the Mayos, who still have grave cultural differences with *mestizos*. The Mayos argue that the *mestizos*' greater literacy and familiarity with the law and contact with politicians or influential landowners increases their power in the community. Nonsense, say the non-Mayos. How can such a tiny percentage control the entire assembly of 971?[23]

It is widely believed both inside and outside of the community that traditional Mayos are less likely than *mestizos* to be assertive or combative about community policy and land tenure issues, which renders them easily intimidated by the better-educated and more aggressive *mestizos*. Vicente often laments, *"No tenemos líderes"* (We lack leaders).

Most of the older, more traditional Mayo men are illiterate and unsophisticated in law and lack the political connections viewed as necessary for success in Mexico. They are hesitant to speak up in the assembly, except in retorts. Several Mayos complained to me that as a result of the presence of powerful non-Mayos, Mayo interests are being undermined, not by outsiders as much as by community members who either have abandoned Mayo culture ("They want to be Mexicans, *yoris*, not Mayos," one old man complained) or who were never Mayo to begin with. In fact, an ongoing complaint of Indians with whom I spoke is that some non-Mayos now claim to be Mayos, and some Mayos claim to be non-Mayos and have joined with the *mestizos* to run the affairs of the community as they see fit.[24] Thus, irreconcilable differences have arisen within the community, and these are a source of continuing complaints to the federal government bureaucracies which administer the *comunidad*. The differences are so profound that one government official lamented that he doubted if they could ever be resolved.

The unstated complaint voiced by the traditional Mayos emerges out of many conversations: the *comunidad* is supposed to protect against outsiders, peasants and *latifundistas* alike, who would appropriate traditional lands for private exploitation. If the *comunidad* is supposed to protect the land rights of its historic families, why is it that nontraditional natives have the upper hand and are able to use the lands for their own purposes?

Modesto Soto, without denying *mestizo* ascendancy, offers a differing perspective, that of a conservative Mayo, a mass-attending Catholic, and former *comisariado*. The *mestizos* have risen in power because they have *visión*, he says. When asked what this *visión* meant to him, he explained that the *mestizos* have "initiative," they plan, they have broad ideas about making things happen, making contacts in the government, obtaining credit, rubbing shoulders with important people. They are well informed about ways of making money, and they are educated and wise in the ways of the law and the political affairs of the region. Might this "initiative" and "vision" not have some negative consequences as well, I asked him? He thought for a while and shook his head, saying only that the Mayos were backward and unwilling to develop the *visión* necessary to further their economic well-being. He did not think it was wise or possible that Mayos should consider as undesirable the qualities that made *mestizos* wealthy and powerful. During our conversation, Modesto Soto referred to *mestizos* as *gente de razón* (people of reason), a term used for centuries by Hispanics to distinguish themselves from what they considered to be inferior beings, namely Indians.[25] I hasten to add that, although Modesto Soto lives in a rather nice, modestly furnished, plastered adobe house, he is quite poor, so much so that after I had spent a couple of hours chatting with him, Vicente asked me anxiously if I was planning to give him a *propina* (gratuity) "*para cigarros o algo*" (for cigarettes or something). "He is very poor, David," Vicente assured me. Don Modesto, unlike most of his successors, clearly did not experience great personal gain from his term as *comisariado*.

When I asked Vicente what he thought about the qualities that don Modesto endorsed, he thought them rather bad traits. "It just means that to get something you have to smash anybody who is in your way. That's how the *yoris* are. They will smash the poor *indio* who is in their way, just to get what they want. And they want everything." Jesús Moroyoqui was even more blunt. "*Yoris* among us hurt us. They don't help at all. We would be better off without them."

Modesto Soto is a staunch defender of Román Yocupicio, the prominent Mayo of the Masiaca community and symbol of a Mayo who adopted Mexican values. Yocupicio joined the Mexican army prior to the revolution and rose to the rank of general and strongman. After the revolution he was elected governor of the state of Sonora, a fact of which Modesto Soto, who knew Yocupicio, is most proud. Some say Yocupicio became crassly opportunistic, preferring to join the Sonoran oligarchy in stealing Mayo lands, until he was finally betrayed and assassinated by the very same circle of wealthy landowners whom he had courted and served. His few defenders, including Modesto Soto, prefer to see him as a lowly Mayo who had *visión*, rose through countless levels of bureaucracy, and through his own ability reached the highest level of government:

"At the end of his *sexenio* [six-year term; re-election is prohibited], he wanted to build a canal from Teachive to lands below, so water could be applied to the fields for irrigation. That way, the wealth of the community would have been greatly increased. The *indígenas* of the *comunidad* refused to accept his scheme. They resisted, and the canal was never built.[26]

"The Mayos of Masiaca are still 60 percent backwards. They didn't understand then and they don't understand now what must be done to develop our community. They just don't have *visión* like the *mestizos*. They don't know about medicine; they use herbs and *curanderos*. They don't know how to have influence. They don't have education. They just aren't modern.

"When I was *comisariado*, [former Sonoran Governor] Biebrich, and after him, Governor [Samuel] Ocaña, came here to visit. Afterwards we had a terrible storm that did huge damage, destroying many homes. I wrote to the governor asking for help. Within one week they had five bulldozers here, cleaning up the mess. Then they helped put in seven deep wells and three small reservoirs. We got a new school. That was because I learned how to work with the government. That was twenty some years ago. Most of the Mayos now don't know how to do that.

"Look at us. We have twenty-three thousand hectares of land that would prosper with irrigation. We've never gotten water for it. We have twenty-three kilometers of coastline good for aquaculture.[27] We tried to petition the government for credit to sow buffelgrass on some big pastures. Nothing came of it. We don't have influence.

"It isn't that there aren't rich Mayos in the community. For example, one man from Teachive owned ranches all over the place. He had hundreds of cows and horses. You would never know it to see him. He didn't have *visión*. He dressed like a poor man. His shirt was always torn, his hat dirty and worn. He didn't even use lace on his *huaraches*. He used spines from the *chírahui* instead. He was dirty and hardly ever bathed. He was rich. That's the difference. If a *mestizo* is rich, you know it."

As Don Modesto told me this, his granddaughter stood quietly in the background. She had just been accepted for fall matriculation at the University of Sonora in Hermosillo. I congratulated her, for she will be one of only two or three members of the community attending college. No one from Teachive has ever gone to college. I asked if she spoke Mayo. She shook her head.

The monthly meetings of the Masiaca community assembly are conducted in Spanish. Mayos of Teachive and San Pedrito mentioned that the Mayo language often takes over when discussions become partisan. On these occasions, they say, they try to translate the discussions into Spanish for the benefit of those *comuneros* not fluent in *la lengua*. Arguments break out often. Issues are not clear and there is no neutral person to clarify them. Traditional Mayo members consistently feel exploited and underserved at the meetings because of their educational disadvantage. This may also be a reflection of their cultural aversion to political assertiveness. Whatever the explanation, race is clearly recognized in the daily intercourse of inhabitants of the region, while class tends to take on less importance. Mayos tend to view *yoris* as wealthy, greedy, manipulative, boorish, and often violent. Mayos who choose to live like *mestizos* tend to adopt the same traits, they say. Mayos tend to attribute undesirable traits to *mestizos*, and accuse them of treating Mayos badly. Still, when pressed, they recognize that some *mestizos* are poor, honest, egalitarian, and hardworking, just as they are. Vicente took me to meet a prominent *mestizo* in Masiaca. After we had spent a few hours talking, we drove away.

"What do you think of Román?" I asked Vicente.

"He is a hard working fellow, but, he is very poor."

"He is a *yori*, though. Do you think he is a good man?" I asked.

"Yes, he is a good man. He is honest and respects Mayos, even though he is a yori."

Vicente had praise for another Mayo-speaking *yori*, a former *comisariado* and advocate for regaining the communal lands illegally seized by wealthy *yoris*. Another *mestizo* who lives in Choacalle was a fine fellow, Vicente also thought. Yet he felt *yoris* as a group were out to take advantage of *indios*. Most Mayos are like Vicente and express varying resentments against "*los ricos*," whom they feel are responsible for most of their ills, from unemployment to inflation to corruption. This amorphous group is overwhelmingly *mestizo* and often hardly more affluent than the Mayos themselves. They constitute a convenient scapegoat for Mayos, whose grumbling denunciation of them is universal.

The Masiaca community, then, is hardly a homogenous, communal-minded political entity. It is torn by ethnic and class differences, so much so that its internal struggles are nearly as great as its external battles, or, in the words of Stern, in connection with *comunidades* of southern Mexico, "The historical origins, functions, and resilience of closed corporate communities has as much to do with internal struggles among natives . . . as they did with the survival of traditions, the desire of exploiters, or the defenses of impoverished Indians against non-indigenous outsiders" (Stern 1983, 24).

The operations of the *comunidad* are deeply affected as well by the overwhelming and systemic corruption of Mexican institutions, including *ejidos* and *comunidades*: money moving in illicit directions frustrates the effectiveness of all social institutions. Community funds, decisions, and resources are all affected by bribery, favoritism, and patronage, as are all institutions in Mexico. The ongoing assimilation of Mayos by the dominant *mestizo* culture through intermarriage and through the pervasiveness of *mestizo* institutions that have suppressed and engulfed Mayo culture, has rendered the community, apart from the *fiesta*, hardly recognizable as an ethnic enclave. Corruption has severely aggravated the problem. Mayos I spoke with assumed that whoever takes the office of *comisariado* will soon become corrupted, no matter how innocent or honest he or she may be beforehand. One man flatly stated: "David, all *comisariados* line their pockets with money that is supposed to help the community. Even some *comisariados* I like put community money in their pockets. All of them." Hardly had the newly elected *comisariado* taken office in 1996 when widespread accusations of embezzlement (apparently well-based) were leveled against him. And, hence, even in the Masiaca *comunidad*, corruption breeds individualism and pits neighbors against each other. The *comunidad* is merely a microcosm of the political history of Mexico.

In fact, Modesto Soto's description of *visión*, which he finds admirable, entails being in a position to exert political pressure through corruption, whether it be through bribes, through patronage, or through favoritism. He sees no other way for the *comunidad* to advance, and thus his concept of *visión* as a goal is inherently detrimental to the traditional community way of life.

In Sonora, even more than in many other Mexican states, to be Indian is at once to be exalted in popular images and denigrated to low social status in practice. From time to time, even Vicente uses the word *indio* to suggest that someone is low-class, drunken, or foolish. Mayo parents, conscious of the discrimination their children will face, tend to deny their "Mayo-ness" and urge their children toward the more socially prestigious *mestizo* world. The Mayos' reluctance to teach their children to speak Mayo is a reflection of their fear that the children will continue to be at a disadvantage, facing discrimination and decreased opportunities due to linguistic inability.[28] Mayos simultaneously affirm and deny their "Mayo-ness," and their community simultaneously affirms and denies its historical congruence with Mayo culture. Modesto Soto, for example, expresses scorn for those Mayos who deny that they are Mayo. "We are *yoremes*," he says. "Why should we deny it. How silly!" His children do not speak Mayo. Neither he nor they attend the *fiestas*. Their behavior, like that of most young people in the *comunidad*, is nearly purely *mestizo*. An outsider could spend many days in the Masiaca community without realizing that it is Mayo.

MASIACA IN REGIONAL HISTORY

Archival materials document the existence of the town of Masiaca and the village of Teachive in 1834 and imply an existence long before that. The boundaries of the *comunidad* have remained roughly the same since that time and probably well before.

Masiaca and Teachive have long, somewhat independent histories which, at least in part, separate them from the Mayo inhabitants of the great river to the north. Historical references to Masiaca are scant.[29] Local legend says that the town was created around the year 1400 by a single Cahita family named Moroyoqui (meaning *es pintor* [is a painter]), consisting of the parents, seven sons, and four daughters. The children of this family reportedly all retained the Moroyoqui name and married within the clan, so that the second generations were all cousins. Regional recognition of this mildly incestuous regime led to the town being known as Masiaca Primo Hermano (Masiaca First Cousin).[30] Others discount this story as a joke, if a callous one.

Among academics, Almada (1952) states that the Jesuit priest Pedro Méndez founded a mission in Masiaca in 1612.[31] This is surely an error, for it is impossible to place Méndez north of the Río Fuerte (in what is now Sinaloa) prior to 1613.[32] The lack of a historical record among the early Jesuits for Masiaca and Teachive suggests that the Masiacans were not connected to the Mayos and were a small enough group that they posed no threat and very little interest to the Spaniards. Masiaca does not appear on any extant regional maps of the Spanish colonial era. Fray Antoino María de los Reyes in 1784 listed and described the missions of Sinaloa and Sonora without mentioning Masiaca (Ramos 1958). Gerhard (1982), in his comprehensive study of the region and of archival documents concerning the region, has no reference to it. It lay off the main route, the *camino real*, which led from the fort of Montesclaros (now El Fuerte) on the Río Fuerte, to the

Río Mayo, following the Río Cuchujaqui through Basiroa north to its point nearest Alamos, then roughly northeast to Alamos via the east side of the Sierra de Alamos, then east to the Río Mayo in the vicinity of Conicárit (Sauer 1932), a village now covered by Lake Mocúzari.[33] The Río Cuchujaqui has dependable water over most of its course, and the Arroyo Tábelo on the Mayo drainage, where an easy route would lead, offers pools of water year round (it also has a sizable population of very old *sabinos* [*Taxodium distichum*], an indicator of permanent water).

The main north-south route, then, bypassed Masiaca by nearly twenty miles. The waters of the Arroyo Masiaca were reliable, though insufficient to maintain a large agricultural population. Hence Masiaca was probably a sparsely populated backwoods town even by contemporary standards and remained so for at least the first seventy years after the first invasion of priests and soldiers from the permanent fort at Montesclaros. It was large enough, though, to warrant a mission.

With the founding of the mines at Promentorios near Alamos in 1679, a second route for a *camino real* was established. This alignment, perhaps less subject to washouts but more mountainous, led from El Fuerte through Masiaca and the Arroyo Masiaca's tributaries to Huasiguari and San Antonio, over the foothills of the west side of the Sierra de Alamos, through the ancient settlement of Tetajiosa, with its permanent water supply, and over the ridge to Promentorios (Aduana). This route exists today, even though the old roadway has been pummeled repeatedly by powerful rainstorms and is impassable by vehicle.

A point of historical controversy is whether or not Masiaca constituted one of the original *pueblos* of the Mayos. Local (Masiaca) historians claim there were eight, of which Masiaca was one. This claim is not substantiated by more general histories. Pérez de Ribas notes only seven towns, all on the Río Mayo.[34] The question is of some moment, since if Masiaca were one of the original pueblos, it would likely have been closely aligned with the Río Mayo and could boast a clearly Mayo origin. If it was not, as seems the case, Masiaca's historical status becomes more murky, for it would have been geographically isolated from the other seven towns and would absent from the historical record, which mentions the others frequently.

Documents nearly two centuries later (1835) refer to a petition to the state government by the "*naturales de Masiaca del Río Mayo*" for a survey to establish and safeguard their *fundo legal*, a commonly owned townsite or lands on which they might build houses, cut firewood, and run livestock (AES 1835, Tomo 187). By that time a church and village already existed in Masiaca, and Teachive and San Antonio were also villages. The natives were represented by one José Valenzuela, who presented the Sonoran government at Arizpe with thirty pesos as payment for the lands thus requested. Valenzuela is a name as popular among Mayos as Smith is among Anglo-Americans,[35] so by 1835 Mayos may well have moved into the area, either freely or fleeing from Mexican avengers of the revolt led by Juan Banderas, which had been quelled only a year earlier. Among other names listed as petitioners, some are noted as originating in Etchojoa, and others at Santa Cruz (now Júpare, near the mouth of the Río Mayo), both of which lend credence to the diaspora hypothesis. Some of the individuals listed are named Moroyoqui, the quintessially Mayo name and still the most common surname in Teachive. It is found throughout the *comunidad* and consistent with the legend concerning the founding of the town of Masiaca by the Moroyoqui family.

In carrying out the Masiacans' request, a letter tells of the conscientious efforts of the state's minion, the *agrimensor* (surveyor), to fulfill the letter of the law:

> I started in the cemetery of the church [of Masiaca] facing the big door, making my benchmark there[36] . . . taking the route to the north, I measured fifty-six *cordeles* along the arroyo, although it was not possible to make a straight measurement because of the impenetrable bushes that blocked it, arriving finally at the last *cordel* where some white outcroppings marked the arroyo's bank, under a huge cottonwood called *bou-tangüeca*, then six *cordeles* more before arriving at the houses, or the village of Teachive, where I was met by Don Jesús Espinosa bearing in his hands his papers proving land titles that set out the limits of San Antonio [his private *hacienda*] which [according to the wealthy rancher] extended downstream to the white outcrops six *cordeles* back, which I then measured and all agreed that the measurement was correct. . . . Then one of the natives, Manuel Ignacio Féliz[37] asked if they couldn't have just a few more *cordeles*, because we were almost to Teachive which is surely what

the Director Don José Almada,[38] *alcalde* of Alamos, had in
mind, even though Don Jesús Espinosa had the papers to prove
it was part of his private lands of San Antonio, which the surveyor agreed was so when he read the title papers . . . and it
would be most just and necessary to the people of the Río
Mayo to have the lands. But the neighbor Espinosa said that he
would not allow that to happen and asked that the survey be
stopped now because the residents of Teachive were forever encroaching on his land beyond any reasonable level of tolerance,
but that he would agree to allow them to continue to plant
their *milpas* [in Teachive] as long as each year they would provide a census and acknowledge the land was his and restrict
their activities to their *milpas* and waters necessary for irrigating
them. (AES 1835, Tomo 187)

It is clear from this description that, in addition to Masiaca, the two
present-day Mayo villages of Teachive and San Antonio existed as
indigenous hamlets in 1835 and had been there long before. The *hacendado* Espinosa claimed the village of Teachive as part of his estate,
which included San Antonio, some fifteen kilometers north of Teachive. (Teachive may have been located about a kilometer upstream from
its present site at that time.) It appears in the documents that Sonoran
authorities were more or less eager to provide land for the Masiacans
and Teachivans, quite probably for no other reason than that they
feared more insurrections if they did not. This surely shows that the
people had a legitimate claim to the lands. Recognition of the request
continued through the move of the Sonoran government from Arizpe
to Ures, and as late as 1841 payment was still being accepted from the
natives for the *fundo legal* (AES 1835, Tomo 187).[39]

This activity must be seen in the context of the new Mexican
republic, which was militarily weak, economically crippled, and politically volatile. With the Banderas rebellion fresh in their minds,
Sonoran civil authorities must have known that a full-scale rebellion by
Cahitas would be almost impossible to put down. Furthermore, every
ranch, village, and town in northeast Sonora was still beleaguered by
devastating Apache raids, which at one point reached as far south as
the Río Mayo. To deal with the constant Apache threat required an
expensive military appropriation and diversion of troops to the north-

east. Anything reasonable that would pacify the Mayos, then, was bound to be acceptable.

At the same time, the government was carrying out provisions of *"La ley para el reparto de tierras a los pueblos indígenas, reduciéndolas a propiedad particular"* (The law for the distribution of lands to native peoples, reducing them to private property), one of the most important pieces of legislation of the 1820s and 1830s and the most important legislative accomplishment of Governor José María Almada, from Alamos. The law gave broad powers to indigenous communities to recover lands taken from them arbitrarily, whether by individuals or by missions. It established provisions assuring that stolen lands were returned in their entirety and that appropriate surveys were carried out (Almada 1952, 37–39; Stagg 1978, 48). It also contained specific provisions requiring that the lands be divided equitably among the natives (Almada 1952, 39), with the implied hope that they would become independent, taxpaying peasants and not stick to their conservative communal ways. There is no record of the division into private parcels ever having been carried out. We know that both Mayos and Yaquis stoutly resisted being taxed (Spicer 1962, 61), to the extent of extending the Banderas rebellion. We can only surmise that in 1834 the Mayos of Masiaca undertook the first part of the restitution, that of reclaiming their aboriginal lands. They somehow forewent the next step, the capitalist transformation into taxpayers, which they neither needed nor desired to be.[40]

For the 1834 declaration to take effect (i.e., for the reclaiming of lands illegally seized), the petitioners needed to establish their long tenancy, which they apparently did to a characteristically skeptical government's satisfaction. The lands of the Masiaca community, mostly arid scrub with little available water, were not highly coveted by powerful and highly placed *mestizos* or creoles. Tension existed, then as now, between the natives and the *hacendados* such as Espinosa, whose land titles to San Antonio had to have been granted in violation of the Mayos' aboriginal rights. San Antonio was then as it is now, a Mayo village of long tradition, situated in rich tropical deciduous forest, and a boundary dispute between the natives and the *hacendado* was inevitable.

Espinosa must ultimately have lost his claim on Teachive, for the land was included within the 1835 limits of the community. Still, as late as 1849, he continued to be listed as the owner (AES 1849, Tomo 238).

Espinosa's stonewalling may well have been a lone protest. He was successful, at least partially, for the enormous estate of the Almada (now Ibarra) family, which in Espinosa's time included San Antonio, to this day still covers tens of thousands of the same acres that it included then. Two former high officials[41] of the community claim that a surveyor informed them that in the late 1940s he had seen a *mojonera* (boundary marker) at a pass between Sibiricahui and the Puerto de Candelario,[42] dominant peaks to the north of the community. This should have been the northern boundary of the community, they claim. The surveyor told them someone from the Ibarra family destroyed the marker and the *comuneros* had no documents to prove that it was an ancient community boundary. Hence, they lost a huge amount of valuable land.

Modesto Soto notes that the survey of 1835 was carried out using landmarks well known locally, not the formal cement monuments that are used today. As the surveyor noted, "It was not possible to make a clearing because we had no ax" (AES 1835, Tomo 187). Well-known trees and places in arroyos were typically noted, both subject to alteration with time. For example, no cottonwoods have survived in the arroyo between Teachive and Masiaca. Clearly, the survey would soon run into trouble if many of its markers could be eliminated by nature in a short period of time. Another survey marker was Guoyguasia (*cola de coyote*, [coyote's tail]), the rocky promontory referred to in the survey and still known on the arroyo.

Modesto Soto cites his family history to establish the validity of the survey and indicate the extraordinary importance to the community of the survey document. The original survey papers, his story goes, fell into the hands of an ancestor named Guadalupe Soto, who wrapped it carefully and placed it in a hole in a *pitahaya* cactus. There it remained until 1904, when another predecessor, Trinidad Soto, removed the documents from the cactus, bound them in leather, and personally delivered them to Mexico City, traveling by horse to Guaymas, by boat to Manzanillo, and then by *berlina* (horse-drawn coach) to Mexico City for formal delivery to the Mexican government on a trip that took three months. While this story is part of oral tradition, it has considerable credibility, given the Mayos' strong emphasis on oral history and the great reverence they have for historical documents.

The survey document became the basis for the formal establishment of the Comunidad Indígena de Masiaca in 1941. It, in turn, implies a historic presence of Indians in the community. A certifying letter of 1946 from the Secretaria de Gobernación states the following:

> The effected citizens [of Masiaca] presented in a timely fashion the primordial titles for their communal lands, that were declared authentic on the 22 of May of 1946 . . . which prove that the communal lands date from 1834, when the formal possession was given to the natives who enjoyed the use of said lands for countless years before and who, in the year 1835, carried out the surveying and measurement of same . . . and who surveyed the surface of 46,487.41 hectares, of lands which they have possessed since time immemorial as communal estates, and which comprise surfaces in excess of those indicated in the ancient title, which they have also possessed.[43] (AES 1946, Tomo 187, num. 16, pp. 18–19, in the possession of don Jesús Moroyoqui of San Pedrito de Masiaca)

All of this establishes that, as of 1834, the natives of Masiaca and its related villages, including Teachive, proved to government officials (undoubtedly over the objections of Mexicans occupying adjacent lands) that they had inhabited the communal lands and had a valid historical claim. In 1835 the lands were formally surveyed; the boundaries were fixed by act of the government in 1841. The title apparently remained unclear for a century, somehow surviving the anti-Indian semipogroms of the *porfiriato*,[44] until 1941, when formal proceedings were undertaken to have the community officially established. The process was completed in 1946. Final formal government recognition came with the completion of the survey in 1951. Masiaca was now a recognized *comunidad*.

What sort of town Masiaca was in the years preceding 1835 is difficult to establish. Leocadio Piña Soto, who died in 1992 at the age of 100, was a former *comisariado* and the greatest historian of the Masiaca community. His handwritten notebooks contain the following entry:

> In 1835, when the *fundo legal* of Masiaca was surveyed, it was already a town and had a church in the same location where it now stands; natives had lived in the town for at least 222 years

when they requested a written proof of their tenure, requesting
that their community be surveyed and a legal title be bestowed
on the pueblo and that it be judged a town with all its rights
and privileges. . . .

[At that time] they already had a church with three great
bronze bells with which they summoned the town council to
the church, as well as the people of the community. The indoc-
trinating priests recognized it as a town and came from the city
of Alamos to Masiaca to teach doctrines to the people in the
church, which also had a cemetery where the dead were buried
according to ancient customs. (Leocadio Piña Soto notebooks,
courtesy of the grandchildren of don Leocadio)

Piña also traced the town and church to 1613, one year later than the
date noted by Almada. Unfortunately, his sourcebooks, which were
said by one of his successors to have been many, appear to have been
destroyed by some of his successors, to the great dismay of others.

In 1848 the town was referred to as the Mission de Masiaca. Las
Bocas, the seaside village and resort twenty kilometers to the southwest, was even then part of the *comunidad*. Because it had a church (a
visita of the *cabecera* of Alamos), it was one of ten villages listed as *admon
espiritual* in a report written for a state senator. The report also lists
"Rancho Las Bocas, 21 leagues to the southeast of Alamos, on the
shores of the sea and inhabited by some native Indians from the Río
Mayo, as a *rancho* of the Mission of the *pueblo* of Masiaca with excellent
potable water and where baths are provided as well" (AES 1848, Tomo
258). The population of Masiaca at that time is listed as 389, with the
admonition that "yellow fever [had] killed so many natives that it was
almost impossible to keep track of the numbers."

The rather unusual size and boundaries of the present community
are related to another oral tradition, given considerable credence by
archival documents. Modesto Soto asserts that during the original
survey, a Mayo who accompanied the surveyor noting the boundaries,
made the comment, in Mayo, "You are leaving out the best parts of the
land."

"What did he say?" the surveyor asked of an interpreter.

"He said that you are leaving out the best lands the community has,"
the interpreter responded.

"Well, let's measure again," the surveyor said. And he did, and thereby included the seaside village of Bachomojaqui, extending northwest along the coast past the village of Las Bocas for twenty-three kilometers, which constitutes the current boundary.

The Mayos owe a great debt to the honest surveyor. This addition of the coast was an asset of indescribable value to the community. Although it is hardly a posh resort, Las Bocas is the most affluent of the community's villages, due to the economic success of its fishermen and the fees charged to tourists who flock to the beach during Holy Week.

The apparent ownership by Mayos of beachfront land has proved too much for some would-be *mestizo* entrepreneurs to tolerate. In 1996 the *municipio* of Huatabampo, at the urging of *mestizos* who wished to develop the beach, claimed usufruct rights to the fifty meters between the high-water mark of the ocean and the interior lands.[45] This move, a bona fide land grab, is based upon a clause in the Mexican constitution which reserves for the public all lands in the intertidal zone.[46] The Mayos respond that their claim precedes that of anyone else, including those who cite the constitution. The lands are rightly part of the *comunidad indígena*, they argue. They have occupied those lands since time immemorial and are not subject to the provision cited by the developers. If the *mestizos* are successful, the "denunciation," or claim, will have grave economic consequences for the *comunidad*, especially for the fishing cooperatives that take advantage of the intertidal area to load their catches and prepare them for marketing.

The 1951 map of the *comunidad* includes a shaded area labeled "*pequenos posesiones*" (small possessions) that roughly corresponds with the greater flood plain of the arroyo. These are, in effect, private lands included within the boundary of the *comunidad*. They include much of the fertile arroyo bottomland and the best grazing lands. Most are "owned" by *mestizos*, some even by absentee landlords. More than 2,000 hectares are thus beyond the jurisdiction of the *comunidad*, although they exist within its boundaries. These exempt lands are a sore point with the *comunidad*. Jesús Moroyoqui fumes that the owners of record have no legal basis for ownership. "Their claims are null and void. They have no legitimate papers to prove they own the land. They still use the land and we don't do anything about it." The same is true of roughly 5,000 disputed hectares that bound the *comunidad* on the north.

Although this land is also claimed by the *comunidad*, it is used as private grazing pasture by the Ibarra family who, the Mayos claim, took it illegally and destroyed the boundary markers to boot.[47]

Two other *comunidades* in the region, Bachoco and Jambiolobampo immediately to the west of the Masiaca community boundaries, were created in 1804, more than thirty years earlier than Masiaca. These *comunidades* are far smaller and less varied, accentuating the size and uniqueness of the Masiaca community. Their creation was probably an inspiration to José Valenzuela and the others who exhorted the government to create the *comunidad* of Masiaca.

HOW THE COMMUNITY FUNCTIONS

Use of community lands

While use of most community lands is available to any member, they may not be sold, mortgaged, or inherited.[48] No taxes are paid on any of the land, only on products derived from it (cattle, crops, etc.).[49] Taxes from production are paid to the state, supposedly deposited in a fund to be returned to the community. According to a former *comisariado*, none of the money is ever seen again.

Although inheritance of community lands is not strictly possible, it exists de facto.[50] Homesites are ceded by application to the governing body. The *comisariado* is empowered to provide home lots to petitioners. Some homes in Teachive are said to have been continuously occupied by the same family for more than a hundred years. No *comunero* has been know to have been evicted from a home. Since communal lands abound, it is comparatively simple to obtain a homesite for a child. It must be done in the name of the *comunero*, however, who can will his or her membership to only one heir.

Group use of land by *comuneros* who band together, can also be granted by the *comisariado* through the formation of a civil or mercantile society within the community. This was the mechanism by which more than thirty individuals formed a group (called Los 35, see chapter 7) to irrigate community lands. Individual beneficial use (as opposed to domestic use) can only be granted by the assembly, and no single person may use or claim more than forty-six hectares for him- or herself. Individuals maintain usufruct ownership of parcels they work, often as part (*socio*) of a subcommunity group. This means that every *comunero* may receive a personal parcel on which he (or she) may raise cows or crops, *and* may join with others and retain a part of the joint project as his or her own. On a parcel a few kilometers downstream from Teachive, *comuneros* banded together to plant corn, beans, and sesame seed (*ajonjolí*) and were permitted to protect the crops with fencing. This right is granted by the community and is not as absolute as a private property right, for it can, in fact, be taken away, even though such re-alloting is virtually unheard of. The *comisariado* may theoretically provide the members with papers granting them the right to use of the land. No one could provide samples of such papers. Although usufruct, the use is de facto perpetual and may be bequeathed to heirs as the owner deems fit, with the tacit approval of the assembly, as long as the heirs are *comuneros*. When a *comunero* dies or wishes to retire, he or she will designate an heir who will fill that position.

Theoretically, the right to private or usufruct use of land can be revoked by the assembly. In reality, non-Mayo *comuneros* (and one Mayo family as well) use large parcels as their private land, even reportedly using these parcels as collateral for gaining credit from private banks. They appear to be confident that their lands are safely assigned. For practical purposes (and for those with political influence), once a right to personal use of land is granted, it will not be taken away. Hence, within the community and within certain theoretical constraints, land is privately owned. In theory, of course, private ownership does not exist; communal lands are still inalienable. They may not be sold, mortgaged, or formally inherited.

The ownership (by tradition, if not by right) of houses leads to social complexities in a village occupied for generations and where families have been huge (twelve children a generation ago was not unusual). Just who will inherit the family house is a question of considerable contention. In one case, the owner is a ninety-year-old woman who lives with a daughter and her husband, who are both nearly sixty. He has no house of his own. When the older woman dies, it is not clear who will inherit the house from her, and her son-in-law may find himself with nowhere to live. This may necessitate his moving to the coast, where several of his children have migrated and built homes. Other children must either acquire a lot from the *comunidad* and construct a house or move away. More often than not, the choice is the latter. For example, most of the children of don Jesús José Nieblas and doña Lidia Zazueta now live in the *municipio* of Cajeme, one hundred kilometers away, where the large city of Ciudad Obregón is located. In another case, a man has six sons, all of whom want the family house when he dies. Only one will get it. The others will have to live elsewhere, probably near Huatabampo. Establishing a separate household in the *comunidad* is often an expense beyond the economic reach of the hopeful individual.

The same is true of a *comunero*: he (or she) must decide which child will inherit the rights associated with being a member of the community. The *comunero* knows that the decision is of momentous importance. The children who are not *comuneros* will retain their homes, only insofar as the *comunero* in the family is pleased to grant them permission. Non-*comuneros* will be second-class citizens, without the right to vote, possess a parcel, or form an association to develop an enterprise within the community. The children of Lidia and Jesús have nearly all left the *comunidad* for that very reason.

Community projects

The *comisariado* from time to time finds it necessary to decree *téquiaques*, community work projects, that can only be accomplished by many people volunteering to work. Examples include the clearing of brush from roadsides, painting of stones along roadways, building of schools, cleaning up of public buildings, and rebuilding washed-out roads. Much of the work on the Masiaca church was such a *téquiac*. If a project is so big that volunteers cannot be expected to complete it (such as the rebuilding and restoring of roads washed out by Hurricane Ismael in 1995), the *comisariado* will call upon the municipal government in Navojoa to provide funds for workers.

The *comisariado* apparently has power to require or even compel *comuneros* to work on *téquiaques*. He can impose sanctions for those who refuse. Vicente says this hardly ever happens, and the penalties for failure to cooperate are unspecified. Not many projects are announced and the burden of work is not heavy. Even so, disputes erupt from time to time. Vicente reports that he was criticized by a woman in the village for not working enough on a *téquiac*. He responded that she didn't understand what his work was and that he was working on other community projects.

I wondered if the *comisariado* might not order a general trash cleanup as a *téquiac*, for outside of individual homes and roadways, trash is deplorably abundant. Vicente answered vaguely in the affirmative. I realized that even if they mobilized for a cleanup, they would have nowhere to dump the gathered trash. It appears that the *téquiac* is used sparingly and only for unequivocally beneficial community projects. The *comisariado* usually wants to be popular and genuinely hopes for community betterment; assigning controversial *téquiaques* would detract from the dignity of the office and possibly arouse passions unnecessarily.

Grazing on communal lands

Livestock, the community's single most important economic resource, roam the communal lands indiscriminately, unless specific fencing provisions are required or requested. One community member planted buffelgrass on a small plot and was given permission to fence it off. One of the non-Mayo *comuneros* has fenced off more than one hundred hectares of the best land and planted buffelgrass. He was able to do this primarily because he "owns" a *pequeño posesion*, has influence in the assembly, and has the money necessary to make the improvements (such as fencing, water tanks, and the purchase of stock) or is in a position to obtain credit to purchase them.[51] In the case of this community member, his cattle prospered, surviving well even through the drought of 1996. Vicente notes that the assembly could revoke the man's right to continue this activity, for it clearly deprives others of the use of that fertile land. Due to the man's power and influence, however, he will continue to prosper, to some extent at the expense of the rest of the community.

Each member is permitted to run twenty-five cows, horses, or mules without special permission. Applications to exceed that number can be approved for an annual fee of 25 pesos (about $3 US). Everyone simply ignores the limit with impunity, claiming it does not even exist on paper. They are able to run many more cows because, according to some, they bribe the community leadership. It hardly matters whether the limit is formal or not, for no official counts, anyway. Figures for the number of cattle grazing run anywhere between 2,000 and 5,000, depending on the year (large numbers of cattle were sold during the prolonged drought of 1995–97) and on the authority consulted.[52] The flat coastal plain to the west of Teachive offers little in the way of forage, so each animal requires a vast acreage to sustain its needs, far more than the twenty-six hectares per animal recommended for areas that receive more rainfall (nearly 150 percent more) than Masiaca.[53] Nearer to Teachive, the natural forage is somewhat better. The figure of twenty-six hectares per animal (cow and calf) is still optimistic, though. CIPES, the state-sponsored agency that conducts research on grazing, considers the entire *comunidad* as desert and not amenable to range manipulation, as in more moist areas (CIPES 1995). If we use a rule of thumb of one cow per fifty hectares as a stocking coefficient (which is still optimistic), the capacity would be somewhat less than 1,000 cows.

Teachivans alone own more than 400 cows, and they occupy only a small portion of the *comunidad*. Their grazing resources are said to be better than many others in the *comunidad*, mostly because the arroyo usually has water in it and provides abundant forage along its banks, and because rainfall is somewhat greater than on the coastal plain. A minimum of thirty families own cows in Teachive; when clan ties are taken into consideration, that is, when we consider that cows are often owned by family members living in different houses, the number of families that own cows is probably closer to fifty. The number of cows per family varies from one to more than fifty. One woman owned sixty. She sold them all in 1995.

In addition to cows, at least two hundred horses (probably considerably more) roam the community's range freely, consuming considerably more forage per animal than cows. They are also subject to a hypothetical, unspecified limit. Goats and sheep, and to an indeterminate extent, burros, are not subject to imposed limits. Consequently, these latter run in great numbers throughout the unfenced community lands, to the detriment of the land's grazing capacity. The smaller livestock consume all edible vegetation not already consumed by cows or other livestock. During the 1996 drought, large herds of from twenty to fifty goats frequently returned early to Teachive from the *monte* because there was no forage to be had. This was a most unusual state of affairs, for goats are noted for their ability to eat and digest vegetable matter that no other herbivore can tolerate. One day in June, Vicente and I set out into the *monte* to see what forage we could find. Goats can balance on their hind legs and stand nearly straight up, extending their long necks and tongue to eat. Within a kilometer of the village we could find no plant matter within the reach of livestock of any kind. The goats had already extended their bodies as far as they could.

No one in the community seems to know for sure how many small livestock forage on communal lands. My estimate is that the number exceeds 3,000, most of them goats. Vicente thinks it is greater. Some families maintain herds of up to a hundred goats. Don Poli Tajia, Vicente's brother, maintains his herd at fifty, milking the lactating does daily and making some cheese to sell. Goats usually require constant attendance to protect them from marauding beasts of prey (coyotes, foxes, bobcats, mountain lions, and, once in a decade, jaguars) and feral dogs, and to keep track of them.[54] Some fortunate herdsmen employ goatherd dogs, two of which can handle a flock of fifty. Goats are often sold to professional buyers, who are always willing to pay the market price. In addition to constituting a resource that can readily be converted to cash, goats provide a source of domestic milk and meat.

Smaller numbers of sheep are found in the community, owing to their lesser economic value and the greater difficulty of maintaining them, due, some residents say, to their noteworthy stupidity. Years ago, natives say, many more sheep were found in the community and were sheared by the women for their wool, which they wove into textiles. María Soledad Moroyoqui, one of the most accomplished *cobijeras* in the village, recalls that prior to the drought of 1950 her family had nearly one hundred sheep. As the drought took its toll, the *aguaje* dried up and they sold off the entire flock. After that, they never raised sheep again. Consequently, all her adult life she has purchased fleeces for weaving. Sheep are also fewer in number than in the past because they are in more direct competition with cattle for forage than are goats. Government pressure to increase cattle production has decreased forage available for sheep as well.

Josefa Soto, Mario Soto's grandmother, once owned a herd rumored to have reached a thousand sheep. It was the envy of the village. The 1950s drought also decimated her herd. Her children found raising sheep boring. No one wanted to spend all their time watching the dumb animals, so when she died they gradually sold off the herd.[55] Today, Mario's wife, Francisca Yocupicio, maintains a herd of seven ewes, shearing them and spinning and weaving the wool.[56] One of the youngest weavers, she is also one of the most skilled. Other women raise ewes sporadically. The work is too much for the return, and competition with cows has proven too much.

The governmental pressure to increase cattle production has not been accompanied by government-provided technical assistance to improve the care of the land. Such techniques as protective and portable fencing, providing additional water sources to assure rotation of pastures, terracing to control runoff and increase biomass, removal of some pastures from grazing either during certain seasons (the arroyo bottom during growing season, for example), or completely through exclosures in areas highly susceptible to erosion, and planting trees to control erosion and increase shade, are not practiced within the *comunidad*. Programs such as these would conserve the community's resources and sustain the long-term productivity of community lands. They would require both clear determination and a substantial subsidy on the part of the government, for putting them into practice would require technical assistance, labor, and materials.

While profound technical difficulties hinder range improvement, the political task of improving management of grazing lands is monumental. The Masiaca community, Sonora, and Mexico in general, grazes all its lands, most of them far beyond their sustainable productivity of the land.[57] Sonoran cattle growers lament the lack of government support in the face of drought, disease, international competition, and falling water tables.[58] Government attempts to control the numbers of cattle on the denuded ranges, or to suggest more conservation-oriented range management practices, are not met with enthusiasm.[59]

Piro Moroyoqui of Teachive runs forty burros on communal lands, a practice that bewilders other villagers. Burros' ability to trample, gnaw, and stunt vegetation is indeed remarkable. They are constantly used as beasts of burden (they are commonly ridden) and are often viewed as family pets. No one was willing to speculate on what anyone would do with forty, however. Indeed, most of Piro's burros are seldom, if ever, put to work. Other burros live carefree lives in the *monte* as well. They subsist on ragged thornscrub throughout their long lives, providing companionship and a certain comfort to their owners, as does a tiny bank account. In spite of their hardiness, some burros died in the drought of 1995–96.

Despite all the drawbacks and depredations of livestock, the dividends from all the cows, goats, sheep, pigs, horses, burros, mules, chickens, and turkeys are real. Goats provide good milk, which is drunk and also made into cheese; kids are slaughtered from time to time and provide the only source of red meat commonly consumed by many families. Poli Tajia eats *cabrita* regularly and has managed to buy a wringer-type washing machine with receipts from selling some of his goats. Some families (including Vicente's) raise pigs. Most do not eat the pork, either because it is worth so much that they cannot afford to consume it, or because they don't like pork. Instead, they sell it to the livestock buyer in Masiaca. Lidia Zazueta, Francisca Yocupicio, and Cornelia Nieblas shear sheep and weave the wool into blankets. Mostly, small livestock is sold, as are cows, which are never butchered in Teachive; they are too valuable to be eaten. Burros carry firewood, water, fencing materials, or anything else small enough to be tied on their back, in addition to transporting men and carts. Mules and horses are put to work as a means of rapid transport or in rounding up animals. It is faster to ride a horse from Masiaca to Teachive than it is to ride by motor vehicle.

Burros are not eaten by Mayos. One individual expressed amazement and scorn in describing the Yaquis' reputation as burro-eaters. "David," he asked, "is it really true that Yaquis eat burro?"

I owned as that I didn't know. I had heard the same rumor.

"¡Que feo!" (How ugly!) he snorted.

Every family hosts a flock of chickens which carry on their own overgrazing, preventing any vegetation from growing around the houses except during periods of heavy rain. Egg production is uneven and never free, for hens hide their nests and must be fed in order to lay eggs predictably. Each day doña Teresa scatters a handful of cracked corn or sorghum for her flock, who scramble feistily for the grain. Chickens easily fly over fences protecting gardens and can devastate the small produce in a matter of minutes. Gardens must be protected from above as well as from the side. Those who raise turkeys must also provide them with feed for them to fatten and protection from virtually any predator, from which the turkeys, in their renowned stupidity, seem too proud to flee. Benigno Buitimea used a broody hen to hatch some wild *chachalacas*, whose eggs he found in a nest. When the pheasantlike birds were fat enough, he said, he and his family would eat them. When the time came to butcher the birds, though, he could not. They endure as household pets.

Community revenues

Modest amounts of money flow into the community from several other sources, including the sale of its natural resources. For example, several men from San Pedrito sell basaltic rock from Pleistocene basaltic floes on the lower slopes of Mesa Masiaca. Empty trucks arrive from Navojoa and Huatabampo (as delta towns, both are rock-poor), and the men laboriously hoist the heavy, black rock into the trucks. Parts of the mesa demonstrate the inroads the rock-vendors have made, for the basalts weather over the eons from a light brown to a characteristic lava-black color. When the top layer is removed, it exposes the still-light layers underneath to the sun and air and the resulting scar can be seen clearly from a distance. The newly exposed rocks will require centuries to weather to the dark black hue of the natural varnish. Once the surface layer is exposed, it will be eons before the layer underneath will be accessible to mining without machinery, for, apart from the top layer, the winds of the ages have filled all imaginable holes with a fine silt, which then packs the surrounding rocks in like stones in a mosaic. Even with the sale of the rocks, depletion is not a concern, for the mesa is huge and can withstand many decades of quarrying. Farther up the hillsides, the basaltic stones become larger. Many weigh a ton or more.

In the vicinity of Sirebampo, an arroyo yields large deposits of fine light-colored sand, another source of revenue. (The Mayo Delta lacks readily abundant supplies of sand suitable for concrete.) A steady stream of dump trucks, sometimes operating twenty-four hours a day, enters and leaves the village, as the sand deposit is transferred to the delta cities (from which it came over the eons). The haulers pay a fee to the community in addition to paying the men who shovel the sand into the trucks. Villagers there have mixed feelings about the steady stream of trucks, for they bring employment. They also create thundering noise at night. Those revenues are earmarked for Sirebampo's schools, and Sirebampans feel that the money reaches them and is not siphoned off by thieves, embezzlers, or "middlemen."

Another source of revenue to the *comunidad* is the lease of lots for vacation homes at the small beach resort of Las Bocas. The beach at Las Bocas is not especially attractive. It is steep and narrow, ending in low clay cliffs, and lacks heavy depositions of light, clean sands, so the village's future as a beach resort is not bright. Furthermore, the area is strewn with garbage. Camahuiroa, a seaside Mayo village ten kilometers to the southeast (and outside the Masiaca community) has a superior beach and more affluent housing. Still, Las Bocas is closer to Navojoa and Ciudad Obregón and has good surf. Its beach is several kilometers long and the construction of new beach dwellings continues at a steady pace. Outsiders pay an annual fee of 150 pesos ($20 US) per lot and build their own residences. The money goes into the community treasury and is used to defray expenses, including pay for those who work for the community. When I asked a *comunero* why the rate was such a pittance, the reply was that the assembly leaders were bought off by the big leaseholders, a thought echoed by several other *comuneros*. Some of the Teachive Mayos also complain that the community funds are not accounted for and the leadership is easily corrupted by crooked exploiters who steal its resources. A group from Los Mochis, Sinaloa, reportedly wished to construct a resort hotel at Las Bocas. They were said to have been turned down because they were unwilling to pay a fair price for the land lease.

During *semana santa* (Holy Week),[60] Las Bocas *comuneros* staff a checkpoint outside the village and collect a ten-pesos (about $1.25) entrance fee from each vehicle. Concessioners also pay a fee to erect beer tents, taco stands, soft-drink booths, carnivals, and other temporary vending operations. Considerable receipts should accrue to the *comunidad*'s treasury, for Las Bocas is an immensely popular destination for Holy Week, with literally thousands of vehicles descending upon the town, resulting in bumper-to-bumper traffic. Accounting procedures are nonexistent, though, and there appears to be ample opportunity for embezzlement, which almost certainly occurs routinely. The *comuneros* of Las Bocas appear to benefit greatly from their seaside location, and would bristle at any suggestion that an accountable collection system be installed.

The sand and gravel in the Arroyo Masiaca are available to any community member willing to attack the streambed with a pick and shovel. Teachivans are heavily involved in selling the aggregate. Older fellows, as well as younger men, excavate gravel. Even during hot June days, they begin early in the morning, becoming drenched with sweat within only a few minutes. The work continues for about six hours without so much as a peep of complaint. They hand-shovel the natural sand and gravel mixture into a large wooden frame covered with wide mesh screen that has been propped up at a steep angle by a pole wedged in each of the upper corners of the box. The screen allows the sand to pass through while it rejects the gravel. The latter is stored in large piles and sold to commercial buyers from Huatabampo, who drive dump trucks to the arroyo and pay thirty pesos (about $5 in mid-1995) per cubic meter (more than two tons of gravel), about a day's production for the average worker. The miner must shovel the gravel into the buyer's truck, a back-breaking and time-consuming task added to the already heavy work of digging and screening the river aggregate. During periods of rain, when the arroyo is running deep, this work is either hindered or delayed until dry weather.

Jesús José "Che Che" Nieblas, and sometimes his older brother Felipe, can be found shoveling into their propped-up screen in the crossing at Teachive, along with six or seven other fellows. After the arroyo floods, others move up to the point where the arroyo enters communal lands, where they dig like badgers. After a few months, the arroyo bottom begins to resemble a great placer mining camp with huge piles and deep pits pimpling and pocking the arroyo bottom. Che Che also runs a few cows on communal lands. When the work becomes too tiring, as it does for all of his generation (Che Che was born in the early 1940s), he wanders into the *monte* in search of his cows, firewood, fruits to glean, or the shade of a *jito*.

In 1993 more than twenty comuneros formed a group to irrigate a parcel of thirty-five hectares (nicknamed Los 35) west of the arroyo to raise alfalfa. They obtained permission from the Secretaria de Agua y Recursos Hidráulicos (SARH),[61] and economic assistance from the National Indigenous Institute (INI), stationed in nearby Etchojoa. INI provided three tractors, piping, fuel, credit for buying seed, and a pump. With this assistance, the partners (*socios*) farmed ten hectares (twenty-five acres) of the total thirty-five, raising alfalfa and other crops. When the alfalfa matured, they harvested it with a baling machine also provided by INI. In July 1995, the harvested *pacas* (bales) were being stored in a warehouse because of a squabble over who owned them. In late 1995 the group sowed beans and corn instead, and were once again pumping considerable water to irrigate the crop. Don Vicente was able to discuss this project in a disinterested fashion, for he was not involved in it and stands neither to gain nor to lose. He, along with nineteen others, has a stake in a nearly defunct silviculture project near Huebampo, ten kilometers away, in which he owns thirteen hectares. That project has been a failure and now lies quiescent.

The extraction of water for irrigating the alfalfa field (a crop of alfalfa requires roughly four million gallons of water per hectare) caused water levels in wells downstream from the pump to drop precipitously, incurring the wrath of those living downstream. For several months, the village of San José was without water. The meager flow of the river also dried up below the crossing at the north end of Teachive, something that almost never happened previously.[62] This experiment demonstrates that the surface waters cannot be further appropriated without dire consequences to the community. They are connected in unknown ways to ground water.

Teachivans are adamant that flows in the arroyo are smaller than in years gone by. If there is any issue they tend to worry about, it is whether there will be enough water in the arroyo. Most Teachivans see the arroyo every day and come to know the health of its flows. The Piedra Bola with its small pool is a popular spot for women to hang out, and, when they have left, for younger men to congregate. When the level of *el aguaje* fell in 1996, the water became scummy and heavily laced with cow dung and urine, a state of affairs that did not sit well with villagers.

Whether the decline in arroyo flow is a reflection of a climatic trend, degradation of the watershed, increased local consumption, or a combination of these, or whether it is a transient, cyclical state, cannot be determined without technical studies. The community has not yet had to face the searing debates that will inevitably arise over allocation of water from the arroyo. As pumps become more readily available to *comuneros*, disputes will arise and the community will be sorely challenged to solve the demands of conflicting interests.

The 3,500 hectares' worth of irrigation water (some *comuneros* say it is actually only 2,000 hectares[63]) has reportedly been allocated to the community from Huites Dam completed on the Río Fuerte in northern Sinaloa in 1995. The water is intended to promote crops for export rather than for subsistence (Barry 1995). *Comuneros* have been assured by government officials that the water will be available, and investor groups from Hermosillo have financed construction of canals to southern Sonora, the closest ending but fifteen miles away. No one is making any bets. Land in a natural amphitheater at the base of Mesa Masiaca, and other flat lands south of Sirebampo, are supposedly designated for clearing and leveling. How these new agricultural enterprises will mesh with the community's present allocation of labor and resources is unclear. Some Mayos grumble that the *mestizo*-oriented leadership appears poised to corner the best lands and commandeer the profits.[64] Rumors have it that contracts have been signed with big-time growers to lease fields with water allocations.[65] Whether or not the community will be able to direct the newly irrigated lands in a manner that provides equitable distribution of the resource and its benefits will depend largely on the technical assistance provided by the Mexican government, which in recent years has adopted a decided bias in favor of private ownership of resources and against communal ownership (Barry 1995). The prospect of the community receiving assistance that will help assure that the benefits accrue to the entire community rather than specific individuals is dim indeed.[66]

The most profitable economic resource of the community is the fishing carried on at Las Bocas, where the Mayos (with the help of INI) have formed a most successful fishing cooperative. The fishermen embark three to a boat in *pangas* (small fishing boats), harvesting shrimp and shellfish in the cool months and fish in the warm months. They dry their nets on the beach with great care, and all who see the great expanse of nylon webbing glistening in the sun must respect the success of the men of the sea. They turn over their catch to the cooperative and receive a high percentage of its worth, the rest going to the cooperative. In every month except January and February they bring in good catches of fish. With the high international price for shrimp ($11 a kilo in 1996), they do well indeed. The work is hazardous, difficult, and seasonal, and the return subject to fluctuations. (The catch of spring 1997 dropped precipitously.) During the hot months the climate at the town is unpleasantly muggy. When the wind dies down, the air is full of biting insects. The rewards are substantial, though, and the fishermen are considered to be affluent. In fact, the fishermen of Las Bocas are by far the most affluent group in the *comunidad*. In spite of their affluence, Vicente feels that they do not live well. He reports that they drink vast amounts of alcohol, dissipating their money in the low life. "Se lo tiran su dinero a cerveza y mujeres (They throw away their money on beer and women)," he says with disdain. Still, as long as they can retain control over the fisheries off the shore of the community, they should be able to continue to live comparatively prosperous lives.

If investors and developers are successful in removing the intertidal zone from control of the *comunidad*, the fishermen will suffer from loss of easy access to the sea and convenient fish-cleaning areas, while the *comunidad* will lose the lease revenues from beach lots.

Beyond the specific resource exploitation in the community, all *comuneros* use the common lands to maximum benefit, if for no other reason than to walk into the *monte* and enjoy the experience of meandering about on land that is their own. Indeed, one of the great advantages of living in the *comunidad* instead of the delta town *ejidos*, which are surrounded by fields, is the psychological benefit of knowing that plenty of land remains available to wander through, land that retains some of its historical freshness and originality. The natives know that Teachive is their home and the *monte* is their land. The community of Masiaca, for all its warts, is their community.

The natural vegetation of the lands in the vicinity of Teachive is richer and more varied than that of the Yaquis, only one hundred kilometers to the north (Martin et al., in press). A wide variety of plant materials makes a semisubsistence way of life more available to the Mayos than to the Yaquis. In the old days, during times of famine, this resource stood the Mayos well. While not capable of sustaining them for extended periods, it would well tide them through short periods of food shortage. Decades of super-overgrazing and constant, relentless harvesting have substantially decreased the availability of these wild resources to the *comunidad*. Only the *pitahayas* and *etchos* continue to produce as they did in the days of old.

For all its virtues, the *comunidad* is finite; it is full and overflowing. Vicente understands clearly that already too many people are trying to extract a living from the communal lands. His children, most of whom already work outside the *comunidad*, will never be economically successful using only local resources. For this reason, he hopes that some of his grandchildren will emigrate to the United States and establish themselves there. His reasoning is based on some sober facts. Without considerable alteration of the current forms of exploitation, that is, dramatic new forms of livestock management, tree planting, erosion control, small industry, or drylands farming, the value of the production of the Masiaca *comunidad* can only decrease. In their current form, the *comunidad*'s resources cannot continue to be exploited indefinitely. As Vicente said to me, as we walked through the battered *monte*, "*Mira, que triste es el monte, David*" (Look how sad the *monte* is, David).

CHAPTER FIVE *Teachive's Worldly Goods*

❧ Teachive is a peasant village. Villagers own the land and use it to provide for their needs. Teachive's peasants have far different relations to their land and to the society around them, however, than the more traditional peasantry. Much of their subsistence, the materials they consume, and nearly all their money comes from outside the *comunidad*. In order to understand the nature of the Teachive peasantry, we must first answer certain questions. What is the source of Teachive's wealth? Where does the money come from that Teachivans spend? To what extent do they rely on the surrounding lands for subsistence?

PEASANT FARMING

It is doubtful that Teachive was ever a self-subsistent village, that is, one that consistently produced its own food and fiber from local resources and bartered or sold a surplus in exchange for those things it could not produce. With the limited rainfall and even more limited soils found near Teachive, a traditional, crop-based, subsistence economy could not have developed, unlike some villages downstream which evolved along a more shallow gradient with better soils, and managed to harvest crops from time to time. Even they, though, could never have been assured of sufficient rainfall or streamflows for reliable, stable farming sufficient to produce a surplus.

In the vicinity of San José and further south, drylands farming by runoff irrigation (called *temporales*) is still practiced in years of good flows on the arroyo. Opportunistic drylands agriculture can be carried out on several hundred hectares of deep, fine soils of terraces along the   133 margins of the arroyo. Such soils retain moisture well, and capillary action from deeper residual moisture keeps soils moist near the surface long enough for a crop to mature. Furthermore, no fertilizer is necessary in the newly delivered soils following a flood. Near Jopopaco, diversion canals have been constructed so that in some years more than one hundred hectares can be irrigated by diverted runoff or pumped goundwater.

Around Teachive *temporales* have existed, though never on more than a small scale. The oldest people in the village agree that decades ago *milpas* (cornfields) were farmed in the vicinity of the village, but there have been only a few since the 1950s. On September 15, 1995, Hurricane Ismael (a name well known to the *comunidad*) dropped a foot of rain on the community. As soon as the rains let up, several *comuneros* with plots south of Masiaca near the arroyo, hastened to their *milpas*, where they plowed and planted beans and corn in the still-sodden muck. Thus, they were able to take advantage of the recently deposited, Nile-like saturated soils, well known for their fertility. Many other downstream *temporales*, especially in the environs of Jopopaco, were also planted at the same time. Sesame seed, watermelon, and garbanzos were planted in addition to corn and beans. No one planted near Teachive.

Even with the record floods of 1995, the crops failed. Prior to the hurricane, *las aguas* (summer rains) had been gravely deficient, and following the hurricane, the *equipatas* (winter rains) failed completely. For three months, humidities were uncharacteristically low and by December the crops had withered and died in the ground. Nothing was harvested. The stunted, poorly developed plants became stubble, food for goats.[1] No measurable rainfall fell through the winter and the long, hot spring, when temperatures exceeded 40°C (104°F) by early May and reached 45°C in a parched June.

So the floodplain planter is faced each year with a tough choice, to plant or not to plant. Even if flooding occurs, a harvest is not a certainty. The seed may germinate and then fail, wasting valuable seed and the considerable labor required to put in a crop. If no flooding occurs, the planters know that no silt will be deposited and soil moisture will be insufficient for producing a crop. Irrigation (pumped by hand from a well), as well as fertilizer for corn crops, will be required, for corn rapidly depletes the soil of nitrogen. Even if water is available, fertilizer is so expensive that it is probably not worth the expenditure. While beans do not require the same amount of fertilizer, their water requirement is nearly as high, and the chance for a profitable harvest is minimal. Because the hybrid seed has no genetic resistance to native pests, the young plants must be sprayed with insecticides. The odds in favor of a good harvest from *temporales* are low. Only a passionate desire to harvest a crop will move a *comunero* to plant under such circumstances.

Milpa activity, then, is confined to the vicinity of the arroyo several kilometers downstream from Teachive and then only on a small scale. Around Teachive, irrigated farming is impracticable without modern pump technology and tractors to till the stony, hard soil. Before the degradation of the arroyo, the stream bottom elevation was higher. Diversion of flows would have been simpler from a gently meandering stream. Still, there is no recent record of diversions around Teachive, only of rain-fed *milpas*. Even historically, irrigation from surface flows was more feasible downstream, where soils are better and the land somewhat flatter. The current irrigation project near Cucajaqui, called Los 35, which is a kilometer south of Teachive, uses a large tractor-powered pump that lifts water from the arroyo at Teachive to an irrigation ditch connected to the distant field.

Still, the 1835 documents refer to *milpas* and irrigating waters at Teachive. Since the drought of the early 1950s the flow and channel of the river have apparently altered substantially, a reasonable supposition based upon studies of arroyo cutting in the adjacent Sonoran Desert region (Hastings and Turner 1965). Prior to arroyo cutting produced by deforestation of the watershed, overgrazing, or undetermined climatic changes, the historic channel probably lay closer to the tops of the arroyo banks. In that case, *milpa* farming would have been possible by simple diversion of streamflows by ditching and diking, as was practiced prior to European contact. Alternately, if rains from *las aguas* were reliable (as most older people claim they were in the past), *milpas* would have been feasible in the deep silty soils of the arroyo margins, now nearly vanished or eroded into grotesque shapes due to the degradation and depression of the arroyo bottom. The hydraulic conditions that residents recall in the arroyo during the last fifty years have precluded *milpa* crops. In Mexico, so great is the lure of farming that a good rule of thumb is that if it is possible to grow a crop, someone will.[2]

Even if rainfall were greater around Teachive, growing a crop is possible only in years when rain is adequate to produce saturation or near-saturation in fields prior to the time of planting. In other words, *milpas* require reliable, heavy rains in July and August. Even with such benevolent conditions, in the absence of flooding, fallow is probably necessary on upland rain-fed milpas after one, or, at the most, two crops. As local planters acknowledge, soil fertility drops quickly after the first year. Furthermore, soil tilth, which helps retain moisture, is also quickly depleted and can only be restored through fallow.

Widespread temporal farming, then, is not possible at Teachive. If subsistence farming was ever possible at Teachive, it was prior to 1950. Whatever farming there was died slowly, unheralded, over a period of time now forgotten. Teachive is nearly completely dependent on food and commodities from without. If commerce with the outside world were cut off, Teachivans would immediately begin to suffer from hunger and would soon begin consuming the local cattle and edible wild plants. When those disappeared, they would slowly starve.

Teachivans are not familiar with sophisticated techniques of agronomy, another indicator of a long separation from planting. Composting is a novel concept for most, which is surprising, given the abundance of animal manures everywhere. Swarms of flies make for considerable unpleasantness as they do the work that well-conceived composting might do more efficiently and productively. It may be that inadequate vegetable matter exists to mix with the manures to produce a workable compost, for whatever edible biomass is not consumed by nomadic horses, mules, goats, sheep, cows, and burros, is gathered to feed to pigs.[3]

The Teachive climate is unfavorable for year-round grazing. Most plant growth takes place during *las aguas*, usually July, August, and September. Some growth occurs following *equipatas*. The timing of those winter rains is even more critical than that for the summer showers. The scanty rainfall throughout the nine months of little or no rain usually produces relatively little biomass. Livestock, of course, must be fed all year round. Since most green forage is gone by fall, the animals must glean rougher matter for the remaining months. As the desperate animals nibble on plants they would prefer to leave uneaten, the overall biomass of the community (as well as that in all of Sonora) is decreasing; that is to say, plant matter converted into animal tissues each year exceeds what is newly produced by photosynthesis the following year (Donald Johnson, COTECOCA, personal communication). The community's plant productivity curve is swinging downward.

A volunteer Japanese government agronomist assigned to the region spoke despairingly of his initial lack of success in recruiting natives to composting and gardening. They had no interest in intensive farming, he said. Gardens, he found to his dismay, were almost certain to be invaded by livestock unless stout fencing were constructed. Even chickens would fly over fences and tear a garden to shreds. No natives seemed inclined to expend the time, effort, or expense of constructing such a livestock-proof fence, he lamented. To make matters worse, his demonstration garden was attacked and his vegetables decimated by leafcutter and harvester ants. Even if the livestock do not eat or trample the gardens, he lamented, the ants will destroy them.[4] He had thought of trap crops, plants of no human usefulness grown as a concession to divert ants from their rampages against the planted gardens. Those plantings, too, would be consumed by livestock. He knew of no solution. His attempts to introduce the culture of fruit trees met with similar defeat. The gradual desertification of the Masiaca landscape owing to vegetation removal and nearly catastrophic overgrazing were providing ideal condition for runaway proliferation of ants, he felt.

Finally, though, the agronomist had success with a garden on the lot of a cooperating village family, who at least temporarily eliminated poultry from their yard. He enlisted their help planting tomatoes, chiles, eggplant, squash, beans, and broccoli. He demonstrated the use of goat manure for fertilizer and companion planting for mutual benefit. The plants sprouted and grew well. Then white flies, a new insect plague in the region, struck. They decimated early harvests, The plants demonstrated adequate resistance, however, and a surprisingly rich crop was harvested. The garden continued until the community pump broke down and irrigation water was no longer available. The experiment required constant and reliable irrigation.

This experience demonstrates that intensive agriculture is possible in the *comunidad* only with a heavy investment in intensive farming technology, for example, infrastructure like a complex water delivery system, soil leveling, plows, centralized accumulation of manures and compostible vegetable matter, livestock-proof fencing, production or allocation of seeds, and, perhaps most important, a means of delivering excess fresh produce to a market. No one in the village can recall any government suggestion of intensive cropping, probably because the labor pool of the *comunidad* is critical to the farming elite of the Mayo Delta, and successful intensive farming might render Teachivans less inclined to venture to the delta to work.

Finally, as everyone in the village knows, no project can be allowed to jeopardize the water available in *el aguaje*, on which most of the village's cattle depend. Old people say that only once in the twentieth century did the pool go dry, in the summer of 1950. Nearly every family now relies in one way or another on the sale of cattle, and in Teachive cattle without *el aguaje* could not exist. If the irrigation project threatens *el aguaje*, the repercussions will be severe, indeed.

Given these impediments to agriculture in the rain-starved thornscrub, it is not surprising that residents of the village say their families have always either bought or bartered for corn and beans, their dietary staples. The basic sources of wealth for the village have always been livestock and firewood, and, to a lesser extent, weaving (Beals 1945). Goats, sheep, cows, pigs, and an occasional horse, have populated the region for centuries. The historic system of barter must have been with downstream people who would exchange corn and beans, which they could raise on floodplain *milpas*, for meat, cheese, and products gathered from the upstream land. It is noteworthy that in Vicente's youth his family sold firewood and livestock and purchased what they needed. Even then, Teachive was not a subsistence community in a classical sense.

Teachivans are peasants entirely within the "free" market system of the Mexican economy.[5]

PEASANT LIVESTOCK-GRAZING

Most natives assert that there are fewer livestock now than in the past, a claim quite plausible when one views the stunted vegetation, lopped trees, and denuded pastures of the *monte*, the bush country that surrounds the village. Except for fenced yards, all 47,000 hectares of the *comunidad* are grazed and grazed hard. Since the grazing habits and food tolerances of goats and cows are rather different (goats can tolerate a broader range of plants than can cattle), the two species can complement each other in a system which uses careful rotation of pastures and alternates grazing times between the two species. In the Masiaca community, pastures are not rotated. Livestock have free access on communal lands to all plants at all times, and what under ideal conditions might be a complementary system, turns into a largely competitive one. One livestock competes with another for diminishing food.

Decades ago the Mexican government, ever vigilant to new sources of export currency and concerned about comparatively low beef productivity on Sonoran ranges, undertook a program of breed and range improvement (Calderón Valdés 1985, 5:267). More cows would mean more export dollars and increased supply for affluent Mexicans in the large cities. A keystone in this effort was the introduction of feed-responsive cattle breeds combined with the introduction of grass species which produce more weight gain in herbivores than do local varieties (Camou Healy 1991). The newly introduced breeds, especially the popular Charolais, fattened more quickly on a diet of nutritious grasses. They also proved to be more tender. That is to say, they are unable to tolerate rugged range conditions and long distances between water sources, and are more susceptible to disease as well.

In contrast, the traditional *criollo* cattle, descendants of ancient, rangy Spanish stock with a genetic splash of Brahma and Zebu, long since had adapted to life in Sonora's hilly, thorny, arid pastures. While these scrubby ranges are lacking in grasses, they are rich in their variety of herbs, shrubs, and trees which the resilient old cows are capable of transforming into meat, albeit a tough, stringy meat. The new breeds do well on relatively flat pastures that have been fenced, cleared, and sown with the introduced grass, buffelgrass (*Pennisetum ciliare*), the other half of the government strategy. Unfortunately, the new cattle do less well in the intact scrub and are far less hardy, that is, drought-and thorn-tolerant. They dislike slopes, require greater water availability, and require more veterinary attention.

Few Mayo members of the Masiaca community have been able to afford the widespread clearing necessary to produce a heavy grass cover and the water availability required by a herd of Charolais. Only non-Mayo *comuneros* were able to afford the modern pastures. One individual sowed buffelgrass in a small pasture north of Teachive. Grass production is higher in that lot (at the expense of all other plant species). Still, the area is insufficient to support more than a single cow and that for only a portion of the year. The new Charolais gain weight, all right, not, however, as they would under ideal conditions, with ample grass and food supplements. And they are costlier to buy and own. Vicente purchased a Charolais (in reality a mongrel Charolais), a cow of which he is proud. It is perhaps a better beef cow than many *criollos* in the region. Given its diet of thornscrub vegetation, it is not by any means a champion cow.

Downstream from Teachive, near San Pedrito, more-affluent, non-Mayo *comuneros* have cleared hundreds of acres and planted buffel-grass, thereby making the introduction of the lucrative Charolais possible. The cows of Teachive, most Zebu/Charolais crosses, are usually a rangy crew, putting on modest weight when the *monte* grows quickly during and following *las aguas*, barely scrounging enough forage to maintain their low weight for the remainder of the year. By late April they have become a sallow lot. During the pounding drought and heat of late spring and early summer, one may count the cows' ribs.

Buffelgrass is hardly an unmixed blessing. In addition to robbing the soil of its natural fertility (thornscrub soils, enriched by an extraordinary variety of leguminous trees and shrubs, are quite rich), buffel-grass flourishes when burned. Green shoots sprout nearly overnight from the black ashes. In the nearby thornscrub, fire is unknown. With each burning, fire kills trees and shrubs at the periphery of the pasture, gradually eating its way into the *monte*. In the burned-over soils, buffelgrass seeds quickly take hold, sprout, and grow. Buffelgrass typically replaces a habitat of immense diversity—more than two hundred plant species are found in the immediate vicinity of Teachive—with one species of grass. Buffelgrass is rapidly expanding its conquest in the Masiaca community, and the native plants are losing ground to the aggressive invader. Most *comuneros* believe buffelgrass is a great improvement and would prefer to have it on their plots. They see the pastures of *yori ganaderos*, where the cows flourish, and judge that with the introduced grass they can do the same for their own cows. Mario Soto runs between twenty and thirty cows of his own and some for his father-in-law. The only member of the Cattlemen's Association in Teachive, he complains that the government does not do enough to help small ranchers drill wells and plant buffelgrass. He has three small fields of buffelgrass, only three hectares each, and during the drought of 1996 the cows ate it all and virtually destroyed the plants. With more buffelgrass, he says, he would be able to raise more cows and make more money. Others agree.[6]

Raising and selling calves represents a slow mining of the soil. With the export of each animal, a tiny portion of a community resource (soil fertility and nonrenewable trace elements) goes with it, a process that only becomes apparent over several decades. Buffelgrass technology accelerates this mining operation, so that its effects become apparent in only a decade or so and require large expenditures of capital to control.[7] It seemed to me that Mario Soto, upon seeing his denuded buffelgrass pasture, realized that he had begun a process of soil degradation that only government assistance (an infusion of others' money) could decelerate.

Comuneros, in general, seem fatalistic about the rate of exploitation of communal lands. More cows mean more money, and since other *comuneros* run too many cows, they will be put at a disadvantage if they fail to run cows as well. More buffelgrass will mean less firewood and other forage, as everyone acknowledges, yet most seem hopeful that they will be able to seed their own parcels. Cutting of firewood is often done when men or women are tired, and cutting down the main trunk of a tree near the village, while perhaps regrettable, is not viewed as a great sin. The casting of garbage away from the home is not considered a serious breach of conduct. Economic necessity, as bills come due and purchases are viewed as necessary, overrides what might otherwise be a community concern.

Apart from the cooperative irrigation project, known as "Los 35," and occasional cooperative plantings on the lower Arroyo Masiaca, there are no communal agricultural activities in the village. Family ties and, to a lesser extent, godparent commitments, produce some reciprocal and cooperative ranching, as is the case with the man who helps care for his cousin's cows in exchange for boarding at her house. Livestock animals are individually owned, and while neighbors will assist marginally and keep an eye on each other's animals, the livestock is viewed as personal property and a sign of economic status. This industrialization of cattle-raising conflicts with traditional Mayo culture, in which such displays are viewed as being in bad taste (see, e.g., Crumrine 1977, 57).

The government's strategy, calling for the preeminence of cattle, taps into a deep-seated Mexican (or Iberian, or, perhaps, human) psychological fixation, a longing to own cattle. The symbol of male achievement (besides having numerous children) in Mexican culture is owning cattle and the land where they roam. Once cattle have been admitted to an area, and once a certain number of cows frequent a range, it is powerfully difficult to lower or eliminate that number. The lust for cows and what they symbolize makes the cow-owning brotherhood one deeply resistant to any change that would decrease cattle numbers or the acreage of pasture. Once Mexico's forests and fields have been converted to pasture, it will be nigh impossible to revert them to forest or field. For a *latifundista* (owner of large estates) with one thousand head of cattle to be told that he must reduce his herd to five hundred is an enormous blow to his ego[8]; for a *campesino* to be told that he or she must decrease a herd from five head to three is economically punishing news. The former is in a position to blackmail, extort, or bribe his way out of the situation. The latter is powerless.

TEACHIVAN PEASANTS IN THEORY AND IN FACT

At first glance, Teachive is a simple peasant community. A closer analysis shows that *comuneros* are peasants only in the sense that they live on their own land. The villagers own their own land, at least to the extent that they are members of the *comunidad* and have an historic claim to land. Although not self-subsistent, they supply themselves with numerous materials from the surrounding bush (see Appendix B). Hinton's (1962) distinction between rich peasants, middle peasants, and poor peasants does not apply in Teachive, for all have a claim in land ownership and no one works for anyone else in an employer-employee or landlord-tenant relationship. To that extent, in spite of considerable income differences, all are middle peasants.

Their status as peasants is modified by two facts that constitute the bleak economic reality of the village: the village could not be sustained without nearly all the people working outside the community (to varying degrees), and the internal resources that provide whatever self-subsistence exists, are diminishing. For example,

Nearly all the men and some of the women and children in the village work either part of the time or full time as *jornaleros*, day-laborers in the fields of nearby Huatabampo. Others work away from home at various jobs and return to the village only on weekends, or at most once during the week. A majority of the village's income derives from the sale of their labor outside the community.

An important source of revenue, the sale of gravel and some sand (and, to a lesser extent fired bricks), is a diminishing or wasting resource. Extraction of the material has a long-term degrading effect on the arroyo, which is the source of the community's water and much of its pasture, as well as much of its beauty.

The waters of Arroyo Masiaca are over-allocated and the increasing population will exacerbate shortages. Upstream manipulation of the watershed by clearing of the forest and overgrazing has probably diminished flows and produced increased siltation of the streambed. The trend will continue.

The raw materials for producing arts and crafts are expensive and some of them are being depleted. The market for fine handmade blankets is largely North American. The amounts earned by the weavers are small, the work physically and psychologically demanding. Wool is increasingly difficult to obtain.

The sale of firewood and the cutting of trees for local house construction and building and for maintaining fences has drastically reduced the number of large trees within several kilometers of the village. Since most of these trees are leguminous, possessing the virtue of fixing nitrogen in the soil, their removal also depletes the soil fertility. Furthermore, the carving of artisan items such as masks and dolls has eliminated soft-wood and carvable hardwood trees in the immediate area of the village.

The population of the village is growing steadily, as large families proliferate.[9] Children hope to live near their parents. Most realize, perhaps dimly, that they will have to look elsewhere for work and permanent residence. The historic strength of the community, the shared awareness of being *yoreme*, with a common history, common language, and shared values, is, according to Teachivans, fast disappearing, as children are taught in Hispanicized schools and remain monolingual Spanish speakers.

The overall biomass of the *comunidad* is diminishing, rendering it less capable of supporting historic livestock populations.

These findings can best be demonstrated through the day-to-day lives of members of the Teachive village. Employment in the village in 1996 broke down roughly as follows:

One family and one man produce rope and hat bands.

One small family produces wire baskets for sale to tourists.

Ten women weave woolen blankets, shawls, sashes, and, occasionally, other items.

Twenty men dig gravel.

About 150 people work as *jornaleros*.

One family makes wooden trays and spoons—*bateas* and *cuchar-ras*—for sale to tourists or outside buyers.

Two men work sporadically at cutting firewood.

Six men work at *albañil*, brick-laying.

Three families (six men) work at brick-making.

Seven men have enough cows to work solely or nearly so at raising them.

One man is a schoolteacher.

Five men are tractor and truck operators.

Two or three men own or have access to operating vehicles.

Varying numbers of men work at collecting buffelgrass seed.

Six men work at bagging buffelgrass seed in a warehouse in Masiaca.

Two women work as housemaids in Navojoa.

One man works as a carpenter's apprentice in Navojoa.

One man works in a sandal shop in Masiaca.

Three women bake rolls and sell them within Teachive.

Three men work primarily on Los 35, the newly irrigated field.

Perhaps five men work sporadically at temporary jobs in the region.

Two men work regularly at a chicken ranch near Navojoa.

None of these categories is exclusive. Some of the gravel diggers also work as *jornaleros*, as do some of the seed baggers. The men who work on Los 35 also work as *jornaleros*, as do, from time to time, nearly all the residents of the village.

Rope-making

Two men (one includes his family; he could not do the work alone and his wife seems quite skilled as well) produce horsehair rope and hat-bands. The family has constructed in the yard outside their house a simple winding machine that weaves the rope from large piles of hair cut from horse tails and manes that are fed into the winding machine. Stakes have been sunk into the ground at set intervals for measuring the length of the rope. The ropemaker charges about one dollar per meter for the rope. His wife and sons assist in making and marketing the rope, which is in great demand by cowboys for its strength and tendency not to tangle. The family also produces belts and hatbands from horsehair, assisted in this by a brother who is incarcerated in Ciudad Obregón and sends partially finished items to them to be completed.

At times it is difficult for the family to secure adequate horsehair to meet demand. When demand for the rope is slack, the ropemaker and his sons work as *jornaleros*. Usually, though, they restrict their work to weaving rope. The family's products are of high quality, irresistible to anyone who cherishes the remotest fantasies of cowboyhood. Sales can bring in forty to fifty pesos a day ($6–7 US), sometimes more. The prevalence of horses with cropped tails in the area is an indicator of the prosperity of the rope-making industry in Teachive. In this family, the wife also weaves blankets.

The other individual works more on his own and, though equally talented, sells substantially fewer ropes and hatbands. He also works as a *jornalero* and has a large herd of cows. When tourists or other visitors appear in the village, he timidly approaches them, offering his wares at embarrassingly low prices.

Weaving

Mayo women have been weaving wool for at least two hundred years. The craft was probably taught or suggested to them by Fray Francisco Joaquín Valdez, who actually brought the wool-weaving industry to the Yaquis in the mid-eighteenth century. (Cahitan peoples wove fine cotton blankets at the time of contact.) *Cobijeras* (blanket-weavers) are highly esteemed in the community. They receive miniscule amounts for their labor. About ten women weave. Of these, three or four produce truly superior textiles. While most of the weavers produce small rugs (approximate two feet by three feet) and larger *matrimoniales* (four feet by six feet), some women produce *fajas* (sashes such as those worn by *pascolas* in festival dancing), shawls, and even handbags. In 1995 one woman was experimenting with sweaters.

Beals (1945) in field studies in 1930–31 noted that poor-quality *cobijas* were produced in large quantities in Masiaca (he does not mention Teachive, probably because at that time he was unaware of the distinction between the larger town and the villages). He also found that "knowledge of what plants were used for other [non-blue] dyes is apparently almost lost" (Beals 1945, 47). Either his research was faulty or blanket-weaving has improved and plant dyes are much better known now, for at least six different vegetable dyes are used (see, e.g., *chiju* in Appendix B). Beals also noted that Masiaca was the principal source of woolen sashes of the kind worn by *pascolas* even today. Two women in the village still weave these rather attractive garments. Some women formerly wove *serapes*, which were lighter blankets, intended to be worn and used as a cover at night. In recent years they have stuck to weaving rugs, which, because the weave is coarser, are less work and require less wool.

Formerly, several families raised sheep for the wool. While a few animals remain, the pastures are much degraded and most of the wool for weaving is now purchased from other Mayos in the irrigated lower Mayo Valley, much of it from around Buaysiacobe and Bacobampo. It is sold by the fleece, the yield of one *borrega* (ewe) at ten pesos per fleece (roughly $1.50 US each). A large *cobija* requires twelve fleeces, or 120 pesos' worth of wool, even more during the winter when the fleeces are more expensive and harder to find. Furthermore, the women must purchase a bus ticket from Teachive to the Mayo Delta at a cost of fourteen pesos. One weaver reported that on the return trip the driver required her to purchase a separate ticket for the bulky parcel of wool, an additional seven pesos.

Sometimes a woman will make a trip to the delta and return without fleeces, for there are none to be had. Fewer sheep are raised now in the region, and of those that remain many are *peligüe*, a breed that produces much meat but no wool. I took several women in a carryall from Teachive to the delta in search of *vellones* (fleeces). They spent most of the day visiting five different places searching for wool. They managed to locate only five fleeces, all of inferior quality. Vicente remembered many places in the delta where sheep used to abound but where only goats and cows are now found. Afterward, Vicente told me, "It was good that you took this trip, David. Now you understand how difficult it is for the women to make their *cobijas* and why they must sell them for high prices." Unfortunately, the market for the blankets has no sympathy for such extenuating circumstances and is slowly drying up.

Preparation of the wool to make it weavable is most time consuming. It must first be washed and cleaned of dirt, plant parts, and sheep smell. Frequently, the fleeces are full of chaff, stickers, and tiny pieces of plants, which must be removed by hand. In former times women made a soap from the fruits of the San Juanico tree (*Jacquinia macrocarpa*), which produced superior cleansing and eliminated the smell of the sheep. Now it is easier for them to use commercial detergents, and all the women of the village have capitulated to that technological innovation.

After washing, the wool is spun, a process that requires roughly a month for a matrimonial blanket, about twice as long as the actual weaving. It is interminable, boring work, requiring continuous, deft rotating of a spindle between the fingers. Fortunately, the work can be done while listening to radio soap operas, talking, thinking, and sometimes, I think, sleeping. I've grown used to chatting with women as they whirl the *malacate* (spindle), which miraculously sucks wool from an amorphous mass and transforms it into yarn.

Dyeing is also labor-intensive. Some women use the natural sheep colors—white, brown, and dark brown (the potent tropical sun bleaches the black sheep color to a dark reddish brown)—exclusively for their blankets and forego this step. For blues, reds, oranges, and yellows, plant dyes are selected. Raw materials for these must be gathered from the *monte*, the dye prepared, the yarn soaked in the dye solution and a mordant applied (in some cases, the urine of children is used). Then the dyed yarn must be washed again to remove any odor or impurities. Setting up the loom and weaving a large blanket requires roughly two weeks of work. The entire production for a large matrimonial requires at least six weeks. For this labor, a woman will net somewhere around 550 pesos (700 pesos minus the cost of the wool and bus tickets), or a little more than $90 US. The better weavers receive somewhat more, the less talented somewhat less. The rate of pay is less than fifty cents per hour, even for the most skilled weavers.

The market for the blankets is unreliable. Most customers are North American tourists. If none are forthcoming (few tourists venture into the village in the hot months between May and October), the women or a family member may journey by bus to Alamos or Navojoa and attempt to sell the blanket there. Mexican buyers typically pay less than North Americans, and the weaver may have to settle for less than her asking price. Vicente and Teresa once took a trip to Alamos, a colonial town frequented by North American tourists, where they tried without success to sell a small blanket. They returned disappointed to Teachive, having wasted two bus fares and an entire day in a futile sales trip. Thus, they had to weigh the consequences of waiting for someone to come to the village, or selling at a painfully small price.

Furthermore, the weavers of Teachive are in competition with weavers in other Mayo villages, such as Sinahuisa and Saneal, and must be concerned about competitive pricing for their wares.[10] The women in the latter villages weave coarser blankets, but they are situated nearer the international highway and have better access to customers. Teachive, after all, languishes at the end of the road. For some Teachive women, income from the sale of textiles is the sole source of income for the household and is irreplaceable. One can scarcely conceive of surviving on the pittance on which the women have learned to make do.

The best weavers are usually older women. The youngest weaver in Teachive is thirty. No younger women are involved in weaving. In addition to paying poorly, the craft is physically punishing: the weaver kneels (stressful on the knees and hips) and must pull and push on the loom (stressful on the back, arms, and shoulders). All the women who weave say they suffer greatly from aches and pains, and they sometimes are not able to weave because one part or another of their body aches. This is not lost on younger women and girls, who, though familiar with weaving techniques, show little inclination to practice the craft. Indeed, the younger women and girls appear to harbor ambitions to move to the big cities, where life is more glamorous and not confined to dull routines such as making blankets. Unless the market improves dramatically, it does not appear that the craft will continue indefinitely.

The end of weaving will signal a change in the role of women in the culture, for a woman's receipts from the sale of her wares are considered her property and foster a spirit of achievement and power unavailable to those who have no independent source of income. In fact, women in Teachive who do not weave have less mobility and are more tied to their homes than women who weave. A woman who wove for years, then for a number of reasons ceased to weave, has become less financially independent as she has become more and more confined to her home. She also communicates less with other women in the village, and spends less time in the *monte* collecting materials for dyeing. Weaving represented her one possibility for transcending a position of subordination to the men of the household. When she gave up her artistry, she surrendered her independence as well. When a woman displays her wares to a customer, she never fails to wear an expression of pride. The weavers are rather adept at discerning the customer's reaction as well.

One of the *cobijeras* owns a few cows and bakes bread as a sideline as well. She is without a man in her household and must work extra hard to support her young son, which she manages to do. She also sells rugs woven by friends and relatives, whose wares, unfortunately for her, are superior to her own.

Improvement of the *cobijeras'* lot is hampered by their independence and isolation. While all are thoroughly familiar with each other and know each other's families intimately, they are highly competitive, even jealous of each other's work. Sisters compete against each other. I discovered the extent of this competitiveness when one of the weavers asked me to bring her some sheep shears from the United States. She believed that with this tool she could obtain wool from local sheep more easily and cheaply. I happily complied and within the month brought her the tool. Before long, I had requests for shears from two more women, which I also fulfilled. On the next visit, two more requested pairs of shears. I suggested that three pairs of shears in the community was more than sufficient for the handful of sheep. Why didn't they share the tools they had, rather than each going to the considerable expense of buying her own? I was met with cold stares. They would no more share shears than Americans would share automobiles. Loaning shears to another weaver might provide a leg up for a competitor.

The competitive atmosphere also appears in the search for fleeces. Fleeces are scarce in the cold months in the region, when the fleeces are left on the sheep for protection against cold. One of the best *cobijeras* had suffered some personal and family misfortunes, and I found her without any wool to weave and no means of leaving her household to venture to the delta where the sheep are found. Vicente and I took her in my carryall to the delta, where we spent an entire day searching for wool. We found only a few inferior fleeces and had to be content with those. We spoke with other weavers, who lamented the scarcity of wool at that time. That year, there were fewer sheep and their wool was of poor quality, the weavers complained. Much to my surprise (but not to theirs), we learned that another woman had obtained good fleeces in a different town, and had kept the information secret so that her competitors would not be able to make their *cobijas*.

Whereas women might benefit greatly by cooperation, sharing techniques, tools, sources of wool, and marketing strategies, they are secretive about all. This individualistic isolation is at odds with the historic sense of community and cooperation that formerly characterized Mayo culture.[11] It is not surprising in the light of the economic desperation they face and the intensely family-competitive *mestizo* culture in which they are immersed. A foreign social worker who worked in Teachive encountered the same isolation and competition; she despaired of inculcating the virtues of cooperation among the fractionalized women, whose decisions are individually rational but socially divisive. The centrifugal economics of Mexican (and global) society overwhelm the centripetal community forces of Teachive.

Day laborers (jornaleros)

A common occurrence on a Sunday afternoon in Teachive is the blast of a horn announcing the arrival of a pickup truck from the fields near Huatabampo calling for *jornaleros* for the following week. That is how the word is spread. Before 6 A.M. on the following (Monday) morning, another, larger truck (or, more recently, an old bus) passes through the village, and men (and women) who wish to work climb into the back, where they stand in cramped spaces while they are driven to the fields more than twenty miles away to labor over the crops: chile, sweet corn, field corn, wheat, cotton, and potatoes for local or national consumption, sesame seed, garbanzos (chick peas), sweet peas, melons, and tomatoes, primarily for export. Pay is between twenty and forty pesos a day ($3–5 US). When work is piecemeal, as it often is during harvests and packing, pay may be greater. At the end of the day, the truck returns the workers to the village. The trip takes more than an hour, so a large portion of their day is spent in transit.

Work as a *jornalero* constitutes by far Teachive's biggest source of employment. Virtually every man in the village, and many women as well, works or has worked as a *jornalero*.[12] In spite of the poverty of Teachive, actual unemployment is very low, making the town an anomaly in Mexico, where rural unemployment typically is in the range of 50 percent. At first, it seemed odd to me that no man reported having worked in the United States, but gradually I came to understand that the abundance of daywork locally removed the incentive to journey north. Because the climate of the Río Mayo Delta permits multiple cropping, there is a constant demand for field laborers.[13] During the season for picking cotton, mid-August through mid-September, entire families go to work, including those who frequently work at other jobs. When tomatoes are being packed, women sometimes outnumber men. Packers often prefer women because they are believed to work faster, more neatly, and damage the produce less. Teachivans prefer to work with other Teachivans, or at least with other Mayos, but this is not always possible.

Only men are identified as *jornaleros*. In spite of the regular participation of women in *jornalero* work, no one I interviewed identified a woman as a *jornalera* per se. Women's field work is viewed as supplementing their work in the home. Women who weave are identified as *cobijeras*, and those who work as maids are so identified; otherwise, their work is viewed as housework sometimes supplemented with outside income. *Jornaleras* are expected to carry on with their home duties as if they did not work in the fields all day.

Some *jornaleros* expressed concern about the presence in the fields of agricultural chemicals, notably insecticides and herbicides, from which they have little protection. Mexican laws regarding pesticides, admirable in concept, are unenforced (see, e.g., Wright 1990).[14] Two of Vicente's sons arrived home a day earlier than expected one weekend. They explained that the chile crop on which they were working was about to be fumigated, and they chose to leave and receive no pay rather than remain and risk exposure to the fumigant.[15]

Sanitary facilities in the fields are nearly nonexistent, so laborers must find toilets the best they can. Water is often not provided, and some workers rely on canal water, which usually contains numerous chemicals and often sewage. Some workers also complain that from time to time employers, for various reasons, fail to pay, either paying less than the promised amount or nothing at all. The workers in this case have no recourse, since, they maintain, the growers are friends of the government, or, in many cases, *are* the government, so it is not reasonable to expect any remedial action from the government. One grower from a well-known ruling family has become notorious for refusing to pay after work is done. None of the workers seem to think that any collective action is possible in such cases; their desperation for work is such that when it is offered they accept, knowing that they are powerless to collect should the grower later refuse to pay them.

Roughly 150 people in Teachive—men, boys, women, and girls—work as *jornaleros*, some intermittently, some as their only source of employment. So many men and women work in the fields of the delta that Teachive could be viewed as a bedroom community, parasitic on greater Huatabampo. During the day, the village's population slumps. The commute is lengthy and expensive (though surely no more so than the daily commutes of millions of suburban North Americans). None of the *jornaleros* can be said to be permanently employed, for their work is strictly on a day-by-day basis. That way, the employer need not provide benefits: the workers receive no social security, no workmen's compensation, no medical benefits, no retirement benefits. Furthermore, there is no such thing as a promotion; a *jornalero* knows that he or she will do exactly the same kind of work every year for the rest of his or her life.

I asked Vicente why people who must work in the distant fields don't move closer to the work. His response was that Teachive is their home and where they have their roots. Besides, he said, there are enormous advantages to living in the *monte*. I found his first answer most appealing and his second answer intriguing, so we leaned back in chairs in the *portal* during the heat of a day in late June and, with Teresa puttering about in the background adding comments, set out to make a list of the things the *monte* provides. Late in the afternoon we were still adding to the list. It is found in Appendix A.

Work in the fields may end as abruptly as it begins. Tasks are physically demanding (requiring, for example, the use of the back-stressing short-handled hoe). Cultivating cotton is risky due to aerial and ground application of pesticides. Cotton is feasted upon by a remarkable array of insects, several of which are historic pests of enormous consequence and have developed resistance to many chemicals. Hence, the number of applications and the dosage of pesticides are annually increased. The workers in the field bear the brunt of the losing battle against nature, being regularly subjected to a chemical shower. Picking cotton is aptly regarded as damaging to hands and faces. When the boll is ready to burst open, irrigation is terminated, the plant dies, and the cotton pops into the world. The dead leaves and branches are sharp and scratchy, wreaking damage on the skin of the hands and posing an ever-present hazard to the face and eyes, especially for shorter adults and children. In 1996 two boys under ten years old were among the cotton pickers of Teachive.[16]

In general, though, the fields of the Mayo Delta are enormously productive and the harvests require large numbers of workers, so this source of employment seems likely to continue, unsatisfactory though it may be.[17] The opening of new fields to the south, as the irrigation systems fed by Huites Dam in Sinaloa are completed, may increase the demand for day laborers. The supreme irony of the situation is that Mayos are now paid low wages to work on lands that once were theirs, while the owners, whose ancestors took the land from the Mayos, live in luxury in Huatabampo, Navojoa, or Ciudad Obregón. In some cases, Mayos work as day laborers in fields that *are* theirs: the lands are owned by Mayo *ejidos*. They are leased out to growers who have the equipment and credit resources necessary to carry out modern farming. The de jure tenants are the de facto owners. In fact, exploitation of leased communal or *ejido* lands is less risky for *latifundistas* than outright ownership, for it frees them from the burdens of taxation and flood losses and from the danger of expropriation by populist politicians.

Other than occasional grumblings, few *jornaleros* complain about the work per se. They acknowledge that it pays poorly, that it is difficult or downright dangerous, and that it is boring. At least, they say, it is *chamba* (work). The specter of unemployment weighs heavily on all men. They have never known what it is like to work for better pay under good working conditions, so their experience is limited to working under conditions of exploitation. For many, work in the fields represents an opportunity to get away from the village and meet people from other communities. For younger men it represents a source of spending money, and for their families an additional income that may enable the family to live somewhat better. One young woman was most enthusiastic about her work (twenty-five pesos per day), which consisted of carrying *garrafones* (jugs) of drinking water to workers who were harvesting chiles at breakneck speed. She felt she was hardly working and expressed astonishment that she would be paid for producing nothing at all.

The *jornaleros* of the Masiaca community represent a bedrock component of Mexico's economy. Many Mexican *jornaleros* are peasants from *ejidos* or communities like Teachive, whose own small acreage and limited resources cannot support them and their family, so they must work on others' lands to survive. Many of them (Barry 1995) travel around the country following the crops and return to their own parcels at planting time. The Mayos of the Masiaca community have the advantage of living close enough to the commercial fields that they can return home each day. Growers prefer to employ them because of their reliability, in part deriving from their nearby residence. An increasing proportion of Mexican *jornaleros*, though, are landless and, as such, are far more desperate than the Mayos. These peasants venture far from home, and evidence of their marginal existence can be seen in the shantytowns of Huatabampo, Navojoa, and Ciudad Obregón. The *jornaleros* of the Masiaca community (and of many Mexican *ejidos*), however, are landowners, or, at least, they have insured access to land. That they are landholders is a clear demonstration that land owner-ship is not necessarily a protection against being forced into the wage labor pool. Indeed, recent Mexican agricultural policy has assumed that *ejiditarios* and *comuneros* will be unable to derive subsistence from their lands and will, as such, constitute a large pool of cheap labor to work in the agribusiness sector (Barry 1995). The *latifundistas* are quite successful in exploiting landed and landless peasants alike. The *jornaleros* of Teachive are a land-owning proletariat employed by an agri-cultural factory in the nineteenth-century tradition.

For classical Marxists, the quasi-peasant status of Teachivans pre-sents an anomaly, for their peasantness shows no sign of disappearing, that is, as long as the *monte* and the arroyo are fecund resources, Teach-ivans will continue to derive use-values from them. The owners of the means of production who pay the wages of the *jornaleros*, have no interest in altering Teachivans' status as quasi-peasants, for it enables them to keep wages low with the knowledge that Teachivans will supplement their low pay with resources gleaned from their lands.[18] In this case, capital benefits significantly from the peasantry.

Sand and gravel operators
Some twenty men from Teachive work in varying degrees producing sand and gravel from the Arroyo Masiaca. A day's work will net a hard worker about forty pesos ($5 US) and a mighty tired back. At times, the streambed resembles a placer mine, with great mounds of displaced

aggregate next to gaping holes in the bottom. The buyers usually are not interested in the coarse river sand and workers leave it behind. Sometimes it is used elsewhere in the community. The bulk of it remains in piles until floods level the mounds.

The operators believe the supply of sand and gravel is infinite. With each flood new supplies are washed down from the hills and mountains above. The depressions fill, the bottom is swept clean. The activity is not without its negative consequences, however; the years of mining have clearly degraded the channel, causing scouring in some areas and eroding banks in others. The general lowering of the gradient in turn lowers the reach immediately downstream and a domino effect is established until only bedrock prevents further degrading (and further accumulation of aggregate). When the larger aggregates are removed, they are replaced by the finer sands, silts, and clays left behind. Muddy floods deposit finely divided sediments in the depressions left by removal of the aggregate. These particles penetrate river gravels and coarser sand, sealing the spaces between the stones and sands, rendering them impermeable and retarding recharge. One of the explanations for decreased downstream flows in recent years may be decreased recharge upstream due to sealing of the previously porous bottom and a subsequent failure of recharge. Whether this will have a long-term effect can only be determined by sophisticated hydrological study. The degradation of the channel, the widening of the banks, and the drying up of the upper reaches of the streambed are warning signs that bode ill for the future.

I discussed these complications with a Mayo familiar with the mining activity. He agreed that the gravel extraction has a negative effect, noting that in his lifetime the upper channel has become far wider and dryer. He added, "When people are poor as we are, we have to have work. For these men there is no other. What else can they do?"

Such fears of channel degradation were realized in 1995, when Hurricane Ismael bore down on the region, dumping nearly a foot of rain on the community in twenty-four hours. Although no house collapsed, a tribute to the quality of Mayo house construction, every building suffered some damage from the high winds and rain. The arroyo ran full, nearly inundating some homes that sit fifteen feet above the arroyo bottom. After the floodwaters subsided, the natives discovered to their dismay that the scouring of the bottom of the arroyo had lowered it more than a meter from its previous level. Iron-ically, much of the transported sediments moved about a mile down-stream, where they raised the level of the streambed at the Masiaca roadway crossing, requiring massive excavation of sand before traffic could pass once again. Hurricane Fausto in September 1996 low-ered the stream bed even more. The meandering, grassy streambed at Teachive has been replaced by an incised channel, obliterating idyllic streamside grazing pastures that supported many cows, sheep, and goats. Parts of the dense and tall riparian forest were washed away and replaced with a rocky, sandy open area. The higher gallery forest may be endangered as well as the water level is lowered. The lowered gra-dient at Teachive will result in poorer grazing, increased channel cut-ting, the death of many streamside trees, and, worst of all, significantly lowered water tables. At the village pump site, the two storms lowered the arroyo bottom by a meter and a half. The well will have to be dug deeper and longer casing installed. Pumping costs will increase, a price that will be spread across all users. It may be that the added costs of pumping and the revenues lost from the disappearance of streamside grazing will more than offset the accumulated money earned by sell-ing the gravel. To put it another way, the income accrued by gravel-extractors has been, in fact, borrowed from the community as a whole, which must now pay it back with interest.[19]

Artisans

Three families (in addition to those families producing textiles and the single family producing rope) produce arts and crafts. One produces baskets woven from strong construction wire, another carves spoons and trays from local woods, and a third produces ceremonial masks and *monos* (carved miniature dancers). In each case, the artisans have no other work (except for occasional day-laboring, when demand is high at harvest time), although the basket-maker assists his cousin in tend-ing her seven cows.

Two, possibly more, individuals also from time to time make *téne-borim*, the long strands of cocoons worn by *fariseos*, *pascolas*, and deer dancers in the *fiestas*. The cocoons are sewn shut and attached to strands of woven *ixtle*, the fiber from local agaves. The rattling noise from the cocoons is produced by tiny pieces of gravel sealed inside. In authentic *téneborim* the gravel is gathered from anthills; ants are said to produce nearly perfectly round bits of gravel and to keep it immaculate, which suits the manufacturers of the *téneborim* perfectly. While some of the rattles are sold to tourists, others are sold to other Mayos for use by *pascolas* and deer dancers in *fiestas* and *fariseos* during Holy Week. Supplies of the cocoons are sorely limited, natives say, because the thornscrub is marginal habitat for the caterpillar. It is more abundant in the tropical deciduous forest to the north. It is nowhere common, hence the production of *téneborim* is necessarily sporadic. Mayos journey to Masiaca and Teachive from towns in the delta to purchase them, because all the original vegetation has been cleared from the *monte* there.

The wire baskets are a relatively new product, appearing in the late 1980s. The wire is a burnt tie-wire, which is purchased by the kilo at hardware stores in Masiaca and Navojoa. The weavers also use the more expensive and pliable bare copper electrical wire. To make the baskets, the wire is stretched with pliers and deftly twisted, clamped, and literally woven into a pattern that produces a strong basket of most agreeable appearance. The first baskets were quaint, primitive affairs, appealing because of their novelty, but hardly aesthetic masterpieces. Experience and study have produced a rapid improvement, and the baskets are now finely crafted. The weaver, a bachelor, works alone and can produce one basket per day. It sells for fifty pesos ($7 US). The material costs only a few pesos, so the net sale is close to the actual sale price. The work is very hard, producing sore hands and blisters. Copper wire costs much more, so these baskets tend to be smaller. The work with copper is easier on the hands, but a more risky investment. The only tools involved are rather simple pliers. The concentration required is considerable. Another family from Teachive and one from Choacalle have recently also taken up the craft, providing perhaps more competition than the limited sales of baskets can justify. One of Vicente's grandsons recently began weaving tiny baskets from copper wire.

Spoons and trays are carved from various native woods, primarily *mezquite*, *palo chino* (*Havardia mexicana*), and *teso* (*Acacia occidentalis*). Most of these carvings, though by no means all, are sold to a North American buyer who visits the village regularly and places orders for the items, usually advancing partial payment. He takes the wooden implements to a shop in the United States, where they are given a smooth finish, turning out as handsome utensils indeed. The people of Teachive view their sales to this North American as an important factor in maintaining the local economy. Working with great dedication, the wood carver can earn up to fifty pesos a day ($7 US). His income is primarily dependent upon the North American market.

The mask and figurine maker works exclusively at producing his wares, sometimes taking them to Alamos or to Navojoa, where shops stock his productions. His work is known throughout the region. With assistance from his wife and family (three of his sons help in varying degrees), he can turn out as many as five completed masks a day, each of which retails for fifty pesos. The *monos*, about fifteen inches tall, are carved from *palo chino*. These finely carved creations depict a dancer in motion, holding a ceremonial knife in one hand and a spear in the other. The figures are sold wearing sewn costumes, a goatskin mask, and tiny representations of *téneborim* (cocoon rattles) made from *sigropo* (*Lycium andersonii*), the entire *mono* resembling the *fariseos* of Mayo Lenten festivities. The masks are carved from *torote prieto* (*Bursera laxiflora*) or *torote copal* (*Bursera lancifolia*). The rough masks are sanded and painted. Holes are drilled above the forehead and on the chin and long tufts of horsehair are worked in, producing the *pascola* effect. Although the masks are produced primarily for tourists, they are also used by *pascola* dancers in the region. Working diligently, the family is able to produce well and may earn more than twenty dollars a day. The husband has a fondness for alcohol, and a rather high percentage of the family earnings go to purchase beer and mescal.

The wood for the masks no longer is available in the vicinity of the village, due to previous lumbering for masks and figurines and the general depletion of the forest. All the woods grow in sufficient quantity nearer to Alamos to the northeast, but they are becoming more and more difficult to obtain. The *desmonte* (clearing) of large tracts of forest in preparation for planting buffelgrass provides a temporary bonanza, since all the trees are uprooted and large specimens of the raw material become available. In the long run, the felling of the forest portends an end to all trees and elimination of the carver's raw material.

As is the case with the *cobijeras*, when tourists do not come to buy the masks, the carver is forced to sell them for lower prices, sometimes for considerably less, which means a considerable drop in family revenue. He and his wife have become good marketers, and they manage to keep stores in the cities, both Alamos and Navojoa, stocked with his wares. Huatabampo is a poorer city, seldom visited by tourists, so he does not bother selling his art there.

Firewood cutters

One, possibly two, men spend a considerable, though an indeterminable, proportion of their time cutting and selling firewood. Since most families harvest their own *leña* from the *monte*, there is no market for firewood in Teachive. Homes in Masiaca, especially those of *mestizos*, are usually in need of firewood, so the *leñeros*, as they are called, have a small market there. They also sell to several Masiaca breadmakers, who heat their ovens with wood. Some brick kilns in Masiaca also require firewood, so much that their requirements are beyond the ability of single woodcutters to supply. The *leñeros* sell what they cannot peddle locally to commercial buyers from Huatabampo and Navojoa, who range through the area in large trucks buying cut firewood from individuals. The current rate is between eight and ten pesos a *carga* (burro load), and a good cutter can cut three or even four *cargas* a day.

Without exception, every family in the village cooks with wood, even those with stoves. The pressure of so many people cutting firewood has greatly reduced the available supply, so the cutters must range far and wide to find a source. Children from the village are regularly sent into the *monte* to find firewood and daily children emerge from the thornscrub dragging branches behind them. Villagers keep a sharp eye wherever they walk for burnable sticks. Men riding bicycles will stack a stick or two on their luggage rack on the way home from work or from the store.

Supplies near the village of the most desirable firewoods, *brasil* (*Haematoxylum brasiletto*), *mezquite* (*Prosopis glandulosa*), and ironwood (*Olneya tesota*) are exhausted. Large stake-bed trucks regularly pass through Masiaca from the north laden with stacked firewood destined for Navojoa and Huatabampo. This demonstrates that local folk are in direct competition with city dwellers for supplies of firewood. No new trees are planted. Regeneration of living trees is slow. The point of diminishing returns has already been reached. Vicente feels that in his lifetime the long tradition of firewood-cutting, whereby a man and his burro venture into the *monte* and return with a load, will come to an end. The problem is not confined to Teachive, for all of Mexico depends on firewood or charcoal for cooking and her once magnificent forests have been leveled or severely reduced in the face of the wood-cutter's or lumberman's ax. The deforestation creates additional soil erosion and loss of soil resources for the community as well. Vicente frankly discusses the problem. "You should have seen how many big trees we used to have here in the *monte*," he says without bitterness. "Now there are only a few small ones or those that are no good for firewood. There is plenty of *to'oro* (*Jatropha cordata*) but it is good for very little."

Brickmakers (ladrilleros)

Six men from three families have formed a small brick manufacturing operation in the community on the west side of the arroyo. At times the enterprise causes some disturbance because of the large fires, the sometimes choking smoke, and the noise on nights when the kiln is fired. The earth-moving operations leave gaping holes. Still, most residents seem content to let the men earn a living. A titter swept through the village on the day that a dead dog was tossed into the kiln for fuel. Otherwise, the operation is uneventful. The bricks are produced by mixing clay soil and water and pouring the thick mass into a mold, then drying it in the sun. The dried bricks are carefully stacked and formed into a large kiln, then fired for 36 to 48 hours, the longer the time, the stronger the brick. Most of the bricks are sold in the Masiaca area. Some are bought by buyers from Navojoa. One of the entrepreneurs has a truck, which he contributes to the enterprise. The men estimate that they are able to clear about 50 pesos each per day for work that allows a good deal of camaraderie and periods of relaxation.

Firing the bricks requires large amounts of fuel, usually firewood. The stock of easily accessible *leña* on the community's lands has long since been depleted, so the *ladrilleros* have located a source outside. A *ganadero* (cattleman) not far from Teachive is in the final stages of clearing the forest and planting buffelgrass on his many thousands of acres. The bulldozers pile the felled trees in long mounds called *chorizos*. For a modest sum, the rancher allows the *ladrilleros* to cull firewood from the *chorizos*. Thus, the destruction of the forest provides firewood for the brick kilns. Obviously, this is a short-term source, for the supply will be spent in a very few years. Other brickmakers in different locations use diesel oil, spent lubricating oils, and even tires and garbage to fire the kilns. Neighbors find this a source of irritation, as the black, pungent smoke fouls their living area. The brick manufacturing enterprise of Teachive has a most uncertain future.

Over a period of years brickmaking operations also produce borrow-pits, excavations from which the clay is removed. As the clay is extracted, these holes enlarge and become neighborhood nuisances, filling with trash and offal. In a recent storm one of the pits, perhaps ten meters square and two meters deep, filled with water. One side then overflowed, initiating a tiny channel in the process. This channel soon became an arroyo and just like that a new eroded ditch running down to the arroyo was created, initiating an erosive process which threatens to cut far back into the middle of the village. In the rainy season, the quarries fill with water and are generally unsightly and provide breeding grounds for mosquitoes, so in the long-term the operation will face questions that arise in larger towns when conflicting land uses occur.

Still, brickmaking itself has a strong future. *Mestizos* believe that a legitimate house, one in which they can declare pride of ownership, must be (1) owner-built, (2) made of brick walls, and (3) framed by concrete foundations, pillars and headers reinforced with steel. It appears that bricks will be in great demand for many years.

Brickmaking is a curious and subtle example of a non-Mayo cultural influence ultimately working to the detriment of the community. Put differently, the industry represents a short-term gain and a long-term liability. The traditional adobe used by all families until recent years is not especially transportable, for the adobes are very heavy and fragile. The massive adobe bricks must also be plastered over rather soon after emplacement, or they will begin to erode from rain and wind. Adobes are not structurally suited for buildings of more than one story without great effort. The fired bricks (*ladrillos*) are more rigid and durable, hence capable of being transported. A house made of *ladrillos* is capable of more than one story, an important social message. (Men will often deliberately leave rods of reinforcing steel jutting from the finished first-story columns, an implication that they intend to construct the socially prestigious second story at a later date.) Adobes are viewed as the building material of poor, low-class people, that is, Indians. The bricks serve a *mestizo*, not a Mayo function, and are a *mestizo* drain on a Mayo resource. The *ladrillo* houses represent a selling off of an *ejido* resource, as the increasing number and size of the gaping borrow pits will testify.

On the other hand, adobes are dried in the sun and their production is hence far less energy-intensive. They are better insulators against heat, cold, wind, and noise. An adobe house is more solid and more permanent. Even children can make them. Their manufacture has virtually no undesirable effects. They are an indigenous building material, and, as such, they are stigmatized.

Bricklayers (albañiles)

Six men from the village work as bricklayers. *Mestizos*, and, increasingly *mestizo*-ized Mayos, prefer homes built of fired brick held together with mortar, the structure stabilized by concrete foundations, pillars, and bond beams, all reinforced with steel. *Mestizos* consider traditional adobe construction and roofs of pole, a cross-hatching and dirt, to be inferior and a sign of poverty. New home construction in Masiaca is usually of the *mestizo* style. A few houses in Teachive are also built of fired brick. In all likelihood new houses will tend to be of brick and concrete as more younger families find the traditional Mayo values unrewarding and a hindrance. The future of bricklaying is bright. Sufficient new construction has taken place to provide fairly reliable employment for these men, who earn forty to fifty pesos a day.

Cattle raising

Seven men in the village devote most of their energy to raising cows. In spite of the increasing cosmopolitan sophistication of Teachivans brought about by television, telephones (there is one in the village), and exposure to large cities, the number of cows owned by an individual is still the most popular index of that person's relative wealth. When I ask Vicente about the relative affluence of an individual, his immediate response is in terms of the number of cows he or she owns. (Affluence in housing is measured by having a house of more than one story; general affluence is measured by the number of cows one has). Nearly every family has at least one cow, although in some cases this applies to extended rather than nuclear families. Vicente, for example, had one cow at the time of this writing. Earlier he had possessed two. One died inexplicably.

Altogether, Teachivans own more than 400 cows, based on an actual count, owner by owner.[20] Numbers for individuals range from 1 cow to 50, with the median number of cows at 10. In periods with more rainfall, this figure would probably be at least 10 percent higher. It varies from the official 1995 figure of 228, which is published by the state department of cattle improvement (Secretaría de Fomento de Ganado). That count lists ten Teachivans as owning bulls; the actual figure is double that. The same registry lists Teachivans as owning 60 goats, but the actual number is in excess of 500. One man alone owns more than 50 goats, and the name of another man owns 40 burros is not even on the list.

The published number is compiled by a cattle inspector stationed in Masiaca, who laboriously fills out a form that includes the name of the owner, the brand, and the number of cows, bulls, calves, heifers, horses, mules, burros, sheep, goats, and pigs. The completed form is filed with the secretariat in Hermosillo, where I found the report. When I read to Vicente the numbers of cows claimed by owners in Teachive, he found many of the claims amusing, and some quite surprising. One owner had fewer cows than he reported. A good half of the fifty owners listed owned more cows than they had reported. One reported eight cows, when he owned at least twenty-five.

I asked Ramón Féliz, the *mestizo* inspector in Masiaca, about the discrepancy between the official record and the actual number of cattle. We sat on the porch of his busy home, where we were repeatedly interrupted by men passing by in trucks inquiring about the price of cows on the hoof. Ramón knows personally all of the cattle owners of Teachive and roughly how many cows they truly own. He rolls his eyes and accepts their word as to the size of their herds. He smiled tolerantly at my inquiry. "There are two reasons for the variation from the report," he explained.

> The official numbers are low for two reasons. First of all, ranchers, especially ranchers with small numbers of cows, do not trust the government under any circumstances. They would prefer that the government not be aware of how many cows they actually have. The people around here are small-time cattle-raisers. Usually they have fewer than 30 cows. Almost always they report fewer cows to me than they actually have. All the inspectors know this.

The second reason for the discrepancy is that the official registry of cows includes only cattle raisers who have registered their brands. To have official sanction for a brand is a pain in the neck and expensive. The owner must travel to Hermosillo— that's a six-hour bus ride. There they have to draw and list their brand, and pay fees and taxes at several agencies, four, I think. Registration is such a nuisance that many who own only a few cows never bother to register their brand, even though they have one, and even though the law is clear that each owner must have a brand. If the officials find out you have cows and no registered brand, they will give you a big fine.

I spoke at length with a Teachivan who owned a few cows and had a brand that was unregistered. He was reluctant to register it. A year later, after he had heard of some penalties assessed against another rancher who had failed to register his brand, he reluctantly made the pilgrimage to Hermosillo and enrolled his brand.

The state agency uses the data from inspectors to estimate actual stocking rates in Sonora. The underreporting (ubiquitous in the state) means that the state significantly underestimates the rates of overgrazing on Sonora's pastures, particularly those of marginal utility, such as the Masiaca grazing lands. The state then estimates its potential beef productivity from the underreported figures and publishes ever-higher goals, which in turn lead to ever-increased overgrazing.

Because there is no meaningful limitation within the *comunidad* on the number of cows permitted, the common pastures are severely overgrazed. During the spring, when all vestiges of grass are gone from the upland pastures, cattle scrounge for any materials they can find, sometimes even eating cactus and agaves. During this time many leguminous trees shed their mature bean pods; each day a small crop drops to the ground. These are eagerly devoured by cattle, burros, goats, and sheep. The fallen beans were the salvation of livestock during the drought of 1996. Had the area been sowed with buffelgrass, most cows would have died. There is no new grass in the arroyo, for whatever little growth occurs there is nibbled off by goats and sheep before it is long enough for cows to devour. Grasses, never prolific in thornscrub, are nonexistent in the hot, dry months. Historical records are absent. A close examination of the *monte* suggests that the root mass of whatever grasses once flourished in the area has long since vanished. Vicente recalls extensive stands of grass between the trees and shrubs of the *monte*, that grew tall when it used to rain. Now it doesn't rain enough to support grass, he laments. The cows, in their desperation, have chewed and stamped away at the roots of these perennial upland bunch grasses, denuding the landscape of its bottom story. The constant pounding from the cows hooves also severely compacts the soil in the adjacent thornscrub, so that when the rains come, the first moisture tends not to penetrate the soil. It runs off, carrying soil particles with it. The pastures yield less each year, more of the topsoil of the uplands is washed into the watercourses, and more livestock starve in times of no rain. Indeed, an examination of soils and arroyos in the vicinity of Teachive following the great storm of September 1995 revealed disturbing increases in soil loss and arroyo cutting from that one storm. Three weeks after the hurricane of September 1996, no grasses were to be found near Teachive. The lowering of the arroyo bottom has also increased the gradient of tributary washes, augmenting the velocity of the runoff and proportionally exacerbating soil loss. The arroyo at Sirebampo, where local men mine sand for sale to outside operators, was similarly affected. The channel and bottom were similarly degraded, and a marked increase in channel cutting was occurring in side washes as well.

Some *comuneros* say a great deal of damage was done to the range by the 1950s drought and that it never really recovered. Graciano Leyba and his uncle Blas from Jopopaco told me how it was before that decade of drought: "We raised cows before the fifties. We sold milk and cheese as well as meat. At one time we had 150 cows here. But the drought came. It killed many of our herd. We had to sell the rest. Some were killed on the new highway and the railroad [which runs near Jopopaco] as well. Since then, we haven't regularly owned cows. Maybe it is just as well. We raise crops instead, at least when it rains, and we can make better money from crops than the others can from cows. Or we could, if it would just rain."

One man claims to have 30 cows, all of which run free range on the common lands. This seems like a lot, and, indeed, given the amount they eat and drink (cows require an average of one hundred liters of water a day in hot weather), it is, so he should be rather well off. The stock are not purebred. They are of *raza mixta* (mixed breeds), usually of Zebu and Brahma with a healthy infusion of ancient mongrel *criollo* blood thrown in. More tender, purebred stock do not fare as well on the trampled pastures of the *comunidad*. Another fellow stated bluntly, "*Nuestra vaca no es buena*" (Our cows aren't very good). The cows of Teachive are usually sold as calves when they are weaned at the end of their first year. They will bring between $100 and $200 US on the market if the owner is lucky.[21] The actual return is considerably less, for the beef is of relatively low quality. From the market price the owner must subtract the costs of vaccinations and any medicines and commercial feeds the cow has needed during its short life, plus seven dollars in transaction taxes and fees. So even if he were successful in selling thirty calves at full price, his net receipts would hardly put him in the category of the wealthy, except by Teachive standards.

By all measures of range vitality—recruitment of new forbs, residual grasses, low soil bulk density, high grass or plant diversity, and preponderance of perennial grasses and forbs—the pastures of Masiaca *ejido* have reached a state of catastrophic overexploitation. The pastures will yield less each year, more of the topsoil of the uplands will be washed into the watercourses, and more livestock will starve in times of no rain.

The cattle of the community are not raised for subsistence or local consumption. Little cheese is made (unlike in the past, when cheese was widely produced and formed an important source of dietary protein). Only Poli Tajia and one woman now make cheese for sale in the town—from goats' milk. The milk from heifers goes to feeding calves so that they will gain weight faster and bring in more cash when they are sold, shortly after weaning. Cows are strictly a commodity and the Masiaca cattle industry represents mining the soil for sale every bit as much as if a mineral were being extracted.

Since the cattle use common pastures, they carry a brand to permit identification. Even those who own but a couple of cattle have their own brand and are frequently proud of it. Vicente, for example, has only one cow, and still he has a brand. Another man has no cows and still he has a brand. The owners usually have a clear idea where their stock are at any given time. Men (and, to a lesser extent, women) love their cows and consider them money in the bank.

El aguaje is the most important watering source for cows. People also use it for bathing and watering other livestock. The irrigation project, Los 35, uses it as the intake point for its irrigation canal. Without *el aguaje* the cattle population would certainly drop drastically, for nearly all of Teachive's cattle depend on *el aguaje*, especially during the late spring drought when other parts of the watercourse will sometimes dry up. No other similar natural body of water exists within the *comunidad*, or, for that matter, within many miles of the *comunidad*.

Goat raising

There are at least fifteen herds of goats in Teachive, ranging from five to more than fifty animals. It is difficult to estimate the economic significance of the herds, since, while some are sold, others are kept for breeding, others for milk, others for meat, and still others as pets. In some cases, more than one family (all related) owns the herds, which may be tended by the grandchildren of the owners. Goats bring a more uniform price on the market than do cattle. Their diminutive weight makes them less an investment than a resource readily convertible to cash in emergencies. The Masiaca cattle buyer also purchases goats. He comes to the village with a portable scale, weighs the animal, and pays cash. If Vicente were to sell all his animals he would receive less than $200 US. Policarpio Tajia, Vicente's brother, has a herd of fifty who are herded and guarded by two dogs whose abilities are noteworthy indeed. The dogs drive the goats gently into the *monte* in the morning and bring them back in the afternoon, allowing the herd to make a detour at *el aguaje* on each sally. The lead goats wear bells, so their clanking sound can be heard well into the distance. Policarpio treats his animals well, for they are worth more than $1,500. He milks the lactating does each day and produces cheese. He also works in the buffelgrass warehouse with Vicente when seed is available.

Teamsters / equipment operators

Five men work from time to time driving trucks and tractors, primarily in the fields around Huatabampo. Since the need for their services varies with the stage of crop production, they are not consistently employed. Their wage, fifty pesos a day, indicates their higher level of skill. Even though only one truck in the community is locally owned, there is considerable prestige associated with obtaining a driver's license and being acknowledged as one who can drive. For the present, the Mayos of Teachive seem cognizant of the great expense associated with owning and operating a vehicle, and they have not made the transition to greater mobility. Indeed, it was a special treat for doña María Teresa Moroyoqui when she rode in the University of Arizona's Chevy Suburban to the *fiesta* at Las Bocas. She had never before ridden in an air-conditioned vehicle and found it most amazing, which, of course, it is.

Mexico is home to great numbers of public vehicles, vans, and trucks. Buses connect even the tiniest of pueblos, and large amounts of commerce are carried on directly out of trucks, which make up an even higher percentage of roadway traffic in Mexico than they do in the United States. This proliferation of trucks and buses in Mexico gives rise to substantial employment opportunities, and bus and truck drivers are held in rather high esteem in terms of the macho index (I have never seen a bus or truck driven by a Mexican woman in southern Sonora). The lack of vehicles in Teachive (and in most of the villages of the *comunidad*) deprives young Teachive men of this employment opportunity.

Seed collectors

An indeterminate and varying number of men work collecting buffel-grass seed. Following the rains during the spring and the fall, the grass produces heavy seed heads. Workers march through pastures or, more frequently, along and through the tall grass on the median of highways, running specially constructed cutters on which collecting bags are mounted. They sell the filled bags to commercial buyers. These harvesters are a common sight on Sonora's highways. The pay for this work can be quite good, as high as 130 pesos a day ($18 US). Normal earnings are about one-half that amount. The higher-paying jobs require that the men be gone from home for extended periods and be willing to follow the ripening seed heads, which take them as far from home as Santa Ana, three hundred miles to the north. They must also pay for their room and board. Away from home, they tend to spend more money than usual on beer. This work is of relatively short duration, so it is not reliable year-round. Teachivans also express anxiety about their personal safety under these working conditions. One man reported that he was threatened by other workers if he did not turn over his money to them. He subsequently returned to Teachive and ceased collecting buffelgrass seed.

Seed baggers

Six men, most of them relatives, including Vicente, his brother, and a son-in-law, work in a small seed-bagging operation in Masiaca. They shovel and sift buffelgrass seed that has been delivered to the warehouse by collectors. The cleaned seed is then packed into large bags and stored for sale in the region. The work is unpleasant and the workers are subjected to an ongoing inundation by clouds of minute plant parts which are irritants to skin, eyes, and lungs. On windy days, the work is difficult indeed, and the workers experience great discomfort in the choking chaff. Their pay is between thirty and thirty-five pesos a day. Some of the same men who work gathering the seed work in the seed-bagging plant. The work is also seasonal, lagging by several weeks behind the collecting of the seed, and ending at a correspondingly later time.[22] In times of drought, buffelgrass produces no seed heads, so there is no work.

Miscellaneous work

One young man works steadily as a carpenter's apprentice in Navojoa. He departs by bus from Teachive on Monday morning, visits his home on Wednesday afternoon, and returns again late Friday afternoon to spend the weekend. He is paid fifty pesos a day. He must provide his own tools. Because homes in Mexico are constructed of concrete and brick and not of lumber, carpenters are far fewer in proportion to the population than they are in the United States, and they are viewed as craftsmen, a status the young Teachivan hopes to attain.

Two brothers took advantage of a sudden boom in construction in Las Bocas and adjacent Camahuiroa. They make forty to fifty pesos a day mixing and pouring concrete. The work will stop as quickly as it started.

Another young man works in a *talabarteria* (leather shop) in Masiaca, which is a regional leather center.[23] He makes *huaraches*, leather sandals. His pay is between thirty and fifty pesos a day, depending on his production. The work is sufficiently close to cowboy activity that it carries with it an aura of *machismo*. In addition to making *huaraches*, shoes, and saddles, the shops buy pelts of mammals, snakes, and lizards from whoever brings them in, fashioning them into fancy belts that are snatched up by would-be cowboys. Especially popular are belts of boa constrictor and armadillo.

One resident is a schoolteacher. He is married to a *mestizo* woman, and his family's standard of living is the highest in the village. He owns an automobile and maintains an evaporative cooler on his house. He also enjoys considerable esteem because Mayos view education as the key to gaining better economic position and better access to justice. His counsel is regularly sought on legal and political matters.

Two women in the village work as live-in housekeepers/maids for wealthy families in Navojoa. (Having a live-in maid is a status symbol in Mexican culture. Indian women are thought be especially desirable for this type of work because they are said to be passive, obedient, neat, and undemanding.) The two women live in Navojoa during the week, a distinct hardship for one, who has six young children cared for by their grandmother. The women are paid 150 pesos a week ($20 US) plus meals. Their employer also provides them with gifts and used clothing for their families. This work is psychologically trying on the women, who feel a strong traditional duty to their husbands and families and experience feelings of self-doubt about their work. They have found no alternatives.

Men in the village, especially younger men, are constantly seeking employment. They may pick up temporary construction jobs (as occurred following the devastation produced by Hurricane Ismael), such as repairing roads, bridges, and public buildings. During regional cattle roundups on adjacent ranches they may also find employment as cowboys for a few days, assisting in brandings, castrations, and inoculations, or in loading steers onto trucks for shipping. Their lives are a constant scrambling for day labor or seasonable jobs. One of Vicente's sons worked for a time as a cowboy near San Antonio to the north. He commuted by horseback, finding the work psychologically satisfying, even though the pay was poor.

Except for the teacher, no Teachive worker can reasonably said to be permanently employed, or to be defined by his or her work (i.e., *be* a carpenter, electrician, accountant, designer, farmer, etc.). In spite of their immense storehouse of practical knowledge, only the maskmaker and rope weavers are known for a particular skill or particular training.

A few young men know how to work leather into artifacts; one is learning carpentry; several know how to make rope. None falls into the category of skilled tradesman. The most difficult skills, those of weaving blankets and making tortillas, are mastered by women; the former pays little, the latter nothing at all. For the men and women of Teachive, life is an unending scramble to find work, any work at all.

TEACHIVE'S ECONOMY: INTERNAL AND EXTERNAL

Almost all of Teachive's money, then, comes from outside the community. If we were to examine each individual's employment record, we would find few, if any, market transactions between or among people of the village. There is little in the way of intercommunity economic activity. Virtually no one works for anyone else in the community, and no one provides significant goods and services for anyone else. Every once in a while someone in town buys a horsehair rope from Adán or from Lencho. One woman and one man occasionally make cheese. Ninfa, Cornelia, and Tomasa bake small loaves of bread, which they sell from house to house on occasion. One fellow is known to be a decent carpenter and takes orders for doors, beds, chairs, and so on, strictly on demand. Otherwise, he works as a *jornalero*.

When I compared Teachive with its ancient roots to the small, rural New Jersey town of my childhood, which was of similar size, I was amazed to find drastic economic relational differences. Whereas in my hometown nearly everyone provided a good or service needed or desired by others in the village, I could think of no instances of similar employment in Teachive. The one meaningful exception is the schoolteacher, and he is paid by the state, not by the community. Teachivans' economic destiny is, for all practical purposes, completely out of their hands. Their worldly goods increasingly come from afar. They do not produce for or serve each other. Theirs is a community based entirely on their historical relation to the land, not on economic ties to each other.

This is remarkable, but it should not be surprising. The history of indigenous peoples in Mexico is a history of superexploitation of their labor.[24] Without the possibility of developing their own internal economy, Mayos, as all Mexican Indians, became part of a huge reserve of labor. Lacking productive land and tools with which to develop a

capital surplus, they have remained at the margins of the world economy. There has never been an opportunity for any of them to amass
the capital necessary for removing themselves from the vast, anonymous pool of cheap Mexican labor.

The Mayos of Teachive live as peasant proletarians. Anchored to
their land, they are too conservative to develop a working class-con-
sciousness. Yet because they are economically adrift, they see themselves as destined perpetually to be wage laborers. Hardly a peasantry,
for they produce relatively little in the way of self-subsistence, they are
at the same time different from landless day-laborers, a distinction
they readily perceive. Their solidarity with each other lies more in their
identification with their community and their ethnicity than with their
economic relationship to the fields in which they work. The unity and
organization necessary to produce true social change is ever fragmented and pulverized by ethnic dissension and their realization that,
no matter how bad things are, at least they are better off than some
who have no land at all. And they have old family and ancient friends.

It is instructive to compare the Mayos' situation with that of the
French peasantry as described by Marx (1914):

> Every single farmer family is almost self-sufficient; itself pro-
> duces directly the greater part of what it consumes; and it earns
> its livelihood more by means of an interchange with nature than
> by intercourse with society. We have the allotted patch of land,
> the farmer and his family; alongside of that another allotted
> patch of land. . . . Thus the large mass of the French nation is
> constituted by the simple addition of equal magnitudes—much
> as a bag of potatoes constitutes a potato-bag. Insofar as mil-
> lions of families live under economic conditions that separate
> their mode of life, their interests and their culture from those of
> the other classes, and that place them in an attitude hostile
> toward the latter, they constitute a class; insofar as there exists
> only a local connection among these farmers, a connection
> which the individuality and exclusiveness of their interests
> prevent from generating among them any unity of interest,
> national connections, and political organization, they do not
> constitute a class. Consequently, they are unable to assert their
> class interests in their own name. (Marx 1914, 145)

How different the Mayos of the *comunidad* are from the French peasants described by Marx! Mayo peasants produce only a small part of what they consume, and as peasants they share objective class interests with other *jornaleros*. Yet they, like French peasants of a hundred years ago, are mostly oblivious to their class interests. Why? Certainly, in part, because of the despair, felt by most Mexicans, that meaningful changes in Mexican society are out of reach, primarily due to the phenomonal success in retaining power enjoyed by the ruling PRI for the last sixty years, and also because Teachivans cherish the illusion that their land will provide them with long-term security. As I have tried to demonstrate, much to my dismay, it will not. In fact, their "peasant" existence is, in Bernal's words (Bernal 1995, 805), "more like any other job, governed by capitalist discipline, rather than offering an alternative to it."

As if to verify Marx's remarks on the peasantry, the ruling PRI party is strongly entrenched in the Masiaca community. By contrast, the nearby *municipio* of Etchojoa, a strongly Mayo county, is the only *municipio* in Sonora that in 1993 elected a slate from the Partido Revolucionario Democrático (PRD), the center-left party of Cuauhtémoc Cárdenas. There are no large *comunidades* in Etchojoa.

Vicente Tajia Yocupicio (photograph by Thomas R. Van Devender)

Vicente Tajia and two grandsons beneath the tree called "El Jitón"

he Mayo church in Masiaca

Jesús Moroyoqui, "El Huírivis" (the Kingbird)

Cerro Terúcuchi, two kilometers north of Teachive

Jesús José (Che Che) Moroyoqui screening gravel for sale

Hauling water home from Arroyo Masiaca

Ninfa's house in Teachive, built ca. 1920

Gravel diggers in the arroyo

Vicente's neighborhood (his house is the middle building)

Driving cows through the village

CHAPTER SIX

The Family

꒰ I asked permission from doña Teresa and don Vicente to reside in their home during my work in Teachive. I wanted to be with a family on a daily basis, to see how they lived and interacted. Besides, there are no accommodations for visitors in the vicinity of Masiaca, and I had nowhere to stay. I had also become quite fond of the family and thought it would add greatly to my experience among the Mayos to be with people for whom I had affection. To my great delight they graciously agreed, showing me almost embarrassing hospitality. They cleared out one of the two rooms in their house and made it my room (I insisted they continue their activities in it). I also wanted to learn as much as I could of the Mayo language.

I described to Vicente the nature of my work and mentioned the fact that I would be referring to him and his family in the book. I offered to provide him with anonymity by changing his and his family's names and altering the location of their home. After some thought, he requested that I leave his name as it really is. That way, he thought, more people could come to know about the Mayos and what kind of people they really are. He also offered to help me learn the Mayo language.

This arrangement was perfect for me. Tucson is a ten-hour drive from Teachive, so I could leave Tucson early in the morning and eat dinner with don Vicente and doña Teresa that same evening.

I first met Vicente Tajia Yocupicio in Teachive in 1993. Plant ecologist Tom Van Devender had joined me in a project to identify the plants used by Mayo Indians. We had come to Teachive because no known systematic plant studies had been done in the area and I had 187 been there several times before and come to know some of the villagers. We explained to a couple of older folk what we hoped to find, and soon a dozen or so people joined us in a walk along the Arroyo Masiaca, identifying for us in Spanish and Mayo the common plants along the watercourse and what they were used for. As we ambled slowly along, Vicente rode up on his bicycle, dismounted and joined the procession, which continued for several hours. When the sun began to sink, he and one other man were the lone diehards. In subsequent visits we learned that Vicente has an extraordinary knowledge of plants, and of the surrounding towns and people as well. While not officially a *curandero* (curer), he is widely known as an authority on the medicinal uses of plants. We have come to rely heavily on his knowledge, even more on his enthusiasm and his extraordinary perceptiveness. I have come to regard him as a close friend.

Don Vicente has a quick, analytic, and relentlessly curious mind. He laments his lack of formal education, which, of course, was not available to him, for there were no schools in Teachive or Masiaca until years after his childhood. He is constantly frustrated by his inability to read (adult literacy programs have not reached Teachive). He is ever on the lookout for new plants and new uses of plants, routinely asking other men in the village if they know of any rare plants. He is ever curious about life in the United States and the general nature of the world outside of Sonora. He alone of the family members is sufficiently confident of our relationship for him to ask me what he considers to be sensitive questions about the United States. Do we really use the death penalty frequently? Do Mexican undocumented aliens get beaten up and killed? Do women really have important jobs? How do Americans manage to have such small families? Did I think his granddaughter would ever be able to find a job in the United States?

A pervasive, unasked question lurked in the background. I knew he had heard rumors and wanted to know, but was too polite to ask. Did gringos really eat children? I asked him if he had heard the ubiquitous stories and wondered about them. He said he had and he did. I assured him that we do not eat babies (it helped that I was a vegetarian and that he could clearly see, after many months, that I eat no meat). He seemed quite satisfied with my answer and appeared thereafter to have harbored no compunctions about entrusting his grandchildren to my company and even occasional supervision.

Vicente was born in Teachive in 1932. His parents were also born in Teachive, his grandparents in other places in the region variously, from the Río Fuerte (where many Mayos still live), the Mayo Delta, and San Antonio, a Mayo village fifteen kilometers to the north. The Mexican revolution had sputtered to an end hardly a decade before his birth, with outbreaks of rebellion in Sonora as late as 1927. The Mayos were then without lands of their own. Legions of Mayos had joined the revolutionary forces of Alvaro Obregón of Huatabampo, who was to become president of the republic. His Mayo troops were, to a large extent, responsible for his military success. Obregón was a charismatic member of the powerful and wealthy Salido family from Alamos, who used some of their vast holdings in the Mayo Delta to produce garbanzos for the world market. The Mayos sided with him because of personal loyalty and because he promised them the return of their lands (which his family, had, among others, appropriated for themselves from the Mayos).

The Mayo fighters returned home victorious to find that the opportunistic Obregón had betrayed them. The ancient oligarchic families, originally the object of revolutionary ire, had learned that they needed only to align themselves with the most probable victors to avoid expropriation. They not only held on to their land, they expanded their holdings as a result of the revolution. The returning Mayos found that their few remaining lands had been distributed to Mexicans and that their families had been dispersed all over the region. Many of them could not even locate the houses from which they had sallied forth in defense of the revolution. It was not until the administration of Lázaro Cárdenas, from 1934 to 1940, that distribution of lands to Mayos took place in the delta and along the Río Mayo and many *ejidos* were formed.

Vicente grew up with these memories fresh in his parents' minds and repeatedly communicated to him. The Mayos' passion to protect and live on their lands is best understood with this history of being uprooted and dispersed from their ancestral lands in the background. Only in the few ancient *comunidades* of the region can natives trace their ancestry on the land for more than a couple of generations.

Vicente's parents and his seven brothers and sisters eked out a living in great poverty on lands ambiguously federal and private, probably part of the original Masiaca community. Because they lacked titled documents, the lands were clearly not their own.[1] They were squatters and had been, as far as the government was concerned, for many generations. "We raised goats and a cow or two, and we sold firewood in Masiaca. In those days four *cargas* [burro loads] of firewood sold for one peso. Imagine that! One peso! It was enough to provide food for one day!" The long era of woodcutting and the countless hours spent wandering the *monte* in search of firewood immersed Vicente in the natural history of the region, for which he still retains an unending curiosity.

"I spoke only Mayo until I was sixteen years old. Then my papá moved us to the delta. I began to learn Spanish there." He still prefers Mayo to Spanish. He derives enormous pleasure in meeting Mayos from other places and chatting in *la lengua*.

In 1946 Miguel Alemán was elected president of Mexico. He abruptly reversed the strongly pro-peasant policies of the Cárdenas administration and moved well beyond the milder pro-private owner-ship orientation of Cárdenas's successor, Avila Camacho (1940–46). Alemán proclaimed that business must come before justice.[2] The gov-ernment's hope for economic growth lay not in distributing lands to the landless. True progress lay in the further enrichment of the already wealthy. Under Alemán's leadership, the Mexican government under-took a program of offering subsidies to large-scale growers and inves-tors to expand irrigated agriculture in the Río Mayo Delta and the contiguous valley of the Río Yaqui. The goal was to enable large growers to have more land, more dependable water, and better trans-portation facilities to market their crops. The industrialization of agriculture was a first step toward industrializing Mexico.

At that time, most of the delta consisted of a seemingly endless plain of thornscrub ribboned with fingers of ephemeral watercourses that flooded in summer and winter and were dry in other seasons. The Mayo Delta was a marshy fan, in the dry season a host of dry or trickling channels, in wet seasons flooded over thousands of acres. To accomplish the rapid expansion of agricultural production, hundreds of thousands of acres of thornscrub and delta marshland had to be cleared, leveled, diked, and ditched for irrigating. This clearing created great demand for agricultural laborers. The fields were to be irrigated by deep wells, installed at government expense.

At the same time, construction was planned and begun for Mocúzari Dam on the Río Mayo (its official name is Presa Adolfo Ruiz Cortines), some fifteen miles upstream from Navojoa. A network of canals was simultaneously constructed to convey water to the distant fields. The earth-filled dam was completed in 1951, and water deliveries began shortly thereafter. Concurrently, an extensive grid of paved highways penetrated the delta region to assist growers with their transportation needs. The government paid for the infrastructure and provided easy credit for *latifundistas* to undertake new plantings. In short, the government provided a new Cadillac and the keys to wealthy landowners, requiring them only to provide the gasoline and oil. No such assistance was provided to the original owners of the lands, the Mayos and their communities, or to the newly formed Mayo *ejidos*.[3]

Vicente's father was one of those who emigrated from Teachive to the coast to work in the new agriculture. "Our family moved to the Saucobe—it's a small town near the [Río] Mayo.[4] We lived there for nearly twenty years. I went to work right away. The other workers were all Mayos, so I didn't need to learn Spanish. Soon, though, I found it was important to be able to understand the orders of the *yori patrón* [boss]. Little by little I learned Spanish, at first just enough to understand the boss. But then I found I needed to communicate with the growing number of *yoris* in the area. I still don't speak Spanish very well. Living among *yoris*, I began to learn about them as well.

"One day General Román Yocupicio came through the fields. Everybody stopped to look at him. He was a Mayo bigwig. He was one of the owners of the fields where I was working, or at least they were in his name. Even *yoris* respected him."

Yocupicio was a Mayo from Choacalle who became a general in the Mexican Revolution (and leader of the federal military forces that helped quell a Yaqui uprising in 1926) and later governor of Sonora. Yocupicio is viewed by many poor Mayos as a traitor to his people, for as general and governor he consistently sided with the *latifundistas* and opposed the land claims of Mayos. As governor he presided over the final division of Mayo lands among *mestizos*. More prominent or affluent Mayos speak proudly of their association with him.

From time to time Vicente returned to Teachive. On one furlough, he married María Teresa Moroyoqui. He describes the wedding: "It wasn't anything, really. We were both young. I was nineteen and she was fifteen. We just decided to marry. It wasn't like in the old days when parents chose their children's marriage partners. For the ceremony we joined many other couples in the commissary hall in Masiaca. A justice of the peace read from some document in the Mexican constitution. That was it! In the old times, parents would not only choose who their children would marry. They would purchase the wedding clothes for them without revealing who their spouse was going to be! That hardly ever happens any more." Teresa, enjoying the memory piped in with comments.

Their first child was born in 1954 while they were living in the delta. When the work in the fields ended, many years later, after the last vestiges of thornscrub had been chopped down, the last concrete for the canals poured, the last ditches dug, and the last water gates installed, Vicente and Teresa and their small but growing family returned for good to Teachive. They lived for a while with his father-in-law. He and Vicente didn't see eye-to-eye on things, so Vicente built his current house in the mid-1960s ("Thank God," he says). Patrilocality and matrilocality in Teachive vary with the family.

Vicente has worked at various jobs in addition to clearing and preparing fields for irrigation. He has cut firewood, cultivated and harvested crops, punched cows, and worked as a consultant to gringo ethnobotanists, never able to accumulate cash, yet managing to provide for his large family and construct a good house. His best-paying long-term work has been collecting buffelgrass seed, work that took him far from home. Currently, he works sifting and bagging the seed in a warehouse in Masiaca for sale throughout the region. Two of his brothers and other relatives work with him as well. Occasionally he works as a *jornalero*. During the cotton harvest he journeys to the fields in the Mayo Delta to pick cotton, and he makes good money during that time, he says. He can pick more than one hundred kilos of cotton a day, more if it is a good crop. When the international highway (Mexico Route 15) was being expanded to four lanes, he worked on construction gangs until the section adjacent to the Masiaca community was finished. During the great 1996 drought, he was employed (along with many others) by the *municipio* of Navojoa, repairing and enlarging dirt roads in the vicinity of Masiaca at thirty pesos a day.

Today, five of Vicente's brothers and sisters survive. One brother lives in the house immediately to the north with his nine children. "Y todos comen" (all of them eat), Vicente says. Two other brothers live in Masiaca, and a fourth lives in Huasaguari, a Mayo village ten kilometers to the north on a tributary of the Arroyo Masiaca. A sister lives in a small town near Navojoa. One brother and one sister are deceased.

The house that Vicente built nearly thirty years ago is a curious mixture of Mayo and *mestizo* elements. It is constructed of adobe covered with plaster and then whitewashed, partially *mestizo*-, partially Mayo-style. The *portal* and part of the house, including the floors, are constructed from concrete, a *mestizo* feature. The roof is of beams covered with slats, covered in turn with mud and plaster, more of a Mayo design and a cooling influence. Don Vicente may have made a mistake in using so much concrete. It retains heat, making the house insufferably hot in summer. On stormy summer nights the two rooms, full of people, become unbearably stuffy. During the chilly mornings of winter and the few days of cold weather, the rooms are snug and most comfortable, however. In general, the house is solid and socially impressive.

The eight-foot-wide *portal* faces east, affording ample protection from the blistering sun throughout the hottest part of the day. During the early afternoon hours of summer, those accustomed to North American climate and air conditioning have few options but to sit and chat the time away while sweating profusely and thinking of cool mountain streams. I suspended a thermometer from the roof of the *portal*. The grandchildren had grand fun reading off the temperatures, which frequently exceeded 40°C (104°F).

The house has two rooms, used primarily for storage and shelter from rain and the chill of winter mornings. In the larger of the two, are a few family pictures, several cots, and a storage chest. A heavy, six-foot, motorless lathe seems to fill the room. José, the youngest son, some day hopes to equip the lathe with a motor. Then the room will become his carpentry shop.

The other room contains some simple shelves, a pole for hanging clothes, a small stereo (nonfunctioning), a sizeable collection of tapes of *norteña* music, several plastic flowers, and Teresa's treadle-type sewing machine. On one wall hung a modest mirror in a decorative frame, a framed picture of a saint, a print of Leonardo's *Last Supper*, and a picture frame with some family photographs mounted inside the glass.

On another wall hangs an old calendar depicting a heroic Aztec warrior. A single, bare lightbulb hangs from the ceiling in the center of the room.

The rooms are swept several times a day and dusted frequently. The door to each room can be locked with a hasp, and a window (no screen) with glass shutters can be locked as well. Iron gratings on the windows guard against uninvited intrusions. These iron bars deter more feral housecats than they do humans. They are also a status symbol, much desired by *mestizos*. Nothing in the home indicates that the household is Mayo and not *mestizo*.

I was most pleased to find the house and the yard free from mosquitoes and biting gnats. Other neighborhoods in the village are plagued with mosquitoes. Whether it is because the public health service sprays the arroyo area a couple of times a year to suppress mosquito populations or because the area is naturally free from the pests, I do not know. Houseflies are a different matter and are an unending nuisance. I considered providing the family with fly paper and fly traps. In view of the flies' role in assisting in the decomposition of animal manures, I thought better of the introduction and decided to endure the onslaught of flies. All the natives complain about cockroaches.

At the southeast corner of the house, extending as an L from the main structure, Vicente has built a small (8 × 10-foot) room, which now serves as the serving and storing kitchen. It has two shuttered windows, one facing the outside yard to the south, the other facing the inner yard to the north. The interior is cramped. A refrigerator, stove, two tiny tables, storage for cases of soda pop, a garbage bucket, and a small set of shelves leave no room, even for a chair.

One gains entrance to the house from the south, passing into the shady *portal* and immediately encountering the house's nerve center, the table, situated in the open air of the *portal*, and where someone is nearly always seated nearby. In the *portal* are a half-dozen chairs of various styles and ages, and the *tinajera* (tripod) in whose clutches nestles the *olla* (water jug). As is the case in almost every Mayo household, when a visitor arrives someone immediately scurries about to produce a chair.

At the rear of the kitchen, around its outside wall, Vicente has constructed a roofless cubicle that he calls the *baño*, literally the bathroom. It has a doorway over which can be draped a curtain. A large bucket and a scoop provide bathwater, and one can quite handily have a refreshing shower, as every member of the family does frequently, down to the youngest children. A drain hole in the outer wall leads to a trench that guides the gray water to one of the trees, that thus receives frequent irrigation. The privy is located some thirty yards to the rear of the house.

The house has two kitchens, the permanent, roofed structure built as part of the main house, the other a separate structure, some ten meters from the house, an enclosed ramada that contains an adobe stove and permanent tables. It is the *real* kitchen. Here Teresa cooks beans and tortillas over a wood fire. During many hours of the day, smoke filters from the ramada. Beans require a minimum of three hours' boiling time, so the fire must be constantly monitored. Preparation of tortillas is also time-consuming and requires years of apprenticeship to acquire competence. Teresa's *comal* (griddle) is a cast-off disc from a field cultivator. It works perfectly, although Vicente (and most men) speak nostalgically of the incomparable flavor of tortillas heated on the old clay-and-adobe griddles universally used before the metal discs became available.

Don Vicente and Teresa, like most Mayos, have a rather ambivalent attitude towards tortillas. Sonora is where most Mexican wheat is grown. Not coincidentally, it is also a bastion for flour tortillas. Sonorans, especially more affluent Sonorans, prefer flour tortillas, which are associated with Spain and Europe, and view corn tortillas, which are associated with Indians, as a necessity to be tolerated as food of the poor, for they are cheaper by far.[5] Indigenous agricultural peoples of Sonora (i.e., Mayos, Opatas, Pimas, and Yaquis) developed their own strains of corn and were eating tortillas long before the arrival of Europeans. For the most part, they continue to eat corn tortillas. Increasingly, they associate flour tortillas (which, incidentally are high in fat and made with nutritionally inferior white flour) with *mestizo* culture, much in the way white bread was associated with affluence in the United States decades ago. Thus, the Indians are increasingly inclined to eat flour tortillas as well.[6] Most older Mayos appear to prefer tortillas made from corn. Younger folk demand flour tortillas. Tortilla imperialism is rattling the foundations of Mayo nutrition.

Teresa addresses this situation by making both kinds of tortillas. Her preparation is even more complicated. Most epicures will agree that the best corn tortillas are made from corn flour hand-ground on a *metate* (grinding stone). Until thirty or so years ago, much of a woman's day was spent stooped over the *metate*, laboriously reducing the corn (previously soaked in a lime solution) to *nixtanal* by grinding with a stone *mano*, then patting the damp mixture into tortillas. In the 1940s, mechanized production of tortillas appeared in the cities and large towns, causing an immediate revolution in women's work. None of these benefits accrued to women in the tiny villages, where economies of scale precluded the installation of the expensive machinery. In the 1950s, hand mills appeared on the scene and women's labor was considerably reduced, accompanied by grumbling from the men who groused that tortillas made from the machine didn't taste as good.

Most of the households in Teachive have such a mill, usually permanently mounted on a stout stump. The parched corn is fed into the hopper and the mill is cranked; the moist flour emerges ready to be patted into tortillas. The mills are responsible for maintaining the upper-body muscle tone of many Mayo women.

In the last decade or so, a new commercial product has reduced women's labor even more. Called *maseca*, it is, quite simply, a packaged corn flour, purchased by the kilogram, ready for making tortillas. It is mixed with water, patted (or pressed) into a tortilla, flopped on a hot *comal*, and just like that, a tortilla is made. *Maseca* has fomented a small-scale revolution. Making tortillas now requires only a comparatively small portion of a woman's day. The resulting tortillas are thicker, heavier, and not as tasty as the more labor-intensive ones. Still, they are tolerably flavorful and the savings in labor are enormous. *Maseca* is now ubiquitous in the homes of the Mexican poor. The catch, of course, is that *maseca* must be purchased and, while inexpensive, it is still considerably more expensive than raw corn.[7]

So Teresa sometimes makes tortillas from ground corn, usually makes them from *maseca*, and frequently makes flour tortillas as well, for her two sons who still live at home are often there and they prefer the more *mestizo* (as opposed to Mayo) flour tortilla.

Although I have assured her repeatedly that I prefer corn to flour tortillas, Teresa continues to make flour tortillas available, convinced that as a "rich," educated *blanco* I must prefer *tortillas de harina* and only request *tortillas de maíz* out of politeness.

Tortillas and beans are the foods of the Mayos, and, along with squash and chiles, have constituted their dietary basics since time immemorial. As Vicente says, "In the morning we have boiled beans, at noon we have fried beans, then at night we have refried beans." And, always, there are tortillas and coffee roasted from green beans. I found this diet to be most agreeable, never, ever, tiring of this most basic and nutritious of combinations, especially because nearly always Teresa prepares a fresh salsa of chopped tomatoes, onions, chiles, and cilantro with a few drops from a lime plucked fresh from a nearby tree.

The Tajia-Moroyoqui household is one of two families in the neighborhood that owns a refrigerator. While small, this appliance represents a true luxury in any Mexican village, for even small refrigerators cost more than $400 US. Theirs was purchased from an itinerant salesman two years earlier, who arranged credit terms so that they could afford it. They planned on buying it as soon as electricity arrived at the village in the mid-1980s.

The refrigerator, which is opened and closed hundreds of times each day, is the basis for a tiny business run by Teresa. She purchases soda pop by the case from a distributor's truck, which makes the rounds of the village each week, and sells it for a minuscule markup. She also pours soda pop or juice into plastic bags and freezes them, selling the resulting ice, a favorite with children and adults alike. This microbusiness adds a small amount to the family coffers, perhaps enough to meet the monthly payments on the refrigerator.

The family also has a small propane gas stove, which is primarily used to boil water, for the bulk of cooking is still carried on in the outdoor kitchen. Tanks of propane gas are purchased in Masiaca, which usually adds another $10 to monthly expenses. In addition to payments on the refrigerator, the family's monthly bills include electricity (approximately $7) and water (approximately $5).

The family diet is varied, for occasionally there are potatoes, eggs, rice, a few vegetables and, from time to time, fresh fruit. After the summer rains, fresh greens supplement the diet. Mayos prefer to roast and grind green coffee beans themselves, producing a thick, aromatic, and satisfying drink. The beans are expensive, so they usually make do with instant Nescafe (which, with a slightly modified diphthong on the first syllable, means "it is not coffee" in Spanish).

The family purchases all its staple foods. On truly special occasions, a chicken will be sacrificed. The victim is usually captured at night while it is helplessly roosting in a tree. One of the young men of the house borrowed my headlamp one evening to do this. Chickens habitually choose one tree for roosting, and the Mayos accommodate their natural preference by constructing a small ladder to assist their ascent. The tree roost protects them from most predators, even owls, who find it difficult to penetrate the dense foliage. Their perch makes them an easy snag for hungry people, and once a month or so, one of their numbers winds up in the pot.

A young buck goat will also be slaughtered from time to time (does are raised for their milk and the offspring they produce), and the meat is made into tacos, *birria* (a stew heavy with shredded meat), and *cocido* (a stew with potatoes, corn, and vegetables). From time to time someone shows up with a small bag of beef, to the delight of all the family. The consumption of meat has a cultural significance, since meat, especially beef, is associated with affluence and *machismo* in the Mexican, especially the Sonoran-ethos. The "good life" involves the consumption of beef. The more you eat it and the more other people know that you eat it, the more respectable you are. Mayos, of course, are not immune from this message, and since they are involved in raising beef themselves, they understand well the significance of being able or unable to afford red meat. Vicente is also fond of *huacabaqui*, a traditional Mayo stew of beef, potato, corn, and onions. Every few days, Teresa serves him a bowl of the stew with a small, bony chunk of meat, which constitutes his meat ration for the period.

When I visit, I always bring along *maseca*, beans, rice, sugar, green coffee beans, oil, cheese, and fresh fruits and vegetables. I once asked Teresa what special treat I might bring her from the city next time I visited. She thought for a while, then said, "Well, David, a cucumber and some lettuce would be very nice."

Daily household expenses are difficult to calculate with precision due to the varying number of mouths to feed. Teresa regularly prepares the morning meal for four (herself, Vicente, and two sons). Throughout the day she also prepares food for up to ten additional children and grandchildren, often with assistance from a daughter and a granddaughter. Basing my calculations on the average consumption of the extended family, the daily outlay is eight pesos for two kilos of corn and corn flower, eight pesos for one kilo of beans, five pesos for one kilo of potatoes, two pesos for one kilo of rice, four pesos for one kilo of wheat flour, two pesos for coffee (instant), four pesos for a kilo of onions, four pesos for a kilo of tomatoes, two pesos for chiles, one peso for herbs and vegetables (cilantro, *epazote*, squash), three pesos for a half-dozen eggs, two pesos for a quarter-liter of oil or shortening, one peso for picante sauce, salt, baking powder, and boullion, and two pesos for sugar, making the total per day forty-eight pesos.[8] In addition, the family consumes several soda pops, which are purchased at two pesos each wholesale from a delivery truck that passes once each week. (Teresa sells them for two-and-a-half pesos each.) This is the basic diet. It varies little throughout the year, except when local cactus fruits ripen, and during the harvest of cash crops such as garbanzos (which are eaten fresh—boiled into a soup), chiles, and watermelons in the delta. Any meat consumed is an additional cost, and on the few occasions when it is available, it is eaten in tiny portions. Vicente's normal daily wage is thirty-five pesos, which he earns by winnowing and packing buffelgrass seed at the packing plant in Masiaca. Obviously, the family cannot survive on his earnings alone. The purchase of corn and beans alone eats up half his income.

Teresa and don Vicente maintain a small garden. It produces mostly herbs, such as cilantro, *epazote* (*Chenopodium ambrosioides*), oregano, mint, and basil, all of which are nonpalatable to livestock. Vegetables stand no chance in that center of insect and animal herbivores. Usually, though, some product of the *monte* is also available, especially in August and September, when *pitahayas* (*Stenocereus thurberi*) mature in enormous numbers. In these months, all the villagers take to the *monte* and the hills and bring home buckets of the delectable fruits, which are consumed in great quantity, and with good reason, for they are as delicious as any fruits available anywhere. During those weeks of satiation, the yard is littered with the skin and spines of the harvested cactus fruits. These are swept up and fed to the family pigs.

Vicente and Teresa have several trees in their yard, the most prominent of which is a large cotton tree, maintained for the excellent shade it provides. A rather short tree (its height will never exceed five or six meters), its virtue is derived from its spreading habit and large leaves. By pruning, propping, and tying the branches, the family has coaxed the tree to produce dense shade over an area twenty feet in diameter, although its lower branches are barely a meter and a half from the ground, so that it is necessary for me to stoop to walk under it. Its shade is greatly appreciated. From time to time, people are ill and will spend the entire day on a cot in the tree's worthy shade. During the hot days between April and November, many animals also find refuge in the cool darkness.

Also located in the shade of the cotton tree is the water spigot, the source of the family's water. This valve is connected to the pump station in the arroyo. One of the grandchildren is assigned the chore of keeping full the earthen *olla* (jug), which rests on a *tinajera* (three-legged stand) in the *portal*, full. Into this *olla*, family members dip a cup that is suspended from a hook just above. The porous clay keeps the water cool and refreshing, even on hot days. From the hose bib a stream of water runs many hours a day, irrigating the household's increasing forest of vegetation. In addition to the water-hungry cotton tree, the yard also hosts a rapidly growing *ceiba* tree (Ceiba sp.), planted by Vicente, which will one day grow to be as enormous in size as the availability of water will permit. There is also a grapefruit tree, which produces modest-sized fruits, a native *júvaro* (*uvulama, Vitex mollis*) transplanted from the arroyo, which will yield a popular cherry-sized fruit that tastes like a plum, and a hedge composed of various smaller trees. In 1990 Vicente planted a native *amapa* (*Tabebuia impeteginosa*), hoping one day to enjoy its burst of pink winter flowers. To date, it has not bloomed. A bougainvillea vine has made modest progress in the *portal*. Its prospect for flourishing is not good, as it endures a constant beating from the human and animal traffic that passes. Beyond the rear fence of the house grow many mesquites, which become larger as one approaches the arroyo, located perhaps fifty yards from the rear of the house. The yard between the front of the house and the street, though fenced, is bereft of vegetation and seldom used for anything. The space appears to be symbolic, a reflection of the Mayos' fondness for open space in their villages.

Various family members are responsible for the care of the livestock. Teresa is the general supervisor. One or two pigs are kept chained to mesquite trees behind the rear fence to limit their marauding and wandering tendencies. They spend their lives there, wallowing in muddy troughs watered daily by the children. The pigs are fed nearly all the family's wet garbage, plus some corn slop. Goats and sheep are taken during the day to the *monte*. They are rounded up each night by Vicente and corralled to protect them from coyotes, marauding dogs and, perhaps, hungry neighbors. Two of Vicente and Teresa's grandsons, young lads, milk the goats for their own use. One holds up a rear leg to keep the doe from bolting, while the other squeezes the udder, directing the stream of milk into a pail. They are especially fond of the fresh milk as an after-school snack. The doe seems quite willing to let the boys milk her and makes no attempt to run away. Two small dogs also are attached to the family and protect the household with great ferocity, though they are treated rather cruelly by family members. Chickens feel free to enter and leave the house and experience only a mild scolding when they jump to the table surface in search of forage.

With Vicente's assistance, José Juan, the youngest son, bought a horse, hardly more than a colt. Within a year it had filled out into a decent animal for riding. It is usually kept in a corral behind the house. (I say "usually" because one day I walked by the corral and saw inside, not the horse but a nearly full-grown calf, which is the property of one of Vicente and Teresa's grandsons.) José grooms the horse constantly and feeds it baled hay, in the hope that it will gain weight and not look quite so skinny. He has a saddle that he purchased in Masiaca (which is a regional center known for the production of leather goods). During his time off, he loves to ride the horse into the *monte*, all the while decked out in his stylish cowboy clothes. A truly handsome young man, he is reported to have female admirers in several of the villages.

José, from time to time, talks of emigrating to the United States to work as a carpenter. He has aspirations to economic success and finds the atmosphere of Teachive stultifying. At the same time, he plans someday to open a carpentry business in his home. José and his older brother Armando still live at home, although they are frequently gone during the week. Teresa waits on them devotedly. The young children also are at the beck and call of these handsome young men.

In the mid-1960s Vicente suffered a dreadful accident. "I was coming home from working in the *monte* one night when I ran into a *murue* that was leaning over the trail. I punctured my eye, right here. From the first, I couldn't see. The pain was terrible and it went on and on. Finally, after more than a month I went to the doctor in Navojoa, and he operated on the eye and took it out. So, now I have a glass eye. It doesn't fit well, so, as you can see, I have to wipe my socket all the time." I asked him if his employer helped defer the expenses of the operation. "No, he's a *latifundista*. He wouldn't give me a cent, so I had to live with the pain until I had the money for the operation." I asked Vicente if I could use some of my expense money to help get a new eye. Within a week, he had a new one.

Even with only one eye, don Vicente's vision is acute and his ability to discern subtle things in the environment is remarkable. In our countless meanderings in the *monte*, his uncanny eye for minute detail never ceased to amaze me—and I have supposedly normal vision. "Ay, David, *mira*" (Oh, David, look!), he will say, and point to some plant or animal sign or an interesting natural feature of the landscape. He is also eager that I should have sufficient quantities of representative specimens of plants with medicinal properties. He will dig up roots on the spot, lop off branches, hack away bark samples, collect flowers, harvest handfuls of leaves, pull off fruits, all with the certain knowledge that they will be of great use to my research. My accidental meeting with Vicente was one of the fortunate events in my life.

María Teresa Moroyqui Zazueta married don Vicente in 1951. She was born in 1937 in Choacalle, the adjoining village to the south. Teresa has six brothers and four sisters, all but one of whom is alive. All live in the Masiaca area, mostly in adjacent Choacalle, where their widowed mother still resides. Teresa's mother, also named María Teresa, is reputed to have been the best rug weaver in the area. She has given up weaving in recent years because it is physically demanding. She is an engaging conversationalist and an important source of information; it is easy to understand why her daughter is also such a remarkable woman.

Teresa, as Vicente's wife is called, has not woven in recent years for the same reason as her mother. An extremely thin woman, she suffers from arthritic joints and muscular aches brought on by incessant work. An older sister, Aurora, still weaves because she is widowed and must support a large family, including a son and daughter-in-law who live with her in great poverty. Aurora's weaving is possibly the best of all that is produced in the village.

Teresa works unceasingly, harder than any man in the village, harder than any woman I have ever known. She arises at four-thirty in the morning to begin preparation of all the food for the many hungry mouths (never fewer than six, often many more) she must feed, and, quite literally, she hardly sits down all day. After having spent several weeks in the house, I grew accustomed to eating alone with Vicente, as their custom requires. One evening I was surprised and delighted when Teresa sat down to partake with us. We needed company, that night, she said, a twinkle in her eye. When I convinced her to take off an evening and attend a Mayo *fiesta* at Las Bocas, twelve miles away, with Vicente and me, she casually pointed out that she hadn't been away like that for several years. When I inquired why she didn't leave more often, she pointed to her grandchildren. "I have them to watch after, David. What would they do without me?" One morning she arose at 3:00 A.M. to prepare food for her youngest son and iron his clothes. I asked her if it wasn't a bit tiring to do all the work. She said only, "It's my duty."

Teresa has a deep mistrust of cameras and for many months declined to have her photograph taken as part of the ethnobotanical project in which I was involved. She viewed me with skepticism at first. Fortunately for me, she had become acquainted some years previously with Barney Burns, an anthropologist and importer of native art, who purchased many of her blankets. His good public relations worked to my benefit, for before long she was willing to chat about a wide variety of topics with me. As for her hyperactivity, don Vicente brings her herbs for teas, including locally gathered salvia (*Hyptis albida*), the tea of which he says helps her relax. Don Vicente is one of Teresa's greatest admirers.

Teresa has strong feelings of community with the other women of Teachive. When I drove her and Vicente to Huatabampo one day, I looked in the back seat where she was seated just as I left their home. She was lying down on the seat. "Are you all right?" I asked, concerned that she might already be carsick after just twenty yards of travel. "Yes, I am fine," she answered in a muffled voice. "She's just hiding," Vicente assured me. Later, though, he confided that she was ashamed to be seen riding in a fancy vehicle and didn't want other women to think she was better than they were, putting on airs, acting important, conceited. Rather than convey that impression, she chose to conceal herself in the back seat.

Teresa also spends many hours laundering clothing on a ribbed washboard. (Her brother-in-law's family next door has a wringer washing machine, the envy of the neighborhood.) She oversees the welfare of chickens, goats, sheep, and two pigs, all of whom must be kept track of, especially in the searing heat of May and June. Grandchildren assist her in this. The children attend school much of the year, and they have games to play and other activities that tend to interfere with animal husbandry, so they must constantly be reminded of their duties. When

Teresa issues an order, she is obeyed. She is especially solicitous about the care of her youngest granddaughter, Lupita, age three, who is the darling of the family. The child is most active, wandering about the yard and across the street in an endless search for new and interesting situations. The older children have strict orders to watch the toddler, who still manages to escape and putter off into the unknown.

With all her responsibilities, it is not surprising that Teresa seldom goes to bed before midnight. How she is able to maintain this schedule of only a few hours of sleep each night is a mystery. Apparently, she has been a person of boundless energy all her life, although at times her face shows a deep weariness. A mother of unending kindness and love (she waits on Vicente most diligently), she is well-informed on many topics. She reads (she was fortunate enough, she reports, to have attended two years of schooling) and matches her husband's curiosity about the world beyond the village.

Doña Teresa is rather more confined to her home than other women in the village. Her limitations are somewhat self-imposed, for Vicente does not appear to place heavy demands on her to limit her activities to the home. She unquestioningly provides him with three meals a day and carries out all normal wifely chores, assuring that his needs come before hers. On those rare occasions when she has no family or grandchildren to watch after, she ventures into the village to visit, sometimes walking the two kilometers to Choacalle to chat with her mother or her sister, who live there.

The women of Teachive occupy an ambiguous power position. They are expected to be good wives, and hence they are usually to be found at home, ensuring that their men and children (and often grandchildren) are taken care of. On the other hand, nearly all the women are responsible in one way or another for a significant portion of the family's income, and, to that extent, control their destiny. Most of the women roam the village at will, visiting with neighbors or venturing into the periphery of the village in search of firewood. In this regard, they exhibit more freedom than is normally seen in *mestizo* towns. It may be that the long absences of husbands, working as *jornaleros*, combined with the long, shared history with their neighbors provides a certain liberation otherwise not available to rural Mexican women. Or it may be that Mayos have different traditions about women's roles. Still, the women's role in family power structure within the family is hardly equal to that of their husbands. In spite of the long hours many of the women spend weaving, their husbands do not cook, clean, and iron for them. Several of the women were intrigued but skeptical when they heard how the women of a Oaxacan village had successfully lowered the homicide rate in their region by organizing and closing down saloons and prohibiting men from wearing firearms (Greenberg 1989).

When in 1996 Teresa suffered a severe injury to a finger, she was unable to manipulate her hand for several weeks. Vicente was forced to do much of the work she normally did. He confessed to me that he was astonished to learn how enormous her responsibilities were. "David, I had no idea how much work she does. Good heavens, all the things she has to do. At the end of the day, I was so tired I had to go to bed, and still many things were left undone."

All family members find it hard to believe that my wife bought and drives her own truck and has her own career, all without my permission. Vicente has reconciled his own experience with my reports that American women raise children alone, travel on their own, and frequent bars alone, without loss of respect. All this is empirical evidence for the widely held Mexican view of North American women as loose hussies.

Teresa and Vicente have eight children, ranging from forty-two to twenty-one years of age. The couple chose their children's names by consulting an almanac of saints' days, a *mestizo*, not a Mayo, custom. Two of the children live in Masiaca, the rest in Teachive. All work at least part time. The eldest daughter, mother to six young children herself, is employed as a maid in a wealthy household in Navojoa. She takes the bus to Navojoa on Monday, returns for the night on Wednesday, leaves for Navojoa once again early Thursday morning, and returns home on Friday afternoon. She is allowed one week of paid vacation each year. When she gave birth, in 1995, she was granted an extended leave of absence, without pay. While she is at work, her children live in their grandparent's house, often sleeping there, even though their home is only a block away. All of the grandchildren except the youngest two, born in 1993 and 1995, are in school. The oldest, born in 1982, and all the others help Teresa with chores, and assist in watching the other children as well.

Another of the couple's daughters lives nearby and has a son who is three years old. A third son has married and has two young children.

He has built his own small house immediately to the east of his parents. (It is of traditional *mestizo*, not Mayo, design; he has apparently absorbed the *mestizo* custom that requires every man to build his own house.) His wife, Vicente and Teresa's daughter-in-law, has Mayo ancestry and understands but does not speak the language. She never leaves home, seldom venturing from the immediate vicinity of her tiny dwelling with separate kitchen and washroom. Their two children are frequently to be found in the Tajia-Moroyoqui household as well.

Another daughter of Teresa and Vicente lives on the east side of the arroyo. She also frequents her parents' house. She has four children, nearly grown, who work as *jornaleros* and aspire to better, *mestizo* occupations. Her husband is a PRI party activist. He is a hard worker who spends considerable time in the *monte* and brings home snakes he has killed, dries and pulverizes the skeletons, and sells the powder, which is reputed to be a tonic.

Two sons, ages twenty-three and twenty-one, are unmarried and still live at home. They are employed in the Mayo Valley and hence gone most of the week. Vicente and Teresa seem to have excellent relationships with most of their sons- and daughters-in-law. They feel that one son-in-law fails to provide adequately for his family.

The result of all this mingling of children and grandchildren, plus a sprinkling of neighbors and cousins, is a lively and usually happy household filled with the exuberance of childhood. The only quiet times during the day occur when the children are in school and their parents are working. At these times, doña Teresa, her granddaughter Lupita, and perhaps a daughter or daughter-in-law are the only people about the home.

For all the physical closeness of the children, occasions in which the family members join together and chat are few or none. The sons do not appear to fraternize, nor do they engage in significant open conversations with their parents. Since the family does not join for meals around a common table, table talk hardly exists. In short, the lives of the Mayos of Vicente's households (and others I have observed) are private and not openly shared with others, even close family members. Any such communications take place in private, and privacy hardly exists. This paucity of intimate conversation is rather strange in Vicente's case, since he has frequently mentioned how he loves to talk and how much he values the endless hours of conversation we have had.

The family's lack of discussions also contrasts greatly with the Seris, hunter-gatherer indigenous people to the northwest, who spend much of their time sharing and commenting on experiences and events. One of the facets of Protestantism attractive to Mayos is the warm treatment and atmosphere of equality that participants find once they are "in the fold." Drunkenness often provides an emotional outlet for repressed sentiments. Revival meetings seem capable of producing the same goal, at a cheaper price.

When they speak to each other, Vicente and Teresa often speak in Mayo in rather hushed tones. All of their children understand Mayo. Several seem reluctant to speak, replying in Spanish to my stumbling inquiries in Mayo. In the presence of their grandchildren, the couple uses Spanish. None of the grandchildren appear to understand any Mayo. Don Vicente expresses the hope that his youngest granddaughter will grow up to speak Mayo and will be well educated to boot. Another grandson, age eleven, shows a remarkable familiarity with plants and animals of the *monte*. In my presence one day, Vicente told the lad that it was high time he began to learn the Mayo language.

Two of Vicente's working sons contribute some of their wages to the household. Multiple incomes help maintain the Moroyoqui-Tajia household, thus verifying the general principal of consolidation, as outlined by Greenhalgh (1985): among the poor, a large family can be economically advantageous over a small one.[9] At this stage in their lives, their children produce a net surplus of income, usually the case when boys (and occasionally girls) reach the age of fourteen or so and begin work as *jornaleros*. The pooling of their resources is a temporary situation that will change when the young men marry and leave the home.

This pooling makes it possible for the family to live somewhat better than many of their neighbors, including buying some appliances. The two grown sons are an important labor asset as well, available to work on house repair or other improvements, or to help in the *monte* with Vicente's cow. In times of scarcity the numerous children can diversify their efforts, resulting in a greater probability of bringing in income where others in the family may fail. With daughters nearby, Teresa also has assistance in any difficult chores or a backup if she becomes ill. Having several grandchildren in the home can also be an asset. One morning Vicente sent two of the boys off to a field several kilometers away to glean dried beans from a failed crop. They returned at the end of the day with several kilos of beans worth more than twenty pesos. No one else in the household could have done the job without leaving other work undone.

The long-term consequences of large families, of course, are more complicated, for the younger sons will have to live elsewhere when they marry or face crowded conditions in the home. The numerous off-spring tend to marry young and reproduce quickly and often, unlike what happens in other cultures where marriage and reproduction may be delayed. The net gains from consolidation are short-lived. Consolidation inevitably leads to division: large families also gravitate against acquiring permanent family wealth, for bitter disputes may arise over inheritance division, or the wealth will be split so many ways that each share is insignificant. For the short term, though, the large family has proved to be an asset.

On the other hand, large families reproduce the patriarchal ethos that maintains women in subordinate roles and engenders a lack of community consciousness.[10] Women's roles are defined rigidly and early. In the home, women and girls are assigned the general role of taking care of men and boys. Young girls, never young boys, are expected to nurture younger siblings, providing the bulk of care for toddlers and small children. Older girls and women care for the children and, most important, the men by cooking, sewing, laundering, cleaning, and listening. When the village pump broke down during the June drought, the arroyo was alive with women and girls washing laundry on rocks. Some older men, but mostly women, fetched water on a *palanca* (yoke); few boys were to be seen. Every additional baby reinforces this model, from which few escape. In Teachive, girls five years old begin caring for toddlers or even babies, while older sisters in turn care for them, and so on up or down the line. Girls also assist with kitchen jobs. Boys are assigned duty watching goats, collecting eggs, milking goats or sheep, going to the store in Masiaca, or gathering wood. Occasionally, they are assigned spot tasks watching children. ("Run and get your little sister. She's out in the road.") They are never assigned general child care. Older boys play at sports such as baseball and soccer, play the guitar, ride burros or horses, or simply run through the village playing a variety of games. Girls watch. When boys reach ten years or thereabouts, they are deemed to be old enough and responsible enough to ride a bicycle into Masiaca to buy something at the store. Girls stay at home. Boys are allowed to attend the *fiestas* and be on their own three or four years earlier than girls.

At the same time, the *mestizo* society's exaltation of the family has been at the expense of the greater society. Numerous negative consequences of the patriarchal family structure occur in Mexico, where social consciousness often appears not to transcend the family. In the Tajia-Moroyoqui household, one frequently encounters the stoic resignation that is common among the poor in Mexico when social injustice occurs. The deep-seated belief that nothing can be done to change the existing order pervades the Mayo ethos, as well as the culture of Mexico. Unless you are a member of an influential family, you cannot hope to be treated with any semblance of justice.

A popular rationale for having large families is also the perceived need for children to care for elderly parents. To the question, why it is necessary to have large families, the programmed rhetorical response is, "Who will take care of you when you are old?" Realistically, though, because pensions in Mexico are a pittance, when they exist at all,[11] and because no one is able or desires to "put something away for a rainy day," parents must view children as an old-age, long-term care insurance policy. It is not simply selfishness that leads to this consideration. It is a logical conclusion based upon Teachivans' perceptions of the society around them. Vicente and Teresa have no resources to fall back on when they can no longer work, except for their children and grandchildren and a tiny pension.

While all of the children and grandchildren attended or will attend primary and secondary schools (grades 1–6) in Teachive, none of the children have attended preparatory school (equivalent to high school). The nearest high school is in Navojoa. Tuition is inexpensive ($8 per month), but attendance requires either that the youth be boarded during the week, an expense the family could not possibly afford, or purchase bus tickets (at $2 per day) and commute. For girls to attend the preparatory school is unthinkable in Teachive. A technical school at San Pedrito provides vocational training in such subjects as animal husbandry, bee culture, and the fundamentals of agriculture. It attracts most of the youths—boys and girls—ages twelve through fourteen, in the region, for they have nowhere else to go. An older granddaughter of Vicente and Teresa attends *la técnica*, a majority of whose pupils are girls. No one from the village has attended college.

Rituals and traditions are mostly absent from the household. Indeed, were it not for the Mayo language spoken among older family members, one would be hard pressed to ascertain that the household is Mayo. Vicente visits many nearby communities during their *fiestas*, often going alone. Holy Week is an exception, for Vicente and María Teresa both love the festivities and traditions that transpire in the village.

During the cool of the early evening of one Maunday Thursday, Vicente and I were chatting, as we were wont to do, when he jumped up and excused himself, explaining that he had to erect the cross. Soon he returned with a large digging bar and a small, ancient cross, some two feet high and eighteen inches across. His next-to-eldest son, Luis, who is seldom seen in the house, soon appeared, and together they dug a hole in the back yard a foot deep and six inches across. Vicente explained that they kept the cross stored behind the kitchen. "Tomorrow is Good Friday, the day the *fariseos* will come by and knock over the cross, David," he explained. "They come to every house in the neighborhood."

That evening he and all the adults in the village were as excited as North Americans are on Christmas Eve. We stayed up late laughing and telling stores. He and Teresa told me with great delight of past ceremonies, and of how when they were little their parents would erect the cross as well. Before we turned in for the night, Teresa told me in a voice uncharacteristically excited, "Tomorrow is the loveliest day of the year."

The following morning we awoke, as always, well before dawn. The penetrating thump of the *fariseos'* drum and the heavy tinkle of their *coyoles* (small bells suspended from a thick belt) could be heard *en la otra banda* (on the other side of the river) as the *fariseos* went from house to house. Before long they appeared at the north end of the village, gradually working their way toward Vicente and Teresa's house. Presently, they came running into the yard, their grotesque masks covered with brightly colored ribbons, their *coyoles* jingling and their *téneborim* (cocoon rattles wound around the legs) swishing with a most agreeable sound. One of them trailed the others. He held out a large tin can, hoping for contributions to help offset the costs of the *fiesta* and their travel through the *comunidad*.

The children were all awake by now and ran excitedly behind, watching in delight as the masked men, beating, pounding all the while, pried at the cross until it was torn from the ground and lay flat on the earth. Then they were off and running to the next house, visiting all the houses in the villages that had crosses, which meant nearly all the homes except for the *evangelistas*, who, of course, would have nothing to do with what they viewed as a pagan blasphemy.

When the *fariseos* had faded into the distance and we could no longer hear the throb of the drum, Vicente walked to the arroyo and cut several large branches of mesquite. He wove them into a handsome arch over the cross, which he placed on a bench. This canopy, he explained, provided the cross with shade and gave it protection for Easter weekend. When the children returned from chasing after the *fariseos*, they gathered the delicate yellow blossoms of brea (*Cercidium praecox*) and sifted them over the cross until it appeared to have been covered by a golden snow. The cross appeared similarly adorned in most of the traditional households of Teachive that day.

Next, Vicente returned to the arroyo and cut a large branch of *citavaro* (*Vallesia glabra*). He proceeded throughout the yard and gently switched each child and adult with the branch, saying "May sickness and harm stay away from you." I asked him to switch me as well.

Vicente speaks of all Teachive adults as equals. He respects some more than others. He has little bad to say about anyone, nor does anyone appear to have anything derogatory to say about him. In his eyes, all the people are equals. He treats others and others treat him with camaraderie and deference. The same is true with Mayos from other villages, even those he has met for the first time. His attitude towards the *mestizos* of Masiaca and Navojoa is quite different. With them, he adopts an air of tentativeness and a touch of submissiveness. He moves through the world of *mestizos* with caution and hesitation.

Vicente and Teresa shun politics. Their hero is Lázaro Cárdenas. They find ex-President Salinas disgusting. They are suspicious of the PRI, INI, the judicial police, bureaucrats, and all city slickers. They adored the Japanese peace corps volunteer who visited them nearly every day in the mid-1990s. They use the social security health services when they need them. Otherwise, they would prefer to have no truck with the government. They are baffled as to how anyone could be an atheist. They love to hear stories of faraway places and odd people and are curious about life in the United States. They can recall few exciting events. They doubt that anything will happen that will change the predictable routine of their lives. They hope for more rain and cooler temperatures. They hope their grandchildren have it better than they do. They do not complain about their poverty. They do not complain about anything and accept their arthritis and rheumatism, which they lament with dignity. They wonder what the future will bring. They doubt if it will be much better or much worse. They hope *yoris* will not succeed in eliminating Mayos.

CHAPTER SEVEN

*The Entanglement:
An Opinionated Analysis
of the Broader Picture*

𝒴 The tranquil appearance of village life in Teachive is only superficial, for the town is slowly sinking into an economic abyss. The community's dependence on the outer world is slowly ripping apart its centripetal fabric. The "outer world" becomes less and less inclined to respond to local conditions as a consideration for what its workers will be paid and is indifferent to the requirements of their way of life. Instead it is international markets that determine the price, just as blankets can be woven by Persian women more cheaply, garbanzos and chiles can just as well be raised in Africa as in Sonora, and the bidders on commodities are indifferent to their origin. In southern Sonora, Masiaca is an economic satellite of Huatabampo and Navojoa, the urban centers where most of the owners of delta lands live. Those two cities, in turn, are underdeveloped satellites of the even greater metropolis, the United States, which benefits the most from Masiaca's underdevelopment by receiving a steady stream of low-priced agricultural products, wrested from the earth by the highly exploited labor of the Masiaca *comuneros*. Teachivans have tolerated the exploitation because their lands provided a margin of subsistence. The fruits, vegetables, firewood, lumber, handicrafts, livestock forage, and religious items harvested from the *monte* made it possible for the *comuneros* to survive while working for low wages.

I have described the material conditions of the village of Teachive and placed them in a historic and regional setting. I have examined the land of the *comunidad* and how the natives use it to sustain themselves. Now I wish to place all of this in a national and international perspective and speculate on the sources of the economic and social hardships faced by the *comuneros*, the larger forces that impinge on the lives of a people who have survived as a people for centuries.

If anything symbolizes the economic decline of Teachive, it is the gradual disappearance of the villager's semisubsistence way of life, their intimacy with the surrounding *monte*. The rich thornscrub that encircles the community is slowly being eaten, cut, trampled, and bulldozed away. Teachivans' familiarity with the diversity of life forms and their many uses is vanishing along with the thornscrub. In spite of the long list of items used by natives of Teachive to carry on a semi-subsistent way of life, the community is decreasingly semisubsistent. Women's role in gathering and preparing wild resources is decreasing, and with it their independence. Men's wandering in the *monte* is losing its productive potential and is being reduced to that of simple protectors of herds that could just as easily be tins of vegetables on a production line.

Why is Teachive so dependent on the "exterior" world for its economic survival? Why couldn't it carry on a bartering tradition with other towns in the region, as it did for decades, and maintain a regional subsistence? The environmental degradation of the *comunidad* brought about by a drying climate, falling water supply, chronic overgrazing, and overharvesting of wild products is one reason. The further question of why Teachive must resort to dependence on the world of agribusiness and tourism for its survival must be addressed. No one answer is possible, of course, and I have tried to suggest some explanations for why the *comunidad* is so limited in its productivity. Several more general factors are also undeniable.

I have no desire to construct a romantic defense of a utopian, precolombian communal system that was supposedly corrupted, then torn apart by the insidious intrusion of disease and European influences. As I have previously noted, even before contact the Mayos had been engaged in intermittent warfare with their Yaqui neighbors, and probably with other adjacent groups as well. I do not wish to infuse Mayos with a morality superior to that of other peoples of the region, indigenous or not, nor do I wish to suggest that if left to their own designs and in control of their own resources, they could achieve an idyllic, productive, harmonious way of life.[1] In their own way, Mayos are as bigoted, narrow, and ethnocentric as most other peoples. The reverse of the myth of the noble Mayo has been the traditional view of Mayo "backwardness," their lack of upward mobility in *mestizo* culture. This view, which suggests that Mayos and their culture are a hindrance to progress and they should either accept assimilation into the mainstream of the Mexican economy or resign themselves to their poverty and cultural deterioration, as a penalty for their backwardness, is equally misleading.

I do not wish to take sides, either, in the arguments between those who, on the one side, denounce *comunidades* and *ejidos* as feudal or precapitalist institutions that prevent the reasonable economic progress of the nation, and those who, on the other side, proclaim the two social institutions as Mexico's only hope for social progress, economic development, and individual fulfillment. The facts are clear: many, if not most Mexican *ejidos* and *comunidades* are economically troubled and, without major structural change, they will self-destruct, leaving the nation with an even greater problem of rural unemployment and demoralization than it already has. The problems vary from place to place, but they always share many of the same economic ills that bedevil Teachive. I cannot pronounce as to whether the problems I have outlined are inherent to *comunidades* and *ejidos*, or are simply a result of poor administration, inadequate attention, and corrupt governmental supervision.[2] The Masiaca community, as I have demonstrated, is laden with conflicts and faces economic duress unknown in its history, due to the ecological degradation of its land and Mexico's financial mess. When I suggest the reasons for the community's decline, I am not suggesting that it would not have faced massive problems even had it been located in a developed nation. Nor do I wish to portray Mayos merely as hapless victims of European conquest or heartless capitalist expansion. I wish to point out the forces leading to Teachive's and Masiaca's deterioration as a first step in arriving at a process by which such communities might survive despite the conflicts of the surrounding society.

LEGACY OF ALIEN CONQUEST

Some of the elements of the economic decline of the Masiaca *comunidad* were assembled at contact with Europeans, brought about by the diseases introduced by the aliens. As Reff (1991) has demonstrated, these catastrophic pathologies physically undermined the native peoples and thereby severely weakened their social systems, forcing them (including the Mayos) to resort to hastily rigged social and political arrangements. While we know nearly nothing of Masiaca in the sixteenth and seventeenth centuries, we can infer that whoever the inhabitants, they were devastated by the same diseases.

Part of what the Mayos were forced to accept as a consequence of their decimated numbers, whether due to military threat or their desperation for a cure, was Christianity, and along with it, a cultural absolutism in which the absolute was the Romanocentric view of the universe. The Euro-version of *Roman* Catholicism (italics intentional) was the basis for absolute government; Catholic doctrines constituted absolute truth; Romano-Iberian-Catholic mores formed the basis of absolute morality. The values of the Roman Empire, passed down in the writings of Virgil (originator of the prototype for the idea of the "white man's burden"), Marcus Aurelius, and Constantine, was codified into an absolute value system and forced upon New World indigenous people with no possibility of rational discussion concerning its correctness or appropriateness. Euro-values and religion constituted required manners. Anything indigenous was deemed inferior, backward, barbarian, or demonic. This is the view the natives had to accept; to demur entailed denunciation as a sorcerer or Satanic force and the risk of death at the hands of a ruthless enemy whose overpowering arsenal included a vastly superior killing apparatus ranging from firearms to smallpox-contaminated blankets.

Whether this new totalitarian system was administered by the iron fist of the Spanish armed forces or the velvet glove of the Jesuits made little difference. The conquerors asserted their imperial ideology and the natives were forced to accept it or death. The forced option meant a slow unraveling of the old ties of custom, language, and ethos in the face of a battle whose outcome was determined at the outset. At no point can we say clearly that *here* the Mayos were conquered by Europeans. Nevertheless, the conquest is nearly complete. All that remains of the traditional Mayo culture are a fading conservatism, decreasingly suspicious of *mestizo* society, the linguistic stubbornness of older Mayo speakers, and precolombian *fiesta* rituals and traditions. These are not powerful defenses against an international conspiracy to produce uni-

formity of consumption patterns and ideology. Mayos still assume
that God, Jesus, the Virgin, and most of the saints are white.

LOSS OF ABORIGINAL LANDS

In a process that began with the Spanish conquest and continues
today, Mayos have been systematically removed from their original
land base.[3] Aboriginal lands have been fragmented into far smaller,
dispersed units, and families have been ruptured and scattered, pre-
cluding the maintenance of a cohesive Mayo consciousness. This process began with the arrival of Europeans and continues today.

The lands restored to the Mayos after the Mexican Revolution, as
ejidos and *comunidades*, represent only a fraction of the Mayos' aboriginal
holdings, and are not the most economically productive lands. When
lands have been returned to them, the Mayos have lacked the necessary
tools with which to make them as economically productive as lands
controlled by the Mexican landed elite. Even in Buaysiacobe, which
evolved from near-destitution in the early 1960s (Erasmus 1967) to
relative prosperity in the 1980s (O'Connor 1989), Mayos who own the
land for the most part do not farm it. Vicente often comments on the
great size of the Masiaca community and expresses his wish that there
were water available to irrigate. "We have so much land, David, but it
has no water, and so we produce very little. Imagine what we could do
with water like the *blancos* have!" I always wished to add, when he made
that remark, "Imagine if you also had the favoritism, subsidies, and
political influence possessed by those very *blancos*."

Government technical assistance, subsidies, and credit are nowhere
available to Mayos to the extent they are to private landowners (German E. et al. 1987). The systemic corruption that continues unabated
in Mexico reinforces the reign of a small number of immensely wealthy
men, who control the vast majority of the land, over an immense
number of the poor, who control only a small portion of the land. On
paper, Mayos control 39,000 hectares (97,000 acres) of irrigable land
through *ejidos* (German E. et al. 1987). As of the late 1970s, 80 percent of
Mayo *ejidal* farmlands were leased to private farmers, who possess the
capital and equipment necessary for preparing, fertilizing, planting,
cultivating, spraying, and harvesting, a practice becoming common
throughout the world. In such cases, actual ownership of the land is

meaningless, because the legal owner is literally separated from the means of production. The wealth generated in the fields of the Mayo *ejidos* flows into the hands of the already wealthy *mestizo* or foreign agricultural interests and the banks that serve them.

For example, an *ejidatario* from Buaysiacobe owns a parcel consisting of twenty hectares of prime irrigated farmland. He could never afford the equipment necessary to work it, nor obtain the credit essential for planting.[4] Instead, he leases the land for $250 a month to an agribusiness farmer who plants several crops a year. The fellow sometimes works as a *jornalero* on his own land.

While such *ejidatarios* may be said legally to own their land, they have no effective control of it. The farming elite of the Mayo Delta have no difficulty obtaining credit and have access to or own the necessary machinery (Barry 1995, 119).[5]

ABSENCE OF ETHNIC LEADERS

Vicente and other *comuneros* lament the absence of Mayo leaders in their midst. By leaders, they mean (principally) men of Mayo roots, with Mayo values, who possess the *visión*, the foresight, the political savvy, needed to represent the interests of the *comunidad* in larger Mexican society, leaders capable of looking beyond their immediate personal interest to the long-term improvement of the *comunidad*, leaders who can confront *mestizo*-ized society and blunt its influence while asserting Mayo influence.

In recent history, two sorts of Mayo leaders stand out. The first is the *cacique*, such as Román Yocupicio, who built an individual power base from Masiaca in the 1930s and operated from it, accepting tribute and doling out rewards based on loyalty and service to him, eventually becoming governor of the state. Few would credit Yocupicio with having advanced the social cause and well-being of the Mayos.[6]

The second sort of leader, unknown to most Teachivans today, but more common in the past, is the charismatic soothsayer, the evangelical prophet, the mystical misfit. Since some charismatic prophets in the 1960s, no one has stepped forward to lead Mayos as a group.[7] The following of such "prophets" was limited by their all-too-specific predictions, none of which came to pass. Neither type of leader has been effective at representing Mayo interests.

Both Crumrine (1977) and O'Connor (1989) point out that traditional Mayos value noncompetitiveness and scorn the accumulation of material goods. These Mayo virtues serve as disadvantages for "getting ahead," and undoubtedly shape a negative attitude toward "leaders," as people who will hold positions of power over others. Several Mayos have expressed a hope for a Mayo who will possess the traits necessary to bring power to the Mayos. None seem to admire the trappings of power associated with such leaders.[8]

The absence of leaders may be an expression of culture, an historical accident, or a legacy of the *porfiriato* (1880–1910) and the latter part of the Mexican Revolution, when anyone resembling a Mayo leader was arrested, detained, assassinated, shipped off as a slave laborer, or disappeared. Whatever the reason, the lack of leadership has hindered the Mayo community's ability to organize and to exert political force. The Yaquis, by contrast, with a more organized ethnic leadership and clear traditional leaders, are more effective at instigating their political demands, at being able to articulate popular goals, mediate internal disputes, and focus popular attention on political objectives.[9]

Still, the older Mayos, especially the men, tend to be steadfast in their desire to see non-Mayos (*yoris*) ejected from the *comunidad* ("We don't want them here," one seventy-year-old *comunero* stated). They form business relationships and even friendships with *yoris*, acquiesce in their political ascendancy, and maintain a stoic acceptance of *mestizo* domination, all the while cherishing a desire to have a pure Mayo homeland. At this point in their long history, Mayos still place ethnicity over class as the most important determinant in social cohesion. The younger Mayo men of Teachive, however, appear to be indifferent to the nationalistic torch that has been transmitted more or less unswervingly for nearly four hundred years. The women appear not to have an opinion on the subject.

I sense that Mayos are disposed to respond overwhelmingly to a leader offering real change and vision. It is doubtful that the Mexican government would ever permit such a leader to survive for long.

THE SPREAD OF INTERNATIONAL AGRIBUSINESS

As Teachivans paid higher and higher prices for imported corn and beans in 1996, they received only token increases in their pay to harvest fresh peas and garbanzos from the fields of the Mayo Delta. The peas went to the United States and Japan, the garbanzos to the Mediterranean. Other typical crops are tomatoes, watermelons, lettuce, and broccoli, all for export, and alfalfa and grain sorghums, for fattening cattle destined for Mexico City and abroad. A comparatively small proportion of crops are raised for local consumption, since returns on crops for export tend to run much higher than those locally consumed, and because the Mexican government promotes agricultural exports as a means of generating foreign currency to repay foreign loans (which are often needed to purchase basic grains for human consumption).

If the Mayos are asked which crops they would like to raise (for most men still aspire to be farmers), the answer is nearly always: corn and beans. Without water, they cannot harvest a crop, so they must sell their labor instead, and the going price of field labor is as internationalized as the oil trade. Nowadays, Teachivans are routinely saddened with news from the grocery stores: *maseca* has gone up again, beans are higher still, potatoes now cost three times what they did a year ago, and so on. Teachivans cherish no hope for improving their lot. A demand for their labor exists only because they happen to live adjacent to more than 100,000 hectares of fertile soils that lie only a few hundred miles south of an unquenchable market for the crops those fields grow. Many of the Delta's crops are alien to the Mayos.

The immense power of international agribusiness, so vast that national governments themselves are unable to control it, has rendered the small producer not only inconsequential, but also obsolete; it has relegated subsistence farming to the realm of nostalgic dreams. Even though small producers may be more efficient than large producers, that is, they produce more crops per unit of energy required for production (Pimentel and Pimentel 1979), conserve resources better (Netting 1993), and maintain production indefinitely, they do not fit into international commerce and, as such, are expendable and usually viewed with indifference or hostility by governments.[10] The neoliberal economists who govern world trade demand privatization of land and all the means of production, meaning that their economic models have no place for corporate communities.

Even among communities, the *comuneros* of the Masiaca community are not small producers in any classical sense. While Teachivans eat corn and beans grown in the United States, an increase in self-subsistence is clearly possible on community lands. Research might well indicate that ancient varieties of corn, long thought lost to Green Revolution varieties, can be raised in the *comunidad*, even under the present dry conditions. The Mexican government, in keeping with its neoliberal policies, has not promoted these possibilities.[11]

So, as remote and peripheral as the Mayos of Teachive may seem to the mainstream world, they are firmly embedded in international industrial mechanisms in which there are no longer farmers, only agriculture with owners and workers. The decisions about which crops are to be planted in the fields in which nearly all the men and women of Teachive work at one time or another, are determined more on the floor of the Chicago Board of Trade than they are in the homes of the owners in Huatabampo and Navojoa. The crops feed into hoppers of the industrial food production strategies of agribusiness that allocate the fruit of the land to the highest international bidders. Decisions about which crop to plant are made not on the basis of local or even domestic need. They are made on a day-to-day basis, as determined by international demand.

The government of Mexico over the last decades has retreated dramatically from its traditional attention to the agrarian component (*sector social*) of its economy, opting instead to enter Mexican agriculture into the world food system, which deals in food as it deals in any other commodity (Barry 1995). Food moves toward the highest bidder or the most powerful government, and food production systems are developed to fit into this enormous complex. That Mexico suffers chronic shortage of corn and beans is irrelevant to the question of what will be planted, except insofar as those commodities show up on computer screens as the highest potential revenue producers for those who control the land. International commodity prices are a factor in the pauperization of Teachivans.

RATIONALIZING THE CATTLE INDUSTRY

For as long as anyone in Teachive can recall, *comuneros* have raised cattle. Most think there were more cows fifty years ago than today. Vicente says there were many more because the pastures could support more. Decisions made in the 1960s by the Mexican government to "rationalize" the cattle industry, that is, organize it along capitalist lines, relegated Mayos to the market role of raising calves on pastures with marginal grazing potential. This slow transformation from subsistence grazing to commodity production has resulted in overgrazing and dependence on the whims of weather and the international market for beef and hides (Camou Healy 1991). Cows have taken on a different role in relation to economic production in Sonora.

Prior to the middle of the twentieth century, rural families kept cows for producing cheese and occasional beef for local consumption. Following a severe outbreak of hoof-and-mouth disease in the 1950s, the Mexican government decided that henceforward smallholders would be ideal for raising calves to be sold as part of a "rationalized" system of beef production. Calves would now be raised by small rural producers, "pre"-fattened by commercial ranchers, fattened by urban feedlot owners, butchered by "modern," "efficient," processing factories, and shipped worldwide to markets paying the highest price, usually the United States. To a great extent, this transformation of production has taken place, and Teachive is not exempt from the new capitalist strategy.

In the rationalized system, cows represent a commodity to be sold, not a subsistence resource for the community. Calves nurse until maturity, depriving the owners of milk and milk products, which they now purchase rather than produce. The Mayos now sell their calves, rather than their cows (usually), and have come to view cattle as a commodity in roughly the same way they view gravel. A calf is money in the bank. A cow is an endowment.

Big ranches abound to the north and east of the *comunidad*.[12] The government has provided subsidies to these large-scale ranchers, assisting them as they increase production by dismantling the native forests which were a natural form of wealth available to many, and replacing the forests with buffelgrass, a derivative wealth, accruing to the landowner and no one else. As of 1995 the Sonoran government offered to pay roughly 30 percent of the cost of *desmonte* (clearing of the forest) for ranchers who would convert their pastures to buffelgrass by providing the necessary machinery—primarily bulldozers—free. With that *desmonte*, an impressive array of potentially valuable resources, not the least of which is the watershed for such riverine systems as the Arroyo Masiaca, has been jeopardized or cashed in for a few cents on the dollar. No more graphic picture exists than a side-by-side comparison in late May of the Mayos' few skinny cows standing in their impoverished pasture on one side of the fence and the pampered stock of the *latifundistas* fattening themselves contentedly in deep grass on the other, while newly formed gullies lead from the *latifundista*'s land onto the Mayos'.[13] The beneficiaries of government largesse attribute their success to their skill and clever management and the Mayos' distress to their backwardness, ignorance, and ineptitude.

The effects of this change from subsistence grazing to market production are subtle. Greenberg (1989), in his study of a Oaxacan indigenous community, noted that the introduction of coffee trees as a cash-crop commodity has had a traumatic effect on the communities where they have been planted. The commodity value of coffee beans created competition, suspicion, sharp disputes over the ownership of trees, and conflicts among villages as well, where none had previously existed.

The change in the Masiaca community from subsistence production of livestock to commodity production of beef has yet to create obvious changes, yet as cows are gradually seen more in terms of their market value rather than as a family resource, conflicts over grazing rights and ownership cannot be avoided. Each cow now represents a known quantity of money which will purchase a known commodity.[14] An extra cow may mean the difference between having and not having a television, new clothing, an operation, or adequate food. If a neighbor is perceived as having a grazing advantage that will lead to acquisition of an equally coveted commodity, clashes over grazing rights cannot be avoided. Already, the clashes are appearing. One man and his father-in-law have forty cows, well above the reputed twenty-five permitted to graze free. He is said to have connections with the community leaders. His excess grazing is resented in varying degrees by other members of the community. More *comuneros* are demanding privately fenced pastures. Vicente one day pointed out to me the herd of a neighbor as we walked through the *monte*. "Look at the herd, how many cows 'poor' Lencho has. He pretends to be poor but has more cows than anyone else. He never helps anyone."

In another case, a woman recently entered into litigation with a neighbor over ownership of a cow. The costs of the litigation nearly equaled the value of the cow. Mario Soto has tried to fence off two small parcels and plant buffelgrass. He cannot manage his cows without more help from the government or from someone he would like to hire but cannot afford to pay.

RACISM

The historical racism of Mexican culture exalts light skin and hair and denigrates dark skin and black hair. The resulting culturewide scorn of Indians perpetuates a sense of inferiority in the Mayo psyche.[15] Yaquis and Seris, other Sonoran native peoples, have thumbed their noses at this racism, professing pride in being different and celebrating the use of their language, thus delaying their cultural decline. Mayos, for historic reasons, lack the tighter social organization of Seris and Yaquis and are less prepared to confront the demeaning attacks on their culture.[16] The absence of the Mayo language among the children of Teachive is not an isolated phenomenon. My research has turned up many individuals in the region who deny that they speak *la lengua* when, in fact, they do. This denial is surely related to the perceived social stigma associated with being an Indian. Don Modesto Soto professes to be puzzled by this tendency, yet his own grandchildren do not speak *la lengua*.

The maintenance of the Masiaca community as a gathering of individuals with common interests and shared history requires a common pride in the land and the traditions of the Mayo culture. The constant deprecation of the Mayo culture by non-Mayos is taking its toll on the cohesiveness and the sense of community of the *comuneros*. Vicente acknowledges that he would tend to have more confidence, other things being equal, in someone who spoke *la lengua* than in someone who spoke only Spanish. Yet, he adds quickly, in business he would rather deal with someone who spoke only Spanish, because such a person would probably be more knowledgeable and skillful in business, be better connected, and have better prices. Nevertheless, he thinks it is better that his children are all married to other Mayos. Had they married *yoris*, their expectations would have been greater. As an example, he cites *mestizo* weddings. *Yoris* are fond of fancy and expensive weddings and run up huge bills to impress other people, he says. And sometimes, in a mixed marriage, *yori* parents look down on the Indian as not worthy.

Evangelical Protestantism appears to be on the rise among Mayos.

It solves the Mayos' feelings of inferiority by affirming the brotherhood of all and downplaying racial and cultural issues. The evangelists exert strong pressure for converts to refrain from expressing traditional Mayo cultural manifestations. They overcome racism by obliterating indigenous behaviors.

OVERPOPULATION

Mexico's population growth is placing unprecedented pressure on its resources.[17] Exploding populations on ejidal and communal lands, especially in the absence of employment alternatives, increase the need to exploit the land's physical resources. The large families enjoyed by Mexicans, Mayos included, guarantee that many more Mayos, or people whose parents were Mayos but who no longer refer to themselves by that term, will be landless and poor in the decades to come. Teachive's population has increased from 194 in 1940 to nearly 600 in 1996. Since cows are the principle source of wealth, the added population pressure has meant more livestock pressure as well.

Women bear the brunt of the large families. They work unceasingly with hardly a day off for childbirth. The lack of reproductive alternatives for women is nowhere more dramatic than in Mexico. Reproductive choices are not available to most women; none are available in Teachive, which is probably moot anyway: birth control pills are not readily available to them either for free or for sale. Two Teachive men talked with me about birth control in the United States. They acknowledged that vasectomies were available free from government clinics. They doubted they could ever submit to such a procedure. Vicente, however, expressed a hope that his younger sons would have smaller families. Too many children created impossible economic hardships, he said.

Mayo men have, to some extent, incorporated the still-prominent *mestizo* view of women as creatures to serve men, to be kept pregnant and sequestered in the house. The model of women as submissive to men is reinforced continuously through television, radio, public advertising, and the church. Living near Vicente and Teresa is a young woman with two young children. Her husband forbids her to leave the house except to do chores in the yard. When the children are at school, she spends much of her day alone in the *portal* of their tiny house.

In spite of its rapidly growing population, the Masiaca *comunidad* still has huge acreages of land used solely for grazing and firewood cutting. Ester Boserup (1981) has published pioneering studies demonstrating that an increase in population can lead to an increase in agriculture intensification and concomitant increased productivity. Under her theory, increased population pressure on lands of the *comunidad* could lead to more intensive human manipulation of resources, thus increasing the lands' productivity. For a variety of reasons (primarily because of the difficulty of obtaining adequate water), this has not yet occurred in the Masiaca community. Increase in intensive agriculture or resource management only occurs, according to Boserup, if people cannot move from a poor and densely populated area to an area where resources are more plentiful. The out-migration of young people from Teachive (and from all towns in the Masiaca community and nearly all of rural Mexico) occurs because they perceive, probably correctly, that life in the cities holds a greater promise for escape from poverty than is likely by their remaining in the villages. Until they are convinced that they have little or nothing to gain by leaving the *comunidad*, intensive agriculture will probably not increase, according to Boserup.

> A growing population exhausts certain types of natural resources, such as timber, virgin land, game, and fresh water supplies, and is forced to reduce its numbers by migration or by changing its traditional use of resources and way of life. Increasing populations must substitute resources, such as labor, for the natural resources that have become scarce. They must invest labor in the creation of amenities or equipment for which there was no need so long as the population was smaller. Thus, the increase of population within an area provides an incentive to replace natural resources by labor and capital. (Boserup 1981)

There are ways by which the community could produce more and support a greater population. Water, through rainfall, surface diversion, or mining of groundwater, of course, is the limiting factor. The community's water resource is casually administered and only vaguely planned. The sole government-sponsored irrigation program is Los 35, an extensive rather than intensive form of productive development.

MALDISTRIBUTION OF INCOME

I calculate that the average family of five in Teachive has a cash income of no more than $2,500 per year, a figure probably representative of *jornaleros'* families throughout the republic.[18] Eighty families are economically active, so we can calculate the amassed annual income of the village optimistically at $200,000, or roughly equivalent to the average annual earnings of a physician or lawyer in the United States, or the monthly income of the average corporate executive in the United States. Average food expenses for a family of five (without meat and little animal protein) are nearly two thousand dollars (see chapter 6), leaving almost no money for anything else. Clearly, all the families must hustle for gleaned food or scratch for additional income.

Prior to the December 1994 devaluation of the peso, Mexico had created more new billionaires than any other nation in the world. The Mexican government has shown no resolve to deal with the nation's astonishing discrepancies in income distribution (Barry 1995). This is hardly surprising, in light of the nearly total control of the government by Mexico's wealthy. Politicians and those well-connected with them interact with wealthy families in an interwoven symbiosis that insulates them from the stark realities of Mexico's poverty and environmental catastrophe. They protect each other, expand their already substantial incomes with newly created government subsidies and windfalls from creative graft, and, alarmed by the social ferment and economic instability produced by the gross inequity their cartels create, prudently ship their amassed fortunes off to foreign banks. A few expendable unfortunates are jettisoned now and then, as peso devaluations and the international press catch some unawares; others are dangled to the public as the government goes through theatrics of social concern. But everywhere the wealthy augment their riches by increasing the poverty of the poor.[19]

With the so-called "structural readjustment" of employment patterns under the emerging world economic order, companies across the globe have "downsized" (i.e., fired) great numbers of employees. In developed nations the "adjustments" have resulted in the elimination of many higher-paying, high-skilled production jobs, the substitution of low-skilled, lower-paying jobs, and the downright elimination of many other jobs. In underdeveloped nations the same mechanisms, plus elimination of jobs through currency devaluation, produces even more disruptive results.[20] In the light of the difficulty developed nations are experiencing in maintaining high, well-paid levels of employment, it is doubtful that debt-ridden, capital-poor Mexico can provide anything approaching full employment for its current population without a radical redistribution of its resources. Its huge numbers of unemployed are certain to expand greatly in every year to come. Young boys frequent gasoline stations instead of attending school, jockeying for position to clean windshields or sell musical tapes to customers. At traffic lights automobile passengers are besieged by petty salespeople, jugglers, fire-breathers, and beggars. At Teachive, when rumors of employment spread through the village, the men seldom wait around for verification. They rush to join the long lines of those seeking work, sometimes successfully, sometimes not.

For their part, *comuneros*, faced with no realistic alternatives, are forced to sell off anything of value merely to survive, and there is less and less to sell each year. When the community pump of Teachive broke down, the community was unable to raise the funds to repair it. It remained idle for more than seven months before the *municipio* agreed to help pick up the tab.

LACK OF DEMOCRATIC INSTITUTIONS

Teachivans seldom discuss matters of electoral politics, a sign that they find it unimportant. In this attitude they are realistic, for the lack of democratic institutions in Mexico has led to a society that endures ongoing hardship and political tyranny without expectation of popular participation in decisions that affect the community. Government programs are instituted in Mexico City or Hermosillo and are set in motion without consulting local citizens as to their advisability, feasibility, or practicability. Bureaucrats in government and in parastatal enterprises (the power company, the national oil company, etc.) assume an attitude of arrogance and indifference to the public. Public works projects are carried out with considerable publicity, but without any real consideration of the needs of the local communities.[21] Mexico's highly authoritarian, powerfully centralized political system has no room for grassroots participation. Politicians do not exhibit any sort of accountability to the constituents who "elect" them in elections nearly always tainted by varying degrees of fraud. The federal judicial police, the country's most hated institution, serve to protect the privileges of the rich by tyrannizing the middle classes and terrorizing the poor.

This absence of democracy is not accidental. The ruling PRI party has always attempted to control all political movements by incorporating into the party those which it deemed to be in its own interest, and repressing those which it opposed. Even such populist Mexican presidents as Lázaro Cárdenas and Luis Echeverría took great steps to stifle the development of popular movements that threatened to be independent of government control. Other presidents have sternly or even violently put down public uprisings that demanded independent political representation. Any attempt to organize politically apart from government sponsorship is still a threat to the government and, if it appears to be gaining popular support, will not be tolerated.

As a result, government projects originate within the party and usually suffer from a lack of consultation at the local level. During the populist Echeverría administration (1970–76), for example, a government-funded silviculture project was proposed near Huebampo, an initiative with excellent potential. It was funded during the administration of President José López Portillo in 1980. Fields of several species of large plant species, including the local trees *mauto* (*Lysiloma divaricatum*), *palo colorado* (*Caesalpinia platyloba*), *guásima* (*Guazuma ulmifolia*), *amapa* (*Tabebuia impetiginosa*), and the shrub *jojoba* (*Simmondsia chilodensis*) were planted in the hope that they would become harvestable and marketable commodities. In the case of *jojoba*, the seeds would be sold for producing oil.

The project has been a complete failure. The plantings still exist. Most of the plants did poorly or grew much more slowly than the project directors had hoped. The *jojoba* yielded only a fraction of the seeds originally projected.[22] Had the federal agents (who dictated which plants would be planted) involved knowledgeable local agriculturalists or natives and the community in the project, they would have learned that the Huebampo climate is too dry for the trees, too wet for *jojoba*, that the unamended soils are inappropriate for *amapa*, *palo colorado*, and *guásima*, and that pure stands of any of the trees will not do well in that climate.[23] Furthermore, no one asked the members of the community what they would do for income during the several years it would take for the plants to mature. Government funds for employing field workers arrived at first. They were quickly diminished, then disappeared completely after a couple of years. As a consequence, no one was able to spend sufficient time caring for the fields and the plants suffered from neglect. The trees selected required more moisture for rapid maturing than they could obtain on the arid coastal plain, so supplemental irrigation was required but not provided. In addition, the last fifteen years have seen the worst dry cycles of the last forty years, perhaps of the last several centuries. The drought compounded the already arid conditions, vastly retarding the growth of the plants.

Refugio Flores, resident of Huebampo and elected *comisariado* of the Masiaca community in 1996, was a key player in the project. He points out that in addition to the above weaknesses, the government also neglected to establish a working organization that could function democratically. Standing outside his traditional Mayo hut in drought-stricken Huebampo, he shook his head in exasperation at the dismal history of the project. "Orders for operation of the project came from Hermosillo or from Mexico City. Nobody asked us what we thought. They said 'You will plant the following species here,' that was the order."

"Did they run tests on the soil?" I asked

"No test. They never consulted the old people. They are the ones who knew the habits of the trees. Any of us could have told them that none of those trees are found around here. They brought the *jojoba* plants from the coast of Hermosillo without asking us. It cost a lot, but we don't know how much. They just said, 'Here is your project. Take care of it!' By 1987 the project was dead." Today, the shrubs and trees languish on the baking plain. Some day some of the trees will be harvested, and perhaps every few years the *jojobas* will yield the oily seed for which they were intended. By that time, however, the project will probably have been forgotten. What could have been a productive, informative project instead faltered nearly from the outset.

The project's failure has been interpreted by many as proof of the impossibility of cultivating regional plants on a commercial scale. What the lack of success proves in reality is that a government that does not involve its citizens in projects purportedly designed to help them, will find its projects withering and its credibility undermined. Mexico has been willing to invest billions of pesos of public moneys in projects to assist agribusiness, yet it has never established a peasant-oriented agricultural research and extension service providing localized expertise for the small rural agriculture producer.[24] The absence of this local, grassroots support is sorely felt and clearly demonstrated by the repeated failure of similar small-scale projects throughout the republic. Many of these were schemes that, with legitimate popular participation and government technical assistance, might have become productive. With the elitist assumptions and paternalism of the Mexican government, they never had a decent chance to succeed.

A corollary of this authoritarianism and paternalism is a pervasive sense of impotence and dependence throughout the community. Complaints abound about the failure of the government to help with this or that, as if popular action or community activities are impossible without initiatives and monetary assistance from "the government." Authoritarianism has resulted in failure of local initiative and, in a sense, an immobilizing demoralization. The words *"el gobierno no hace nada"* (the government doesn't do anything) have become the reflex slogan of a people whose will to exert personal power has been undermined and depreciated.[25]

POLICIES OF INTERNATIONAL
LENDING ORGANIZATIONS AND NAFTA

Teachivans had little to say about the North American Free Trade Agreement when it was adopted, except that they were skeptical. In fact, they have few opinions on politics or international matters. Except for their loathing of ex-President Carlos Salinas de Gortari, on whom they blame all of Mexico's economic woes, and their conviction that presidential candidate Luis Donaldo Colosio was murdered by the former president, national and international issues are almost never a topic of discussions among them. Complex issues such as international trade agreements and lending policies of multinational banks are as remote from their conversations as talk about nuclear physics. They do talk about the cost of food and clothing. They discuss which crops are due to be harvested and when. They ponder the availability of basic foods and of water and propane gas. They worry about crimes reported in the region and complain of the failure of younger generations to exhibit respect for their elders.

They have been repeatedly staggered by a seemingly endless round of price increases since the devaluation of the peso in December 1994.

They have seen the price of *maseca* quadruple, beans and potatoes triple, and flour, sugar, tomatoes, and cooking oil double, all while their wages have remained mostly constant and work has become more difficult to find. They have seen Conasupo, the government-subsidized (and scandal-ridden) retail outlet for basic foods, providing fewer and fewer products and the availability of these products more and more limited.[26] The cost of bus tickets has increased 60 percent. Medicines have generally doubled in price, some increasing by 400 percent. Teachivans see this as a result of NAFTA (North American Free Trade Agreement) and are correspondingly opposed. They heard of the denunciation of NAFTA by the Zapatista rebels in Chiapas and nodded in agreement.

To some extent the price increases in food are a function of the drought that affected eleven Mexican states in 1995 and 1996. To a greater extent the inflation is attributable to austerity measures required by international funding agencies and the passage of NAFTA. The Zapatistas' manifesto made that clear.

The pressure on Mexico by international monetary agencies to adopt neoliberal fiscal policies (a sharp reduction in public investment, elimination of subsidies in the public sector on foods and necessities, selling off of public enterprises to private companies, and the elimination of protective tariffs) so as to enable Mexico to pay off its foreign debt, combined with Mexico's near bankruptcy meant, in 1995 and 1996, a dramatic decrease of federal money available to most of the nation plus an end to subsidies on basic foodstuffs, which had been a bedrock policy of Mexican politics for the last four decades. In 1995 the state of Sonora faced budget shortages as well, and curtailed most of its rural improvement social programs. The tremors from this double economic earthquake reached the Mayos. Public works projects such as road paving, installation of potable water systems, and construction of new schools ended, schoolteachers' salaries fell to or below subsistence levels,[27] and credit for marginal agricultural operations (i.e., those not connected with large corporations and Mexico's landed elite) dried up. Much of the Masiaca community was without running water because of inadequate delivery systems or lack of funds to repair broken systems. The pump on which the entire neighboring town of Yocogigua relies broke down, and no funds or expertise were available to repair it for over a year. A switch on Teachive's community pump burned out in late June 1996, during the hottest part of the year and the worst part of an extended dry spell. Five months later, it had still not been repaired. These are examples of local crises which, in turn, have increased the reliance by Mayos on exterior sources of revenue, that is, day-labor and the sale of already meager resources.

As painful as these austerity measures have been for Mexicans, especially poor Mexicans by the millions, they are hardly unpredicted. Mexico's international status is still one of dependency.[28] The country exports tropical fruits, vegetables produced for the winter market, incremental amounts of added value from *maquiladores* (assembly plants) paying very low wages, and raw materials, especially metals. It imports finished goods, machinery, electronic equipment, and, increasingly, basic foodstuffs. Mexico's once-flaunted oil reserves are vanishing, its anticipated oil revenues having evaporated with the onslaught of unprecedented (even for Mexico) corruption and a drop in the international price of oil. When the International Monetary Fund ordered Mexico to undertake austerity measures, it complied without a murmur of protest. When the United States made an emergency loan to the failing Zedillo government in 1995, and again in late–1996, Mexico made its first and second payments early—by borrowing money from European banks to help repay the loan. In order to secure these foreign loans, the country had to promise to cut back on goods and services for its own people.[29]

The Mexican wealthy, during the years of oil euphoria in the 1980s and thereafter, moved their profits out of the country and into foreign, devaluation-proof banks, a move no different from the more primitive extraction of wealth from a colony by an imperial power, except that in this case the imperial powers were Mexicans. The impoverishment of the Mexican economy by devaluation (and the subsequent inflation unmatched by increases in wages) represents a tax laid on the backs of the already poor to pay the bills for the high living of the nation's wealthy during the "golden days" of López-Portillo, de La Madrid, and Salinas.[30] The situation is analogous to the burdens placed on the peasantry or peons of the old *haciendas*. During the decade of the 1980s Mexico created more billionaires than any other nation in the world. It also created more poor people than any other nation in the western hemisphere.

The endorsement and ratification of the North American Free

Trade Agreement (TLC in Mexico) by the Salinas administration placed an even heavier burden on Mexico's poor. The peasants of Masiaca cannot compete in producing grain with the mechanized rain-fed corn belt in the United States.[31] In trade battles, the more powerful and resourceful always wins. As the overwhelming power in NAFTA, the United States stands to become further enriched at the expense of Mexico, to perpetuate its hegemony as an industrial nation and guaranteeing that Mexico will forever be relegated to colonial status. Mexicans will continue to supply the raw materials, agricultural products, and an industrial reserve of cheap labor to assemble appliances for foreign kitchens, sew clothing for foreign bodies, and grow luxury foods for foreign plates. The devaluation of 1994 forced prices to rise dramatically. The rise has not been accompanied by corresponding increases in real wages. In 1994 a *jornalero* could expect to earn from twenty-five to thirty-five pesos a day. The higher figure has hardly increased, although the lower figure appears to have increased slightly, so that the average is now thirty to forty pesos a day. To date, Mexico cannot point to a single benefit the nation at large has received as the result of NAFTA.[32]

International loans must be repaid with hard currencies. These can only be collected as cash received from the sale of export commodities, or from money foreigners spend inside Mexico's borders. Mexico has had to increase its exports while decreasing its internal expenditures in order to gather the currency to pay off the loans and avoid default. The nation as a whole thus acts very much like the Masiaca *comunidad*: it sells off its resources in order to survive.

It is easy to point to the environmental degradation of the Masiaca community and similar *ejidos* and communities throughout Mexico and to deride these communities for allowing the degradation to take place, invoking the so-called "tragedy of the commons." Such a simplistic analysis overlooks the tiny range of options available to the natives. Teachivans do not seem overly upset with the sad state of their communal resources. They occasionally lament the woeful loss of biomass, noting the decrease in the number and size of trees and the absence of livestock forage. They do not wax eloquent over the vanishing bounty of the *monte*. They resent the few individuals who run too many cows or cut down trees unnecessarily. The *comuneros* are not willfully fouling their own nests, selling off their estates "an acre and a cow at a time." They are not plundering their lands so that they may drive luxury cars, eat tastefully prepared foods shipped in by air express, and live in gated communities. It is not thoughtlessness, it is desperation that leads to their overharvesting of their resources. This is the reverse of the case of the *latifundista* ranchers who destroy their forests and convert all pastures to buffelgrass in order to maximize production and short-term profits, and maintain a lifestyle of luxury and a position of social power.

For more than any other reason, the commons is being overexploited so as to perpetuate an international economy (and its local *compradores*) that maintains a few in luxury and many in poverty. The pressures the Mayos put on their natural resources are, in general, a reflection not of greed, nor of inability collectively to manage a resource, but rather of far deeper economic forces which leave the natives with few options. They would rather not see the ecological well-being of their lands compromised. So far, however, no alternatives have appeared on the horizon. Their response to "*la crisis*," as Mexico's profound economic slump is popularly known, is to extract what they can find to sell simply to survive. The denuded pastures around Teachive can be partially traced to the practical effects of the international lending agencies, so-called "aid" programs whose loans are offered subject to socially painful conditions, and, perhaps, to NAFTA.

INTERNATIONAL DRUG TRADE
AND IRRATIONAL DRUG POLICIES

While Teachive is not demonstrably caught up in drug trade, it is widely known that some of its residents have an at least marginal affiliation to the traffickers. Navojoa is known as a regional distribution center. San Bernardo on the Río Mayo is a known hotbed of production. The *sierras* of nearby Sinaloa are notorious for harboring crops and *mafiosos*. Crops are grown in the Sierra de Alamos as well. All are part of a huge network of drug smuggling targeting consumers in the United States. In return, the United States has adopted drug policies guaranteed to maintain the high value of marijuana and opium crops. The United States spends more than $10 thousand million annually on its touted antidrug smuggling campaign. It has extorted promises of crackdowns from a long series of Mexican presidents, at least one of whom (Salinas de Gortari) had alleged ties to *narcotraficantes* while he was deploying the military and the federal judicial police into the countryside to attack Mexican citizens, ostensibly to eliminate illegal crops. The connections of the governor of Sonora (Beltrones) with drug lords was the subject of numerous international news stories in 1997.

The most obvious local effect of the drug wars is in the use of large ranches (and to a lesser extent, industries) for money-laundering operations. In the larger picture, however, the potential profits from the international trade in illegal plants and plant products is so lucrative that many Mexican politicians are directly or indirectly involved in drug operations. Most Teachivans assume that their state and national leaders profit from drug traffic.

Drug searches by the military and the police are routine and ubiquitous. They are equally unproductive. As a highly educated Sonoran said, "They all know when the shipments are coming and shut down for a while until the shipment has passed." The Mayos accept the harassment and bullying of the police stoically, knowing they have no recourse. The young people, however, are aware of the high wages paid to those involved in the trade, and, according to some Teachivans, are being lured into it as an alternative to their grim future as semi-employed *jornaleros*. They are also seduced into a milieu of unmatched violence that views death by murder as a routine part of daily operations.

CORRUPTION AND THE HERITAGE OF PATRONAGE

One advantage of the poverty Teachivans experience is their relative freedom from the need to bribe public officials. They simply cannot afford to, so the possibility seldom arises. The tradition of entrenched patronage, traced back to Spanish rule, and the debilitating, systemic corruption that characterizes Mexican society, penetrates so deeply to all aspects of that society that it has become a part of the Mayo psyche as well. The hopelessness that any change can be made, and the stoicism and cynicism that are the offspring of corruption, make hope for social change a chimera. Corruption, and its corollary, the arbitrary exercise of power, are assumed to be a part of daily life in Teachive, as in all of Mexico. All police, bureaucrats, and public officials are assumed bribable, with good reason. Some examples will illustrate the problem.

The pummeling dirt road that connects Masiaca with the international highway eight kilometers away was paved ten years ago, according to official government documents. Authorities in Mexico City and the state assert that the road is paved, for money was apparently appropriated and it was certified as paved. The major problem with this claim is that the road is not paved and never has been. Natives say the money wound up in politicians' pockets, while those who live there must endure the terrible road, so rough that a parallel track has evolved in the *monte* immediately adjacent and is used more than the developed roadway, even though it is only a one-lane roadway and vehicles cannot pass on it.

A more local example of corruption is also instructive. A well-known federal agency in Mexico is DIF, the agency of Development of the Whole Family. Each community is supposed to have an office that assists in guaranteeing nutrition for children and help for families in need of basic supplies and services. Funds were allocated to Teachive for a DIF building, which all other villages have. The funds were supposed to go for constructing a new building, which would be a symbol for the village and for the government. A local woman took the funds, had her own home painted a brilliant green (including the letters DIF), and, the accusation goes, apparently made off with the rest of the money. No building exists and none will exist. Villagers are indignant and residents of other villages scoff. All realize that nothing can be done, for the feeling is that the woman was able to get away with the embezzlement because she had some political connections that make her untouchable. They assume that any appeal would be useless and might even get the appellant into trouble.

Incidents like these, at a federal or local level, leave residents with no recourse. When the much despised federal judicial police harass or steal from the people, there is no recourse, no system of justice to appeal to. The people quietly submit, hoping to maintain their dignity.

A further example, natives charge, is that of the National Indigenous Institute, which allegedly appropriated many thousands of pesos to assist with the harvest of alfalfa from an agricultural project in the *monte* southwest of Teachive. The money was appropriated, the natives believe, but wound up in a politician's pocket and not in the project.

The details of the project reveal a melange of corruption and patronage.[33] The story, as constructed from interviews with *socios* of the project,[34] is as follows: In 1993 officials from INI approached the *asamblea* and suggested that they form a cooperative to farm land within the *comunidad*. Thirty-four members signed up as *socios*, partners in the enterprise. This number gradually decreased to the twenty-four *socios* currently involved. They were allocated a parcel of thirty-five hectares by the *comunidad*, with promises of credit and machinery from INI. They elected a president and a treasurer, who, other *socios* say, do not work in the field. Instead, they restrict their efforts to administration and bookwork. Some of the *socios*, though not all, went to work clearing the land of thornscrub, an onerous task so great that they were able to clear only twelve of the thirty-five hectares. When that was finished, they fenced the cleared land, using fence provided (at a charge) by INI.

The next task was to construct a canal to *el aguaje* just north of Teachive, the most reliable source of surface water in the *comunidad*. Engineering consultants were provided (at a charge) by INI. According to one *socio*, the consultants' engineering experience was entirely theoretical and they had no idea how to construct a ditch, so the *socios* wound up building it themselves, using a length of transparent hose as a level to ensure the proper gradient for the nearly mile-long canal. It was necessary to construct a small bridge over the ditch to permit vehicle access to the *monte* north of the ditch. INI provided a pump, and the *socios* purchased (with credit) the piping and earthworks necessary to construct the ditch head. The pump, borrowed (at a fee) from a school in the delta, was belt-operated from the flywheel of a tractor, so that during operation the noise was loud enough to be heard in the most distant part of the village.

Alonso Moroyoqui helped work on the ditch. He talked to me about his work on the project, preferring to sit in my vehicle and talk rather than in his home, where he might be overheard. "As soon as the ditch was built, we started the plowing. No, they didn't do any studies of the soil. INI provided the tractors on credit, and they charged us for the drivers, too.[35] We had several *socios* who know how to operate the tractor. But INI made us use their INI people. We don't even know how much they paid them! They gave us three tractors. Junk! One broke down right away. It never plowed an inch of land. The others weren't much better. They were always breaking down and needing parts. Even now, as you can see, none of the tractors are running. There they sit, in Mario Soto's yard."

At INI's recommendation, the *socios* planted alfalfa, purchasing seed and commercial fertilizer with credit. The fertilizer was applied, along with the seed, without studies of natural soil fertility to determine how much, if any, might be needed and the correct application. None of the work by the *socios* was compensated except for the irrigators, who had the critical responsibility of siphoning water from the main ditch to the furrows. Six weeks later the *socios* harvested the first bales, using a baler provided (at a charge) by INI. The harvest was poor, and immediately a dispute erupted concerning the division of the paltry bales of the harvest. According to the administration, each *socio* received five or six bales, a claim poorer members dispute. Alonso says he received nothing.

Not all *socios* worked equally. Many had livestock to tend to.[36] The poorer *socios* without livestock spent their entire days working in the fields. They felt that they should receive a larger share because they worked more. Others insisted that the division be equal. The poorer *socios* especially felt that the president and the treasurer (better educated and connected than the poor members) should not receive an equal share, for they did almost no visible work. No consensus was reached. The point was hardly worth debating because the harvest was scant, the bales were of poor quality, and little income was realized.

Six weeks later, a second harvest was made, hardly better than the first. A third harvest followed and was slightly better. The fourth and last was more satisfactory, and the *socios* looked forward to the income. INI officials seized the harvest as part of the project's repayment of credit, and the *socios* were left with nothing, or at most, a few bales of little value.

Even in these discouraging circumstances, the project proceeded. The *socios* planted sorghum for livestock food. The yield was small, and the harvest came when the price of feed crops was depressed, so no market could be found and the *socios* simply fed the harvested sorghum to their own livestock, a most disappointing result for an anticipated cash crop. Next they planted beans, but the lack of agronomic expertise among the *socios* was painfully felt, and the crop failed completely.

For their next endeavor, in the fall of 1995, the *socios* planted five hectares of corn. The very modesty of this crop is an indicator of the project's gradual failure, for even under the best of circumstances, the harvest of five hectares of corn divided twenty-four ways will yield a pittance to each member. The harvest was completed in March of 1996 and was marginally acceptable. Considerable confusion remains among the poorer *socios* as to what became of the corn. No accounting of distribution of the crop has been made, and some of the *socios* feel cheated. Some received three sacks of corn; others claim they received none. Nevertheless, plans were made to continue planting.

Some *socios* feel that the soil is fertile, water is available, and labor ample. All that is lacking is machinery. It is obvious, though, that little expertise has been available to the cooperative, for the soil is high in clay and quite compact; without considerable soil amendments, working it will become more difficult. Agronomic assistance has not been provided, and without it hopes will run out soon. My discussions with some *socios* indicated that they have little if any experience in commercial cropping, and have little comprehension of the need for technical knowledge and marketing expertise when raising crops for commercial sale. No one has a clear idea of how or when the tractors will be repaired, and they acknowledge that without them water cannot be pumped and the fields cannot be plowed. Whether the community can supply water indefinitely for the irrigation of a large field is also highly questionable. At this point, the project must be considered a dismal failure.

Vicente declined an opportunity to join the cooperative endeavor. He says he didn't want to have anything to do with INI. Perhaps his stand was a reflection of his early bad experience on the agricultural experiment at Huebampo. While INI promotes itself as an agency advocating for indigenous people, it is noteworthy that few people in the community view it as anything more than a cynical government agency seeking only to promote the well-being of its personnel. One *comunero* viewed INI officials in the same light as the federal judicial police.

Pervasive corruption, racism, imperialist economic penetration, overpopulation, lack of democracy, the overwhelming greed of the wealthy, impoverishment of the land, lack of leadership: all these things represent an overwhelming barrier to the economic and cultural survival of the Mayos of Teachive and the Masiaca community. The crush of global economies, the immense power of international and national elites who leave no room for marginal and atavistic communities such as Teachive, seem to spell certain doom for the Masiaca community as a viable meeting of individuals with a shared history, common goals, and mutual interests. Still, the *comunidad* has great resources, mostly untapped, because the *comuneros* have never had an opportunity to tap them. Knowledge of this, perhaps unconscious, is the source of Vicente's naive yet infectious optimism and of his ingenuous enthusiasm for life and his home. If only the rains would return, he muses, things would be better in Teachive. He is ready to work, to experiment with new ways. Thousands of people like Vicente are available to bring energy to creative development projects. For decades observers have been pronouncing Mayo culture as "vanishing" or "dying." Yet the *fiestas* continue, the *pascolas* dance, and the *fariseos* parade. The *monte* has been ravaged before and it has recovered. Perhaps it can recover once again. Mayos have been dispossessed of their lands, scattered, and demoralized in the past and they have recovered. As long as people like Vicente wander through the *monte* cataloging the myriad organisms that might prove useful to his community, dreaming about what might be, the future holds out hope for them and for all of us. When such people no longer collect plants and store knowledge, the day of judgment will be nigh at hand.

CHAPTER EIGHT *Afterword*

❧ In the spring of 1997, I returned to Teachive following an absence of several months. Vicente was just arriving at his home. He was riding his bicycle, on which he carried a small *carga* of freshly cut brasilwood. He had been far out in the *monte*, he said, looking for the nearest brasil.

The change in the *comunidad* was notable. "I have bad news for you, David," Vicente said after our initial greetings. "Jesús Moroyoqui, 'El Huírivis,' died. It was sudden, probably a heart attack, that's what they say." I was staggered by the loss. Jesús was a powerful voice in the *comunidad*, an articulate spokesman for conservative Mayos. I had intended to stop by and visit with him. When I passed by his house, it was nearly empty.

Equally stunning was the loss of Rosendo, a talented musician from San Pedrito. Well known throughout the *comunidad*, he was an accomplished harpist, a maker of instruments who taught younger people to play. He was easily identifiable at the *fiestas*, slouching inside the *ramadón*, his hat cocked on his head in an eccentric manner. A cow had stepped on his foot and the injury had become infected. Treatment had been unsuccessful. He died of tetanus at the age of forty-five, leaving behind five children. His family was selling cassette tapes of his music at inflated prices.

The community pump had still not been repaired after seven months of silence. The town looked brown and drab. Teachivans still had to lug buckets of water from the arroyo on *palancas* (yokes). During my visit, the water came back on without warning. The electric company had been paid for a new motor and overdue electric bills had been collected. There was general rejoicing. Almost simultaneously people 243 sprayed their dusty yards everywhere in town. Older people especially rejoiced, liberated from the tiring treks to haul water.

Los 35 was viewed as a dead project. No more work had been done. The tractors lay idle, crippled. The field was a wasteland of eroded soil covered with long-dead weeds. Some people expected reprisals from INI, as the officials tried to recoup their agency's heavy losses.

Near Vicente's house a little cultural center had been built through the leadership of Míchiko, the Japanese community development volunteer. A small, clean adobe building, it was referred to as "La Casa Míchiko," in honor of the young woman. She held daily workshops on knitting and cooking in the house, as well as neighborhood meetings. Women were nearly always present in the center, learning new techniques and sharing weaving tips with others.

Vicente announced gleefully that the Masiaca priest had been censured by his superiors for his neglect of the Mayos. He had been ordered to accept their festivals, Vicente said. Others could not verify this.

The spring of 1997 promised a worse drought than that of 1996. There had been no *equipatas*, and Hurricane Fausto in 1996 had delivered far less rain than had Ismael in 1995. The dust was worse and the *monte* harsher than it had been a year earlier.

Toño Gámez, a strong supporter of the ruling PRI party organized a bus to carry Teachivans to a rally in Navojoa for the PRI candidate for governor. Only a handful of people showed up for the free bus ride.

Rumor had it that within a few weeks federal officials would meet with the assembly of the *comunidad* to ascertain if the *comuneros* wished to abolish the *comunidad* and replace it with an *ejido*. Once *comuneros* became *ejidatarios*, they could vote to privatize parcels and turn some or all of the communal lands into private property. Vicente didn't think the assembly would accept the proposition. He couldn't imagine abolishing the *comunidad*.

A boom in arts and crafts production had struck Cucajaqui. Women had begun again to weave blankets and to embroider. Men were carving trays and utensils, and weaving wire baskets. Several people had begun making *morrales* (handbags woven from *ixtle*). One fellow had begun carving *pascola* masks.

I paid a visit to doña Buenaventura, now ninety-one. As we sat in the breezeway of her ancient house, she told me in a quavering voice that Juan, one of her grandsons, had been murdered a month earlier in his home just across the way, leaving behind four children, including a baby. Her ancient face was bathed with tears as she described the incident. "God must hate me, David. Another death in my family!" Juan had been at home celebrating the baptism of his little son when Candelario, one of the sons of Cornelia Nieblas had come to the house. Outside was Alonso, godfather to Juan and, ironically, to Candelario as well. Alonso greeted Candelario and asked him what he needed. Candelario said casually that he needed to see Juan for a minute. Alonso summoned Juan. Candelario shot him three times with a high-powered revolver and fled.

No one offered a motive for the killing. Several people speculated that Candelario was a low-life type undoubtedly involved in drug traffic. The Nieblas bunch was always courting trouble, always sneaky, people said. Maybe Juan knew something Candelario wanted to know or something Candelario didn't want him to know.

Buenaventura and her daughter María Soledad went to the state police. They came to the house and asked a few questions. Candelario was nowhere to be found in the village. Wouldn't they try to find him and bring him to justice, María asked? The policeman answered: María would have to pay 1,000 pesos (about $140 US) to have an investigation undertaken. If it was a difficult case, she would have to pay more. Wasn't it the job of the police to bring justice to the people, she asked? The police left without answering, saying only that the investigation would begin when they received the money. Vicente told me angrily that if María paid the money, the police would just spend it on a party and wouldn't do an investigation anyway. "They don't care about the death of a poor *indio*," he said.

María Soledad was despondent. Her family had experienced many deaths, by accidents and by a suicide, but this was the worst. "We've always heard of these things happening in other places, in Navojoa or Huatabampo, but we never thought it could happen here. Now we know we aren't safe at all. It's probably drugs. Murder, right here in Teachive. And we can't even get justice!"

Vicente shared her alarm. "This is very bad for Teachive, David," he said. "Juan has several brothers. They won't forget this. They will want vengeance for Juan's death. They will kill somebody from Cornelia's family. Then there will be retaliation. It will never stop." He said it was a sure sign that *narcos* (drug dealers) were influencing Teachive. This was the worst sign he could imagine for the town and the community.

As Vicente related this, his twelve-year-old grandson stood at his side, adding details, fascinated yet horrified by the murder.

And life went on in Teachive.

Don Vicente's List of the Benefits of Living in the Masiaca Community

❧ The following list, assembled by don Vicente, represents his opinion of the advantages of living in the Masiaca community, where there is monte, over those of living in the more affluent ejidos of the Mayo Delta, which abut agricultural lands where many jornaleros work. Don Vicente developed the list one day after I idly asked him to tell me the advantages of living in Teachive. The second part of don Vicente's list follows as Appendix B and includes plants and plant materials he and his family and neighbors actually gather from the monte and use in their household. As to the benefits of living in the monte:

You have the right to go anywhere you want, along private paths, to quiet places, to the monte where you can see all the trees and plants.

You have the right to gather firewood.

You have the right to have animals, that is, livestock, running freely.

You have the right to land of your own, with plenty of space.

There is the presence of game animals, maybe not many, but at least some.

There is the availability of sharpening stones on the ground. (In the Delta stones are rare in the fine soils).

247

[I found this odd, but came to understand, as Vicente opened my eyes, that for people who live near the land, stones can be of incomparable value. I then also understood why trucks come to the Masiaca community to buy rock for all phases of construction in Huatabampo and Navojoa.]

There is an abundance of rattlesnakes in the monte. [While Vicente has little to do with them, two men, including one son-in-law, kill the snakes and skin them. Then they dry and sell the skin. They also clean the skeleton and grind the bones into a powder, which they sell as a medicine to rejuvenate those who need rejuvenation.]

Finally, and perhaps most important, there is the availability of all the plants of the monte (see Appendix B).

Don Vicente's List of Plants Used in the Tajia-Moroyoqui Household

❧ Below is a partial list of plants actually used in the Tajia-Moroyoqui household, nearly all of them gathered in the nearby monte (many other plants are known to don Vicente that do not occur commonly near Teachive). Field identifications were accomplished with the considerable assistance of Thomas R. Van Devender of the Arizona-Sonora Desert Museum, who spent many days with me in the field and who is warmly received in Teachive. Further information can be found in Martin et al., in press. The Mayo name is given first, with the Spanish name (if known) in parentheses, followed by the scientific name and family.

Aaqui (*pitahaya*)—*Stenocereus thurberi,* Cactaceae. The organ pipe cactus is used for many purposes, but is most important for its fruit, a dietary staple for the Mayo in the months of August and September. The cactus is also a good source of building material. *Pitahayas* are the most important single wild food source for the people of the region. Some women still make *tamales* from the fruit. The dried ribs are gathered for fencing material.

Agiya (*guásima*)—*Guazuma ulmifolia,* Sterculiaceae. A most worthy tree found along the arroyo. Its bark is kept and boiled into a tea for liver problems. Its fruits are boiled for kidney problems and used as a coffee substitute. Its wood is used for making chairs, tables, and other furniture. Every tree within a few kilometers of Teachive shows scarring from lopped-off limbs and stripped bark.

Ba'aco—*Phaulothamnus spinescens,* Achatocarpaceae. The leaves are heartily eaten by goats. The translucent fruits are gobbled up by birds, especially *cenzontle* (mockingbird), of whose song the Mayos are particularly fond.

Bacaporo (*guacaporo*)—*Parkinsonia aculeata*, Fabaceae. The Mexican *palo verde*'s bark is brewed into a tea and taken for cough and fever. Its thorns are nasty, however, and other barks are preferred. I suspect this tree was introduced rather than native, for it never seems to grow far from people.

Bachomo (*batamote*)—*Baccharis salicifolia*, Asteraceae. This common seepwillow produces a soap that will neutralize body odor (a problem gringos have, according to certain blunt and crass Mayos). A few leaves are commonly slipped into shoes and worn beneath the feet to eliminate foot odor. I asked don Vicente for some. He presented me with a handful and it seemed to be effective.

Bahuío (*guayavillo*)—*Acacia coulteri*, Fabaceae. This small-to-medium-sized tree is found in abundance on Mesa Masiaca. Its wood is exceptionally strong, making excellent posts and *vigas*. It is fine firewood, which is a shame since it is such an excellent wood for construction.

Baiguo (*palo dulce*)—*Eysenhardtia polystachya*, Fabaceae. This large shrub or small tree has a myriad of uses. Its wood is very hard, making it ideal for implement handles. Combined with *tajimsi*, it produces a fine red dye. Its herbage is relished by livestock, and it is said to have curative powers for the livestock that consume it. I presumed it would be scarce due to overharvesting by man and beast, but it is rather common in the *monte*, never growing in abundance, but well distributed. It is a candidate for cultivation as a forage plant.

Baijuo (*garambullo*)—*Pisonia capitata*, Nyctaginaceae. Although the shrub is formidably armed, forming dense, impenetrable thickets and covered with vicious spines, goats and burros eat the leaves eagerly, hence its importance.

Bais cápore (*saituna*)—*Ziziphus amole*, Rhamnaceae. The fruits of this small tree are eaten and the bark is used to expel amoebas. It can also provide excellent shade when in leaf.

Bauguo (*pochote*)—*Ceiba acuminata*, Bombacaceae. One must travel up the Arroyo Masiaca for some distance to find these kapoks nowadays. In times of hunger, the roots were eaten, and still could be, according to Vicente.

Bausabu (*tescalama*)—*Ficus petiolaris*, Moraceae. One must travel a few kilometers upstream on Arroyo Masiaca to find these rock figs. They are worth the effort for their sheer beauty and cool shade, if nothing else. Their sap is viewed as peculiarly efficacious in curing bruises and hernias. Don Vicente demonstrated how the bark of the roots, which often flow over rocks in a great blotch of yellow, are carefully scraped and the gum collected. This is rubbed onto a rag, which is then wrapped around the injured area. He keeps some of the stuff on hand. He also says one can eat the figs in a pinch, but they are best left to the animals. The popularity of the remedy may explain its greatly diminished range. Whereas it once was found at Teachive, one must now travel upstream nearly to San Antonio to find the great trees.

Bíbino (*salvia, chani*)—*Hyptis albida*, Labiatae. One of three members of the lavender genus found in the region, all with medicinal uses such as cleansing foreign objects from the eye, curing earaches, curing *pasmo*, a neurasthenic disorder in which the victim appears disoriented and irrationally fearful, and as a pleasant room fumigant. Don Vicente collects this for regular use in his home. On one occasion he snared some branches from a hillside, telling me that it would make a good tea to help Teresa sleep.

Ca'aro (*palo verde*)—*Cercidium floridum*, Fabaceae. The leaves and beans are good fodder for livestock. The wood makes passable firewood.

Caguorara (*guayparín*)—*Diospyros sonorae*, Ebenaceae. The Sonoran persimmon is not common in the area. Individual trees yield abundant fruits, which are eaten and the seeds ground into an *atole*, which, according to don Vicente is most tasty. The tree may have been brought to the area by human beings many generations ago, for it appears to be found only in association with people.

Chíchel (*toji*)—*Struthanthus palmeri*, Loranthaceae. This mistletoe has long, narrow leaves and grows on a variety of trees. It is said to be good for many things, including as a tea for diabetes, as an infusion for healing sores, and as a fodder for livestock.

Chiju (*añil*)—*Indigofera suffruticosa*, Fabaceae. The indigo plant is a fast-growing annual found in deep soils. Its leaves produce a deep blue used to dye wool. Doña Teresa (and every other women who weaves) uses it and gives excellent instructions for preparation of the dye, actually providing a demonstration. Although it is not rare, *chiju* tends to grow in isolated thickets. Whenever I find a patch, I collect a bagfull and take it to someone in Teachive. An old woman who died in early 1996 was known to have made the best *chiju* of all.

Chino (*palo chino*)—*Havardia mexicanum*, Fabaceae. A mesquitelike tree that grows quite large, it has red wood that is carved into fine figurines by Teachivans. The bark is used for dye as well. The strong wood can be used for beams and posts, for which it is most attractive.

Chírajo (*guinolo*)—*Acacia cochliacantha*, Fabaceae. Boat-thorned acacia, known also as *chírahui*, is a common, medium-sized leguminous tree with reddish spines that enlarge and turn gray with age. The large spines are used to brew a tea for curing urinary problems and prostatitis. (Don Vicente preferred to visit a doctor when he complained of the symptoms.) The wood makes decent firewood. In times of drought, burros strip bark from the trees and seem to derive nourishment from it, much to the detriment of the tree. It is an aggressive invader of overgrazed pastures, hence its numbers are on the increase.

Choal (*quelite*)—*Chenopodium cf mexicanum*, Chenopodiaceae. A lamb's quarter, gathered and eaten as a green. Usually, though, livestock get there first.

Chogua (*cholla*)—*Opuntia fulgida*, Cactaceae. The fruits are eaten for their taste and to relieve upset stomach.

Choi (*brea*)—*Cercidium praecox*, Fabaceae. The Sonoran *palo verde* not only provides an important source of forage for livestock (especially goats, who gobble up the fallen beans as though they were popcorn and stand on their hind legs straining to reach the lower branches), but also exudes a golden sap (*chu'uca*), eaten as a sweet and taken also as a remedy for respiratory problems. Don Vicente and his oldest grandson collected some to alleviate my asthma, assuring me it would help. He also sent me to doña Buenaventura, a woman of more than ninety years who lives on the east side of the arroyo to learn more about *choi*. She reported that in the old times older women would burn the root of *C. praecox*, mix the ashes in a tub with a pig carcass (she rather giggled at this) and water, and cook the godawful mess for a couple of days. Out of this would come a liquid, which would be poured into clay molds, and which functioned as a tolerable soap. The tree flowers profusely in April. The brilliant yellow-gold blossoms are gathered by children and sprinkled on the house cross on Good Friday.

Choya guani (*guarequi*)—*Ibervillea sonorae*, Cucurbitaceae. A gourd whose thin-stalked vine rises from an enormous, semisubmerged storage root, surely one of the most interesting plants in the region. Vicente distinguishes between male and female *choya guani* by their shapes, pointing out that males are good for ailments in women and vice-versa. The root is widely used and highly valued for rheumatism, diabetes, and cancer. Don Vicente demonstrated how to cut off a small piece from the huge corm and stick it between the toes to alleviate the pains of rheumatism. *Guareques* are quite common in the coastal scrub, which is surprising, given their wide popularity. They are sold along the highway by natives.

Cócorit (*chiltepín*)—*Capsicum baccatum*, Solanaceae. The fiery little chile is found in every household, growing wild along the arroyo. No meal is complete without it. Upstream on the Arroyo Masiaca a few kilometers from San Antonio, don Vicente, Tom Van Devender, and I were snooping among the plants along the stream when I happened upon a robust bush of ripened *chiltepín* fruits the size of peas, resembling tiny persimmons. I picked and ate one rather complacently and was instantly overcome by a volcanic eruption in my mouth. My companions gave me little sympathy (everyone knows *chiltepines* are hot and are not for sissies). When the burning did not subside after fifteen minutes, don Vicente investigated the plant more closely. After examining it, he looked at me in wonder and exclaimed, "Ay, David, no wonder. This is a *chiltepín de la sierra!* They are very, very hot!" In the late summer and early fall, the chiles are ready to harvest. At times, entire families will venture into the *monte* and collect the cherished fruits.

Cósahui—*Krameria greyi*, Krameriaceae. The ratany of the Sonoran desert is made into a tea and taken for kidney and back pains, apparently acting as a diuretic. It is regularly used in the Tajia-Moroyoqui household. Teresa found it helpful when she suffered from aching back while weaving *cobijas*.

Cuépari (*golondrina, spurge*)—*Euphorbia* sp., Euphorbiaceae. Although ubiquitous in disturbed soils, the *cuépari* are collected and stored by many families in Teachive. Goats eat the young plants quickly.

Cuépari is brewed into a tea and taken for ulcers and digestive problems. It is also applied to areas of the skin that have lost pigmentation for whatever cause. Vicente assures me that he has used it and it is highly effective.

Cu'u (*mescal*)—*Agave angustifolia*, Agavaceae. The pointed, long leaves of this agave are chopped from the agave head. The heads are then slow roasted (*tatemadas*) in a pit for several days, after which they and the leaf remainders adnate to the head are consumed. The leaves are eaten much as artichoke leaves. They are very sweet, almost excessively so, and I could eat but one. They are relished by the natives, who find the strong molasseslike flavor most agreeable. Don Vicente views them as a rare treat, since their numbers have dwindled in recent years. There is a long period between the last *pitahaya* fruits in early all and the first *etcho* fruits in late spring. The natural diet of the Mayos had lacked sweets during this period. The *cu'u* filled a void. Other men harvest the heads to brew into *vino* or *mescal*, a fiery distillate, the local moonshine. Diminishing numbers of agaves have put a brake to this time-honored practice. The uncooked leaves are also scraped by others to make *ixtle*, a fiber that is twisted into twine, especially for sewing the cocoons of *téneborim*. Doña María Teresa Zazueta, Teresa's mother, who still makes cord from the agave leaves, reports that the best rope of all used to be made from *ixtle* and that she and others still make it from time to time. Until recently, several people in Teachive made *morrales*, handbags from the *ixtle*. They would last forever. Plastic ones are cheaper now. Beals (1945) noted widespread bagweaving in Masiaca in 1930. He states that the weavers were exclusively men, a practice that apparently no longer exists in Teachive. Erasmus (1967) found considerable weaving of *morrales* in Las Bocas in the mid-twentieth century. Don Reyes Baisegua of Sirebampo made a couple of *morrales de ixtle* for me in 1995.

Cu'uca (*vinorama*)—*Acacia farnesiana*, Fabaceae. The leaves and beans are good fodder for goats. Some people use the root to heal insect stings and bites.

Cuta nahuilla (*palo piojo*)—*Brongniartia alamosana*, Fabaceae. This small tree frequents hills nearby Teachive. It is abundant on Ayajcahui (Fox Hill) two kilometers to the north. Although the name means "good for nothing tree ("louse tree" in Spanish), it yields tolerably good firewood. In the late fall its legumes dry out and explode, the sudden sound causing temporary elevations of blood pressure in nearby humans.

Cuta síquiri (*palo colorado*)—*Caesalpinia platyloba*, Fabaceae. A small tree (it grows larger at higher elevations, never exceeding more than about eight inches in diameter), it is harvested ruthlessly for its strong, durable wood. Nearly every house contains beams of this fabulous wood, which is, in theory, protected. Don Vicente notes that the government will punish natives who cut the trees without a permit. Owners of big tracts of land carry out wholesale demolition of their forests, including all the *cuta síquiri*, with impunity.

Ejéa (*palo fierro*)—*Olneya tesota*, Fabaceae. Ironwood is used less in Teachive than farther north, where it is more common. Still, it is recognized as an excellent firewood and a good wood for carving. No other wood is as hard or as durable, even though it is brittle. Those fortunate enough to have a ramada or *portal* with posts of ironwood will never see them fail from rot or from weakness. The dead wood used for posts may have endured as long as nine hundred years. Some of the largest *ejéas* in existence grow near the village of Sinahuisa, nearby on the coastal plain. At the edge of the plaza in Masiaca is the dead trunk of an ancient *ejéa* nearly a meter thick, that shows no sign of rotting. It is a local landmark. Vicente observes that *ejéas* do not grow south of Teachive, which means their southern limit roughly corresponds with the southernmost locality for *saguaro* as well. Both plants are key species in the Sonoran Desert.

Etcho—*Pachycereus pecten-aboriginum*, Cactaceae. It is one of the two great cacti of everyday importance to Teachive. The fruits are eaten, the seeds made into tortillas (tasty) and *atole* (similar to cream of wheat), the surprisingly durable wood used for all manner of purposes including furniture-making and as *vigas* in houses, and the flesh regularly used as a home remedy. Doña Teresa Moroyoqui made some tortillas from the seeds that another woman had collected. Their flavor was reminiscent of blueberry pancakes. She also prepared some *miel*, a syrup, from the fruit. She recalled that her grandmother made cooking oil from the seeds of the *etcho*. Before there was lard, she said, the old people would smash some seeds on a *comal*, or griddle, and the oil would coat it. They even squeezed oil from the seeds. The great cacti are also an important source of shade. Decades ago, *etchos* were planted in tight rows to make fences. Now up to ten meters tall and growing tightly together in impenetrable columns, these long rows remain effective barriers. As fences, they have long since been replaced with barbed wire. María Soledad Moroyoqui has used a *salsapayeca* (tamping stick) made of *etcho* wood for nearly thirty years.

Guaro (*verdolaga*)—*Portulaca umbraticola*, Portulacaceae. The purslane is gathered and eaten as a green in summer.

Güey (*bledo*)—*Amaranthus palmeri*, Amaranthaceae. These explode from the bare ground, appearing in enormous numbers during *las aguas*, the summer rains. They are gathered while still tender and eagerly consumed by adults, children, and livestock alike, a race taking place to see who can get to them first. Well they might, for they are delectable, tastier than any spinach. These are probably available in delta villages as well. Amaranths are raised for grain by Guarijíos to the north, but I have not recorded such a use among the Mayos of the region.

Güicobo (*güiloche*)—*Diphysa occidentalis*, Fabaceae. This large shrub or small tree sends out several straight, skinny trunks from a common base. The wood is very hard and straight-grained, making ideal poles, clubs, and canes, for which is it harvested. Some folks also use it in making roof *latas*; in other areas the braces for stools are made from *guiloche*. Nearly every plant shows signs of previous harvesting, indicating it is useful indeed.

Guo'otobo (*vara prieta*)—*Cordia parviflora*, Boraginaceae. A scraggly bush becoming quite large, it explodes with leaves and delicate white blossoms following substantial rains. The leaves are stiff, the branches irregular. Sections of the shrub are cut and used to beat wool. Thus, they are said to clean it and render it more amenable to spinning and weaving. All weavers use string heddles of guo'otobo. The branches are specifically harvested during Holy Week and are used in ceremonies by the *alaguássim* and by the *pascolas* to beat the ground, as they call out "Gloria, Gloria" to the crucified Jesus.

Jévero (*chilicote, peonía*)—*Erythrina flabelliformes*, Fabaceae. The coral bean tree was once common on nearby hillsides. Larger specimens are now found only in more moist and remote forests to the north and east. The soft but durable wood is made into corks, masks, benches, and figurines. Don Serapio Gámez still uses the wood for corks to plug holes in the *calabasas* (squashes) he makes into *bulis* (canteens).

Jícamuchi (*palo piojo blanco*)—*Caesalpinia caladenia; Caesalpinia palmeri,* Fabaceae. This small tree or large shrub is important fodder for goats and sheep. It also produces a decent firewood. The two species are so similar as to be constantly confused by local experts. They also tax the experienced botanist.

Jíchiquia (*escoba*)—*Desmanthus covillei,* Fabaceae. This rather nondescript leguminous shrub is eagerly sought for making brooms, a function which seems rather pedestrian and uninteresting, until one sees firsthand the Mayos' obsession with cleanliness and the need for inexpensive brooms. It is an important shrub. Don Vicente was pleased one day to come upon a large population growing a couple of kilometers from his house. He cut enough branches to make a broom and vowed to return for more.

Jiógo (*chicura*)—*Ambrosia ambrosioides,* Asteraceae. This ubiquitous annual grows very tall and thick in the arroyo bottom. It is eaten with relish by beasts of burden. A tea is made and drunk by women after giving birth to cleanse them and help them return to a normal menstrual cycle.

Jito—*Forchhammeria watsonii,* Capparaceae. The shade is a refuge from the blistering sun; the fruits are boiled and eaten. Tom Van Devender christened the *jito* "the lollipop tree," with good reason, for in the spring drought, when all else is dreary, the trees stand out in the *monte* like gigantic lollipops. *Jitos* are respected by the Mayos. I have searched in vain for tiny, young plants. I fear that the trampling of the *monte* by cattle is preventing recruitment of replacement trees.

Jócono—*Havardia sonorae,* Fabaceae. A small tree with numerous small, sharp thorns, its leafage is eaten by goats. It is a good firewood, and at times the branches and trunks are used in building houses. The thorns are most intimidating. It is viewed by ranchers as a pest, for where it grows, it can be difficult to eradicate. Around Teachive, it is quite common.

Jopo (*palo blanco*)—*Piscidia mollis,* Fabaceae. A large, oaklike tree, the wood is strong, though not especially hard. It is ideal for posts and, because it is dense and resists rotting, it is also good for bases of posts. The leaves are spread over a roasting agave to protect the steaming head and leaves from dirt and to help keep steam from escaping. The leaves are not bitter and the heat does not impart any flavor to the succulent agave.

Joso—*Albizia sinaloensis*, Fabaceae. In the region of Masiaca this tree grows into a graceful giant up to thirty meters tall. Its bark is yellowish or white. The bark is used in Masiaca for curing leather, producing a white color. The wood is carved into large spoons and other utensils. Also, the wood is used for roasting, although the flame is not particularly hot.

Jósoina (*papache*)—*Randia echinocarpa*, Rubiaceae. This strange large shrub that seems to grow in arches yields even stranger tennis-ball-sized fruits with immense, dull, decurved spines protruding randomly. These fruits, when ripe, are eagerly harvested and enjoyed, especially by children. Adults also claim they are good. I have not observed their practice conforming to their pronouncements. (This may be because Teachive is a bit low in altitude and arid for the *papache* bush.) I found the fruits to be rather bitter and could eat but one and preferred to make it an annual affair. The pulp is said also to be good for many ailments, including stomach distress and diabetes, for which it is highly recommended by many Mayos. Doña María Soledad Moroyoqui, a Teachive weaver, claims that when eaten on an empty stomach, the fruits kill amoebas and other parasites. Vicente claims that if you make a hole in the ripe fruit and let the juice drip out, the resulting liquid is refreshing. I think I'll let him enjoy it without any comment from me.

Ju'upa (*mezquite*)—*Prosopis glandulosa*, Fabaceae. Mesquite grows everywhere, maturing into huge trees along the arroyo. It, like *brasil*, is used by every family in Teachive, for firewood, for lumber, for *péchita* (beans) eaten by livestock and formerly by people (who prefer the beans from *P. velutina*, rare in the region), for its sap (candy and a dye), its roots (medicine and a brown dye), its shade, and so on. It is probably far more common now than in the past, benefiting from seed dispersal by burros, mules, cows, and goats, and able to withstand the onslaught of livestock better than other trees. Some of the grand old individuals have been recently sacrificed to construct new houses for Teachive's growing population. On Good Friday, Vicente (and most Teachivans) cut some small branches and wove them into an arbor covering the house cross. During the terrible drought of 1995–96, after all the grass and edible shrubs had been consumed, the *péchita* (beans) of May and June were the only food left for livestock. Each morning a new crop of the legumes would fall to the ground and be eagerly consumed by cows, goats, and sheep. The mesquite alone kept the livestock alive.

Júchaco (*brasil*)—*Haematoxylum brasiletto*, Fabaceae. A small tree once found throughout the *monte*, it is now rather scarce, due to overharvesting. A slow-growing wood, *brasil* trees of usable size have virtually vanished from the vicinity of the villages. This loss is a great shame, for *brasil* has a multitude of uses from firewood (the best available) to dyes to medicine. No home in Teachive persists without sooner or later using *júchaco*, this most versatile tree, in one way or another. Dyes made from the heartwood are especially noteworthy, the degree of saturation of red being a function of the duration of dyeing. Julieta Zazueta mixes the heartwood with the root of *sa'apo* and boils them to make a fast, red dye. Don Vicente also touts it as a remedy for *tiricia* (sadness or depression).

Jupachumi (*cola de zorillo*)—*Petavaria alliacea*, Phytolaccaceae. The root of this herb is peeled, chopped, and placed in a small flask of alcohol. The vapors are breathed in to cure colds, sniffles, and asthma. A tea is also brewed to cure *empacho*, or bad digestion. Don Vicente is quite enthusiastic about its powers and has urged me to use it. The actual translation of the Mayo *jupachumi* is "skunk's ass."

Jupachumi (*palo zorillo*)—*Senna atomaria*, Fabaceae. This small, graceful tree is widely used for posts and beams. It makes decent firewood as well. It flowers in late spring, adding a touch of bright yellow to the drab landscape.

Júpaque cara (*mesquite hormiguillo*)—*Condalia globosa*, Rhamnaceae. Longer trunks are used for fence posts, the spines left on. The leaves are eaten by goats. When the plant is young, the tender branches are nibbled off as well.

Júsairo (*vara prieta*)—*Croton flavescens*, Euphorbiaceae. Among other things, the *júsairo* leaves turn red in the fall and spring, adding a rare touch of red to the landscape. The shrub, sometimes nearly a small tree, is used for a variety of stomach ailments ranging from stomach ache to diarrhea to *empacho*, a folk ailment of the digestive system.

Júapostuguo (*palo santo*)—*Ipomoea arborescens*, Convolvulaceae. The morning glory tree provides emergency food for burros, who devour the bark hungrily and, in extreme drought, for cows, who examine it disdainfully, then seem to shrug and munch away. The gum, or sap, is used in various places to cure toothache in molars, which are said to disintegrate over a few weeks' time once they have had the gum applied (hence caution is recommended in the application). The blossoms fall to the ground in late winter and are eagerly eaten by livestock. A local woman reports that the flowers brewed into a tea are a remedy for high blood pressure. Vicente, who suffers from hypertension, was eager to collect some of the flowers. He had to wait until December when we could drive to the nearby hills to collect the flowers, which are winter bloomers, opening only when the tree is leafless. Although it is common in the region, *júapostuguo* does not grow near the village, being confined to slightly wetter slopes and better soils a few kilometers to the north. It grows close enough to town that Vicente was willing to walk to find it if necessary. Vicente attributes the decline in numbers to the rampages of burros, and to the drying trend in the climate. In full flower, the trees are visible from afar, as the large white blossoms at the tip of the branches reflect sunlight.

Júapostuqui, *Bachata*—*Opuntia* sp., Cactaceae. A chollalike cactus with rather vicious spines. It is abundant in the *monte* near Teachive. The root is brewed into a tea and taken for prostate problems.

Júaposvare (*igualama, uvulama*)—*Vitex mollis*, Verbenaceae. A medium-sized tree found along the arroyo; in August it yields black, cherry-size fruits which are eagerly eaten. I found them bitter when I first tried them, but Teresa stewed them with a little sugar and the result was something like plums. Don Vicente suggests they are tasty eaten with goat's milk. The *igualama* flowers in spring, the delicate lavender blossoms spreading a delightful perfume over the landscape. Sitting in Vicente's *portal*, I could detect the perfume from the tree, ten meters away.

Juvavena—*Atamisquia emarginata*, Capparaceae. It is necessary to walk a kilometer from don Vicente's house to find this large shrub. For molar pain, the tender branches are pounded to a pulp, then boiled. The resulting liquid is applied to the tooth. In recent years, the seed of the avocado has been found to be more effective. For mange, the same pulp is used and the effected skin bathed. It is thought to cure the mange.

Júyaguo (*guayacán*)—*Guaiacum coulteri*, Zygophyllaceae. The delicate lavender-blue flower of this small tree is brewed into a tea and widely taken for asthma. The tough, durable (closely related to *lignum vitae*) wood is used in the construction of looms. Branches are woven to make walls, and then covered with mud, making for a solid, long-lasting wall.

Mabes (*tonchi*)—*Marsdenia edulis*, Asclepiadaceae. A vine in the milkweed family. Children gather the young pods and bring them home, where they are eaten with great relish.

Máchaguo (*Tepeguaje*)—*Lysiloma watsonii*, Fabaceae. Often a large, angular tree, it is used for lumber. More regularly, its bark is taken in a tea for gastritis and other stomach problems and for "female" problems, whose etiology requires a conceptual framework based on the ontological elements "hot" and "cold," quite different from the standard Western assumptions. Vicente explains that many (but not all) diseases are caused by consuming cold or cool foods, the list of which is quite varied. *Tepeguaje* is one means of overcoming this imbalance. Scarce locally, it is more abundant farther up Arroyo Masiaca and near Yocogigua to the east. A supply of the bark is kept in the Tajia-Moroyoqui household and used frequently.

Macochini (*guamúchil*)—*Pithecellobium dulce*, Fabaceae. This widespread tree, although not as common in the village as elsewhere, is found in Teachive, as in other towns near Masiaca. It is probably a human-introduced species, never found far away from humans. It yields highly edible beans which most natives eat eagerly, many toasting them first in a *comal*. They have a sweet taste, reminiscent of a rather dry plum, and can pucker the mouth when harvested prematurely. Children gather the pods, which turn red when ripe, and chew on the beans for a snack. The reddish wood is also sometimes used as lumber, although don Vicente was not enthusiastic about it. The trees are highly valued for shade as well as for fruit. The bark is used in curing leather, though not widely, since it is said to smell rather bad.

Mambia (*chichiquelite*)—*Solanum douglassi*, Solanaceae. Relished as a green, especially when prepared with sauteed onions, garlic, tomatoes, lime, and salt. With that combination, almost anything would taste good. Following a very heavy rain, Vicente and I found an arroyo in which the rapid-growing plant abounded. We gathered large bagfuls and presented them to doña Teresa, who was delighted. She prepared the greens by stewing them and by sauteeing them as above.

Mayo (*mauto*)—*Lysiloma divaricatum*, Fabaceae. An excellent firewood, good, tough lumber for building, growing into thick, straight, heavy poles. Most of the larger trees in the region were harvested long ago, although trunks tend to regenerate quickly. The bark is made into a tea for diarrhea and to tan leather. Some natives gather the bark and sell it in Masiaca to the leather workers there. Someday a project to plant and raise *mauto* for firewood, bark, and poles will get underway.

Miona—*Commecarpus scandens*, Nyctaginaceae. The leaves, branches, and roots are boiled into a tea that is taken for sore kidneys.

Mochis—*Boerhavia* sp., Nyctaginaceae. The leaves are boiled into a tea taken to relieve measles.

Mo'oso—*Aster spinosa*, Asteraceae. This pretty purple aster grows abundantly along overgrazed bottomlands. Vicente touts it as a good remedy for inflamed tonsils. The leaves are brewed into a tea, which is gargled.

Murue (*jaboncillo, ocotillo macho*)—*Fouquieria macdougallii*, Fouquieriaceae. As the Spanish name indicates, soap can be made from the plant, especially from the bark. Don Vicente notes that it is efficacious on dandruff. It is also planted to make living fences. The cut stalks sprout almost immediately if planted before *las aguas*. They also bloom frequently, which makes the fences more than a mere deterrent to livestock and humans.

Na'atoria (*baiburilla*)—*Dorstenia drakeana*, Moraceae. The root of this small, large-leafed perennial is mashed and made into a poultice which is rubbed on the face to heal *boca torcida* or *alferecía* (twisted mouth), probably a reference to Bell's palsy. One of Vicente's grandchildren used it with satisfying results. It no longer grows in the vicinity of Teachive, owing to the drying out of the climate, according to Vicente. It still can be found upstream near San Antonio. The same is true for another Moraceae, *Ficus petiolaris*, the rock fig, which was far more common in the region when Vicente was young.

Navo (*nopal*)—*Opuntia wilcoxii*, Cactaceae. The prickly pear is valuable for livestock, which in times of drought eat the mature pads, and for humans, who eat the tender pads (*nopalitos*) and the fruits (*tunas*). Tacos made from the *nopalitos* are most appealing. The fruits are refreshingly juicy and, once one gets used to chewing the seeds, substantial. I suspect that the pads, a bright green, are an important source of vitamins, for the Mayos' diet appears to be lacking in fresh vegetables much of the year. There are several varieties of *navos* with varying properties.

Nésuquia (*uña de gato*)—*Mimosa distachya*, Fabaceae. Goats eat the leaves and the beans. It also makes acceptable firewood.

Ona jújugo (*huele a sal*)—*Adelia virgata*, Euphorbiaceae. A small or large shrub, frequently with straight branches that are used for fencing or, in emergency, for firewood.

Onore (*biznaga*)—*Ferocactus herrerae*, Cactaceae. While the fruits of the barrel cactus are left for livestock to consume, Mayos hack off the waxy epidermis and spines with a machete and roast the inside flesh with sugar, pronouncing the cooked starch to be delicious. They are correct. Unfortunately, these often large cacti (as tall as two meters), though not rare, are never common. No one will ever be saved by drinking the water contained therein.

Orégano—*Lippia palmeri*, Verbenaceae. Highly aromatic bushes of the herb grow wild on calcareous soils not far from Teachive. It is harvested in commercial quantities by the Mayos of San Antonio, not far away. No home is without it.

Palo mulato—*Bursera grandifolia*, Burseraceae. A medium-sized tree, formerly found on the farthest hillsides of the *comunidad*, now found only in the forest a few kilometers to the north, and northeast, where it becomes increasingly common on more moist slopes. The bark makes a refreshing, reddish tea, taken as a tonic or simply as a refreshment; the wood is carved into masks. Don Vicente keeps a supply of bark in the house, as do I.

Paros pusi (*ojo de liebre*)—*Solanum tridynamum*, Solanaceae. This prolific annual grows on disturbed soils throughout the region. It features attractive purple-blue flowers with yellow centers. The leaves are made into a concentrated tea and poured into the ears of people who suffer from deafness. It is said to open up the ear canal. Whether it has been tried successfully on older people, I do not know. Vicente assures me that it would be effective on people who have been deaf for a long time.

Pi'isi (*papache borracho*)—*Randia obcordata*, Rubaiceae. This large, slim shrub is favored by goats. The cherry-size fruits are edible, and virtually everyone in the community has tried them. They seem to produce a dizziness when more than one is eaten, hence the Spanish name. A larva infests many of the fruits. Woodpeckers come searching for the larvae, making a pea-sized hole in the fruit while extracting their prey. The fruit then dries out in the arid winds. Boys pick these dessicated fruits and blow into the hole, producing a whistle that can be heard over long distances.

Pómajo (*palo de asta, cabo de acha*)—*Cordia sonorae*, Boraginaceae. A small, erect tree (hence its Spanish name, which means "flagpole tree") whose straight, hard wood is used regularly to make handles for implements. It makes great clubs.

Pohútela (*toji*)—*Phoradendron californicum*, Loranthaceae. A bushy, leafless mistletoe that prefers mesquites and other legumes. It is widely viewed as brewable into a tea that is effective for lowering blood pressure. Vicente, however, does not use it. The fruits are eagerly devoured by phainopeplas whose Mayo name is also pohútela.

Sa'apo (*sangrengado*)—*Jatropha cinerea*, Euphorbiaceae. A large shrub with blunt branches that drip sap when cut or broken. This sap is placed directly on a bruise, cut, abrasion, fever blister, or sore and is believed to cure such injuries rapidly. It is used daily by people who work in the *monte*. Don Vicente demonstrated its application on a cut on his hand. He has not used it on cold sores or the painful cracks some people are prone to get in the corners of their mouths. His brother has used it for these with success, he says. The sap burns and a layer of skin will eventually peel off, leaving the skin free of the sores, he claims. A mere drop on clothing will stain irrevocably. Julieta Zazueta, a *cobijera*, uses the root as a mordant with *brasil* wood in preparing a bright red dye for her woolen blankets.

Samo, causamo (*sámota*)—*Coursetia glandulosa*, Fabaceae. The springy branches of this large shrub or small tree are used to make chairs. Dried branches make acceptable firewood. A lac produced by an insect frequently appears on the branches. It is widely used in Sonora under the name Goma Sonora as a cure for intestinal complaints.

Sanarogua (*mataneni*)—*Callaeum macroptera*, Malpighiaceae. For livestock with sores that refuse to heal, you mix the root with rattlesnake fat and apply it to the wound. It will heal quickly. Vicente assures me that this is truly effective—and on humans as well.

Saya—*Amoreuxia gonzalezii*, Bixaceae. A nifty little plant eaten entirely, roots and all. Usually, though, just the root is eaten, roasted or raw. It is much relished in Teachive. Unfortunately, it is nowhere common. People and animals alike rush to harvest the plants, which are conspicuous by their showy orange flower. Their flavor is greatly enhanced with lime juice. I'm baffled as to why they are not domesticated.

Sibiri (*cholla*)—*Opuntia thurberi*, Cactaceae. The green, tender young spines are eaten before they become dry and sharp as a cure for diarrhea and "*pujos*," bloody stools. This and Chogua are revered as remedies, although don Vicente has had no need to use them in recent years, he said. During the growing season the spines are green and succulent and can be easily plucked from the cactus and eaten.

Sigropo—*Lycium andersonii*, *L. berlandieri*, Solanaceae. The thin branches are cut into small sections and threaded into necklaces, especially rosaries, for they are nearly hollow inside and a needle can easily pass through. Local artisans weave imitation *téneborim* on dolls resembling *fariseos*.

Sina—*Stenocereus alamosana*, Cactaceae. A rambling small columnar cactus whose small fruits are especially relished. They are also reported to help ease the pains of rheumatism and to alleviate the pain and swelling of insect stings. Vicente collected the husks of ripe fruit to boil into a tea for soothing his granddaughter's heat rash.

Sire—(*granadilla, morito*)—*Malpighia emarginata*, Malpighiaceae. Its bright red fruits the size of blueberries appear regularly in the Tajia-Moroyoqui household in late July and early August and are eaten with enthusiasm. They taste all right, but are rather dry and unsatisfying.

Sitavaro—*Vallesia glabra*, Apocynaceae. A vinelike shrub rather common in the arroyo, often growing into dense, user-friendly thickets and even into a tree. For pinkeye or other eye problems, Teachivans break off a tiny stem and place a drop of the exuding milky sap into the corner of the affected eye. It is also believed in some quarters to possess strong healing powers against evil forces. It is a favorite source of greenery for covering the *fiesta* ramadas during Holy Week. The shrub or small tree is found in great abundance along the arroyo. When I had an eye infection, don Vicente showed me how to use it and inquired afterwards if it had helped. It hadn't done any harm. Doña Lidia Zazueta made a small *cobija* that bore small figures dyed with *sitavaro* root. It produces a mustard-like color. On Good Friday, Vicente cut a branch and gently beat each member of the family, saying, "May harm and sickness stay away from you." He uses *sitavaro* for this, he explains, because the branches and leaves are soft and will not scratch or otherwise injure anyone during the ceremony.

Táboaca (*tabachín*)—*Caesalpinia pulcherrima*, Fabaceae. This shrub is quite common in the more moist areas of the community. It produces showy red and yellow blooms up to twelve centimeters across. For twisted mouth (perhaps Bell's palsy) a poultice is made by mashing the root and rubbed on the paralyzed part of the face. Vicente assured me that although it sounds far-fetched, it does, in fact, work.

Táchino (*cardo*)—*Argemone ochroleuca*, Papaveraceae. Benigno Buitimea drinks a tea from the leaves to alleviate the symptoms of diabetes. It is also rumored to be good for prostatitis.

Tajimsi—*Krameria erecta*, Krameriaceae. Bark from the roots of this shrub is used to help heal sores that refuse to heal naturally; also a source of red dye when combined with *palo dulce*. Vicente dug up a specimen to show me, gave me half, and took the rest home. Don Reyes Baisegua of Sirebampo assured me that *tajimsi* was an excellent remedy.

Tapichogua (*copalquín*)—*Hintonia latiflora*, Rubiaceae. *Copalquín* is a small tree used regularly as a lumber wood for fences and cross beams in roofing. It is valued even more for the curative properties of its bark, which is reputed to make a superb tonic and cure stomach and intestinal ailments. Vicente swears by it, as do multitudes of Mexicans who purchase it in markets for its curative powers. Benigno Buitimea, a diabetic, maintains a sizeable bundle of bark strips hanging from the ceiling of his house and regularly drinks a tea made from the bark. He doesn't mind the bitterness which others find distasteful. *Tapichogua* is often the first plant mentioned when one asks Mayos what sorts of medicinal plants they know. Trees seem to tolerate considerable bark harvesting without appearing much the worse for wear. The tea is usually drunk with a pinch of cinnamon to combat the bitterness.

Tásiro (*San Juanico*)—*Jacquinia macrocarpa*, Theophrastaceae. This strange tree is commonly found in the *monte* around Teachive (and in tropical deciduous forest as well). It bears copious small, narrow leaves whose apex forms a needle-sharp point. Doña Teresa Moroyoqui and other women use the flowers to make a yellow dye for their weaving. Of old, the fruits were made into a shampoo that left the wool and their hair squeaky clean and nice-smelling. Now, alas, detergents are simpler to obtain. Doña Buenaventura Mendoza was out in the *monte* one day gathering the flowers when I went to visit her. She stated that tea from the flowers would strengthen her heart. She had brought quite a pile with her. They must be harvested before the rains come, she said, or they will be no good for dye or for medicine. Harvesting flowers and fruits is hard on the hands, for it is impossible not to receive a multitude of tiny stabs from the needle-sharp leaves.

Tatachinole—*Tournefortia hartweggii*, Boraginaceae. The root is used for a wash to soothe the pains of rheumatism. A tea is made, said to be good for kidneys, although it is not widely used in Teachive.

Teso—*Acacia occidentalis*, Fabaceae. A large, leguminous tree, it is found commonly to the north and east of Teachive and along dry washes throughout the community. Fine utensils are carved from the strong wood. The wood is strong and suitable for use in building.

Teta segua (*flor de piedra*)—*Selaginella novolensis*, Selaginellaceae. The resurrection plant, found on rock faces of the Arroyo Masiaca some kilometers away from Teachive. Vicente keeps it in his home. The entire plant is soaked in water, the water then drunk to relieve kidney problems, kidney stones, and gall stones. He is convinced it works and has treated himself with it, combining it with a tea of *cósahui*. Kidney problems appear to be common among natives of the region. This common pathology may be related to the intense heat of the coastal region, which promotes rapid loss of body water through sweating.

To'obo (*amapa*)—*Tabebuia impetiginosa*, Bignoniaceae. A tropical tree now uncommon in the region due to overharvesting. Most older houses, particularly those of Masiaca's more affluent residents, contain beams of *amapa*. Formerly it was found along the arroyo and in the forests a few kilometers to the northeast. Now only isolated individual specimens remain along the more moist arroyos distant from the *pueblos*. The tree flowers a brilliant pink when leafless in winter. The wood resists rot and termite infestations and so is favored in the construction of houses. Vicente is raising an *amapa* in his backyard. It is five years old and has not yet bloomed.

To'oro (*papelío*)—*Jatropha cordata*, Euphorbiaceae. This common small tree with exfoliating bark produces a wood, don Vicente says, that when sucked on will cure bee and wasp stings. He hasn't used it for that purpose, but, he says, his brother has. He hacked off a twig for me to try and I found it to be most astringent. A large sheet of the bark is also useful for wrapping freshly made cheese to keep it fresh, an asset in a region of hot climate and many goats and cows, with refrigeration generally unavailable. The tree is also an aesthetic boon to the region, for it leafs out early and turns green whether or not it rains, bringing some measure of consolation to the natives in times of summer drought. In July it produces a delicate pink flower.

To'oro (*torote*)—*Bursera fagaroides*, Burseracea. Oddly scarce near Teachive, it is common in most parts of the thornscrub. Although it is not viewed as useful, the dead wood is still thrown into the kiln firewood for baking bricks. Birds also love the dried fruits, which cling to the apparently dead branches for many months.

To'oro chucuri (*torote prieto*)—*Bursera laxiflora*, Burseraceae. This large shrub grows to tree size as well. Its wood is used by Benigno Buitimea to carve *pascola* masks. The bark is brewed into a tea said to be effective for coughs. When *cu'u* (agave) is roasted, a few branches of the *to'oro chucuri* are thrown on first and when burned impart a delicious flavor to the sweet-flavored leaves and head. Its resins smell strongly of incense.

Tubchi (*abolío, amolillo*)—*Sapindus saponaria*, Sapindaceae. An often large tree with bright green leaves, it occurs sporadically but frequently in the region. The seeds are polished and made into necklaces used by *fiesteros* and others. The wood is used in building houses. It is not very strong.

Uose náacata (*oreja de león*)—*Perityle cordifolia*, Asteraceae. A bright green herb with pretty yellow flowers, found on volcanic rocks high on the hillsides, especially on Cerro Terúcuchi and Ayajcahui. Juan Féliz swears that the following happened: His grandfather had told him that a tea brewed from the whole plant would put the drinker to sleep. He and a friend were curious. They were reluctant to try it themselves, so they boiled up a tea and poured it into a dog's water dish. The animal drank the liquid and directly fell into a deep slumber from which it could barely be aroused.

Usim yuera (*matachamaco, palo verde*)—*Agonandra racemosa*, Opiliaceae. The tree is found along arroyos, never common but hardly ever absent. The bright green leaves tend to droop, providing help in identification. Vicente pronounces the wood to be very good in building houses.

Yoco sutu, uose sutu (*palo fierro*)—*Chloroleucon mangense*, Fabaceae. The beans are excellent livestock food. The wood, though brittle, is very strong and useful for fenceposts. The trees' outer branches tend to descend, providing umbrellalike shade, so that livestock can stay in the same place for many hours without losing the cool protection.

Yoroguo (*cacachila*)—*Karwinskia humboldtiana*, Rhamnaceae. The wood of this small, tough tree is used for posts and firewood. The leaves are brewed into a tea for fever and for hepatitis. Victims of the latter are also bathed with the infusion.

APPENDIX C *Plants Listed by Scientific Name*

SCIENTIFIC NAME	MAYO NAME	SPANISH NAME
Acacia cochliacantha	chírajo	guinolo, chírahui
Acacia coulteri	bagüío	guayavillo
Acacia farnesiana	cu'uca	vinorama
Acacia occidentalis	teso	teso
Adelia virgata	ono jujuga	huele a sal
Agave angustifolia	cu'u	lechuguilla
Agonandra racemosa	usim yuera	palo verde
Albizia sinaloensis	joso	palo joso
Amaranthus palmeri	güey	bledo
Ambrosia ambrosioides	jiógo	chicura
Amoreuxia gonzalezii	saya	saya
Argemone ochroleuca	táchino	cardo
Atamisquia emarginata	juvavena	
Baccharis salicifolia	bachomo	batamote
Boerhavia sp.	mochis	
Brongniartia alamosana	cuta nahuila	palo piojo
Bursera fagaroides	to'oro	torote
Bursera grandifolia	to'oro mulato	palo mulato
Bursera laxiflora	to'oro chucuri	torote prieto
Caesalpinia caladenia	jícamuchi	palo piojo blanco
Caesalpinia palmeri	jícamuchi	palo piojo blanco
Caesalpinia platyloba	cuta síquiri	palo colorado
Caesalpinia pulcherrima	táboaca	tavachín
Callaeum macroptera	sanarogua	mataneni
Candelia globosa	júpaque cara	

271

SCIENTIFIC NAME	MAYO NAME	SPANISH NAME
Capsicum baccatum	cócorit	chiltepín
Cercidium floridum	ca'aro	palo verde
Cercidium praecox	choi	brea
Chenopodium cf. mexicanum	choal	quelite
Chloroleucon mangense	yocosuto, uosesuto	palo fierro
Cordia parviflora	guo'tobo	vara prieta
Cordia sonorae	pómajo	palo de asta
Coursetia glandulosa	samo	sámota
Croton flavescens	júsairo	vara prieta
Desmanthus covillei	jíchiquia	escoba
Diospyros sonorae	caguorara	guayparín
Diphysa occidentalis	güicobo	güiloche
Dorstenia drakeana	na'atoria	baiborilla
Erythrina flabelliformis	jévero	chilicote, peonía
Euphorbia sp.	cuépari	golondrina
Eysenhardtia polystachya	baiguo	palo dulce
Ferocactus herrerae	ónore	biznaga
Ficus petiolaris	bausabu	tescalama
Forchhammeria watsonii	jito	palo jito
Fouquieria macdougalii	murue	jaboncillo, ocotillo macho
Guaiacum coulteri	júyaguo	guayacán
Guazuma ulmifolia	ájiya	guásima
Haematoxylum brasiletto	júchago	brasil
Havardia mexicanum	chino	palo chino
Havardia sonorae	jócono	jócono
Hintonia latiflora	tapichogua	copalquín
Hyptis albida	bíbino	salvia, chani
Ibervillea sonorae	choya guani	guareque
Indigofera suffruticosa	chiju	añil
Ipomoea arborescens	jútugo	palo santo
Jacquinia macrocarpa	tásiro	San Juanico
Jatropha cinerea	sa'apo	sangrengado
Jatropha cordata	to'oro	papelío
Karwinskia humboldtiana	yoroguo	cacachila
Krameria erecta	tajimsi	
Krameria grayi	cósahui	cósahui

SCIENTIFIC NAME	MAYO NAME	SPANISH NAME
Lippia palmeri	orégano	orégano
Lycium andersonii	sigropo	
Lycium berlandieri	sigropo	
Lysiloma divericatum	mayo	mauto
Lysiloma watsoniii	máchaguo	tepeguaje
Malpighia emarginata	sire	granadilla
Marsdenia edulis	mabes	tonchi
Mimosa distachya	nésuquia	uña de gato
Olneya tesota	ejéa	palo fierro
Opuntia fulgida	chogua	choya
Opuntia leptocallis	jíjica	cholla
Opuntia sp.	bachata	cholla
Opuntia thurberi	sibiri	choya
Opuntia wilcoxii	navo	nopal
Pachycereus pecten-aboriginum	etcho	etcho
Parkinsonia aculeata	bacaporo, guacaporo	guacaporo
Perityle cordifolia	yoco na'ácata	oreja de león
Petavaria alliacea	jupachumi	cola de zorillo
Phaulothamnus spinescens	ba'aco	
Piscidia mollis	jopo	palo blanco
Pisonia capitata	baiguo	garambullo
Pithecellobium dulce	macochini	guamúchil
Portulaca umbraticola	guaro	verdulaga
Prosopis glandulosa	ju'upa	mezquite
Randia echinocarpa	jósoina	papache
Randia obcordata	pi'isi	papache borracho
Salaginella novolensis	teta segua	flor de piedra
Sapindus saponaria	tubchi	abolío, amolillo
Senna atomaria	jupachumi	palo zorillo
Solanum douglassi	mambia	chichiquelite
Solanum tridynamum	paros pusi	ojo de liebre
Stenocereus alamosana	sina	sina
Struthanthus palmeri	chíchel	toji
Tabebuia impetiginosa	to'obo	amapa
Vallesia glabra	sitavaro	sitavaro
Vitex mollis	júvare	igualama, uvulama
Ziziphus amole	bais cápore	saituna

Glossary of Spanish (and Mayo) Terms

agrimensor—surveyor

aguaje—water hole, pool

ajonjolí—sesame seed

alaguássim—fiesta official

albañil—bricklaying

alcalde—mayor

aleluia—halleluia, name for
  evangélicos

alguates—glochids, tiny cactus
  spines

alpez (alférez)—chief fiesta
  official

amapa—tree (Tabebuia
  impetiginosa)

artesanías—arts and crafts

asamblea—assembly

atole—porridge

baño—bath

batea—wooden tray

bacote—agave pole for harvesting
  pitahayas

bajada—sloping alluvial fan

berlina—horsedrawn carriage

birria—stew of shredded meat

blanco—white, non-Mayo

borrega—ewe

brujo—witch or shaman

cabecera—mission headquarters

cabrita—kid (young goat) meat

cacique—strongman, tyrant, local
  dictator

calzones—traditional baggy white
  muslin trousers

camino real—official or royal
  highway

campesino—peasant, rural dweller

carga—a load or order

catre—cot

chachalaca—pheasant–like bird

chamba—employment

cholugo—coatimundi

chorizo—sausage; here it refers to
  the long pile of upturned trees
  and brush that is left when
  clearing pastures

ciclón—hurricane

cobija—blanket

cobijera—blanket weaver

cocido—cooked; vegetable and
  beef stew

275

cocina—kitchen

colorado—red

comal—griddle

comisariaría—the political entity presided over by a *comisario*

comisario—commissar, commissioner

comisariado—commissar, as pronounced in the Masiaca community.

comunero—member of the *comunidad*

comunidad—community, communally owned land, reservation

conejo—cottontail rabbit

conquistadores—conquerors

consejo de vigilancia—watchdog official

conti—Lenten Mayo procession

cordel—measurement of length

cordillera—large mountain range

coyoles—bronze bells worn by *pascolas*

criollo—creole; in this case, the tough, rangy, longhorned cattle introduced by the Spaniards

cronista—chronicler, historian

cruda—hangover

cuaresma—Lent

cucharra—large spoon

curandero—curer

curandismo—curing

desmonte—clearing

ejidatario—member of an ejido

ejido—communally owned land

elote—ear of corn

emborracharse—to get drunk

empacho—a digestive disorder that results from an imbalance of hot and cold

equipatas—winter rains

etcho—large columnar cactus

evangélico—evangelical

evangelista—an evangelical Protestant

fábrica—factory

faja—sash

fariseos—Pharisees, fiesta dancers

federales—federal police

fiesta—festival

fiestero—fiesta organizer

flojo—lazy

fundo legal—registered town lands

ganadero—rancher

garrafón—large water jug

gente de razón—people of reason (a term used by Spaniards and mestizos to distinguish themselves from Native peoples)

guacabaqui (Mayo)—beef and vegetable soup

hacendado—owner of a hacienda

hacienda—landed estate

hechicero—sorcerer

hermanos de la fe—brothers of the faith, evangelicals

hiel—bile

horcones—support posts

huaraches—leather sandals

indígena—indigenous, native

indio—Indian

ixtle—burlap woven from agave fiber

jícamuchi—small tree (Caesalpinia palmeri)

jito—small tree, Forchhammeria watsonii

jojoba—shrub whose seeds produce oil (Simmondsia chinensis)

jornalero—day laborer

joso—large tree (Albizia sinaloensis)

judiciales—state police

la lengua—the (Mayo) language

ladrillero—brickmaker

ladrillo—brick

las aguas—summer rains

latas—wooden cross-pieces

la técnica—trade school

latifundista—owner of large estate

leña—firewood

leñero—woodcutter

limpieza—cleanliness

limpio—clean

los ricos—the rich

machismo—cult of masculinity

maestro—master, teacher, lay catechist

mafiosos—organized criminals, drug lords

maquiladora—foreign-owned assembly plant

mal puesto—bewitched or under a spell

malacate—spindle

mapache—raccoon

maseca—corn flour

matachín—member of fiesta dance group

material—gravel, material

matrimonial—large blanket

mauto—tree (Lysiloma microphyllum)

mayor—major, older, principal

mediador—mediator, agent

menor—minor, younger, assistant

mescal—distilled agave liquor

mestizo—person of mixed Indian and Caucasian ancestry.

metate—flat or scooped grinding stone

mezquite—mesquite tree

miel—honey, syrup

milpa—cornfield (usually not irrigated)

mojonera—boundary marker

mono—doll, carved figurine

monte—the bush, uncleared forest

morral—handbag of agave fiber

municipio—county

murue (Mayo)—ocotillo (Fouquieria macdougalii)

músico—musician

narco—drug dealer

narcotraficante—dealer in drug traffic

naturales—natives

norteña—northern

olla—jug, pot

paca—bale (of hay)

palanca—yoke for carrying buckets

palo colorado—red stick, the tree *Caesalpinia platyloba*

panal—beehive

panga—small fishing boat

parina—fiesta official

pascola—traditional Mayo dance

pasmo—ailment characterized by emotional or physical distress resulting from physical or emotional trauma

patrón—boss

peligüé—sheep for meat production

pequeña posesión—smallholding, inholding

piedra—rock, stone

pila—storage tank

pintor—painter

pistear—to drink alcohol

pisto—distilled liquor

pitahaya—organ pipe cactus; also the fruit

pitahayal—forest of organ pipe cacti

porfiriato—the period of Mexican history under President Porfirio Díaz, 1880–1910

portal—shaded porch

preparatoria—prep school

prestanombre—a name loaned to another to skirt landowning restrictions

promesa—promise, commitment, vow

propina—gratuity, tip

pueblo—people, village

ramadón—pascola ramada

raza mixta—mixed breed

rebozo—shawl

repartamiento—system of forced labor

respeto—respect

roce—influence

sabino—bald cypress

saituna—small tree (*Zizyphus amole*)

seca—dry

sector social—social sector

semana santa—Holy week

serape—blanket, meant to be worn

sexenio—six-year term

sierra—mountain range

socio—member, partner

son—folk song

susto—ailment caused by shock or fright

talabartería—leatherworking shop

tamal—corn mash

técnica—technical school

temporal—dryland farm plot watered by flooding

téneborim—cocoons sewn with pebbles inside and strung into rattles for dancers

téquiac (Mayo)—community work

tinaco—elevated water tank

tuna—prickly pear fruit

tinajera—tripod supporting a water jug

trabajador—worker

vaquero—cowboy

vellón—sheep's fleece

venado, venadito—deer, deer dancer

venganza—vengeance

vigas—beams

visión—vision, foresight

visita—village church served by a
    priest from a larger church

yoreme—Mayo

yori—mestizo or non-Indian

zorillo—skunk

zarca—cloudy, gray–white

Notes

1. Don Vicente Tajia has been my friend and companion during my visits to Teachive. The honorific title "*don*" is used to denote respect. Esteemed men and women over fifty or thereabouts are frequently referred to as *don* or *doña*. The name Teachive is said by some to be derived from the Cahita *teta* (stone) and *chibilem* (scattered), which would translate simply as "scattered stones." Vicente believes the derivation to be *técola* (round stones) and *chibila* (scattered), or, in Spanish, *piedras redondas regadas* ("scattered round stones"). Larry Hagberg of the Summer Institute of Linguistics has studied the Mayo language extensively and finds Vicente's translation a reasonable one.

2. The term *monte* refers simply to the surrounding bush, the natural vegetation. The phrase "Irse al monte" can mean anything from going for a hike, to going to the toilet, to gathering cactus fruit or firewood.

3. Of the *jito* (*Forchhammeria watsonii*), Gentry (1942) says, "The tree has a very individual appearance, suggestive of old olive trees in ancient Judea. In the burning days of late spring it is about the only tree that offers shade to weary beasts and man."

4. Natives of the region refer to the peculiar dry season color of thornscrub, a nearly uniform gray-brown, as *mojino*.

5. The geographical coordinates for Teachive are 26°47'10"N, 109°14'W. Elevation is 75 meters. Masiaca is located at 26'46"N, 109°13'W and 50 meters elevation.

6. In all cases those who assisted in the field, unless in their official capacity, were compensated for their help.

7. I use as a watershed date the 1951 completion of Mocúzari Dam on

the Río Mayo, which thereafter assured a dependable supply of irrigation water to farms in the delta and permitted the economic transformation of the region. The transformation is a matter of degree, for large-scale irrigated agriculture began in the Mayo Delta in the 1880s. I suspect that it is no mere coincidence that the strongly anti-collective President Miguel Alemán also signed the Masiaca *comunidad* into official existence in the same year (1951), thereby assuring an abundant supply of cheap labor for the delta, from which there would be no unrest and demands for land.

8. Lest I be accused of romantic exaggeration, let me point out that the 1994 uprising in Chiapas involved little more than two hundred poorly armed, mainly illiterate peasants. Stock exchanges all over the world were rocked by the events in Chiapas. As of mid-1997 the rebellious forces continue to wield international influence.

CHAPTER 1

1. About six million years ago what is now Baja California was literally torn and rifted away from the continent. The newly formed peninsula hurried to the northwest, a direction it still tends at the rate of up to five centimeters a year. This extraordinary stretch and pull tore off a chunk from the mainland as it rifted away, creating the delta of the Río Mayo (Lonsdale 1989).

2. *Nojme* = highest (*punto mas alto*); *cahui* = mountain (*cerro*).

3. Freezes have been offically recorded in the Fuerte Valley to the south, and in the river valleys to the north, but no one recalls a freeze on lands of the *comunidad*.

4. Snow frequently falls at Yécora at 1,500 meters in the Río Yaqui Basin, and in the easternmost (and highest) mountains of the Río Mayo drainage. Yet it is unknown in the ranges best known in the Mayo region, the Sierra de Alamos at 1,760 meters, the Sierra Saguaribo at 2,000 meters, and the Sierra Charuco at slightly over 2,000 meters. Because the Mayo Basin is encircled by the larger mountains of the Río Yaqui and Río Fuerte Basins, the former is shielded from the colder air masses from the north and east. Consequently, winters are milder on the Mayo and snow is unknown at elevations where it commonly falls outside the basin to the north and east.

5. Local people are well acquainted with the birds of predawn (as well as many others). Vicente was able to list thirty-nine species of birds

known from around Teachive and to identify the myriad birds of night by their calls. One of them, the Buff-collared nightjar, is called the *préstame tu cuchillo* (lend me your knife) in imitation of its call.

6. *Norteña* music is rather like U.S. country music. It includes many ballads and songs of broken hearts accompanied by guitar, accordion, and string bass. Its uniformity is noticeable.

7. The women's custom of wearing an ersatz shawl may be the only vestige of native costume remaining in the region. Yaqui women still wear colorful woven *rebozos*, which they wind and swirl effortlessly to provide a headcover and partial veil and in which they carry infants and packages. Many Mayo women achieve the same effect with textiles designed for other purposes, but they appear not to carry infants in their shawls.

8. On December 21, it is light by 6:30 A.M. and dark by 6:00 P.M.

9. No rain fell in Teachive between September 15, 1995 and July 1, 1996. A heavy rain fell on September 14, 1996. As of April 1, 1997, no rain had fallen since the previous September.

10. White-faced parrots are most common, sometimes in huge numbers. Natives capture them as chicks and keep them in cages. Lilac-crowned parrots are seen less frequently. Men sometimes find birds' nests and bring fledglings home to entertain the family. One family thus raised a Harris hawk, which they kept until it was a strong-flying adult. *Chachalaca* eggs are eagerly sought, for they can be hatched by hens and grow to nearly the size of turkeys.

11. A few trees, notably *Forchhammeria watsonii* and *Jacquinia macrocarpa*, retain their leaves throughout the year. *Lysiloma watsonii*, found in foothills thornscrub to the north and east, leafs out as early as late April.

12. In the spring of 1995, however, extensive pumping of water above the village led to drying up of the water course, causing wells to dry up. Many of the pools dried up as well.

13. *Albizia sinaloensis*. While *josos* are common in southern Mayo country, they are rare in the Río Yaqui, not having been identified in the drainage by botanists until 1996. See description in Appendix.

CHAPTER 2

1. Spicer (1962) and O'Connor (1989) have compiled useful histories of the Mayo. I have attempted in this chapter not to duplicate their work except for unavoidably important historical events.

Carl Sauer was a highly influential geographer and anthropologist, who contributed much to our understanding of the early history of northwest Mexico. I am doubly indebted to him, for it was he who urged the young Howard Scott Gentry to explore the upper Río Mayo in search of Guarijío Indians. Gentry published *Río Mayo Plants* in 1942, after spending more than four years in the region. I was influenced, in turn, by Gentry's work and his urgings that the explorations in the Río Mayo be continued. The present work is the product of my interest in Teachive's plants, stemming from my desire to add to Gentry's contribution.

2. In addition to Mayo and Yaqui, Cahitan languages include the extinct Baciroa, Huite, Macoyahui, Sinaloa, Tehueco, and Zuaque.

3. Whether the Aztecs would have been interested in a people of such limited material wealth as the Cahitas is questionable. See Padden (1967).

4. Pfefferkorn's *Sonora: A Description of the Province* was not written until 140 years after the arrival of the Jesuits in Sonora.

5. The Crown had great interest in the discovery of precious metals. The coastal plain of Sinaloa is narrower and its rivers are shorter than those of Sonora. The closeness of the mountains to the coast meant that mineralization of the mountains was not far from any of Sinaloa's numerous indigenous people. Most of the non-clerics who came early to the region came in search of precious metals. For example, Pérez de Ribas notes of Francisco de Ibarra that he "set out from Culiacán and from there (with a great number of soldiers), entered the province of Sinaloa [which included the Río Mayo]. He traversed through the province and visited all its peoples . . . and seeing it populated by so many peoples . . . and that the colors with which the Indians adorned and painted themselves, were signs of mines, (because those colors were taken from the mines) he determined that he would leave a populated estate on the river they call Zuaque [Fuerte]" (Pérez de Ribas 1645: Bk. 1, ch. 9).

Peréz de Ribas also attributes the arrival of Hurdaide to the Crown's interest in metals. "The Count of Monterrey, viceroy of New Spain, having been notified by people who know that in the province of Sinaloa there were thickly-veined mines that promised great riches, whose discovery would be of great importance to the king and his vassals, dispached with this news and information his official order and charge to the captain of Sinaloa [Hurdaide]." (Bk. 2, ch. 24.) García (1967) notes that "The mines of Copala [near Mazatlán] were destroyed during the uprising of the Tepehuanes of 1616." (All translations mine.) Hurdaide's expedition against the Chínipas was also motivated by rumors of silver. (ch. 47)

6. Frank (1972) notes that the most underdeveloped parts of Latin America are the areas with the greatest riches at the time of contact; in contrast, the areas where development took place were those areas with little to export. The Mayos fall in between. Their agriculture resources were exploited by the Spaniards prior to the discovery of silver at Alamos.

7. Alvar Núñez Cabeza de Vaca had been shipwrecked in Florida and then marooned in Texas in 1526. He wandered westward for nearly eight years, living with natives, curing them, and learning their languages. (Cabeza de Vaca, 1972)

8. Brading (1971) notes that Ibarra's career as governor and explorer was possible because of an inheritance from his uncle, who made an incalculable fortune in the silver mines at Zacatecas.

9. Such contemporary descriptions of Hurdaide as provided by Pérez de Ribas, suggest that he was sufficiently astute militarily that he would not recruit local warriors merely as cannon fodder. (Acosta, 1983, p. 46)

10. Pérez de Ribas (1634, bk. 4, ch. 1) "The word Mayo in the Mayo language means "limit, perhaps due to this river's being between two others whose people make continuing war with the Mayos and don't allow them to leave from their 'limits'." (translation mine.)

11. Historians rely almost exclusively on Pérez de Ribas's account of the Yaqui campaign. He was not present for the battles, however, and relied on others' accounts. In exalting the achievements of Hurdaide, he relates an incident in which the Yaquis purportedly set fire to the brush around a hill on which Spaniards had established a defensive position. Hurdaide gathered sick and wounded horses and drove them away, knowing they would head for the river. The Yaquis were deceived by this strategy and took the herd of horses for Hurdaide's men, following them and leaving the way clear for the Spaniards to retreat. The problem with this account is that the coastal thornscrub, in which the fighting took place, does not burn, even during the scorching dry season, and cannot be ignited except for scattered

individual shrubs (in order to plant buffelgrass, ranchers must clear the pastures by hand, wait for the cut brush to dry, then burn it). The account is either a great exaggeration or a fabrication, if not by Pérez de Ribas, then by one of his informants.

12. Pérez de Ribas owned that he was distressed to find "an abuse among the Mayos, that was difficult to correct: this was, that it was quite easy for pregnant women to obtain abortions." Divine intervention assisted in eradicating this blasphemy, however. Of an old midwife, he records that "the old woman had the devil in her, to do abortions for pregnant women, exhorting them and giving them remedies to carry it out. God took mercy on this old woman, because he moved her heart to request baptism, which she received and the next morning she awoke dead" (translation mine). No inquest is recorded. (Pérez de Ribas 1645, bk. 4, ch. 3)

13. Pérez de Ribas says of the arrival of Pedro de Méndez: "The Mayos received Padre Méndez, with singular demonstrations of joy, venturing out to receive him two or three leagues before his arrival at their pueblos, and all of them raised their triumphal arches fashioned from tree branches, which are the Mayos' tapestries." (1645, bk. 4, ch. 3)

14. While there is no reason to believe that the historic differences in military prowess between Yaquis and Mayos is based on character, there has been, nonetheless, a clear historical difference between the two. Hu DeHart (1984, 277) notes that the Mayo region is less blessed with topography lending itself to guerrilla warfare. While this is true of the Mayo Delta, it is not true of the Masiaca *comunidad*, where numerous hills and mountains, plus the well-watered Sierra de Alamos would suffice for temporary guerrilla hideouts. Water is, in general, more abundant in the Mayo region and toward the south, while in the Yaqui region reliable surface water is confined to the Río Yaqui and agriculture is confined to the delta area. The proliferation of villages in the Mayo Delta and south contrasts with the denser concentration of the Yaqui Delta. The more dispersed populations probably led to a more dispersed culture as well, and a less clearly defined sense of a cultural unity.

15. The "reduced" pueblos were: Batacosa, Camoa, Cohuirimpo, Conicárit, Júpare, Navojoa, Tepahui, and Tesia. Jesuit sources (Pérez de Ribas 1645) divide the Mayos into three greater subdivisions: Camoa (the upstream Mayos), Navojoa (midstream), and Etchojoa (delta).

It is noteworthy that Masiaca does not easily fit into any of these divisions.

16. In describing the arrival and activity of Fray Pedro Méndez, Bannon (1947) reveals his allegiance to the long list of writers who evoke the cultural superiority of Europeans. He characterizes as sorcerers (*hechiceros*) Mayo spiritual and medicinal practitioners who objected to the Jesuits present, dismissing their objections as mere jealousy. (Ambrose Bierce would have defined a sorcerer as a practitioner from someone else's religion.) He also attributes to the Jesuits success in vastly improving agriculture almost overnight, thereby alleviating perpetual impending starvation among Mayos, a claim that simply cannot be substantiated by the historical record. It is perhaps difficult for a Jesuit to be objective about the exploits of those in his own order, but such cultural chauvinism by a sophisticated scholar demonstrates how deeply some cultural myths have penetrated.

17. Pérez de Ribas 1645, bk. 2, ch. 48.

18. By "Sonoran," Pfefferkorn means indigenous Sonoran.

19. Although we can only infer the deliberations that took place, there must have been many. Evidence for this is necessarily oblique. If we consider the numerous rebellions that characterized the Spanish colonial occupation of northwest Mexico, however, a long tradition of planning and deliberations must have existed. The nature of the revolts usually involved tactics and strategies that presupposed carefully laid plans. Rebellions included the Tepehuanes in 1616; Aibinos in 1622; Tarahumaras in 1648; Eastern Pueblos in 1680; Opatas in 1687; Lower Pimas in 1690; Opatas in 1696; Seris, Apaches and Upper Pimas 1680–1700; Cahitas in 1740; and the general uprising including the Pimas, Opatas, Seris, and Apaches in the 1750s.

20. Reff (1991, 256–57) successfully debunks the myth of Jesuit-spawned technological revolution among New World natives. In spite of claims to the contrary, wheat, cattle, and the metal plow were scarcely used among indigenous people until well into the nineteenth century. Pfefferkorn acknowledges that Sonorans preferred wild game, horse, and mule meat to beef, which they appear to have resisted for aesthetic (and, perhaps, cultural) reasons. Indeed, among natives of the northwest, only the horse seems quickly to have gained wide acceptance, and that by Comanches and Apaches, much to the dismay of Spaniards. Likewise, cattle were highly valued only by the

Seris, who rustled them at will, thus providing an excuse for Spanish and Mexican extermination campaigns. Today, corn tortillas are said to be the food of Indians, while flour tortillas are the food of *gente de razón*, indicating that wheat never made a great impact on indigenous Sonorans, and the introduction of wheat proved to benefit only colonists.

Pfefferkorn (1949) grudgingly admits that the European diet was less wholesome than the native Sonoran diet: "The food supplies of the Sonorans . . . are in part bad, in part insipid and nauseating. And yet these people live contentedly, reach a great age, and are much more healthy on such a fare than are others whose daily board consists only of artificial and highly spiced dishes" (200). This admission seems to undercut the common claim that European horticulture and husbandry benefited the natives of the New World.

21. In return, the best the New World natives could send to Europe was syphilis. The exchange was highly unequal.

22. Reff (1991) notes that the smallpox virus can be communicated through clothing and can remain virulent while stored on blankets for more than one year. In addition to the danger of direct contamination through nasal discharge and saliva, phenomenal amounts of innoculum could thus have been stored up by Spaniards who presented Indians with European textiles.

23. The mission population of Sinaloa and Sonora, already far below the preconquest levels of indigenous populations, fell from 90,000 in 1638 to roughly 52,000 in 1678 (Reff 1991, 202). Pfefferkorn (1949) noted a loss of half the population of Sonora between 1700 and 1767, when he was expelled along with all other Jesuits.

24. Reff (1991) notes epidemics of 1616–17, 1619–23, 1623–25, and several between 1636 and 1660. That any natives of Mexico survived at all seems miraculous and a tribute to their genetic toughness (or, perhaps, to whatever "primitive" religion they practiced).

25. See, for example, Pérez de Ribas 1645, bk. 2, ch. 47.

26. It is also clear from the narrative that natives quickly learned to invoke the Devil to explain their deviance from the true way. Pérez de Ribas goes to great lengths to detail the descriptions of The Adversary provided by various Indian groups. These garish portraits strike a gleeful note in those who have worked among native peoples and learned how their subjects often take great delight in pulling the legs

of highly trained observers. I once spent several weeks doing an ethnobotanical study with a Mayo, dutifully jotting down all of his comments. I learned only later from his daughter that he amused himself from time to time by inventing all manner of preposterous tales about uses of plants, sometimes wondering when I would catch on. When I confronted him with one especially egregious exaggeration, he chuckled happily for some time.

27. Polzer (1976, 62) is careful to point out that "the religious were not permitted to inflict physical punishment. Actual physical punishment was dealt out by a person other than the religious." Apparently, the clergy could not abide the taint of physical violence, hence they delegated the frequent corporal punishments to those less close to God.

28. Brading (1971, 146), however, notes that "Mexican mine-workers, far from being the oppressed peons of legend, constituted a free, well-paid geographically mobile labour force which in many areas acted as the virtual partners of the owners. . . . The vast majority of Mexican miners—they did not number more than 45,000 individuals—worked voluntarily."

29. For an excellent discussion of the machinations of miners, missionaries, and Indians, see Calderón Valdés (1985, 2:102–10).

30. If Brading (1971) is correct, the Jesuits may have protested too loudly at the recruitment of indigenous men to work in the mines. The Indians may well have viewed mine work as desirable, while the Jesuits resented the loss of influence over the men, hence inflating their "concerns" about the effects of mining on the Indians.

31. Several operating mines persist today in the Río Mayo region, primarily in the upper portion, including El Pilar, Moris, Ocampo, and Santa María.

32. In 1996 Sonora was Mexico's principal producer of copper, and newly reopened gold mines made it the leading producer of gold as well. Mining still draws southerners in search of work to the state.

33. The view of natives as subhuman is still current in Sonora, where *mestizos* often refer to themselves as *gente* or *gente de razón*, in contrast to Indians, who are simply referred to as *indios*, frequently used as a pejorative term.

34. Gerhard (1982, 274) notes without citation that Mayos rebelled again in 1769 at a place called Charay, in present-day Sinaloa.

35. The popular belief that weaving and blanket-making were Spanish innovations brought to incompetent and ignorant natives is a clear example of the assumption of European cultural superiority. Spaniards everywhere in Mexico marveled at the exquisite textiles and varied dyes produced in the New World. In general, scholars believe that postconquest textiles never reached the high levels of those produced prior to European contact. Wool is not a superior material. In fact, cotton is preferable in hot weather. Wool is, however, easier to obtain than cotton, and sheds water, a virtue in cool, rainy weather.

36. In December 1995, I visited the last Guarijío weaver, who lives in the remote village of Bavícora. She pronounced her weaving days to be over and vaguely lamented the absence of successors.

37. This reluctance to pay taxes continues among Yaquis in the United States today. As one who worked with the Tucson Yaqui community, I found it amusing and frustrating that they refuse (passively) to pay property taxes, meaning that huge bills for back taxes are run up on their homes.

38. The threat from the Cahita rebellion extended as far as El Fuerte, Sinaloa where the authorities, as a security measure, decided to move the capital from El Fuerte south to Cosalá near Culiacán (Nakamaya 1975, 75).

39. One historian blamed Juan Banderas for all future conflict between the Cahitas and the government: "Having been dormant for so many years, the hatred that Jusacamea [Juan Banderas] had aroused in his people continued to plague Sonora into the present century" (Stagg 1978, 40).

40. Federalists favored states' rights and a weak central government, while centralists preferred a strong central government and relatively weak states. These distinctions were frequently glossed over, however, as warlords tended to attract followers on the basis of their personalities rather than their ideologies.

41. For a brief history of the French invasion, see Chisem (1990, 157–68).

42. Pesquiera probably bore a festering resentment against indigenous people. Born of creole parents, he was educated in Spain and France. He insinuated himself into Sonoran politics and rose quickly to command a garrison at Baviácora on the Río Sonora, ultimately becoming governor of the state. His promising career suffered a

severe setback at the battle of the Stinking Well (Pozo Hediondo) on January 20, 1851, where his dashing troops were handed a crushing defeat at the hands of a small army of Apaches. Twenty-six of Pesquiera's troops died in the contest and forty-three were wounded. Pesquiera himself was wounded and knocked from the saddle. He was forced to run for his life, an ignominious taint for a vaunted Sonoran. The Apache force proceeded to steal 1,300 horses and raid the defenseless town of Bacoachi, which they sacked and pillaged. Pesquiera recovered quickly, managing to be elected to the state legislature the following year, and ultimately became one of Sonora's most famous and successful strongmen (Almada 1952). As governor, his programs included the colonization and agricultural development of the Río Mayo and Río Yaqui lands, both programs contingent upon the submission of the Yaqui and Mayo peoples (Hu DeHart 1984, 58.) In 1872, he also proposed the establishment of "Pesquiera Colony," a model *mestizo* town to be built according to the most modern plans between Navojoa and Júpare. It was never built.

43. For a fictionalized but intriguing account of the life of Teresa Urrea, see Domecq 1990.

44. Erasmus cites the outbreak of a new prophetic movement in 1957, when "God" appeared to a young Mayo, and demanded a resurgence of the *fiestas*. Word of this revelation quickly spread through the Mayo region, resulting in an increase in *fiestas* and an embellishment of the appearance of "God." See Erasmus (1967, 102–3).

45. During the Porfiriato large numbers of Yaquis were deported to Oaxaca and the Yucatán where they worked as slave laborers on sugar cane and henequen plantations. Others fled north to the United States, where they formed communities in exile. Three such Yaqui "towns" remain in Tucson, one in Marana, and one in Guadalupe, a suburb of Phoenix. Frequently, Mayos joined in the exodus as well and were incorporated into the Yaqui communities. These *barrios* retain Yaqui customs and still distinguish themselves from *mestizo*, or Mexican, immigrants. In 1976 a reservation for Yaquis was created southwest of Tucson. Mayos were not sufficiently represented to merit separate consideration.

46. At the forefront of the enterprise to make the Yaqui and Mayo valleys into one huge agricultural enterprise was a remarkably resilient entrepreneur and opportunist named Carlos Conant. A native

of Guaymas, he rose rapidly in the military, but proved adept at siding with losers. At one point he was exiled from Sonora, using his enforced vacation to open a mine near Ocampo on the Río Mayo in Chihuahua, where in 1883 he conscripted a small army to put down a strike. Returning to Sonora in 1888, he was given a concession by the Porfirio Díaz regime to survey and develop the Mayo and Yaqui Deltas as a first step toward "opening" the deltas to modern agriculture. He went broke, but sold out to others, ultimately, the Richardson Construction Company, which purchased the delta scheme in 1905 and was to dominate delta economics and politics for nearly forty years. For an account of Conant's schemes, see Dabdoub (1964, 267–91).

47. This is not to imply that Mayos per se had ever formed a clear-cut, distinctive culture. Over the centuries, they had intermarried with Yaquis and Opatas to the north, and Zoaques, Huites, Baciroas, and Zoas to the south. As I will discuss below, Mayo culture was more vaguely defined than Yaqui culture. Still, a clear identification of themselves as *yoremem* pervaded and still pervades the region, and references to Mayo culture are perfectly justifiable. See, for example, German E. et al. 1987.

48. O'Connor (1989) describes a brief uprising in 1910 by the Mayo Totoliguoqui and a few followers. Its goal was to oust non-Mayos from Mayo lands. Though the Mayos were armed only with bows and arrows, the pathetic revolt was violently put down by the Mexican military. It is the last recorded armed struggle of Mayos against outsiders.

49. Robertson (1968, 21–22) describes parenthetically how Mayos from the Río Fuerte stormed the Navojoa garrison in 1915 during the height of the Mexican Revolution. His comments are disturbingly brief.

50. Calles made a practice of eliminating his enemies or those with whom he merely disagreed. He developed a secret police that became notorious for using torture on political prisoners. His opposition in the late 1920s, including the Cristeros (a rabidly pro-Catholic military movement centered in west-central Mexico), responded in kind to his violence. It was not a good period for Mexico.

51. Calles, although known for his anticlericalism and radicalism, was first and foremost aligned with wealthy growers and ranchers. His

vision of Sonora included the transformation of the deltas of the Río Mayo and Río Yaqui into highly efficient export-oriented modern farms. The indigenous *comunidades* and *ejidos* stood in the way of that vision and were hence an expendable anachronism.

52. The most prominent of evangelical groups is La Iglesia de Diós Completo.

53. See, for example, Erasmus (1967), German E. et al. (1987), and O'Connor (1989) for analyses of the problems in Mayo *ejidos*.

54. Reff (1991, 150) surmises that Basiroa may have been affected by the epidemic of 1606–07. It is highly likely that Masiaca would have been affected as well, since the two towns are only thirty kilometers apart. The inevitable loss of population accompanied by the scourge of disease may have so decreased Masiaca's population that it became even less strategic in historical events, possibly explaining its obscurity. Basiroa, which has but a tiny Mayo population, may have lost its ethnicity when it was struck by repeated epidemics as well. Apparently, Reff notes, Baciroans left the *sierra* (their town was located on the lower Río Cuchujaqui, a valley, not a *serrano* settlement) and relocated at Concárit and Tepahui, both villages on the Río Mayo or its tributaries.

55. Gerhard considers the languages of these groups to be Mayo, further confusing what he refers to as a confusing situation. It is doubtful that Ahomes, Choix, Huites, and Zuaques, would have agreed to call their language Mayo, even though today their descendants consider themselves to be Mayo speakers.

CHAPTER 3

1. The lack of grasses and other plants is entirely a function of human and animal use. An abandoned house on the east side of the arroyo, empty because of the indecision of its absent owner, is surrounded by a stout fence. Within the protected boundaries, no livestock have been able to graze for several years. Viewing those protected lands, one can glean a vision of how the region might look if livestock were not allowed to consume every last bit of edible forage. The ground within the fence is covered with a heavy mat of grasses and shrubs. On Cerro Terúcuchi, among the rocks inaccessible to goats, numerous bunch and perennial grasses are found.

2. The actual phrase is "hace muchos años, mas de cien años."

3. She reports that, while Yaquis were wild and destructive, they only burned and pillaged the Mayo towns. They brought no personal harm to Mayos. With *yoris* (*mestizos*), however, it was a different story. The Yaquis killed all of them they could.

4. Channel meander and widening, plus the relentless onslaught of livestock, have obliterated all signs of old Teachive. The original site had advantages over the present site, for it is on higher ground and the surrounding thornscrub is somewhat richer in trees for firewood.

5. The name is not as drab as may appear, for much of the *comunidad* of Masiaca is devoid of stones. Where they abound, others come to fetch them.

6. Masiaca = *masia* (centipede) and *cahui* (hill).

7. One such is a *mestiza* who married into the Mayo family of her husband. He is said to treat her shamelessly, hardly bothering to look after her or their children's needs.

8. Nor is there any detectable Mayo physiognomy. Various pronouncements about a Mayo phenotype are hogwash. Mayos may tend to be slightly shorter and heavier than Yaquis, but the differences, if they exist, are so slight that they could only be established by an exhaustive statistical study. When I try to guess if a stranger is Mayo, I am correct roughly 50 percent of the time.

9. Lower on the coastal plain the woven, mud-covered *carrizo* style is more common. Teachive has closer access to trees used for *vigas*, *horcones*, and posts than do towns in the delta or nearer the Sea of Cortés.

10. Amapa = *Tabebouia impetiginosa*; mauto = *Lysiloma divaricatum*; mezquite = *Prosopis glandulosa*; palo colorado = *Caesalpinia platyloba*. See Appendix B.

11. It is satisfactory from the women's standpoint, for it heats up more quickly and requires less curing. Men say that tortillas cooked on the old earthen griddles taste better. But, of course, they don't have to cook them.

12. Within the last two decades several women in town organized a project to have a (Catholic) church built, adding onto a current building which was not in use. Bricks and cement were purchased with the funds collected and the supplies were stored on the east bank. Residents claim that subsequently some funds were stolen and

the bricks and cement began to disappear. Since that time, the idea has been dropped, and Teachive still has no church or visiting priest.

In 1996 members of the Teachive Iglesia de Diós Completo, the evangelical church headquartered in Ciudad Obregón, acquired a pastor. Work immediately began on a substantial ramada, which was soon completed. Thus, Teachive became an anomaly: it is a Mexican village with no Catholic church, only a Protestant church.

13. The church was first shown to me by a Mayo *ejidatario* from Yocogigua, twenty kilometers distant. He spent a good hour detailing the history of construction of the church and explaining the history of the saints and the mural of San Miguel. He (along with many others) had contributed labor and materials to build the church, in spite of his great poverty.

14. Technically, the term *comisariado* refers to the office of the commissioner, and the office-holder is a *comisario*. In the Masiaca *comunidad*, however, the office-holder is universally referred to as the *comisariado*.

15. I spoke to a middle-aged man who sat working in his *portal*. I greeted him in Mayo; he answered me in Spanish. Another Mayo man who was present asked him why he didn't answer me in Mayo. The fellow replied simply that his parents had never taught him to speak Mayo.

16. I suspect that Vicente keeps track of his age, however, because when he reaches sixty-four he will be eligible for a modest pension.

17. Members of the evangelical church do not attend.

18. The celebration date of flag day may differ from that of the national holiday. In 1996, for example, the *fiesta* was nearly a week after the holiday because the fiesta of San Antonio, a Mayo *ejido* sixteen kilometers to the north conflicted with it. The schedule of the *fiestas* is not dictated by national calendars.

19. Bacabachi and San Antonio, villages not far from community boundaries, have well-known *fiestas*.

20. This test must be applied with caution, however. Teachive's best weaver and a fine source of cultural information never attends *fiestas*. The reason, I have concluded, is that she and her mother live alone; her husband left her years ago, a brother and a sister have been killed, and her father is long dead. As a single woman, she would not feel comfortable in the *fiesta*. She is very much a Mayo, but does not participate in *fiestas*.

21. Wolf (1959) describes the role of the *cargo*, or obligation to support

community activites, temporally and financially, as a cultural adhesive in Meso-American cultures. That is, members of the community would view the role of *fiestero* as cyclically obligatory. In Masiaca, however, the role of *fiestero* has become largely, if not entirely, manipulative. Individuals assume the role of *fiestero* as part of a *promesa* and *manda*—a promise to the Virgin to be a *fiestero* in return for a perceived favor.

22. Individuals, from time to time, will sponsor *fiestas* in their homes. These include *pascola* dancers and are usually open to the public.

23. The term is derived from the Spanish *alférez*, or standard-bearer.

24. All the musicians are men. They are a tightly-knit bunch, and it is inconceivable that a woman could fit into the circle of musicians.

25. Erasmus (1967, 65) wrote that in 1958 the number of *fiesteros* had dropped from the traditional twenty-four to seven. He thus prophesied the demise of the *fiesta* in the Masiaca *comunidad*. During the Holy Week *contis* (processions) of 1996, *fiesteros* marched in a prestigious place. Nine were present, and others were involved but not in that procession. Erasmus further noted that *fiesteros* were preponderantly from the poorer ranks. "The Indian who is able to improve his financial situation generally wants to identify with Yoris and becomes part of Mexican lower- or, more rarely, middle-class society" (86). While this is still somewhat true, none of the *fiesteros* in 1996 could be said to have been middle-class and they represented a variety of income levels.

26. For an excellent description of the requirements and hardships of being a *fiestero*, see Erasmus (1967, 85–106). In the thirty years since the publication of that manuscript, the role of *fiestero* has changed considerably, but not to the extent that his findings predicted.

27. The 1996 Fiesta of San Pedro at Las Bocas was diminished by the mediocre performance of the deer dancer. He was not the first choice, but was the best available. His routines were mechanical and repetitive, not inspired and varied as they should be with a good deer dancer. Onlookers lost interest in his dance after only a few ten-minute performances, to the distress of the *fiesteros*.

28. *Pascolas* have a demonic connotation, while the *venados* are divinely connected. At the ceremonies' opening, the *pascolas* ask the Virgin Mary for advance forgiveness for their ribald and irreverent conduct. The *venados* need not do so.

29. Erasmus (1967) found in his studies in 1948 and 1958 that Río Mayo

pascolas and *venados* accepted money for performing. Río Fuerte Mayos, however, found this practice mercenary, viewing their performances as part of a lifetime dedication to God.

For an extended (though often confusing) description of the cultural aspects of the Mayo *fiesta*, see Crumrine (1977). Beals (1945) has a clearer, though less detailed, description.

The typical dancer is paid 200–300 pesos for a *fiesta*, more for Holy Week. Considering that a day's wages in the fields brings in about 40 pesos, they are well-paid.

30. O'Connor (1989) describes in detail some other complications arising from commercialization of the fiestas.

31. The Spanish brought with them the technology of distillation, which New World natives adopted with a vengeance. Agaves had been harvested throughout Mexico to make *pulque*, a mildly alcoholic, nutritious beer. Gradually, the distillation of agave brew spread, and for centuries it has captured the imagination of many men. While production of *pulque* has nearly vanished, distillation of agave spirits has soared. Entrepreneurial production has flourished, especially in the northwest where producers operate tiny stills and sell the liquid illegally. Known in Sonora as *jimeros*, they gather the heads of agaves and carry them on burros to their clandestine stills, where they produce a moonshine known variously as *bacanora*, *mescal*, *lechuguilla*, or *vino*. Recently, the Sonoran government, weary of the losing battle of locating and eradicating the thousands of illegal stills, legalized the practice, provided that the *jimero* obtain a license. No self-respecting *jimeros* have responded.

32. *Fiesteros* formerly butchered a steer as part of their duties (Erasmus 1967). They distributed meat and other food to godchildren, who were expected to give back twelvefold what they received. This practice has apparently become sporadic in Masiaca and Teachive, quite probably because the cost was too high.

33. The water is potable but not purified or treated. Few rural villages in Mexico have water systems delivering drinkable water.

34. When the pump motor burned out in June 1996, the villagers unsuccessfully petitioned the municipal, state, and federal government to provide a new pump.

35. The pump broke down in June 1996 at the height of the worst drought in Sonoran history. Watering of the new trees ended

abruptly. Soon, many of the newly planted trees showed signs of stress. Some began to die. Villagers hand-dug small pothole-sized wells in the arroyo from which they carried water to their homes, the men using *palancas* (poles on which buckets are hung at either end), the women using their heads.

36. Choacalle and Cucajaqui both have *tinacos*, but neither functions except as a landmark. They are hardly isolated examples. During the late 1970s and well into the 1980s, the federal government funded the construction of thousands of these elevated tanks. I know of none that still functions.

37. Francisco Gámez in San José carves *pascola* masks and makes drums. His father, don Serapio Gámez fashions *bulis* (canteens) from gourds. His sister Elodia weaves rugs. A family in Choacalle weaves baskets from wire, a woman weaves fine rugs, and another man carves trays from mesquite and teso wood. Don Reyes Baisegua of Sirebampo occasionally weaves *morrales* (handbags) from *ixtle* (agave fibers). Other than a few assorted occasional handicrafts, the artisan productions in the community are limited to those from Teachive.

    Other villages in the region in which women weave include Bacabachi, Chírajobampo, Choacalle, Los Buayums, Saneal, San José, and Sinahuisa. The quality of their blankets does not appear to be as good as those of the best weavers of Teachive.

38. In her study of the region's economy, O'Connor (1989) found Jopopaco to be more affluent than the other villages in the community, and decidedly toward the *mestizo* end of the continuum. The sense of community in that village is independent of its "Mayo-ness."

39. Doña Lidia Zazueta sometimes visits several of her children, who live in Pueblo de Yaqui in the Yaqui Delta. Teresa Moroyoqui has cousins in Hermosillo. Vicente has a sister who lives on an *ejido* near Navojoa. Thus, travel outside the village is not unusual for older people, but few have ventured more than one hundred miles from Teachive, and most have never been beyond the Mayo Delta. Virtually none of the village's children had ever seen the sea when I began working on this book in 1995.

40. *Matachines* wear elaborate headdresses and dance as a group. They are featured throughout the Catholic southwestern U.S. and northwest Mexico. Their name is Spanish, but parts of the dance may predate the conquest.

41. The priest who visits Las Bocas, by contrast, is known to be sympathetic to the *fiestas* and blesses them with his presence and support. He goes so far as to hold confirmation ceremonies in conjunction with the June 28 Fiesta of Saint Peter. He is widely admired by the Mayos of the region.

42. The assembly of the community elects a *comisariado* (chairman) who has considerable power. The losing candidate traditionally is appointed as *consejo de vigiliancia* (vigilant advisor), whose job is to make sure the *comisariado* does what he is supposed to do.

43. "Nos trató con indiferencia."

44. Mayos from Jopopaco, Teachive, San Pedrito, and San José shared this opinion.

45. The hierarchy of the Catholic Church in Mexico has a long history of siding with the wealthy landowners and against the poor. Much of Mexico's anticlerical tradition derives from the church's historic hostility to democracy and its alignment with conservative monied interests, as well as its ancient practice of accumulating huge amounts of land and buildings while the bulk of Mexicans were landless. Friedrich (1970) studied the destruction of the historic subsistence base of a Tarascan community in Michoacán around 1890. By draining a lagoon that had provided the community's wealth, *mestizos* used their political power to gain enormous wealth, with the ultimate result the impoverishment of a previously prosperous subsistence-based community. As the fortunes of the indigenous folk declined, "the *mestizos* of the region ardently supported the Catholic Church and were in turn backed by the local priests, such reciprocity reinforcing the prestige of both groups" (47). The clergy then became ideological defenders of the *mestizos*, who thus "stole" the land from the community: "Acceptance of poverty and of suffering were constantly urged from the pulpit and in the confessional pew, and the fires of Hell were predicted for those daring souls who challenged the landlords' right to the black soil." This tradition continues throughout Mexico with the church's identification with the Partido de Acción Nacional (PAN), the conservative party which is generally considered to be activated by an alliance of church leaders and the wealthy. There are, of course, important and notable exceptions, such as individual priests, and even an occasional bishop, who are outspoken advocates for indigenous people and the poor.

46. The statue of the Virgin Mary inside the Masiaca church presents Mary as a light-skinned, porcelain-complexioned European. Vicente was astounded to hear that Mary's actual skin color was probably at least as dark as that of the Mayos and quite possibly darker. Nuestra Señora de Guadalupe, the patron saint of Mexico whose image is seen in all churches, is portrayed with a more olive skin, perhaps more Mediterranean, but still lighter than one would expect for Mary. Mayos in general are convinced that God, Mary, and the Saints are predominantly light- or white-skinned.

47. In *The Death of Ramón Gonzales*, Angus Wright quotes a Mexican intellectual as saying "When it comes to a commitment to real change [a national movement] can't be taken seriously. The loyalties are to family, to little groups, to patronage networks, not to wider programs or principles" (1990, 72). This is an excellent characterization of *mestizo* society. Mayos tend to have more community-consciousness than do *mestizos*. This vaguely social consciousness may be breaking down in the face of increasing *mestizo* influence.

48. Members of the largest evangelical group, *La Evangélica Iglesia de Dios Completo* (the Full Gospel Church of God) do not view themselves as Protestants. I have subsumed them under Protestantism because they are so considered in the United States, where the missionary movement that founded the Mexican church originated. I explained this to Eduarda Zazueta of Teachive, who was adamant that her church was not Protestant, but she remained unconvinced.

49. Cucajaqui is viewed in the community as very poor and very Mayo. Teachivans often speak disparagingly of Cucajaquians, noting their high incidence of alcoholism and unemployment. They say that Cucujaquians are darker, dress more conservatively (the women wear longer skirts), speak a more pure Mayo, and walk differently.

50. Erasmus noted in 1958 that Protestants ridiculed the *fiestas* and the exaltation of the saints, apparently predicting the rise of Protestantism at the expense of folk Catholicism. If this has taken place, its progress has been slow indeed.

51. The church still instructs wives to be subordinate to their husbands and to be homemakers, however.

52. Agnus Wright, in *The Death of Ramón González* (1990, 115), cites anthropologist Robert Hinshaw, who found that elsewhere in Mexico becoming a Protestant or *aleluia* was an effective means of avoiding the

financial obligations of being a member of a community, especially the costs associated with *fiestas*. Becoming a Protestant, with its repudiation of costly *fiestas*, was a way to accumulate wealth.

53. Some supporters of the *fiestas* would not disagree with this point.

54. Juan Féliz and Eduarda Zazueta Leyba.

55. This practice is an excellent development for small towns, even though the turnover is annual and there may be a significant gap between the departure of the outgoing physician and the arrival of the next. After the rural internship, the physician returns to medical school to complete a residency or specialization and select his or her final place of practice. Sonora has gained some doctors this way. The interns find Sonora to their liking and decide to make it their home.

56. Mayos analyze physical ailments based on heat and cold, explaining etiology and symptoms on the basis of those two humours. Most childhood ailments (other than severe infectious diseases) are attributed to the mother's failure to avoid excess heat or cold while pregnant, while nursing, or while caring for young children. Infirmities of adults, too, are diagnosed either by childhood exposure to improper temperatures, or failure to be aware of the effects of temperature on the body.

57. The family has been repeatedly struck by tragedy. Three of six children have been killed, two in accidents, one by her own hand. A grandson was recently murdered.

58. Teresa Valdivia Dounce in her book, *Sierra de Nadie* (1995), cites a doctor in a rather typical Mexican town who estimated that 90 percent of the male population suffered from alcoholism.

59. This was in late 1995. Since then, the prices of corn and beans have skyrocketed, while beer has merely crept up, so the comparison is subject to market fluctuations. Count on the price of beer to continue to rise steadily.

60. Thus it is that the biggest change in the lives of those who convert to evangelical Protestantism is giving up drinking. As long as they abstain from alcohol, it is difficult for them to socialize with non-Protestants, for such socializing is usually done around alcohol.

61. In 1996 Bancomer closed its branch bank in Alamos, an affluent town of seven thousand inhabitants. Only cities with more than thirty thousand people are sure to have banks. Banks also charge for cashing checks, moreso if the check is written in dollars.

62. I once ran into such a salesman in the Guarijío village of Conejos, thirteen kilometers from the nearest vehicle roadway. He sold only trinkets and clothing.

63. See, for example, Greenberg 1989. Defense of family honor in the Oaxacan community he studied threatened to eradicate the male population.

CHAPTER 4

1. No formal opposition to the final legal description of the community appears in the historical record. This may seem odd, given that the date was during the *sexenio* of Miguel Alemán, notorious for his collusion with Mexico's *latifundio* class and an implacable opponent of *ejidos* and *comunidades.* The absence of controversy may be explained by the fact that the community, virtually without irrigable lands of its own, constitutes an excellent reserve of cheap labor for the vast agribusiness holdings in the Mayo Delta, a fact not lost on the planners of the Mayo Irrigation District.

2. While the Spanish word *boca* means "mouth" or "mouth of a river," which makes sense in that Las Bocas is situated at the mouth of the Arroyo Masiaca, some Mayos contend that in their language *bo'ca* means "stretched out," referring to a beach where the natives could stretch out.

3. According to don Loreto Ortega of San José (which abounds with the surname Ortega), the village did not exist per se until 1803. At that time it contained six dwellings. The residents dug a well and struck good water on October 9, San José's Day. Thus, they named the village after the saint who helped them reach water. Don Loreto says that Teachive had existed for many years before the founding of San José.

In general, I confess to harboring a mild resentment against the Spanish imperialism that established the custom of superimposing (or even imposing) religious place names over existing indigenous labels. There are hundreds of Santa Bárbaras, San Josés, and San Antonios in Mexico, and I find the names monotonous and utterly nondescript. These names usually served a particular religious and political purpose. Once a place took on a Spanish religious name, no one could doubt who had influence there, or that the preexisting culture had been or was being suppressed. I find indigenous place names are far more expressive and interesting. Two Mayo place names, in particular, strike my fancy: Buayums ("loose diapers") and Buaysiacobe ("he lost it three times in the river"). Other Mayo locations have intriguing names as well: Jambiolabampo ("old woman in the water"); Macoyahui ("the echo of something or someone hatcheted to pieces"); Etchoropo ("pile of *etchos*"); Moroncárit ("sorcerer's house"); Mocúzari ("where the owl hooted"); and Tepahui ("very fat"). There are dozens more. In some cases, the conquering Spaniards simply transformed an aboriginal name. One outstanding example of this more subtle imperialism is the landmark peak near San Carlos called Tetacahui ("stony hill," in Yaqui). It is of great significance to the Yaquis. It has been renamed Tetas de Cabra ("goat teats"), supposedly because the enormous pillars at its summit resemble—goat teats. The similarity of sound between the old and the new names is startling.

4. The 1990 population figures for villages in the *comunidad* are as follows: Las Animas, 93; Bochomojaqui, 100; Las Bocas, 474; Chichibojoro, 109; Choacalle, 257; Cucajaqui, 190; Huebampo, 111; Jopopaco, 613; Masiaca, 1,280; Piedra Baya, 10; San José, 596; San Pedrito, 195; Sirebampo, 478; Teachive, 503 (INEGI 1990).

   Growth of the community has been steady since detailed census data became available in 1940. In those fifty years, Masiaca grew from 379 to 1,280 inhabitants. During the same period, Teachive grew from 194 to 503, San José grew from 306 to 596, and Jopopaco grew from 198 to 613. It is not possible to determine the total population of the *comunidad* from previous census data. Many villages were not included in the 1940 and 1950 censuses. The 1980 census figures yield a total of 4,007 for the *comunidad*, while in 1990 the total was 5,009. The most recent figure, however, probably reflects a more rigorous census than the previous figure, and it would be imprudent to assume a population increase of 25 percent for the *comunidad* in the decade of the 1980s. On the other hand, it is possible that the explosion in family size from the 1960s through the 1990s resulted in such an increase.

5. The Masiaca community crosses municipal boundaries, making for some administrative awkwardness. The town of Masiaca is in the *municipio* of Navojoa, while Las Bocas, Chichibojoro, and Sirebampo are in Huatabampo. The entire community originally was part of the

municipio of Alamos. The change of boundaries took place during the administration of governor Román Yocupicio, a Mayo from Masiaca, who, for political reasons, wanted Masiaca, his nominal home, to be included in Navojoa, where he had considerable land holdings. During a later administration, parts of the community were removed to the *municipio* of Huatabampo for different political reasons. Further moves may emerge with new administrations. After the floods in the wake of Hurricane Ismael, the *municipio* of Navojoa paid residents of the *comunidad* to clear roads, repair bridges, etc., but only those who lived within the *municipio*. Thus, some *comuneros* were eligible, others, who lived in the *municipio* of Huatabampo, had no such opportunity.

Indian reservations in the United States also cross county lines (even state lines, in the case of the Navajo Reservation). However, in the United States, on-reservation policies are entirely or nearly entirely preempted from state or county control. Members of *comunidades* in Mexico are subject to all applicable laws, federal and local. *Comuneros'* rights are limited to considerations of land tenure. Since it is the historic and contemporary policy of the Mexican government ultimately to assimilate indigenous people into mainstream Mexican society, no exemptions to any laws are granted to *comunidades* and an historic paternalistic attitude, such as that of the U.S. government to American Indians, is far less obvious in Mexico.

6. *Municipios* have their own elected government, quite similar to county governments in the United States.

7. Sheridan's illuminating work focuses on the *comunidad* of Cucurpe, in northern Sonora. Cucurpe was granted the status of a *comunidad agraria* (as opposed to a *comunidad indígena*) in the 1970s. None of its *comuneros* are *indígenas*. Still, they trace their occupation of the communal lands back many generations. The town celebrates an Easter *fiesta* that, unknown to the participants, demonstrates strong links to Opata ceremonies of the nineteenth century.

8. This office is usually pronounced *comisario*. However, in the Masiaca comunidad the officer is referred to as the *comisariado*.

9. I discussed with two former *comisariados* the fact that this impoverished fellow from the poorest town in the *comunidad* had become *comisariado*. What did they think about it? They shrugged and said merely that he had insufficient *roce social* (political and social influence) to be effective.

10. Las Bocas has a fluctuating population because it is a resort. Still, only *comuneros* are members of the assembly, and they are all Mayos. The remainder of the population lives on leased lots and are not *comuneros*.

11. Sonoran Indians refer to *mestizos* (and sometimes North Americans as well) as *yoris*.

12. Antonio Almada y Reyes came to Alamos from León, Spain, in 1783 and founded the mighty dynasty. He was the great-great-grandfather of historian Francisco Almada, whose *Diccionario de historia, geografía y biografía sonorenses* (1952) has become a standard Sonoran reference work.

13. This is even more true with the revision of Article 27 of the Mexican constitution, which establishes guidelines whereby *ejidos* may select to allow their members to gain full title to their parcels and to sell, rent, or lease them as if they were private property.

14. *Comunidades* may, however, vote to turn the *comunidad* into an *ejido*, which then, according to 1992 legislation, may be privatized. This happened at San Pedro de la Cueva in central Sonora.

15. The basic definitions, rules, and regulations, but not all of them, are found in a document entitled "Legislación Agraria," published by the Procuraduría Agraria of the Reforma Agraria.

16. This issue remains unresolved. According to O'Connor, (1989, 197), INI urged a new census that would expand the list of *comuneros* to include more children of Mayos, thus guaranteeing increased Mayo control over the *comunidad*. The second census was never completed.

17. Yet, according to O'Connor (1989, 107) the INI intervened within the *comunidad* to assist Mayos in asserting more firm control over *mestizos* in the assembly.

18. While the original rationale for legal creation of *comunidades* was to give formal legitimacy to indigenous groups' occupation of their lands, not all *comunidades* are made up of *indígenas*. The *comunidad agraria* of the eastern Sonoran *municipio* of Bacadéhuachi, for example, was created in 1981 during the administration of José López Portillo. It comprises more than 11,000 hectares, including the land the town occupies. None of the *comuneros* is an *indígena*, for Bacadéhuachi has been a *mestizo* town for more than a century. The *comunidad* is referred to simply as the Buenas Comunales de Bacadéhuachi. It consisted originally of 167 *comuneros*, all of whom were *mestizos*, and fifteen of whom immediately declined to participate because they preferred to

be incorporated into an *ejido*, meaning they could be dealt a parcel which would be their own land. To be eligible to enroll, a *comunero* was required to trace ancestry for at least two generations in Bacadé-huachi. Ironically, in the process of creating the *comunidad*, archivists discovered that Bacadéhuachi lacked a *fundo legal*. This is not a trivial omission, since it means that none of the town residents have provable titles to their lots. The more affluent members of the town declined to participate in the *comunidad* (they felt they had no need to, since they already owned land, in some cases, much, much land), so the creation of the *comunidad* left them legally vulnerable to eviction from the homes. When the omission was discovered, the state government immediately became involved and has been "working on" getting the proper papers and land titles. In all other aspects, the *comunidad* of Bacadéhuachi functions in the the same way as the *comunidad* de Masiaca.

19. O'Connor's list, while well-considered, should not be applied too strictly. My colleagues and I have suggested that familiarity with Mayo terminology for plants is also an excellent test for "Mayoness" (Yetman et al. 1996).

20. This information is confirmed by Ing. Leon Demetrio Beltrán, *visitador agrario* of the *procuraduría agraria*.

21. Historic documents refer to the original inhabitants of the community not as Mayos or *indígenas*, but as *naturales* (naturals or natives), a clear indication of the government's attempt even then (1835) to deny the significance of ethnicity as a factor in communities.

22. See O'Connor (1989) for an excellent discussion of Mayo cultural values.

23. See O'Connor (1989, 113) for an explanation of perceptions about who *really* controls the *comunidad*.

24. Among Seris, another Sonoran indigenous group, interracial marriage is uncommon and frowned upon; among Yaquis to the north it is frowned upon and not the norm; among Mayos it is common.

25. This demeaning tradition has endured for more than four hundred years. "In New Spain race as much as class determined a person's position in society. The population separated into three broad categories—Spaniards, both European and American; *castas*, i.e., *mestizos*, *mulattos* and other permutations; and Indians. Those categories, into which individuals were enrolled at baptism, described civic and fiscal

status rather than genetic formation. Most 'Spaniards' were *mestizos*; many *castas* were acculturated Indians; and Indians, especially their *caciques*, could often be *mestizos*. Each group, it should be emphasized, possessed distinct civic rights and fiscal obligations. Quite commonly, however, a simple contrast was drawn between the *gente de razón*, the Hispanic community, and the Indians, a dichotomy which stressed the sharp division which still existed between the two great communities which inhabited New Spain" (Brading 1971, 20). Brading also notes (21) that mobility to the highest social class (*gente decente*, or "decent" folk) was virtually impossible for Indians and *castas*. Yet all who were socially ambitious strove to become viewed as Spaniards, whether or not blood or origin justified it. If we replace the term "Spaniard" with "light-skinned," the same social stratification exists in Mexico today.

26. The project would not have succeeded, for it would have robbed upstream users of water while helping downstream users. The overall water budget available would have been painfully small as well. Erasmus (1967) noted of Masiaca *comuneros* that they "have preferred to continue their relatively unrewarding exploitation of the thorn forest by cutting firewood, making lime, weaving maguey fiber products, and pasturing livestock and view any talk of opening these lands up to irrigation as a threat to their way of life." A more thorough probing of the *comuneros'* opposition might well have revealed a more rational basis for their disquietudes.

27. Soto is voicing a common naive view of irrigation—that water is available if only the proper political pressure is brought to bear. The fact is that all surface waters are overallocated and all known groundwaters are being withdrawn in excess of recharge in Mexico's northwest. Similarly with aquaculture, a common view is that all that it takes is some credit and the project will be a success. Shrimp and oyster farms in Sonora have been plagued with viral infections that destroy the crop and endanger native organisms in the sea, however. Aquaculture is an extremely risky enterprise. Aquacultural projects in Southeast Asia have wrought incalculable environmental and economic damage on the host nations (*Arizona Daily Star*, June 2, 1996).

28. Although spoken Mayo is fast disappearing, it has been exhaustively studied and numerous works document the language. Dictionaries are available. In 1996 a radio station began broadcasting from Etcho-

joa in Cahita (Mayo and Yaqui) and Guarijío. A small but vigorous movement in the *municipio* of Etchojoa to have the Mayo language taught in schools seems to be gaining regional strength. Mayo is taught in some Sinaloan Mayo villages.

29. The only archival documents I have located for Masiaca and its villages are in the state archives in Hermosillo. They begin in 1834 and are cited herein. The municipal archives in Alamos, where the most important documents should be located (Masiaca was in the *municipio* of Alamos till 1934 and all records since independence and even before would have been kept there), are in a state of catastrophic disarray. The archives are in great piles on the floor of a moldy, unattended room of the *presidencia* in Alamos. The mountain of papers, souvenirs, and posters, mostly of recent dates, are covered with cockroach, bat, and bird feces. Despite many hours of searching, I was unable to locate any document of any kind prior to 1870. The local archivist is a political appointee who mumbled an excuse about having too much other work to do to clean up the archives, but he has no other work. It is doubtful that any valuable historical materials remain in that morass of jumbled papers.

To establish the historic continuity of families of members of the *comunidad*, that is, to determine their lineal descent and to gather a feel for the historic continuity of the *comunidad*, the logical source would be baptismal and marriage records, but all such records prior to the twentieth century appear to have been lost. Historical records of the Masiaca church do not exist. Some say they were destroyed during the anticlerical raids of the late 1920s. The clergy rely on the local judicial registry, which has birth, death, and marriage records since 1899. No other archives exist in Masiaca. Other records, as reported to me by the Masiaca judge, were lost "during the revolution," which is a convenient phrase invoked to explain missing records. Early records from the Alamos church were transferred to Navojoa (the *cabecera*), where, if they exist, they remain undiscovered to this date. The church in Masiaca is now attached to Huatabampo, which has no registry for Masiaca. According to the archivist of El Fuerte, Sinaloa, the site of Montesclaros and the supposed repository of early Jesuit and military records, all historic archives there were lost in a fire in 1949. The blaze erupted spontaneously, he explained to me, because of repeated soaking and drying of the documents and the accumulated animal wastes.

30. Don Tomás Valdez of Alamos and Modesto Soto both related this story.

31. Almada does not state his sources, to the detriment of all his successors.

32. See Pérez de Ribas 1645, bk. 4, ch. 2.

33. Masiaca does not appear on Eusebio Kino's well-known map of 1701 (published in many sources, including Dabdoub 1964). Kino followed *el camino real* from Montesclaros to Alamos and would have had no reason to pass through Masiaca. Once on the Río Mayo, he would have become acquainted with all the important Mayo towns as he passed downstream from Conicárit. The same would have been true for the Río Yaqui, where the eight towns are located closely together in the Yaqui Delta.

34. The seven towns are Conicárit, Camoa, Tesia, Navojoa, Cohuirimpo, Etchojoa, and Júpare (Santa Cruz). The site of Conicárit lies under the waters of Presa Mocúzari. Cohuirimpo has been swallowed up by Navojoa and intervening fields. The remaining towns are extant. Hu DeHart (1984, 98) lists without explanation the Mayo pueblos as Navojoa, Tesia, Camoa, San Pedro, Echojoa (sic), Masiaca, Cuirimpo, and Santa Cruz (Júpare). She unaccountably implies that Masiaca lies on the Río Mayo.

35. The great major league baseball pitcher Fernando Valenzuela is a Mayo.

36. The beginning of the *agrimensor*'s report is in accord with the Laws of the Indies, which required the *fundo legal* to be surveyed with the church door as benchmark. See Varegge 1993.

37. The surname *Féliz* is common in Teachive today.

38. Son of the scion Antonio Almada y Reyes, don Juan was governor of the state of Occidente (Sonora) from 1828 to 1830 (Almada 1952).

39. The *fundo legal* is the basic footprint of the town, based on a legal description and laid out in accordance with the Laws of the Indies. Those whose property lies within a *fundo legal* have the right to build houses, collect firewood, and run livestock. The *fundo legal* is a town's legal certification, its public affirmation.

40. A curious example of revisionist history is found in Stagg (1978). An Almada descendant, he does not discuss the effect of the "Almada Law" on communities. He characterizes it as a "radical" law passed to protect natives (48). He makes no reference to its calculated effect of breaking up communally owned lands into tax paying parcels.

"The fact that a great landowner like José María was the author of such radical and far reaching law was a credit to his father's influence and the teachings of his uncle, Father José Almada. It would have brought joy to that simple, kindly priest and to Antonia and Bishop de los Reyes to know that the Almadas were concerned with the welfare of the Indians. If the Almada Law did not accomplish all that its author had intended, it was due to selfish interests and the corrupt politicians who succeeded him" (49). The "Indians" whose welfare was thus looked after stoutly resisted the implementation of the law, except for its provisions whereby they could recover lands stolen from them. The Masiaca *comunidad* did so to great benefit, but refused to acknowledge the more specific provisions of the law, which required that they break the parcels up into acreages of specific sizes.

41. Benito Alcaraz and Juan Crisóstomo Ortega. In 1993 the "owner" of the disputed land bulldozed a wide swath up the southern slope of the Sierra Sibiricahui to the south of Puerto de Candelario, creating a roadway of sorts and ending on an inclined mesa, which was also cleared. Natives of Teachive found the action puzzling, for the clearing could serve no earthly purpose as an impossibly steep road that leads to nowhere. The action and the massive scar on the hillside may well have served as an "improvement" made by an owner, strengthening a claim to ownership in case the title to the lands is ever questioned by *comuneros*.

42. Sibiricahui means "cholla (cactus) hill."

43. The wording specifically mentions *naturales*, or natives, which would clearly preclude communal lands from being awarded to non-natives, as happened early in the twentieth century. The original documents buttress the Mayos' claim that the lands of the community should be confined to Mayos.

44. The term *porfiriato* refers to the period when Porfirio Díaz was president (dictator) of Mexico, roughly from 1880 to 1910. During that time, millions of Mexican Indians, including Mayos and Yaquis, were dispossessed of their lands, which were taken over by outsiders who promised to make them productive on a capitalist scale.

45. *El Independiente* (Hermosillo), June 1, 1996.

46. The provision was inserted to prevent the takeover of beaches by foreigners and the wealthy to the exclusion of the public.

47. The problem of inholdings, or *pequeños posesiones*, is not unique to the Masiaca *comunidad*. The Mayo community of Baimena on the Río Fuerte in Sinaloa consists of 21,000 hectares with a mere 205 *comuneros*, but *mestizos* there control much of the prime land in the form of *pequeños posesiones* as well. Mayo officials in Baimena claim that the matter is in the courts and they are optimistic that the *mestizos* will be evicted or have their holdings vastly reduced.

48. Article 27 of the Mexican constitution states that *comunidad* status includes "la protección especial a las tierras comunales que las hace inalienables, imprescriptibles e inembargables" (Mexican Constitution, Art. 99, III).

49. In 1996 the taxes included twenty-five pesos for the sale of a cow and eighteen pesos for a certificate of permission (*guia*). A cattle inspector stationed in Masiaca collects the tax and the fee and turns them over to the government. An owner of a cow may not dispose of it in any way without informing the inspector. These restrictions extend even to an individual who wishes to slaughter a cow for personal use. The inspector points out that it is to the advantage of those wishing to transport cattle to have the permits. With the papers in hand, they will not face extortion from police, who will demand payment for not confiscating the cattle that are so obviously stolen.

50. Article 101 of Article 27 of the Mexican constitution states: "La comunidad implica el estado individual de comunero y, en su caso, le permite a su titular el uso y disfrute de su parcela y la cesión de sus derechos sobre la misma en favor de sus familiares y avecindados, así como el aprovechamiento y beneficio de los bienes de uso común." In other words, the *comunidad* may create a presumption of continuous use of lands in usufruct. A *comunero* may bequeath his or her parcel to children or to fellow settlers. Nevertheless, the *comunidad*, as a higher power, retains the right to revoke that use.

51. Part, if not all, of his holdings are shown on the map to be *pequeños posesiones*, smallholdings, which are ambiguously private, although included within the community boundaries. On these lands the possessors have more than an usufructary privilege, and they are inclined to treat them as private, a status vigorously protested by the *comunidad*.

52. The 1995 Masiaca inspector's report for the Secretaría de Fomento de Ganado listed approximately 1,300 cows and 35 bulls in the com-

munity. The figures are approximate because some questions remain as to the inclusion or exclusion of Piedra Baya within the community for purposes of the report. This report is probably low by 50 percent, since, according to the inspector, nearly all respondents underreport their numbers, usually by at least half. In addition, many do not bother to report to the inspector at all, since they have not registered their brand in Hermosillo and would be subject to a fine if they were to register their cows. The number does not include heifers or calves. It is safe to assume, then, that there were at least 3,000 cows on communal lands in 1995.

53. COTECOCA (Comité Técnico Consultivo para la Determinación de los Coeficientes de Agostadero), an arm of the Mexican government, recommends one animal unit (cow and calf) per 26 hectares in relatively well-watered central Sonora, an area that receives roughly 50 percent more rainfall and is more than a thousand feet higher than the Masiaca *comunidad*. A pasture's capacity cannot be based upon a linear scale relative to rainfall, since biomass productivity increases dramatically with rainfall up to a certain point. In other words, it is likely that one cow per 80–100 hectares is the maximum realistic sustainable grazing capacity for the Masiaca *comunidad*. In desert uplands of Arizona in the 1950s the figure was generally one cow per section (640 acres = 259 hectares).

54. They also recognize that herding sheep or goats is mind-numbing work. One Mayo suggested to me that the work is so boring that it can stunt the mental and social growth in the lads to whom the responsibility is delegated. Whether or not this belief also applies to girls has not been stated.

55. That the *monte* could have supported such an enormous herd attests to a far lusher epoch prior to the great drought of the 1950s. By all testimony there was far more grass, many more trees, more water in the arroyo, and more abundant firewood. The drought of the 1950s is the only time in living memory that the *aguaje* went dry. At that time, says Buenaventura Mendoza, people had to carry water all the way from Masiaca, nearly two kilometers distant.

56. In addition, Carlota Alcaraz maintains a herd of fifteen sheep that she keeps near the *aguaje*. Doña Lidia Zazueta kept a herd of seven sheep until 1994.

57. For example, José Trinidad Chávez (Camou Healy 1991, 211), a researcher for the Centro de Investigaciones de Alimentación y Desa-

rollo, cites figures indicating an average overstocking of over 400 percent in central Sonora. In other words, in the area studied (which is representative of all of Sonora), there are four times as many cattle as the range can support without loss of biomass and degradation of the overall resource.

58. "Buscan ganaderos apoyo en la capital," *El Imparcial*, Hermosillo, March 3, 1997.

59. Mario Soto is a member of the Cattlemen's Association. He complained bitterly during the 1996 drought that the government provided only marginal assistance to small-time cattle-raisers such as him. Government aid was limited to a grant of four hundred pesos, which purchased sixteen bales of hay, sufficient to feed his cows for a couple of days. He felt that only wealthy ranchers and those near to Hermosillo received any meaningful relief. Still, he acknowledged that the state government provides machinery to assist ranchers to clear their lands in preparation for planting buffelgrass.

60. During Holy Week all government offices close and it is customary for bureaucrats to head to the beach. Las Bocas is closest to Navojoa and to Ciudad Obregón as well and is inundated with revelers.

61. In Mexico, all watercourses are deemed national resources and as such are placed under the jurisdiction of SARH. Similarly, all surface waters are claimed by the federal government. Ground waters, however, are viewed as private property.

62. Buenaventura Mendoza reports that in 1950 the *aguaje* went dry (the only time anyone has known that to happen) and the arroyo ceased to flow. With that exception, Teachivans say, that arroyo had never dried up until the pumping began.

63. Juan Crisóstomo Ortega.

64. It is assumed that *mestizo comuneros* will corner lands either by getting the assembly to increase the individual allocation, or by hiring other *comuneros* to obtain parcels and then rent them to *mestizos*. The assumption has some historic basis, since *mestizos* control the majority of *pequeños posesiones* (small holdings) within the *comunidad* and have done rather well by them. Nevertheless, there does not appear to be any concrete evidence that anything has been signed, sealed, and delivered to anyone in the *comunidad* regarding Río Fuerte water.

65. In mid-1996 extensive clearing for canal construction and leveling for irrigation had begun near Agiabampo to the south of Masiaca and in several Sonoran *ejidos* along Mexico Route 15. The intense drought of

1996 dried the flows of the Río Fuerte, however, and the new Colosio Reservoir at Huites contained almost no water, not even enough to generate electricity through the sparkling new turbines. Widespread rumors predict conflict between Sonora and Sinaloa over allocation of the waters from the new reservoir, much in the way that armed strife took place between the states of Nuevo Leon and Tamaulipas over stored waters. It is widely believed that Sinaloa will manage to grab a larger share of the water than originally believed. One of Sonora's greatest losses when Sonoran Luis Donaldo Colosio, the PRI candidate for the 1994 presidency was assassinated, was the certainty that Río Fuerte water would arrive in Sonora. Mayos from Teachive are convinced that *mestizo comuneros* have already made deals with the authorities to assure that they will be in a position to benefit first from any water that comes to the *comunidad*. I have been unable to verify these rumors.

66. I am not endorsing communal over private plots, or vice-versa, but rather hoping for a distribution that is not based on political influence or a family connection. Netting (1993) demonstrated convincingly that following the reversion to family, as opposed to communal, farming in China in the late 1970s, the Gini (index of equality of resource distribution) declined rather than advanced, to the great surprise of the government and socialist critics of China's abandonment of the commune system. In other words, income distribution was more egalitarian after the return to family farming than when the farming was done through communes (257).

CHAPTER 5

1. The failure was probably a direct or indirect outgrowth of the Green Revolution. Hybrid varieties of corn and beans have replaced the old strains that were selected over generations for their adaptability to local conditions, including drought. The farmers of the *comunidad* ceased many years ago to save their seed. They were assured by government and private agricultural agents that the hybrid varieties would produce more, and indeed they did. The specialized varieties have little tolerance for drought, however, for their high productivity is predicated on inputs of water, fertilizer, and pesticides, without which their yield drops dramatically. In short, had the villagers

planted the seeds of old, they would undoubtedly have seen a harvest. Having surrendered their old, conservative seed to the high-powered new generation seeds, they lost all hope of harvesting. Worst of all, the new seeds do not breed true, and so new seed must be purchased each year. Wright (1990) summarizes the effects of the Green Revolution on a peasant community such as Masiaca as follows: "The effect of the Rockefeller program was to eliminate the system of security and stability built into agriculture by thousands of years of peasant technology practiced under widely varying circumstances and adapted to those differing conditions" (180). "What should be clear from the history of the Green Revolution in Mexico is that it was a very specific political project designed in a very particular political context and carried out by technicians whose self-justifications had only the slightest relevance to the real purposes of the project. It was carried out in order to defeat a popular political movement with a different conception of the improvement of human life, and it so far has succeeded in that task" (186).

2. Nabhan (1982) describes his astonishment at seeing from the air a newly plowed *milpa* following an unusually heavy rain in what had recently been a dry wash in the remote and arid Pinacate volcanic range in northwest Sonora.

3. Biomass is the sum total of the mass of vegetable matter.

4. Ants plague Teachive households, more so in times of drought, when the relative productivity of human households attracts them. Most natives resort to a variety of poisons to suppress ant populations, which always rebound before long. Local yards abound with leaf-cutter, harvester, and fire ants in a huge variety of species.

5. As Bernal puts it: "Contemporary peasants do not operate outside of capitalism, though they may occupy a special place within it. Where peasants must purchase essential consumption items or agriculture inputs, peasant farming cannot be the basis of an autonomous economy with its own logic. The conditions of household farming and the strategies pursued by peasant households in allocating agricultural resources are then responsible to national and international economic conditions. In this case, the substantive rationality of peasant economy is subordinated to the rationality of the market. Familial bonds and the high value accorded to satisfying household subsistence needs are neither dissolved nor replaced by market calculations.

Rather, these enduring values and relationships are acted upon and activated within the terms set by the market" (Bernal 1994, 805).

6. The Sonoran government provides machinery free of charge to clear land in preparation for planting buffelgrass. It is at cross-purposes with its own research arm, CIPES, which strongly recommends against planting buffelgrass in the Teachive area and calls upon ranchers not to strip pastures completely of their vegetation.

7. Adequate maintenance of buffelgrass requires burning, deep plowing, and physical or chemical removal of unwanted plants (CIPES 1995).

8. Under Article 27 of the Mexican constitution, a *pequeña propriedad* (small landholding) consists of the land necessary to raise up to five hundred cows. More than that number constitutes a *latifundia*, which is repudiated by the constitution. To be limited to five hundred cows is an insult to a successful *ganadero*, and the law is seldom observed in Sonora.

9. One of the older women in the village, for example, has 12 children, 75 grandchildren, and somewhere around 125 great-grandchildren.

10. The women are actually in competition with other women all over the world. Mexican weavers (men and women) from Oaxaca produce cheaper wool blankets. The weavers of India, Pakistan, and Afghanistan produce high-quality blankets and rugs far more cheaply than the Mayo women can produce them.

11. See, for example, Crumrine 1977, 117–20.

12. Doña Aurora Moroyoqui of Choacalle, born ca. 1935, worked hard as a *jornalera* in 1996 to earn her contribution as a *fiestera*.

13. While it is tempting to classify the agribusiness of the Río Mayo Delta (which merges imperceptibly with that of the delta of the Río Yaqui) as an *economic enclave*, I have chosen not to do so. Wolf and Hansen (1972) characterize an enclave as a region producing products "on which each country must rely [and] tend to be produced in relatively restricted areas, by relatively few enterprises, often surrounded by a vast hinterland which participates but little in the strategic processes of production and distribution (7)." Usually the products of such enclaves are destined for export and are a strategic source of foreign currency. At times the Mayo Delta functions as an enclave, in that virtually all its products are exported, much of the agricultural inputs and machinery are imported, and the labor force

is located immediately adjacent. It has relatively insignificant relations with what Wolf and Hansen call the *hinterland*, that is, the region outside the enclave. The *jornaleros* of Teachive are at that point part of the enclave. Depending on numerous variables, for example, governmental policy, international prices (demand), the presence of pests or pathogens that attack certain crops, and so on, the products may be dedicated for local, regional, and national consumption. When this occurs, the delta ceases to function as an enclave. It becomes part of the national food distribution system; its products are consumed by those who harvest them, plus other nationals. At this point, the enclave economy becomes instead a "siphon" economy, distributing the products throughout the hinterland and beyond (13). The physiographic/social context in which the enclave is located constitutes the "matrix" (usually one of poverty and underdevelopment). The *comunidad* of Masiaca is sometimes part of the matrix, sometimes part of the enclave, sometimes neither, depending on the vicissitudes of international commerce and the vagaries of Mexican politics.

14. Chlorinated hydrocarbons, largely banned in the United States, are commonly found, if the number of disposed containers is any indicator. Public health workers routinely spray rural homes with DDT to control malaria-bearing mosquitos.

15. For a detailed narrative about pesticides in Mexico and their effect on Mexicans, see Wright (1990).

16. Cotton is one of only a few modern crops that have not seen dramatic increases in yields following the Green Revolution.

17. Much has been written of the Green Revolution and its negative effects on Mexico's poor. In general, its benefits have accrued to the wealthy, which should surprise no one, given its sponsorship by the Rockefeller Foundation, which today continues to dominate agricultural research in Mexico (see Jennings 1988). In 1938 populist President Lázaro Cárdenas expropriated all Mexican oil operations. In so doing, he particularly enraged the Rockefeller interests, who "owned" a majority of the seized oil industry. They managed to slip back into Mexico under the guise of their sponsorship of the Green Revolution, in a move that might be called The Rockefellers' Revenge.

The most articulate, knowledgeable, and strident critic of the Rockefeller initiative, which was begun under the leadership of then

Vice-President Henry Wallace in the early 1940s, was none other than the eminent geographer Carl Sauer. Jennings cites Sauer's prescient warning:

> A good aggressive bunch of American agronomists and plant breeders could ruin the native resources for good and all by pushing their American commercial stocks. . . . And Mexican agriculture cannot be pointed toward standardization on a few commercial types without upsetting native economy and culture hopelessly. The example of Iowa is about the most dangerous of all for Mexico. Unless the Americans understand that, they'd better keep out of this country entirely. That must be approached from an appreciation of native economies as being basically sound. (Jennings 1988, 51)

18. Reports continually circulate in the Río Mayo Delta that Mayos of delta villages harbor strong resentments against the *jornaleros* from the *comunidades*. Critics charge that the *jornaleros*, because they have access to the *monte*, are willing to work for less and consequently drive down wages that are paid to *ejidatarios* who lack the resources of the *monte*. Vicente reports that the delta Mayos refer to *comuneros* as *chupa piedras*—(rock suckers) because they are willing to work for so little that they must derive livelihood from sucking the rocks. He responds that the *monte* is worth more than the wages received by the *ejidatarios* of the delta. See Appendix A.

19. Left to nature, the streambed would quickly revegetate, new trees would sprout up, silt banks would be reestablished, and flows retarded. Grazing pressure, however, literally nips new vegetation in the bud, preventing the initiation of succession necessary for the reemergence of a new gallery forest.

20. A cow is considered a bull, a cow plus a calf, or a heifer. A calf is not counted as a cow, but as part of its mother until it is weaned. A heifer is not considered a cow until she gives birth, usually at the age of two.

21. During the drought of 1996 the value of a calf decreased by more than 50 percent. Some brought as little as $40 US. The going price was five pesos a kilo, and calves were weighing in at around 100 kilos,

far less than the 170 kilos which is considered minimal normal weight for a calf at weaning.

22. In June 1996 it had not rained in Masiaca for nine months. Most of the buffelgrass in the region was dead or nibbled to the ground. There was no seed left to work and the bagging warehouse had been silent for several days when two semi-truckloads of seed arrived from Nuevo León. Knowing that the market for the seed in Sonora would be greatly stimulated by the drought, entrepreneurs from drought-stricken Nuevo León had sacrificed their seed to the better odds in Sonora, where buffelgrass production is greater. The seed took a week to bag.

23. Five *talabarterías* (leather shops) in Masiaca produce finished leather goods. They are owned primarily by *mestizos* and most of the workers are *mestizos*. The leather industry employs more than thirty people to various degrees. The operations include collecting tanning agents, primarily tree barks (see Appendix B), purchasing the hides, curing them, and cutting, sewing, and producing *huaraches*, shoes, and saddles.

24. Wolf (1985) has described the function of communities as reserves of labor for *hacendados*.

CHAPTER 6

1. Prior to 1941, when the government acknowledged the validity of the Masiaca residents' petition for constituting a community, the legal classification of the lands was ambiguously *comunidad* (under the constitution) or, alternately, *terrenos nacionales*—national lands belonging to the national government. The petition of 1835 under the law of restitution, commonly known as the Almada Law (for it had been passed by José María Almada), still held sway, although not sufficiently to protect the community lands from all comers.

2. It was also under Alemán that the Rockefeller Foundation's programs to alter the structure of Mexico's agriculture away from peasant production for the domestic market to corporate production for the international market began. Mocúzari Dam is a clear symbol of Mexico's acceptance of the Rockefeller model of industrialized agriculture. For an excellent and revealing background account of the Foundation's activities, see Jennings (1988).

3. Erasmus (1967) describes Buaysiacobe in the 1950s as a demoralized, poverty-stricken enclave, torn apart by dissension and corruption. O'Connor (1989) found it in the 1980s to be the most prosperous Mayo town.

4. The name means sau = saguaro, cobe = corner: *rincón de sahuaros* (saguaro corner).

5. Sonorans use the term *guacho* to refer to southerners, especially southern Indians. It is a derogatory label, connoting oafishness and social backwardness. Sonorans tend to blame the state's economic problems on "*guachos*." Mayos also use the term to refer to those from the south. *Guachos* are said to prefer corn to flour tortillas.

6. Angus Wright makes an important observation on the ascendency of flour over corn tortillas in Mexico. Mexican industrial agricultural policy (under the auspices of the Rockefeller Foundation—led Green Revolution) "changed the food patterns of the nation, with wheat favored over corn, the North American researchers going a long way to accomplish what the wheat-loving Spanish had attempted to enforce on Mexican farmers for three hundred years" (184). In commenting on the proposals of the Rockefeller Foundation to transform Mexican agriculture, Carl Sauer (Jennings 1988, 52) argued that a combination of corn and beans was the foundation of an excellent diet and that there was no need to change it. The introduction of commercial white bread, begun in the 1950s, was a blow to the diet of Mexico.

7. With the passage of the North American Free Trade Agreement (NAFTA), Mexico agreed to eliminate subsidies to crops, including grains, which will be phased out over fifteen years. The price of corn then became higher, because for decades the Mexican government had subsidized its price, paying farmers more than the international price, and selling it cheaply for making tortillas. The lifting of price supports and the end to marketing subsidies coincides with a steep rise in the international price of corn, as world stockpiles dwindled, for partially unrelated reasons (Mexican irrigation farmers now have little incentive to raise corn, which delivers far less return than specialty crops raised on the same acreage). This has meant a rapid increases in the price of tortillas. The "market" price for *maseca* has increased from less than one peso per kilo in 1994 to nearly four pesos per kilo in 1996. To cushion the blow this potentially devastat-

ing inflation would represent to the legions of Mexico's poor for whom corn tortillas are the basic food, the government continues (1997) to subsidize the price of kernel corn and *maseca* through the national food distributor, Conasupo. This appears to be in violation of NAFTA.

8. At the time of this study, the drought of 1995–96 had driven the price of beans—pinto or the local *mayacova*—to ten pesos a kilo, more than twice their price in the United States. The price of *maseca* rose from less than one peso to 3.8 pesos per kilo. Kernel corn doubled in price as well, increasing from one peso to two pesos a kilo. These price increases drastically reduced local consumption of beans, much to the detriment of the natives' nutritional well-being, I assume.

9. Specifically, Greenhalph distinguishes among four phases of family income in her study area in Taiwan: (1) expansion, from marriage to the birth of the first son; (2) maturation, from birth of the first son to marriage of the first son; (3) consolidation, from marriage of the first son to division of dispersion of the first son, and (4) division, from division of dispersion of the last son (1985, 587). She argues that varying family wealth during these phases demonstrates that inequality in Taiwanese peasantry is demographic, that is, varying over time as a function of phases of family dynamics, rather than social, i.e., varying with the evolution of the peasantry into social classes and changing relations to the means of production. The income of Teachivans indicates that both factors are present: if isolated Teachive families are studied and compared over time, the inequalities among them would surely lie in the former (demographic). Viewed from a regional perspective, however, the inequalities between Teachive families and other (e.g., *mestizo*) families in the region are probably more a function of class (social) differences. Only empirical studies will establish which is the more important determinant.

Greenhalph concludes her study by urging that "government planners should distinguish between the temporary poor, where poverty is demographic, and the more permanent poor, whose poverty is political and economic in origin, and design different policies for each group." Teachivans clearly fall into the latter group.

10. Netting (1993) notes that one consequence of China's abrupt turn from communal to household-dominated agriculture is a reversion to the inferior status of women. "Women's contributions . . . are now

less clearly identifiable, since they no longer earn discrete numbers of work points, but are merely laborers in the household work force. . . . Household responsibility may merely have restored patriarchal power over subordinate women and children" (255).

11. Vicente has applied for his pension, which will be roughly $100 US a month.

CHAPTER 7

1. Netting (1993) notes, however, "Where peasant communities have not been broken up or dispossessed by external elites with state support, the tendency has not been for smallholders to accumulate and become commercial entrepreneurs using machinery and wage laborers." Had the Mayos not been evicted from their historical lands and had government subsidies been available to a Mayo peasantry rather than to a landed oligarchy, the intense social stratification of the Río Mayo might never have occurred.

2. Some *comunidades* and *ejidos* are comparatively well off. The Mayo *comunidad* of Baimena on the Río Fuerte is affluent by comparison with Masiaca. It has comparatively well-watered lands, more rainfall, more fertile soil, and a richer vegetation. Similarly, the *ejido* of Los Capomos, a Mayo *ejido* some thirty kilometers distant, is more affluent than non-delta Mayo *ejidos* in Sonora, blessed with better rainfall and superb soil.

3. Mayos, of course, did not always inhabit this land. Their ancestors, Uto-Aztecan speakers who wandered into the Mayo Valley more (possibly much more) than a millennium ago, undoubtedly imposed themselves on earlier settlers, possibly with the same violence or implied violence as the Spaniards later imposed on the Mayos. Mayo's physical differences from Yaquis *may* be explained by intermarriage with the peoples previously living along the Río Mayo, with whom the interlopers intermarried. Without proclaiming Mayos as the *original* inhabitants of the Mayo lands, we can nevertheless acknowledge the strong bond between the people and their lands.

4. Erasmus (1967) found *ejidos* to be rife with discord and corruption, internally in that *ejido* officials absconded with funds, appointed their relatives to important posts, and used the office to personal benefit,

and externally, in that the same officials entered into collusion with outsiders (especially government agents) to funnel funds their own way. Mayo *ejidos* have been no more exempt from corruption and inefficiency than non-Mayo *ejidos*.

5. Marcela Vásquez León and Thomas McGuire (1994) have documented the Mexican government's policy of deliberately sabotaging the livelihood of small fishermen in Sonora by promulgating regulations governing shrimp harvesting. The new regulations were written and endorsed by the owners of large shrimping companies operating in deep waters who compete with individual boat owners operating near the shore. These laws place drastic limits and severe penalties on small-time fishermen who attempt to carry on their traditional fishing methods in their traditional locations. The laws go so far as to incorporate into law patently false environmental grounds for restricting the techniques used by traditional shrimpers, and to alter fishing boundaries and dates of harvest to the maximum benefit of the commercial shrimpers (owned by the wealthy) and the ultimate economic destruction of the poor or marginal fishermen.

6. Yocupicio receives mixed reviews in Masiaca. Elsewhere, among historians, there is greater unanimity: he was a ruthless, scheming politician who used his office to enrich himself and supported public projects only insofar as they enhanced his career. One prestigious Sonoran historian described Yocupicio to me in one phrase: "He was a *sono*fabitch."

7. Crumrine (1977, 1–5) describes meeting in 1961 with the last regionally famous Mayo prophet, to whom he gives the pseudonym Damian Bohoroqui. Although Damian was a regional celebrity, claiming to be or to represent God, no such prophet was well-known in Teachive. Vicente, who was in his late twenties during the prophet's period of cosmic visions, does not recall having heard of him, remembering only vague representation of prophets.

8. Hardly three months into the term of the *comsariado* elected in 1996, his term of office was compromised by allegations that he was misappropriating funds. Opponents accused him of sequestering community funds for drinking and carousing. His supporters claimed that the opponents were nervous because he was uncovering a history of illegal financial dealings by previous *comisariados*. The controversy threatened to split the community even more deeply.

9. Probably at the price of deep and bitter internal conflicts, in 1994, Yaqui factions engaged in armed conflict against each other, resulting in two groups' claiming legitimacy. Some traditional Yaquis accused the Mexican and Sonoran government of deliberately exploiting tribal differences to weaken Yaqui political power.

10. Pimental et al. (1997) estimate that the recipients of irrigation water in Mexico pay only 11 percent of the actual cost of that water. Nearly all of the products of irrigation are exported to Mexico's large cities or abroad.

11. Mayo subsistence farmers practiced (and a handful still practice) tricultural farming, combining corn, beans, and squash in the same field. This type of agriculture is not compatible with intensive livestock grazing, but it has enormous advantages in overall productivity. Javier Trujillo de Arriaga has shown that triculture can outproduce Green Revolution technology on the high plains of Tlaxcala and has numerous additional benefits as well. But it does not fit neatly into commercial export agricultural models (cited in Wright 1990, 156). My own research has found Mayos in Sinaloa mixing sesame planted as a cash crop, with beans, squash, and watermelon for subsistence.

12. Article 27 of the Mexican constitution explicitly repudiates *latifundios*, that is, landed estates. It legitimizes *pequeñas propriedades* (small landholdings), which are defined for ranching as "that which does not exceed for an individual the surface necessary to maintain up to 500 head of adult cattle or their equivalent in young cattle . . . in accordance with the forage capacity of the lands" (Mexican Constitution, Article 27, XV). The lands immediately to the north of the *comunidad* are owned by the Ibarra family of Alamos. The family apparently owns or controls more than twenty thousand hectares of land, on which it runs many thousands of cows, avoiding violation of the constitution by dividing ownership among spouses and children, even though such measures are seldom necessary among friends of the government.

13. The area where this occurs, to the north of Teachive, involves lands claimed by the *comunidad* but in the hands of the Ibarra family.

14. Perhaps the best-known market variables in Sonora are the price paid for *maseca* and that paid for beef on the hoof. As with all commodities, the price paid for cows on the hoof fluctuates with supply and demand. The local buyer in Masiaca keeps in close touch with

feedlots or shippers in the cities and knows to the minute the price they will pay. He communicates this on a daily basis, or even more frequently, when prices are volatile. The price is communicated quickly to everyone in the community.

15. In 1995 I interviewed a Mexican immigrant in California, who had moved there in the 1960s from San Bernardo on the Río Mayo. He described collecting plants with a North American botanist in the mountains to the northwest. One day he found a population of rare plants. "In that region," he said, "there were no people. Only Indians" (*No había gente, puro índios*).

16. Erasmus (1967), for example, notes: "The Indian component of the Mayo River population is not, as can be seen, so homogeneous as that of the Yaqui reservation. It offers much more of a continuum, or social gradient, of differences in attitudes and habits. There are many Mayos who openly denounce the ceremonial traditions, and many who, as the Mexicans express it, 'want to be Yori.' The latter are Mayos who would like to have their Indian backgrounds forgotten and wish to disassociate themselves from all things Indian. . . . One reason many Mayos cling to their traditional ways is that they see no alternative. The Indian occupies the lowest status in the local class structure, although his Indianness is as much a social as a biological phenomenon. Though it is possible for Indians to rise, few do so." (106–7)

17. Grindle (1988) notes that in 1980, 800,000 individuals joined the Mexican labor market. By 1985 the number had increased to 1 million a year and was expected to exceed that number every year through the end of the century.

    A disturbing development in Mexico's struggle to feed, clothe, house, and educate its population is the effect of global warming (Liverman and O'Brien 1991). Virtually every long-range climatic forecast is for Mexico's climate to become hotter and drier, with the inevitable consequence of less agricultural productivity from fewer acres of crops. Mexico's response to dwindling water resources has been to construct more dams as quickly as possible. Dams are ultimately water wasters (evaporation losses increase dramatically with exposed surface area) and silt traps.

18. I assume that each family will sell three calves at $150 or goats in an equivalent amount, and have two *jornaleros* who work an average of

two hundred days a year at thirty-five pesos a day. A *cobijera* will net no more than $1,000 per year, and only one or two of the weavers can hope to earn that much.

Vicente's family exceeds this amount, for he has one son who has permanent employment and another who works nearly every day. In addition, Teresa realizes a small income from the sale of soda pop and iced fruit drinks. One of his sons, however, is desperately poor, finding only occasional employment while trying to raise a family of five. One of his daughters is married to a man who works with Vicente in the buffelgrass seed warehouse. For a while, one of his sons worked with him as well, but he was laid off, meaning that the father must now support the family of five on his meager income (thirty-five pesos a day) from the factory, all the while sending one son to preparatory school in Navojoa in the desperate hope that the son will become successful and move beyond being a *jornalero*.

19. Vicente and I witnessed a dark and foreboding example of the astonishing greed of Mexico's oligarchy. Near the headwaters of the Arroyo Masiaca in the Sierra de Alamos sits the tiny semi-ghost town of Las Rastras, inhabited by three Mayo families. One of their number, Luis Valenzuela, guided us up the watercourse as we searched for plants with human uses. To the north and west of the arroyo lay vast pastures, stripped of forest and planted with buffelgrass. This enormous tract is owned by a wealthy family from Navojoa. At the limit of the family lands, on the slopes of the Sierra de Alamos, a fence demarked the private ranch lands from the *terrenos nacionales* (federal or public lands) on the mountain. Under Mexican law, these public domains are open to the public for beneficial use. They are a resource for all to use, especially to graze livestock. At the fenceline we could not help but be struck with the contrast between the private lands, in which the grass grew rich and tall, and the federal lands, which were nearly stripped of all grass. We asked Luis who was grazing on the federal lands that they would be so overgrazed. He replied that the wealthy rancher ran all of his cows on the federal lands until all the grass was gone, then transferred his herd to his personal lands, which had excellent forage. In other words, the wealthy rancher stole the common forage, depriving the poor, small-time ranchers of all benefit, then, only when he had wrecked the resource, did he begin to use his own lands. This was the real "Tragedy of the Commons."

20. The December 1994 peso devaluation created an overnight crisis in meeting payments on foreign debts, which are payable in dollars or other international currency. The value of the peso dropped from 3.1 to the dollar to more than 6 to the dollar. In order to meet these payment deadlines, the Mexican government required quick, huge loans, one of which came from the United States. To produce the funds to repay these loans, the government was forced drastically to curtail government programs and divert their funds into debt payments. Many thousands of Mexicans who had achieved a marginally middle-class standard of living in government-dependent employment, were thrown out of work as the government eliminated jobs, using the funds saved to pay off loans. Simultaneously, imported goods, on which Mexico has become totally dependent in the last two decades, doubled in price overnight, producing an instant decrease in the buying power of the peso. Although the Zedillo government pledged to hold the line on inflation, over the first six months of 1995 the prices of *maseca*, beans, and gasoline skyrocketed, followed by nearly every other commodity. Wages, of course, did not keep pace, and the *jornaleros* of Teachive experienced only a homeopathic increase in their pay. A curious example of how inflationary the devaluation proved to be is illustrated by the plight faced by a Mexican friend of mine. He and his wife were in the process of building a new house in a major Sonoran city. During construction, they found that as a result of NAFTA, doors, windows, and hardware produced in the United States had become competitive in price with those produced in Mexico. Desiring the better quality of U.S. goods, they posted their order and made their deposit with a U.S. firm. A week after the devaluation, the shipment arrived. It had more than doubled in cost, resulting in an immediate increase of nearly $4,000 in the cost of the house. My friends had to divert funds from savings and scrimp frantically to pay for the shipment, without which they would have had no house. The Mexican government faced precisely the same situation on an enormous scale.

21. Teresa Valdivia Dounce (1995) relates that while she was employed as an anthropologist by the National Indigenous Institute her plan to assist the isolated Guarijío Indians of Sonora in obtaining rights to their land by distributing to them copies of Mexico's agrarian law was squelched by her superiors at INI. She was prohibited from distributing copies of the law to primarily illiterate Indians. The

rationale for the prohibition was that distributing the law would incite the Indians to do bad things.

22. Blás Leyva pointed out with a smile that although female *jojobas* are the productive shrub, yielding the oily fruit, the plantings yielded an overwhelming majority of male plants, which yield only flowers. The consulting agronomists were not aware that *jojoba* is dioecious.

23. Carl Sauer called for anthropology-based agricultural research to determine how productivity could be increased while drawing on Mexico's vast cultural resources. His voice was lost in the crowd of Rockefeller-sponsored researchers who denigrated Mexico's native resources and called for introducing high-technology, foreign-developed agricultural models instead. See Jennings (1988, 50–54).

24. Clifton (1990) notes (based on historical interactions between U.S. Indians and the U.S. government) that "the fundamental, conflicting elements of the goals of most modern Indian groups . . . simply put . . . are obtaining absolute political autarchy while perpetuating utter fiscal dependence" (5). Mexico's government has, in contrast, unswayingly viewed the social integration of Indians as its goal, while retaining a highly paternalistic relation to indigenous groups. It is unencumbered by the legions of treaties which color the historical relation of the United States and Indian groups. The *ideological* and, to that extent, fiscal dependence of Mexican Indians, including Mayos, on the government is every bit as "utter" as in the United States, though the ascendancy of autarchy shows various degrees of development among natives, none as intensely proclaimed as among U.S. Indians.

25. In July 1996, supplies of *maseca* to the Conasupo in Masiaca and another in Jopopaco were strictly rationed. The meager shipments sold out almost instantly. *Maseca* could not be found at any store within the *comunidad* for several days at a time.

26. The Teachive schoolteacher was paid roughly 3,000 pesos a month, about $400 US.

27. For an especially prescient analysis of the long-term effect of the policies of international lending agencies, see Payer (1974). An excellent analysis of the U.S. role in the agencies and their effects on underdeveloped countries can be found in Bello (1994).

28. Mexico has a long history of bending to the will of international financial institutions. Barry (1995) observes: "From 1980 to 1991 Mex-

ico received thirteen structural and sectoral adjustment loans from the World Bank, more than any other country. It also signed six agreements with the International Monetary Fund, all of which brought increased pressure to liberalize trade and investment. After Mexico acceded to multilateral pressure to join the GATT in 1986, the World Bank granted the country a huge loan. During the Salinas administration, the World Bank further opened the spigots of loans with low-interest rates and easy payback terms" (43).

29. A popular joke had it that López-Portillo made every Mexican a millionaire. He managed this, of course, by overseeing an era of hyperinflation, with the result that in 1995 the peso was worth one-six-hundredth of what it had been worth in 1972.

30. Ironically, the powerful grain barons of the Yaqui Valley are also facing disaster as they try in vain to compete with grains imported from the United States, which is blessed with the world's most favorable agricultural climate. While Yaqui Valley soils and growing conditions are ideal for many hybrid wheats, the crops must be heavily irrigated and doused with agricultural inputs not necessary in the United States. As of this writing, Río Yaqui *latifundistas* were desperately seeking an alternative crop. So far, they have been spared the appearance of Karnal blunt, a rust which has decreased the marketability of the U.S. crop of durum wheat.

31. Certain export-oriented sectors, especially farmers producing cash crops destined for export (e.g., table grapes, asparagus, and chiles) have benefited from devaluation, but even they acknowledge that their benefits are short-lived, for they must import agricultural equipment and purchase agricultural inputs. The prices of both have escalated dramatically as the peso remains in competition with other world currencies, almost always to Mexicans' disadvantage.

Higher-quality consumer goods have also become readily available—to those who can afford them. Following devaluation, these goods immediately doubled in price, bankrupting many who had purchased them for resale. Mexico had for decades protected its industries with high tariffs. Most observers agree that in the absence of competition, Mexican industry failed to produce high-quality products and thus could not compete with those produced abroad. The new competition has killed many of these industries. All to the good, respond some.

32. Erasmus in 1967 found rampant corruption in the *ejido* of Buaysia-cobe. So many people, including Ejido Bank leaders, bank personnel, *ejido* leaders, purchasers, and vendors, were involved in bribes, kick-backs, padding of accounts, and outright embezzlement, that no one trusted anyone else in the *ejido*. Those earning less invariably blamed their lack of success on corrupt management (Erasmus 1967). Corruption breeds universal blame-throwing.

33. Mario Soto, treasurer of the project and an advocate for continuing, and Alonso Moroyoqui, an extremely poor *comunero*, agreed on the details of this analysis, although their interest in the project differed.

34. According to *socios*, the charge for use of the tractors is based on the number of hectares plowed, the typical charge being eighty pesos ($11 US in 1996) per hectare.

35. Mario Soto, for example, owns between twenty and thirty head (his own description) and manages some cows for his father as well.

36. The roughly twelve *socios* who had no other work constitute the poorest of Masiaca's residents. With no other income resource, they threw themselves into the irrigation project vigorously and still hope for success, even in the light of the project's disappointing results. Their status fits Bernal's characterization well: "When peasants cannot support themselves solely through agriculture, they seek to market their labor elsewhere. In the competitive labor market, the more skilled, educated, and youthful individuals find wage or salaried work or enter commerce. The rest of the population is effectively marginalized because the capitalist economy cannot absorb their labor directly. This 'surplus' labor, then, by its characteristics is not so much a reserve industrial labor pool as it is a reserve labor pool for the least productive, least developed sector of the economy—peasant agriculture" (Bernal 1994).

References

ARCHIVAL MATERIALS

Archivos del Estado de Sonora, Hermosillo, Sonora. 1835. Tomo 135.
Archivos del Estado de Sonora, Hermosillo, Sonora. 1835. Tomo 187.
Archivos del Estado de Sonora, Hermosillo, Sonora. 1848. Tomo 238.
Archivos del Estado de Sonora, Hermosillo, Sonora. 1848. Tomo 258.

BOOKS AND ARTICLES

Acosta, R. 1983. *Apuntes historicos sonorenses*. Hermosillo: Gobierno del estado de Sonora.

Alegre, F. J. 1888. *La historia de la compañía de Jesús en Nueva España*. Special collections, University of Arizona Library, Tucson.

Almada, F. R. 1952. *Diccionario de historia, geografía, y biografía sonorense.* Hermosillo: Gobierno del Estado.

Arbelaez, M. S. 1991. The Sonoran missions and Indian raids of the eighteenth century. *Journal of the Southwest* 33:366–77.

Arizona Daily Star. 1996. Shrimp farms wreck Third World lives, group says. June 2.

Bannon, J. 1947. Black robe frontiersman: Pedro Méndez, S.J. *Hispanic American Historical Review* 27:61–86.

Barry, T. 1995. *Zapata's revenge*. Boston: South End Press.

Beals, R. 1945. *The contemporary culture of the Cahita Indians*. Washington: Smithsonian Institution Bureau of Indian Ethnography, no. 142.

Bello, W. 1994. Dark victory: The United States, structural adjustment, and global poverty. Oakland: Institute for Food and Development Policy.

Bernal, V. 1994. Peasants, capitalism and (ir)rationality. *American Ethnologist* 21:792–810.

Bolton, H. 1936. *Rim of Cristendom*. Tucson: University of Arizona Press.

Boserup, E. 1981. Population and technological change: A study of long-term trends. Chicago: University of Chicago Press.

Brading, D. 1971. *Miners and merchants in Bourbon Mexico, 1763–1810*. Cambridge: Cambridge University Press.

Brunk, S. 1995. *Emiliano Zapata: Revolution and betrayal in Mexico*. Albuquerque: University of New Mexico Press.

Cabeza de Vaca, A. 1972. *The narrative of Alvar Núñez Cabeza de Vaca*. Translated by Fanny Bandelier. Barre, Massachusetts: The Imprint Society.

Calderón Valdés, S. (editor). 1985. *Historia general de Sonora*. 5 volumes. Hermosillo: Gobierno del estado.

Camou Healy, E. 1991. *Potreros, vegas y mahuechis*. Hermosillo: Gobierno del estado de Sonora.

Chisem, J. 1990. *Apuntes para la historia de Guaymas*. Hermosillo: Gobierno del estado de Sonora.

CIPES. 1995. *Guía práctica para el establecimiento, manejo y utilización del zacate buffel*. Carbó, Sonora: Patronato del centro de investigaciones pecuarias del estado de Sonora.

Clifton, J. 1990. The invented Indian: Cultural fictions and government policies. New Brunswick, NJ: Transaction Press.

Crosby, H. 1994. *Antigua California*. Albuquerque: University of New Mexico Press.

Crumrine, R. 1977. *The Mayo Indians of Sonora: A people who refuse to die*. Tucson: University of Arizona Press.

Crumrine, R. 1983. Mayo. In A. Ortiz (editor), *Handbook of North American Indians*. Washington: Smithsonian Institution.

Dabdoub, C. 1964. *La historia de el valle del Yaqui*. Hermosillo: Gobierno del estado.

Domecq, B. 1990. *La insoleta historia de la Santa de Cabora*. Mexico, D.F.: Planeta.

Dounce, T. 1995. *Sierra de nadie*. Mexico: Instituto Nacional Indígena.

Dunbier, R. 1968. *The Sonoran Desert*. Tucson: University of Arizona Press.

Erasmus, C, 1967. Culture change in northwest Mexico. In J. Steward (editor), *Contemporary change in traditional societies*. Volume III. Urbana: University of Illinois Press.

Frank, A. G. 1972. *Lumpenbourgeoisie: Lumpendevelopment.* New York: Monthly Review Press.

Friedrich, P. 1970. *Agrarian reform in a Mexican village.* Englewood Cliffs, NJ: Prentice-Hall.

Fontana, B., B. Burns, and E. Faubert. 1977. *The other southwest.* Phoenix: The Heard Museum.

Gentry, H. S. 1942. *Río Mayo plants.* Washington: Carnegie Institution.

Gerhard, P. 1982. *The northern frontier of New Spain.* Princeton: Princeton University Press.

German E., J. L., L. Ríos R., C. E. Flores G., and O. S. Ayala P. 1987. *Genesis y desarollo de la cultura mayo de Sonora.* Sonora: Instituto tecnológico de Ciudad Obregón, Sonora.

González, L. 1974. *San José de Gracia: Mexican village in transition.* Austin: University of Texas Press.

Greenhalgh, S. 1985. Is inequality demographically induced? The family cycle and the distribution of income in Taiwan. *American Anthropologist* 87: 571–94.

Greenberg, J. 1989. *Blood ties.* Tucson: University of Arizona Press.

Griffith, J. 1967. Río Mayo pascola masks: A study in style. M.A. thesis, University of Arizona.

Grindle, M. 1988. Searching for rural development: Labor migration and employment in Mexico. Ithaca: Cornell University Press.

Hall, L. 1981. *Alvaro Obregón: Power and revolution in Mexico 1911–1920.* College Station: Texas A & M University Press.

Hammond, G., and A. Rey. 1928. *Obregon's history of 16th century exploration in Western America.* Los Angeles: Wetzel Publishing Company.

Hastings, J. R., and R. R. Humphrey. 1969. *Climatological data and statistics for Sonora and northern Sinaloa.* University of Arizona technical reports on the meteorology and climatology of arid regions, No 19.

Hasting, J. R., and R. M. Turner. 1965. The changing mile: An ecological study of vegetation change with time in the lower mile of an arid and semiarid region. Tucson: University of Arizona Press.

Hinton, W. 1967. *Fan Shen.* New York: Vantage Press.

Hobsbawm, E. 1994. *The Age of Extremes: The short twentieth century, 1914–1991.* London: Michael Joseph.

Hu DeHart, E. 1984. *Yaqui resistance and survival.* Madison: University of Wisconsin Press.

INEGI. 1990. *XI Censo general de población y vivienda, 1990*. Mexico City: Instituto nacional de estadística, geografía e informatica.

Jennings, B. 1988. *Foundations of international agricultural research: Science and politics in Mexican agriculture*. London: Westview Press.

Liverman, D., and K. O'Brien. 1991. Global warming and climate change in Mexico. *Global Environmental Change* 1991 (December): 351–64.

Lonsdale, P. 1989. Geology and tectonic history of the Gulf of California. In Winterer, E., D. Hussong, and R. Decker (editors), *The Eastern Pacific Ocean and Hawaii*, Geological Society of America, Geology of North America N: 499–521.

López, F. B., A. H. Ramírez, and C. Y. Martínez C. 1995. Los Mayos de Huites, desplazados por la presa. Unpublished manifesto. Subdirección de antropología de la dirección de procuración de justicia del INI.

Martin, P., D. Yetman, T. Van Devender, P. Jenkins, M. Fishbein, and R. Wilson. In press. *Gentry's Río Mayo Plants*. Tucson: University of Arizona Press.

Marx, K. 1914. *The eighteenth brumaire of Louis Bonaparte*. Chicago: Charles Kerr & Co.

Morfi, A. de. 1967. *Diario y derrotero (1777–1781)*. Monterrey: Instituto Tecnológico y de Estudios Superiores de Monterrey.

Nabhan, G. 1982. *The desert smells like rain*. San Francisco: North Point Press.

Nakamaya, A. 1975. *Sinaloa: El drama y sus actores*. Mexico City: Instituto Nacional de Antropología y Historia.

Navarro García, L. 1967. *Sonora and Sinaloa in the seventeenth century*. Sevilla: University of Seville.

Nentvig, J. 1951. *Rudo Ensayo*. Tucson: Arizona Silhoutte.

Netting, R. 1993. Smallholders, householders: Farm families and the ecology of intensive, sustainable agriculture. Stanford: Stanford University Press.

Obregón, A. 1959. *Ocho mil kilómetros en campaña*. Mexico City: Fondo de cultura económica.

Obregón, B. 1988. *Historia de los descubrimientos antiguous y modernos de la Nueva España escrita por el conquistador en el año de 1584*. Mexico, D.F.: Editorial Porrua.

O'Connor, M. 1989. *Descendants of Totoliguoque*. University of California

Publications in Anthropology. Berkeley: University of California Press.

Padden, R. 1967. *The hummingbird and the hawk*. Columbus: Ohio State University Press.

Payer, C. 1974. *The debt trap*. New York: Monthly Review Press.

Pérez de Ribas, A. 1645. *Crónicos de los triunfos de nuestra santa fe*. Original copy in University of Arizona Library Special Collections.

Pfefferkorn, I. 1949. *Sonora: A description of the province* (translated and edited by T. Treutlein). Albuquerque: University of New Mexico Press.

Pimentel, D., and M. Pimentel. 1979. *Food, energy & society*. London: Edward Arnold.

Pimental, D., J. Houser, E. Preiss, O. White, H. Fang, L. Mesnick, T. Barsky, S. Tariche, J. Schreck, and S. Alpert. 1997. Water resources: Agriculture, the environment, and society. *Bioscience* 47:97–112.

Polzer, C. 1976. *Rules and precepts of the Jesuit missions of Northwestern New Spain, 1550–1600*. Tucson: University of Arizona Press.

Procuraduría Agraria. 1995. *Legislación agraria*. Mexico City: Procuraduría agraria.

Ramos, R. 1958. *Fray Antonio María de los Reyes: Relación hecha el año 1784 de las misiones establecidos in Sinaloa and Sonora*. Mexico City: Ediciones Culturales del Gobierno del Estado de Sinaloa.

Reff, D. 1991. *Disease, depopulation, and culture changes in northwestern New Spain, 1518–1764*. Salt Lake City: University of Utah Press.

Robertson, A. 1968. *My life among the savage natives of New Spain*. Los Angeles: Ward Ritchie Press.

Sauer, C. 1932. *Road to Cíbola*. Berkeley: University of California Press.

Sauer, C. 1934. *Distribution of aboriginal tribes and languages of northwest Mexico*. Berkeley: University of California Press.

Sauer, C. 1981. Aboriginal populations of northwest Mexico. In Carl Sauer, *Selected essays 1963–1975*. Berkeley: Turtle Island Foundation.

Sheridan, T. 1988. *Where the dove calls: The political ecology of a peasant corporate community in northwestern Mexico*. Tucson: University of Arizona Press.

Spicer, E. 1962. *Cycles of conquest*. Tucson: University of Arizona Press.

Spicer, E. 1980. *The Yaquis: A cultural history*. Tucson: University of Arizona Press.

Stagg, A. 1978. *The Almadas and Alamos, 1783–1867.* Tucson: University of Arizona Press.

Stern, S. 1983. The struggle for solidarity. *Radical History* 27:21–45.

Troncoso, F. P. 1905. *Las guerras con las tribus yaqui y mayo del estado de Sonora.* Mexico, D.F.: Departamento del estado mayor.

Valenzuela Yocupicio, H. 1984. *Utilización de las plantas en la comunidad mayo de los Buayums, Municipio de Navojoa.* Dirección general de culturas populares. Secretaria de Educación Popular. Manuscript in University of Arizona Special Collections.

Varegge, N. 1993. Transformation of Spanish urban landscapes in the American southwest, 1821–1900. *Journal of the Southwest* 35:371–459.

Vásquez León, M., and T. Mcguire. 1993. La iniciativa privada in the Mexican shrimp industry. *Mast* 6 (1/2): 59–72.

Vazquez, R. E. 1955. *Geografía del estado de Sonora.* Mexico City: Pluma y lápiz de Mexico.

Villa, E. 1951. *La historia del estado de Sonora.* Hermosillo: Editorial Sonora.

Wallerstein, I. 1980. *The modern-world system II: Mercantilism and the consolidation of the European world-economy, 1600–1750.* New York: Academic Press.

West, R. C. 1993. *Sonora: Its geographical personality.* Austin: University of Texas Press.

Wolf, E. 1959. *Sons of the shaking earth.* Chicago: University of Chicago Press.

Wolf, E. 1966. *Peasants.* Englewood Cliffs, NJ: Prentice-Hall.

Wolf, E. 1969. *Peasant wars of the twentieth century.* New York: Harper & Row.

Wolf, E., and E. Hansen. 1972. *The human condition in Latin America.* London: Oxford University Press.

Wolf, E. 1985. The vicissitudes of the closed coroporate peasant community. *American Ethnologist* 13:325–29.

Wright, A. 1990. *The death of Ramón González.* Austin: University of Texas Press.

Yetman, D. 1995. Caminos of San Bernardo revisited. *Journal of the Southwest* 37:142–56.

Yetman, D., T. R. Van Devender, P. Jenkins, and M. Fishbein. 1995. *The Río Mayo: A history of studies. Journal of the Southwest* 37:294–345.

Yetman, D., T. R. Van Devender, A. L. Reina Guerrero, and G. Valenzuela Gámez. 1995. Where have all the Mayos gone? An ethnobotanist's lament. Unpublished manuscript.

Yetman, D., T. R. Van Devender, and R. López Estudillo. In press. Monte mojino: People and trees in the Mayo region. In R. Robichaux (editor), *The tropical deciduous forest of the Alamos, Sonora Region*. Tucson: University of Arizona Press.

Zembrano, P. 1969. *Diccionario bio-bibliográfico de la compañía de Jesús en México*. Volume 9. Mexico: Editorial Jus.

Zuñiga, I. [1835] 1948. *Rapida ojeada al estado de Sonora, territorios de California y Arizona*. Reprint, Mexico, D.F.: Editor Vargas.

Index